Nietzsche as Postmodernist

SUNY Series in Contemporary Continental Philosophy

Dennis J. Schmidt, Editor

Nietzsche
as
Postmodernist

Essays Pro and Contra

**Edited and with an Introduction
by
Clayton Koelb**

THE STATE UNIVERSITY OF NEW YORK PRESS

Published by
State University of New York Press, Albany

© 1990   State University of New York

For information, address State University of New York
Press, State University Plaza, Albany, N.Y. 12246

Library of Congress Cataloging-in-Publication Data

Nietzsche as postmodernist : essays pro and contra / edited, with an
    introduction, by Clayton Koelb.
        p.   cm. — (SUNY series in contemporary continental
    philosophy)
        ISBN 0-7914-0341-6. — ISBN 0-7914-0342-4 (pbk.)
        1. Nietzsche, Friedrich Wilhelm, 1844-1900.   2. Postmodernism.
    3. Deconstruction.   I. Koelb, Clayton, 1942- . II. Series.
    B3317.N489   1990
    193—dc20   89-27506
                                                                  CIP

10 9 8 7 6 5 4 3 2 1

Contents

Acknowledgments

This project began with a conference of the International Association for Philosophy and Literature held at the University of Kansas in 1987. I am grateful to the association for its encouragement and support, above all to Gary Shapiro, who organized the conference, gave valuable advice about the volume's contents, and even contributed an essay. All of us who participated in the IAPL Nietzsche session owe a debt of gratitude to Peter Heller, who read and commented on all the papers and offered welcome suggestions for revisions. I thank him personally for the substantial improvements he brought about in my own essay as well as for his long-term support for the project.

I am pleased to thank the Division of the Humanities and the Department of Germanic Languages and Literatures at the University of Chicago for assistance with telephone and mailing costs and for other courtesies. Several scholars who were not able to contribute essays provided valuable assistance of various kinds; they include David Allison, Samuel Jaffe, and Stephen H. Watson. Thanks are also due to two anonymous press readers, who made numerous suggestions for improving the volume.

Finally, I acknowledge a few special permissions. Portions of Maudemarie Clark's "Language and Deconstruction" appeared previously in *International Studies in Philosophy* 19 (1987). I am grateful to the editor for permission to reprint. Part of my essay "Reading as a Philosophical Strategy" was published in *Inventions of Reading: Rhetoric and the Literary Imagination* by Clayton Koelb (copyright ©1988 by Cornell University) and is used here by permission of the publisher, Cornell University Press.

Introduction:
So What's the Story?

Clayton Koelb

Any discussion of Nietzsche's relation to postmodernism presupposes that there are answers, albeit not definitive ones, to two questions: "What is 'postmodernism'?" and "What is 'Nietzsche'?" The second question, I will argue here, offers the germ of an answer to the first, for both are versions of the more fundamental and perhaps more interesting question "What's the story?"

At first blush it would appear that the first question is by far the more difficult one, since the term "postmodern" is still at a formative stage and has not yet reached the consistency of usage that would make most of us comfortable with it. Even those who go to considerable lengths to inform themselves on the matter sometimes emerge no wiser than before. Stanley Fish testifies to such an experience: "The whole modernism/postmodernism context of discussion simply mystifies me because I don't have any handle on any of your terms. I've been looking at *Innovation-Renovation*, edited by Ihab and Sally Hassan, that has Lyotard and a bunch of others debating the issue, and I read it diligently, but with an increasing sense of how distant I am from its concerns."[1] This confession inevitably makes one apprehensive and prompts one to wonder about the advisability of rushing in where Fish has feared to tread. If the significance (and indeed usefulness) of the term "postmodern" eludes so influential and informed a theorist as he, perhaps the term is not worth wrangling over. Perhaps the answer to the question "So what's the story of postmodernism?" is *"So what?*'s the story."[2]

There is much to suggest, however, that the debate over the meaning of "postmodernism," if not the term itself, has already proven its value to those engaged in philosophy, criticism, and others of the human sciences. The publication of Jean Francois Lyotard's essay *The Postmodern Condition: A Report on Knowledge* (French edition 1979, English translation 1984) has provoked a reaction quite out of proportion to the modest ambitions of the book, which from one point of view very much resembles a minor detour from the main road of Lyotard's career as a philosopher.[3] It seems that he unexpectedly hit a major nerve in the academic body politic with his little needle. Lyotard's name is on everyone's lips, not because he is the author of *La Phénoménologie; Discours, figure; Economie libidinale*, and so on, but because he is a leading authority on postmodernity. The magnitude of the reaction—whether appropriate or not in the context of Lyotard's philosophical project—testifies to the cultural importance of the issues now associated with the term "postmodern."

Lyotard's impact surely has more to do with those issues than with any special glamor attached to the term itself. As early as 1960, Harry Levin could cite the word as an established part of the historian's vocabulary: "Today we live in what has been categorized—by whom but Arnold Toynbee?—as the Post-Modern Period."[4] Levin's announced topic—"What Was Modernism?"—declares its sense of temporal distance from a modernism which was even then assumed to be definitively finished. A "Post-Modernism" that is simply the time that comes after modernism has been part of the intellectual scene for more than a generation, then, and as a notion is hardly likely to kindle excitement in the 1980s. Lyotard's success as a prophet of postmodernism has nothing to do with his ability to create fashionable terminology. It was not the term, which was already old, but his use of it that brought about the reaction.

Certainly one of the most radical things he did with the term was to deny explicitly that postmodernity is simply that which comes after the modern. With deliberate effrontery he proposed just the opposite: "A work can become modern only if it is first postmodern. Postmodernism thus understood is not modernism at its end but in the nascent state, and this state is constant."[5] The immediate effect of this assertion—beyond its intended shock effect—is to move the notion of postmodernism out of a particular historical time slot (such as the present) and let it loose to attach itself to a modernity that is ever aborning. Modernity, furthermore, emerges as a concept with considerable potential for escaping history. Lyotard defines "modern aesthetics" not by reference to a specific historical configuration but as "an aesthetics of the sublime, though a nostalgic one" (*PC* 81). We might imagine, quite correctly as it turns out, that modernity thus defined would appear in historical contexts far in advance of the "modern Period." Lyotard's act of detemporalizing both the modern and the postmodern is complete when he proposes that "the essay (Montaigne) is postmodern, while the fragment (*The Athaeneum* [*sic*]) is modern " (*PC* 81).

Part of the attraction of Lyotard's version of the postmodern is that its applicability extends far beyond the present cultural situation. This is not to deny that *The Postmodern Condition* is centrally concerned with understanding the present cultural situation but rather to point out how Lyotard's notion allows the present (contemporary postmodernity) to be understood as part of an intellectual formation that surpasses the present. Lyotard's "postmodernism" is clearly less a period concept than a philosophical category, and as such it allows the contemporary cultural scene to play a far more dignified role than the one to which it is regularly assigned by such alarmed observers as Levin. Lyotard may be no less alarmed than others, but the condition he diagnoses is not simply the symptom of exhaustion and decadence; it possesses its own vitality and, perhaps more important, its own epistemology. Lyotard's concept of postmodernism allows us to take contemporary culture seriously and therefore allows us to take ourselves seriously, even if much of what we are engaged in is the undermining of traditional notions of seriousness.

When Lyotard defines postmodernism as "incredulity toward metanarratives" (*PC* xxiv) and structures his argument toward a "recognition of the heteromorphous nature of language games" (*PC* 66), he substantially raises the stakes in the game of current cultural history. It is true, to be sure, that other commentators had already made important moves in the same direction: Ihab Hassan had certainly done so in 1971 with *The Dismemberment of Orpheus*, to cite just one example. But Lyotard offers a set of terms and concepts that makes it possible to understand the studied superficiality encountered so often in contemporary art and architecture as part of an intellectual enterprise that is as respectable as Montaigne's tentative "essays" at self-understanding by means of the commonplace and even the trivial. To put it briefly, and in words better than my own, he has shown how and why the artifacts of contemporary culture are "superficial—out of profundity."[6]

That the words are Nietzsche's and their object the ancient Greeks indicates, I think, something of the far-reaching implications of Lyotard's ruminations. Not only Montaigne with his essays but the Greeks with their myths of the Olympians can be understood as post-modern. There is obviously a danger that the notion of postmodernism will quickly become so encompassing that it ceases to have any useful meaning—and indeed already things have gone so far that, as Babette Babich observes in her essay in this volume, it is a stock claim that the term "postmodernism" is "perniciously chimerical." A word that can mean so many different things at once, it is argued, cannot help us to understand anything. Those who warn of this danger—including some contributors to this volume—could easily cite examples of other intriguing concepts that have grown so massive that there is and perhaps can be no consensus as to their meaning. The term "tragedy" (another notion that inhabits the discourse of both criticism and philosophy) experienced just such growth during the two centuries since 1750 and is now arguably as much an evaluative term as a genre-designating one.[7]

It almost seems that "postmodern" has acquired, thanks to Lyotard, an attraction very similar to that of "tragic." I do not mean with these words to anoint postmodernity with the same chrism that attaches to "tragedy"; the notion of tragedy is, after all, the product of more than two millennia of cultural development, while the postmodern is an upstart only a few decades old. It is possible that discussion of the nature of tragedy will continue long after all interest in the postmodern has ceased. But even if this statement turns out to be true, one essential point of kinship between the two concepts remains, for both offer the possibility of summing up in a single word the most complex and fundamental impulses underlying an entire culture. Whether either term could ever succeed in realizing this possibility remains an open question, of course, but the possibility never ceases to intrigue us. The examples of Nietzsche's pursuit of "tragedy" and Lyotard's pursuit of "postmodernism" suggest strongly that the effort is worthwhile even if it fails of perfect closure.

If one can argue—as I seem to be doing here—that the very project of trying to gather a cultural complex into the domain of a single highly charged term/concept is characteristically Nietzschean, then one must grant that the production of post-modernity (as a philosophical concept, that is, and not necessarily as a historical phenomenon) begins with Nietzsche. It is clear enough that other components in the configuration of the post-modern derive from Nietzsche. Lyotard alerts us to this point when he notes that a presupposition

which takes us in the direction of postmodern culture... defines the set of rules one must accept in order to play the speculative game. Such an appraisal assumes first that we accept that the "positive" sciences represent the general mode of knowledge and second, that we understand this language to imply certain formal and axiomatic presuppositions that it must always make explicit. This is exactly what Nietzsche is doing, though with a different terminology, when he shows that "European nihilism" resulted from the truth requirement of science being turned against itself. [*PC* 39]

Fredric Jameson sees in the *The Postmodern Condition* "an unexpected modulation towards a Nietzschean thematics of history" in that Lyotard's characterization of narrative as an oblivious rather than a memorializing activity "recalls the great and still influential essay of Nietzsche on the debilitating influence of historiography and of the fidelity to the past and the dead that an obsession with history seems to encourage" (*PC* xii). Even more instructive is Jameson's identification of postmodernism with "a commitment to surface and to the *superficial* in all senses of the word" (*PC* xviii). He does not mention Nietzsche here, but he does not have to; few of Nietzsche's notions are more famous than his assertion that Greek culture was based on a deliberate (and philosophically "profound") cultivation of the superficial.

Actually, it is likely that few would argue with the proposition that Nietzsche initiated many of the basic ideas which stand behind the broad concept of postmodernism as expounded by Lyotard and others. Certainly Lyotard's definition, with its stress on "incredulity toward metanarratives," develops a well-known strain in Nietzsche's thought though with different terminology. The issue of Nietzsche's participation in the creation of the current concept of postmodernism is therefore not one to spark much debate. The more troubling question, and the one this volume addresses, is whether or not Nietzsche's work exemplifies the postmodern condition. Most of us can agree that he paved the way for the philosophical concept of postmodernism—in many, if not all, its principal themes—but was he himself a postmodernist? Even some of those who readily admit that Nietzsche helped to found the idea of postmodernity doubt that his writing is in any important way postmodern. Certainly he was interested, for example, in the way in which the ancient Greeks were superficial out of profundity, but many would claim that there is plenty of evidence indicating that he had no desire to appear superficial in his own writing or to offer superficiality as a positive value. Certainly Nietzsche is critical of the science and philosophy of his day, casting doubt on their efforts at self-legitimation, but does not his work as a whole aim toward the creation of its own metanarrative and thus its own version of modernism?

It follows that the most vexing question, the one that most frequently divides Nietzsche scholars into warring camps, involves the Nietzschean metanarrative. I have cited that question at the beginning of this introduction in its simplest and most polemical form as "What is 'Nietzsche'?" We can expand this formulation into something more specific: "What is the master story which explains or governs Nietzsche's project as a philologist/philosopher?" If we could offer a clear and convincing answer to this question, we would accomplish two things. First we would be able to organize and simplify what is on the surface a dauntingly heterogeneous body of writing, providing for ourselves and other readers a set of principles for deciding what will "count" as paradigmatically Nietzschean. Second, we would help to settle the modern-postmodern debate in favor of modernity, since presumably only a modernist writer and not a postmodern one would produce an oeuvre calling for self-legitimation by metanarrative. If, on the other hand, we could show definitively that no single story will order and explain all of Nietzsche's work—could show in fact that the work itself regularly subverts the possibility of such a story—we would accomplish two other things: we would eliminate the necessity of attempting to find in Nietzsche a consistent system of thought, and we would go far toward establishing him as a paradigmatically postmodern writer.

The questions surrounding the issue of "Nietzsche as postmodernist" are therefore centrally important to discussion of Nietzsche, whether or not one cares what "postmodernism" might be. The issues central to the debate about postmodernism happen to coincide closely with the issues around which have clustered the most fundamental and interesting disagreements about Nietzsche. The issue of narrative can serve as a paradigm, and the work of Gary Shapiro, one of the contributors to this volume, can serve as illustration. Shapiro's *Nietzschean Narratives* is clearly a book focusing on Nietzsche and not on the question of postmodernism, but the questions with which it deals are frequently those we recall from Lyotard's *The Postmodern Condition*. Shapiro addressed the problem of Nietzschean narrative because it is a problem of long standing in the literature; it did not just pop up in the last few years in response to Lyotard. Shapiro argues that Nietzsche does not, as is often alleged, treat narrative with wholesale skepticism and that he is a pluralistic narrative thinker who recognizes the inevitability of narration. This narrative pluralism expresses itself in what Shapiro calls the "many voices" of Nietzsche's writing, which include modes of discourse deriving from science, history, the novel, and other sources. Nietzsche's many narrative strategies demonstrate both his dependence on narrative thinking and his unwillingness to submit to a single master story. Shapiro discovers a Nietzsche whose narrative skepticism is directed at metanarratives but not at narrative in general; his work would in fact be impossible without his interest in various modes of storytelling and his desire to exploit them.

The premise guiding the project of *Nietzsche as Postmodernist* is that the questions "What is 'postmodernism'?" and "What is 'Nietzsche'?" are deeply intertwined. It is difficult to discuss postmodernism without invoking Nietzschean themes, and it is difficult to discuss Nietzsche without involving issues now widely associated with postmodernity. The reason is in part—one must acknowledge it from the outset—that both "Nietzsche" (as a cultural phenomenon) and "post-modernism" (as a cultural concept) cut such a wide swathe. Both are complex and pregnant with meaning but also often frustratingly difficult to pin down. The two overlap to some degree simply because they are both so big. But the congruence of the two questions is a matter not just of magnitude or of interpretability but of specific issues. The essays gathered here speak to these specific issues in ways I will discuss below.

I would argue, furthermore (adding at once the disclaimer that this is solely my argument and not one to which the contributors necessarily subscribe) that the question of Nietzsche and that of postmodernism go together in another way. The need to ask again and again "What is 'Nietzsche'?" and to ponder whether or not any straightforward answer is possible is itself a symptom of the postmodern condition. The urgency of the question betrays our uneasiness with the master stories that have been offered until now and indeed for many of us an uneasiness with the very idea of finding a master story according to which we could order all of Nietzsche's writing. Certainly a similar discomfort might be (and has been) directed at the metanarratives constructed around other influential thinkers—Marx and Freud are notable examples—but at those around Nietzsche more than anyone.

Nietzsche's work really seems to call for the kind of incredulity cited by Lyotard, not only or even principally because of what he says, but also because of the aggressively heterogeneous ways in which he presents his material. If often appears as if no single "Nietzsche" emerges for analysis from all these essays, aphorisms, fragments, verses, and outright fictions. The Nietzschean corpus might seem indeed to be a great anthology assembled by an editor whose principals of selection have never been satisfactorily explained. No one, certainly not Nietzsche himself, has produced an "editor's introduction" for this anthology to which one can reliably turn for a definitive exposition of such principles. If we did not have substantial historical evidence that all of this writing in fact flowed from the pen of a single human organism, there would be little justification for talking about "Nietzsche" at all. And even this criterion of individual authorship, of the unity of human selfhood, meets with a growing reaction of postmodern skepticism.

Lyotard's formulation of "incredulity toward metanarratives" could be restated in humbler and more specifically historical terms as a rejection of the great romantic and neoromantic (in other words, "modern") assumption of organic unity. When applied to texts, this rejection brings about a move away from the New Critical consensus of the mid-twentieth century, which was built on Coleridge's theory of the text as organism, toward deconstruction and its insistence on the necessity of textual self-undoing. When applied to persons, it leads to a radicalizing of Freud's insight into the lack of self-presence within the self and to greater emphasis on temporal differentiation in the life of the human organism. (Is the Dante of the *Vita Nuova* the "same person" as the one who courted the living Beatrice? Dante's title implies that perhaps he is not.) When applied to thinking, the rejection implies that the allegedly fundamental philosophical law of noncontradiction ("not A and Not-A") is untenable: not only do we violate it regularly but we *must* violate it in order to think. When applied to epistemology, it suggests (as Derrida finds when reading Plato's *Phaedrus*) that untruth is the precondition for truth.

The promise of the metanarrative is integration: under its aegis everything will somehow fit together. The incredulity of postmodernism is based on experience that this promise is never actually fulfilled, that even the most successful metanarratives inevitably omit something. Perhaps the most important insight of contemporary theory is that narratives (of all kinds, including philosophical or scientific explanations) can come into being only if they leave something out. The possibility of narrative arises only as a result of acts of exclusion. One of the principal conclusions reached by Paul de Man and the circle of American deconstructors is "that 'truths' can only be shored up by strategic exclusions, by declaring opposition where there is complicity, by denying the possibility of randomness, by proclaiming a provisional origin or point of departure as ground."[8] The fulfillment of the promise of metanarrative must therefore always include its breaking.

When we debate the question of Nietzsche's postmodernity, we are ultimately concerned with the question, "So what's the story?" In other words, we wonder whether or not we could (and whether or not we should want to) write the story that would put it all together. Those who believe that he is not postmodern do not simply propose that he is something else (Robert Gooding-Williams argues, for example, that he is basically modern) but, more important, insist that his work is *comprehensible*, in the root sense of that term as "capable of being taken together." Those who assert that he *is* postmodern offer evidence that Nietzsche knowingly engages in the exclusions, complicities, and aleatory acts that make discourse possible but preclude this sort of comprehensibility. Both sides of the debate seek to understand Nietzsche, but they have very different notions of what "understanding" means. Those who suspect that discovering the truth always entails covering something up and those who believe in the possibility of discovering the "whole truth" share one thing, however: a conviction that the effort of inquiry remains necessary and worthwhile.

I have divided the volume into five sections, mostly as a matter of convenience, but in part to signal what I see as certain main trends in the debate about Nietzsche and postmodernism. The first part offers a group of essays each of which assesses Nietzsche in relation to and through the eyes of one or more later (modern or postmodern) thinkers. To illuminate basic Nietzschean concepts, Debra B. Bergoffen uses Lacan; Gary Shapiro Derrida and, to a lesser extent Foucault; and Rebecca Comay uses Heidegger and Benjamin. Comay's "Redeeming Revenge" addresses an issue of considerable importance in recent discussions of postmodernism when she examines the "politics of memory" in Nietzsche's writing. The question of remembering and forgetting, we recall, is central to Lyotard's discussion of the temporality of narrative. Lyotard's paradoxical hypothesis is that "a collectivity that takes narrative as its key form of competence has no need to remember its past" (*PC* 22). Fredric Jameson suggests that this is a Nietzschean idea, fundamentally akin to the "aktive Vergesslichkeit" with which we are familiar from the *Genealogy of Morals.*

Comay shifts the discussion of postmodern memory to a different site, that of revenge and *Widerwille.* With the help of Benjamin and Heidegger, Comay reads Nietzsche "a step beyond Nietzsche" (a step that Nietzsche had himself already taken) toward a notion of remembering that goes "beyond recuperation, beyond affirmation, beyond the eternal stamp of presence" toward a "transvaluation of revenge." Memory becomes the site of counterwill, *Wiederkunft* the place of *Wilderwille*, where we find "against" (*wider*) complicit with "again" (*wieder*). Because Comay's project aims, as she says, not to reconcile Nietzsche with himself but "to try to think where he might, most profoundly, differ from himself," it must be seen as an argument in favor of reading him as a postmodernist.

Gary Shapiro listens in on the activity of genealogy in the text of the *Genealogy of Morals* with an ear tuned to discursive movements to be repeated in the works of later thinkers. Shapiro insists, and argues that Nietzsche insists, upon the "uncanny" quality of the *Genealogy*, on its "disruption of nostalgia and hope." This disruption occurs in part because Nietzche consistently attacks "the positivist metanarrative of science" and partly because he disperses himself into many heterogeneous voices, each of which speaks in the text with an equal claim to the authority of the author.

The uncanniness of Nietzsche's *Genealogy* emerges with special clarity when we examine two recent but very different attempts to come to terms with it, one by Foucault and the other by Derrida. Contrary to expectation, Derrida's repetition of the *Genealogy* in *Of Grammatology* (which for the most part refrains from naming Nietzsche) rather than Foucault's "Nietzsche, Genealogy, History" (which announces itself as a commentary on Nietzsche's text) emerges as the more Nietzschean in its principles and practices. Foucault wants to see in Nietzsche a "genealogist who understands his business" and thereby inappropriately limits the plurality of the *Genealogy;* Derrida, on the other hand, "repeats or translates" it "by reconsidering the project of several putative sciences which are shown to be impossible sciences."

Debra B. Bergoffen offers a version of the postmodern Nietzsche who rejects the law of noncontradiction in favor of "a logic which affirms disjointed terms." This is the logic of the "Madman," whose announcement of the death of God, far from the nihilistic assertion it is frequently assumed to be, actually helps to free Nietzschean perspectivism from its implications of nihilism. Bergoffen argues that Nietzsche's Madman helps us to rethink the relationship between perspectivism and nihilism by suggesting that the two are linked only from the point of view of a "centered subject in a metaphysically anchored world." By proposing a decentered perspective and cutting the world loose from its metaphysical moorings, Nietzsche sets perspectivism free from nihilism.

Bergoffen, enlisting the help of Lacan, reads the affirmation of God's death as a rethinking of the desire for the absolute, as an abandonment of the demand for absoluteness, as a replacement of absolute centeredness by a notion of a (subjective) interpretive center. The desire for the absolute does not vanish; instead, it reemerges as a voice which speaks "the desire of desire rather than the desire of fulfillment." What emerges is a new kind of philosophy, a perspectivism that stresses pluralist contextuality rather than an absolute center. The death of God does not foreclose human desire but rather liberates it into creative playfulness.

Part 2 deals with deconstruction, a topic that does not figure in Lyotard's discussion of postmodernism but which, as I suggested above, is implied by its assumptions. Maudemarie Clark criticizes the deconstructive approach to Nietzsche in one of its most influential forms, the work of Paul de Man. While granting that Nietzsche may in other respects be properly considered postmodern, Clark argues that the notions about language and truth attributed to him by de Man are not really Nietzsche's—or at least not fundamentally and abidingly his. She acknowledges that de Man's reading of *The Birth of Tragedy* has a powerful attraction, explaining as it does contradictions in the text that cannot plausibly be attributed to carelessness, but she attacks the claim that these contradictions are the results of the figurative nature of language. Assumptions about values, Clark says, are far more responsible for the contradictions. "What surfaces . . . is the conflict between acceptance of Schopenhauer's values and his desire to reject them."

There is really no connection, in Clark's view, between the claims about language made in "On Truth and Lie in an Extra-moral Sense" and the contradictions in *The Birth of Tragedy*. The arguments of "On Truth and Lie," furthermore, are not to be taken seriously. Indeed the young Nietzsche did state them with conviction, but he did not maintain them throughout his life, as is shown perhaps by the fact that he never published the essay. Clark finds Nietzsche's position here, which de Man accepts, to be clearly mistaken, to be rejected in favor of a Davidsonian concept of metaphor that she sketches out at the close of her discussion.

Daniel Conway, on the other hand, finds deconstruction central to Nietzsche's work as a philosopher. He identifies Nietzsche's post-modernity as residing in his strategy of deconstructing his own textual authority. Like de Man, Conway sees in deconstruction not an "assault on the author" which illuminates aspects of textuality to which the author was blind but rather a way in which texts ("literary" texts, in de Man's terms) take their own blindness into account. Conway professes to depart from de Man, however, with his contention that Nietzschean self-deconstruction leads ultimately to an "authorless reconstruction" that allows the text to reassert its unity.

Thus Spake Zarathustra offers a particularly apt example of this strategy, especially in its second part, where the text is marked by frequent jolting discontinuities. These discontinuities are not evidence that Nietzsche was carelessly playing with language; Conway maintains that they are the means by which Nietzsche undermines the authority of his own character Zarathustra and forces the reader to move beyond the impasse in which Zarathustra must remain. "He knows that God is dead, but he is powerless to inform his own practices with this knowledge." By thus deliberately abrogating, through his character, his own textual authority, Nietzsche makes certain that the reader will not replace God with either Zarathustra or Nietzsche himself. "Any reader who still reveres Nietzsche's authority in the wake of Zarathustra's dismal failure and 'demise' has missed the point of *Zarathustra*." Parts 3 and 4 then take up the task of "reconstructing" the project on the authority, not of the author or his spokesman, but of the book's readers.

Richard Weisberg takes up again the question of de Man's reading of Nietzsche, directing a critique against de Man's interpretation of the word *hinzugedichtet* in the *Genealogy of Morals*. But Weisberg's critique really goes far beyond de Man to attack one of the most fundamental tenets of postmodern readings of Nietzsche: the belief that his work aimed to undermine the traditional philosophical value of "truth." The Nietzsche of Weisberg's essay is clearly and uncompromisingly a "seeker after truth" whose many iconoclastic opinions were directed not at the value of truth itself but at the value of numerous distortions, misinterpretations, and perversions of otherwise truthful texts.

It is certainly true, Weisberg grants, that Nietzsche undercuts, particularly in his later works, the basis of Western metaphysics, but this skeptical effort does not by any means imply that he had abandoned belief in truth or sought to destroy epistemology. Far from giving up on the possibility of true meaning, Nietzsche insisted on it again and again. One locus for such meaning is the text "as text," which serves as the agency by which the seeker of truth chooses to be controlled "in einer Richtung" (by a single constraint), as Nietzsche puts it. The text is a form of *Stoff* (matter), and as such it is "clearly privileged...above system, history, and especially concept" in Nietzsche's hierarchy of values. By engaging with the text as Stoff, Nietzsche's reader ruminates over it with a sensitivity to all its linguistic and structural subtleties. Nietzsche offers a message, not of post-modernism, but of "textual reverence" in the service of truth.

In part 3 is gathered a set of essays treating Nietzsche as a rhetorician concerned not only with the theory of rhetoric (Crawford) and of writing (Parkes) but also with the philosophical practice of rhetorical reading (Koelb). Graham Parkes moves in the direction of a "post-Derridean" reading of *Thus Spake Zarathustra*, paying special attention to the topic of reading and writing. Parkes wonders why, if Nietzsche is indeed a postmodern, self-deconstructing writer, he produced a book so full of directly quoted speeches and so empty of acts of reading, writing, and indirectly reported narrative. Nietzsche's Zarathustra often resembles Plato's Socrates ("he who does not write") more than he does a postmodern grammatologist, and one wonders whether Nietzsche did not himself share Plato's apparent discomfort with the idea of writing philosophy. Does not the very title of *Thus Spake Zarathustra* privilege the spoken word over the written one?

Parkes suggests that, for all the speechmaking that goes on in *Zarathustra*, there is also "a movement afoot away from the 'speaking' alluded to in the book's title" that leads toward a recasting of the notion of writing as dancing. The act of writing is, like dancing, "a divine affair which requires an inversion of the natural attitude: standing on one's head, one's ear to the ground, keeps one's feet pointed towards heaven." This sort of writing, then, involves the whole body in a continuous process of response to the "music" of becoming. It is not a secondary activity parasitic upon "living" speech but instead the result of a total commitment of the resources of life. The apparent logocentrism of *Zarathustra* can therefore be understood as part of an enterprise whose goal is grammatological.

My own contribution investigates the intersection of rhetoric and philosophy, but it focuses less on the now familiar issue of self-deconstruction than on the inventive function of rhetorical reading. One of the implications of the positions taken in "On Truth and Lie in an Extra-moral Sense" is that "truth" cannot be distinguished from the figurative structures of even the most ordinary and prosaic language This preception could lead to the melancholy (and very unpostmodern) conclusion that one ought to try somehow to circumvent language altogether in order to avoid its contaminating metaphoricity, or it could lead to a decision to join forces with language in an effort to exploit it as a fertile source of philosophical thinking.

Nietzsche displays his postmodernity by taking the latter course, especially in *The Gay Science*, which exemplifies his decision not to shun rhetoric but to immerse himself in it. He uses all the resources of literary language—including versification, mythmaking, and abundant wordplay—to produce a work which announces itself as both joyful and scientific at once and which demonstrates the integration of rhetorical or poetic invention into philosophical discourse. The result is a book that "sees the familiar as a problem" by finding in the commonplaces of everyday discourse the stimulus for refined philosophical thinking.

Claudia Crawford looks at Nietzsche's theory of rhetoric as part of an "agonistics" of ideological discourse that has often been erroneously interpreted as a kind of nihilism. She bases her argument on an aspect of Nietzsche's thinking that has received relatively little attention from Nietzsche scholars in general and from the "new" (postmodern) Nietzscheans in particular: his notion of "physiology." Crawford indicates the prominence of physiology in Nietzsche's theory of rhetoric, noting how the "Course on Rhetoric" grounds discourse on a set of organic "excitations" rather than on "Dinge an sich." These excitations, however, always take place in an individual who is equipped with a set of beliefs, so that "our physiological and unconscious operations are not free from ideological influence."

Crawford's postmodern Nietzsche understands "objects" not as the causes or initiators of language but rather as the products of what we call today, after Foucault, discursive practices. Ideological criticism is one such discursive practice, and its goal is not the discovery of truth but the alteration of power relations. Nietzsche's model of rhetoric, which is both physiological and ideological, shows how the "tricky" agonistics of language seek to effect such alterations.

Part 4 offers several perspectives on the question of the self, whether conceived as the subject of consciousness, the locus of experience that guarantees meaning and unity, or the site of creativity. Kathleen Higgins finds in Nietzsche's work a defense of the value of subjectivity, a defense which would disqualify him from participation in postmodernism. Although skeptical about the value of the term "postmodern" as the designation of a unitary phenomenon, Higgins finds certain main contentions made by most or many who claim to speak from a postmodern perspective, chief among them a rejection of "the full human subject" as a locus for meaning. The postmodern writer is one who "is somewhere else, someone who was someone else the last time, someone who will be someone else the next time." Is Nietzsche one of these postmodernists?

He may at first look like one, because indeed much of what he says appears to advocate "a fragmented, perspectivist orientation toward our experience." But when we look more closely, we find deep disagreements between Nietzsche's perspectivism and contemporary postmodernism. Nietzsche's writing, Higgins argues, does not display postmodern discomfort with subjectivity; on the contrary, his writing "aims at direct and personally invested encounter" with the world. Analogously, Nietzsche may appear to share the postmodern impatience with modern historicism, but Higgins finds Nietzsche moving in a direction contrary to that of postmodernism. His critique of historicism proposes to move "not backward into a more distanced theoretical vantage [like the postmodernists], but forward—not toward a stance of further detachment, but toward a state of immediate involvement." Once again, Nietzsche appears to be far more committed to the value of subjectivity than any self-respecting postmodernist would admit to being.

The Nietzsche proposed by Charles E. Scott, on the other hand, wants nothing more than the "overcoming" of this kind of subjectivity. Scott's Nietzsche is classically postmodern, in that he is concerned centrally with the issues of superficiality and narrativity. At stake in Scott's argument is in fact the question of the philosophical value of a narrative practice that seeks aggressively to be a kind of surface that is not the cover for something else more basic, therefore not the manifest appearance of a latent consciousness. That narrative practice may be described as "self-overcoming," to use Nietzsche's own terminology, or as "recoiling," to use Scott's explanatory metaphor.

"Recoiling is one of the primary movements of self-overcoming and is a movement of masking in Nietzsche's writing that reveals no meaning at all." This lack of meaning is not the result of meaning's disappearance—as it would be perhaps in the work of a modern thinker—but is the fact which Nietzsche's recoils seek to expose. Scott emphasizes the *movement* of recoiling, of self-overcoming, that takes place in Nietzsche's genealogical accounts. Nietzsche's writing is fundamentally narrative in that it constructs a process that we follow as we read, but it is never *metanarrative* because it never promises unity, wholeness, or closure. Scott's Nietzsche makes us experience a "discursive movement . . . that puts the genealogy beyond the reach of any instance of consciousness or experience." This Nietzsche seeks to know but does not necessarily want to be wise. Such a knowing without wisdom is perhaps one of the most intriguing symptoms of the postmodern condition.

Robert Gooding-Williams offers evidence in favor of reading Nietzsche as a modernist who cherishes one of the most traditional values associated with the self, creativity. In his analysis of the famous "Three Metamorphoses" speech that opens part 1 of *Thus Spake Zarathustra*, Gooding-Williams finds a kind of program for creating new values by a process of living through and finally living out "the Christian-Platonic cultural inheritance which repeatedly besets" Zarathustra. By living out various metamorphoses of the spirit, Zarathustra becomes the creator of new values and thus becomes as well a paradigmatic modernist.

Gooding-Williams finds the principal theme of *Thus Spake Zarathustra* to be "the *avant-garde* pursuit of novelty and originality which typifies modernist literary and artistic practices." It will not do, then, to categorize Nietzsche simply as a postmodernist, no matter what his affinities with or legacies to postmodernism might be in other respects. "If Nietzsche is in fact a postmodernist, then his postmodernism is a distinctly (and paradoxically) modernist postmodernism." We might understand it—though Gooding-Williams does not draw this conclusion—as modernism in that peculiar nascent state described by Lyotard and named by him as "postmodern." In any event, Gooding-Williams is surely pointing out in *Zarathustra* a convergence point between the modern and the postmodern that is entirely consistent with Lyotard's hypothesis.

Part 5 offers a discussion of postmodernism itself with particular reference to Nietzsche. The two concluding essays argue—each of them very vigorously—the pro and contra positions to which the volume's subtitle alludes. Babette E. Babich sets forth a case for understanding Nietzsche's work as postmodern in the philosophical sense outlined by Lyotard, though perhaps Babich would want to go further even than Lyotard dared to venture. She too sees the main issues at stake in Nietzsche's choice of his unorthodox philosophical style as those that Lyotard considers the hallmarks of postmodernism: the critique of master narratives and the inevitability of language games. Furthermore, she sees in Nietzsche the founder of the critical project which postmodernism represents, even though his founding role is not always acknowledged by those who employ his ideas.

Even Lyotard, Babich asserts, keeps his discussion of Nietzsche to a minimum and ultimately fails to "endorse the explosive significance of Nietzsche's diagnosis for his own depiction of the postmodern." That diagnosis is most characteristically visible not in Nietzsche's pronouncements but in his style, which Babich finds to be a paradigmatic exemplification of the communication strategy we now call postmodern. This style is characterized by "concinnity," that is, a "playing of and between" the heterogeneous elements that make up the Nietzschean text. Nietzsche's radical articulation of the postmodern condition is often left unacknowledged, or acknowledged only obliquely, in the current debate about postmodernism, but it remains fundamental. What we have identified as the postmodern condition of knowledge is really the post-Nietzschean condition, a situation in which we have, with his help, learned to reconsider the relevance of "the question of the question, the ability to question, and to think."

Robert C. Solomon argues just as energetically against our understanding Nietzsche as a postmodernist and indeed against any easy acceptance of "postmodernism" as a useful historical/philosophical concept. Solomon suggests that the debate about postmodernism has not only failed to help understand Nietzsche (or anything else) but has actually contributed to an increase in misunderstanding by promoting distortions and diversions from "substantive issues," Solomon's Nietzsche may be a canonical source for many of those who think of themselves as postmodernists, but he is not a spokesman for postmodernism. On the contrary, his writings are full of warnings against the very positions now identified with the postmodern condition.

Solomon focuses on the notion of pluralism—central, he feels, to most definitions of the postmodern—and investigates the question of Nietzsche's alleged perspectivism. Only in his "middle" period did he pursue perspectivism: "The mature Nietzsche (from *Zarathustra* on, at any rate) was no perspectivist, not much of a pluralist and, consequently, not much of a postmodernist either." Only the Nietzsche of the "middle" period, if any, can be regarded as committed to a position congruent with postmodernism. But even here questions arise. Solomon takes the notion of *ressentiment* as his test case and finds that it simply cannot be correctly understood as an element in a postmodern philosophy. Nietzschean resentment reveals itself in Solomon's analysis, on the contrary, as a source of postmodernism against which Nietzsche launched one of his most forceful protests. Nietzsche is therefore the prophet of postmodernism only in the sense that Jeremiah is the prophet of Israel's fall: he saw the conditions which would lead to it and warned loudly against them.

It is perhaps only to be expected that a reader of *Nietzsche as Postmodernist*, after hearing so many voices raised on both sides of the debate about postmodernism, might finish the book only to suspect that postmodern criticism may be the very "putative but impossible science" to which Gary Shapiro alludes in part 1. If so, it suggests that postmodern criticism in fact stands or falls by its own postmodernity, its own unwillingness to make of itself a master narrative. It stands if the impossibility of master narratives can be accepted as a condition for all discourse, for then its own refusla to offer one is merely evidence of candor and consistency. It falls if we conclude instead that a master narrative is the one thing a proper field of inquiry cannot do without, for then postmodernism's refusal all too greatly resembles a self-serving rewriting of the rules of intellectual activity. Proponents argue on the one hand that postmodernism does not do something it knows cannot be done; opponents argue on the other that postmodernists have merely declared impossible something that they themselves are incapable of achieving.

The reader who suspects that he or she is surrounded by soldiers fighting a battle over the value of a putative but impossible science may also recognize that such a suspicion does not in itself offer evidence in support of either party, for it is as easily reconcilable with a defense of postmodernism as with an all-out attack upon it. While those who criticize postmodernism will suppose that "putative but impossible" menas "hopelessly inadequate" and "useless for serious thinking," those who defend it will tell you that those same words describe precisely the most interesting and worthwhile projects of which the human mind is capable. What is at stake here may be what Barbara Smith calls a "conceptual taste" and not, after all, a set of claims about the way the world "really" is.[9] If so, we need to revise the nostrum "There's no arguing about taste" to "There's no end to arguing about taste." Indeed, if Smith and the postmodernists are right, there may be nothing else worth arguing about. The story of Nietzsche—which can stand as an abridged version of the story of philosophy and the story of literature—may be nothing as much as the always-incomplete narrative of that argument.

Part 1
Postmodern Perspectives

1

Redeeming Revenge:
Nietzsche, Benjamin, Heidegger, and the Politics of Memory

Rebecca Comay

"It was"—that is the name of the will's gnashing of teeth and most secret melancholy...This, indeed this alone, is what revenge [*Rache*] is: The will's ill will [*Widerwille*] against time and its "it was"....

I led you away from these when I taught you, "The will is a creator." All "it was" is a fragment, a riddle, a dreadful accident—until the creative will says to it, "But thus I willed it." Until the creative will says to it, "But thus I will it; thus shall I will it."

But has the will spoken thus? And when will that happen? Has the will been unharnessed from its own folly? Has the will yet become its own redeemer and joy-bringer? Has it unlearned [*verlernt*] the spirit of revenge and all gnashing of teeth? And who taught it reconciliation with time and something higher than any reconciliation?

—Nietzsche, *Thus Spoke Zarathustra*, "On Redemption"

Not man or men but the struggling, oppressed class itself is the subject of historical knowledge. In Marx it appears as the last enslaved class, as the avenging class [*die rächende Klasse*] that completes the task of liberation in the name of generations of the untrodden....Social Democracy thought fit to assign to the working class the role of redeemer of future generations, in this way cutting the sinews of its greatest strength. This training made the working class unlearn [*verlernen*] both its hatred and its spirit of sacrifice, for both are nourished by the image of enslaved ancestors rather than by the ideal of liberated grandchildren.

—Benjamin, "Theses on the Philosophy of History"

21

The structure of my argument is slightly circuitous, textually indirect. I intend to do two things: to effect two returns. *First, to return Nietzsche to Heidegger*—by way of Benjamin: a writer who wrote contemporaneously with Heidegger's major Nietzsche studies, and who was in his life and death a rather lucid political observer of the times. *Second, to return Nietzsche to himself*: not, certainly to reconcile him with himself, but to try to think where he might, most profoundly, differ from himself. Notably on the question of "the return" itself. In particular, I would like to think about the way in which the thought of such a return which is not reconciliation—neither appeasement nor pity, neither compensation nor identification—opens again the questions of redemption and revenge.

It is a question ultimately of power and the will, and the limits of both as they collide with the given and with each other and with themselves. A question of facing history as "fragment, riddle, and dreadful accident." A question of the "it was." Question that Benjamin sharpens, Heidegger at times blunts—bringing out the double edges in Nietzsche's own thought.

The detour is difficult and far from obvious, for a few basic reasons. First, because of whatever obstacles Heidegger himself may have thrown in the path of redeeming Nietzsche for the thought of time and history beyond the metaphysics of a subject enternalizing itself in its self-asserting positing of the world as standing product.

Second, because Benjamin himself had little good to say about Nietzsche by name. (Scholem names Nietzsche as one of the two writers—Freud is the second—with whom Benjamin came least to terms.[1]) His most explicit pronouncements on Nietzsche tend to brand him as an idealist of one stripe or another: trying to resuscitate the ancient Hellenic spirit of tragedy over against the fractured allegories of the Baroque *Trauerspiel;*[2] fetishizing "creativity" over the mundanities of the "blast furnace and airplane";[3] exalting the aristocratic *Übermensch* over the disenchanted *Unmensch* described by a Brecht, a Kraus, and so on.[4] And nowhere is Benjamin more manifestly troubled than on the subject of the "eternal return" itself (with which he seems to have been acquainted mainly through Karl Löwith's theological, ultimately cosmological, reading),[5] and which he sees to express the ideology of capitulation in its most pernicious, because most consoling, form. For the "return" officially signifies, for Benjamin, the flattening reduction of time to the static repetition of the identical: the leitmotif of the political economy of commodity production (the incessant circulation of what Benjamin calls the *Immerwiedergleiches*) on the one hand,[6] and the leitmotif of the psychological economy of neurosis (the repetition-compulsion of obsessionality), on the other.[7] It expresses, that is to say, the recuperative ideology of capitalism itself in its fullest pathological dimension (and Benjamin was perhaps the first to try to think between Marx and Freud to really *think* the psychopathology of the political). So it is in any case a classic instance of a reader who speaks most of someone where he speaks least about him by name.

Third, because Nietzsche himself would surely have resisted this exercise most vigorously. One can only here imagine what Nietzsche's response to this Jewish, Marxist, thinker would be (Benjamin is emphatically both), who can speak in the same text of both the Messianic redemption of humanity and the socialist equalization of property. Who begins his last, most enigmatic text with an image of a sleight of hand, a mechanical collusion between "theology" and "historical materialism"—both stooped and fettered, both *sitting down* (un-Nietzschean postures), each the other's slave. It is hard not to imagine Nietzsche's jeers. For the two poles of Benjamin's thinking would seem at first glance to collapse squarely into what Nietzsche designates as two most powerful versions of the ascetic ideal, two versions of a life-denying herd mentality in its most debased form.

Not to mention, fourth, the manifest tensions between Benjamin and Heidegger. (And we know that Benjamin spoke most deprecatingly of Heidegger,[8] and that Heidegger seems not to have read Benjamin). I mean the very real tensions between someone attempting to think the political economy of culture and the thinker of Being. Between someone who stubbornly called himself a dialectician and someone who insisted on a certain release from that mode of thinking. Let alone the very great political differences between Benjamin and Heidegger—nowhere more so, of course, than during the 1930's, a time when all these issues press particularly hard.

So all the difficulties of bringing three thinkers together on a single set of questions press hard here. But my point is not to stage for its own sake a particular debate or dialogue—Nietzsche, Heidegger, Benjamin—but rather to try to think the real political meaning of confronting the past, of negotiating the future, ultimately of living with the radical untimeliness of the present as of every time. More precisely: my question is about memory and action, about the ways in which the past returns and gets repeated, but perhaps too about the recurrent impossibility of return, and about the way such return, both possible and impossible, relates to the possibility of action. For in one sense return can be said to be the real meaning of action, both in its potency and at its limit.

Adorno argued that those who "pick up the tab" for civilization,[9] the victims of every society—and most especially the victims of our time, the society of surplus which has opened the space of leisure providing the very possibility of surplus "theory"—have the right to be remembered. One might add that such a memory of victimization, a memory, indeed, of being forgotten, is the real motor of action insofar as it is ultimately this anger that drives all political critique and change.

Nietzsche knew such anger. He too was concerned with memory, with the pressure of the "it was," with what he describes as a heavy stone, a prison. He sought to refuse the pity and appeasement of Christianity in the face of such a weight—the merely teeth-gnashing pose of those who go limp in the face of history, diluting mourning into lament, diluting rage into outrage. His concern, like Heidegger's, like Benjamin's, was rather to face the full force and pressure of history, to let its stone weigh hard—and to resist: not to reconcile or to alleviate all that weight. Such resistance and such refusal to reconcile emerges most clearly in the fight and anger that informs the *Uses and Disadvantages of History*, to which I will shortly turn.

But the fifth and final difficulty here involves simply the special peculiarity of Benjamin's final essay on history, the *Theses on the Philosophy of History*. It is a text that manages to open up Nietzsche's own conflicted sense of history and politics, making necessary and possible a repetition of the question raised by Heidegger at the end of "Who Is Nietzsche's Zarathustra?," when he asks whether the thought of the eternal recurrence can be thought beyond metaphysics, whether that "closed door" can be, for a moment, pried open.

It is a strange and complex text, one which speaks of memory and action, of the fragility of all memory, and of how such fragility can itself become the potent fuel of action. It is a text which asks, without asking, whether the thought of return without reconciliation can itself contribute to a nonmetaphysical sense of history and what that could mean for politics today.

It is a strange text to turn to for this most Heideggerean, but also most non-Heideggerean, of questions. For in this text Benjamin speaks of revenge positively, speaks in one breath of both redemption and revenge. Not redemption *from* revenge, but precisely redemption *as* revenge. A strange text to turn to. For "revenge" has officially, for Nietzsche (and Heidegger seems to buy into this definition) the most metaphysical of all structures: the symptom of an intolerance or "ill will" toward time and its transiency, the symptom of the slave economy of retribution and exchange, the symptom of reactivity in its most abject form.

Official doctrine and orthodox readings aside: what I would like to ask is whether "revenge" itself may be a thought which remains the great "unthought" in Nietzsche's thought. For I believe that the concept of "revenge" may need to be refunctioned and rethought, and that such rethinking may be most potent when it follows the axis of history and politics: an axis which Nietzsche himself for a time begins to loosen, which Heidegger too abruptly closes, and which Benjamin violently blasts open.

I

Three questions concerning revenge: (1) Can the concept of revenge, refunctioned, permit us to think the eternal return in its postmetaphysical truth? Freed, that is to say, from the need to imprint time with the character of eternity, paralyzing all action in the static affirmation of the status quo? (2) Can such a refunctioned concept help us determine the possibilities of a politics beyond the logic of retributive exchange? (3) Can such a concept help us to think "ill will" (Nietzsche's word, *Widerwille*, is telling) as the site not of illness—not the paralysis of disgust or "repugnance"—but as the site of a *resistance of the will* that runs counter to the given and hence even ultimately to itself? Can the desire for revenge transform or transvalue itself into the imperative of resistance? An imperative which would disrupt the very metaphysics of the will as self-assertive subject and hence dislodge the classical politics always attendant upon such metaphysics?

It is not the word "revenge" I want to fix on here, but rather a cluster of concepts which articulate a possibility of a history and a politics which would be freed from revenge in the official sense defined by Nietzsche and by Heidegger. Freed for something not quite apparent.

That official, debilitated, sense of revenge is easy enough to define. The attitude of "revenge" betrays a paralysis in the face of history's "it was." Revenge has three aspects.[10] It is: (1) an inability to reforge the "it was" into a "thus I willed it, thus I will it, thus shall I will it"—an inability which remains a simple passivity and acquiescence before the pastness of the past, turning the past into a rigid ground or cause, the present into a consequence, unleashing a psychology of moral responsibility determined by an entire metaphysics of the subject; (2) a turn, consequently, to otherworldliness, to "fables" of reward and punishment, to a life-denying deferral to the eternal time of final judgment—a real refusal of return and action and thus a static affirmation of the present; (3) a blinking in the face of what presents itself as "riddle, fragment, and dreadful accident" that has relinquished the creative drive to draw or "thicken" (Nietzsche's word is *dichten*) time into One—a complacent atomism or dispersion which is just a fetishizing of the fragmentary.

All of which is to be overcome and redeemed, redeemed by being "unlearned" [*verlernt*], according to the letter of Nietzsche's doctrine, in the affirmations of *amor fati*, by the willed renewal of time's own pastness, by the "poetic" unification of the fragment.

Benjamin's implicit challenge to Nietzsche, I think, is to raise the very question of whether revenge can be rethought, redeemed, nonmetaphysically. It is a question of whether revenge can be thought nonretributively—beyond the logic of punishment and exchange, with the otherworldliness that such logic always drags in its wake. It is a question, then, of whether revenge can be thought non-fetishistically —beyond the atomizing fragmentations of an exchange society. To the point where the eternality of return is finally freed from Christianity's appeasing stamp of the eternal. To the point where the self-assertive will meets a limit which is not mere abnegation.

II

In "Who Is Nietzsche's Zarathustra?" Heidegger outlines the ways in which he believes that Nietzsche's attempt to overcome the metaphysical spirit of revenge against the "it was"—that is, Nietzsche's affirmation of time's incandescent transience in the eternal return of the ephemeral—is a failed attempt.[11] Failed insofar as Nietzsche's own sense of eternity ends up, according to Heidegger, collapsing the ecstatic modalities of time into the standing "sameness" of the present, committing Nietzsche despite himself to the vulgar conception of time as a static series of nowpoints, together with the metaphysics of subjectivity that such a conception always harbors. Together with the politics of self-assertion that such as metaphysics always threatens. Preparing the way for the planetary domination of the earth that is to culminate in the infinite spiralings of mass technology. Forcing Nietzsche despite himself, finally, to succumb— "exuberantly"[12]—to the very spirit of revenge he had sought most strenuously to overcome. Or according to Heidegger's last words on the matter: "What is left for us to say, if not this: Zarathustra's doctrine does not bring redemption from revenge?"[13]

Now is not the time to dwell on the various ways in which Heidegger may or may not have misread by underreading Nietzsche's text here; many of these ways have been well-enough rehearsed by now and can be elaborated with some facility. There is the way, for example, in which Heidegger fails to emphasize fully how the chapter on Redemption is itself already, profoundly, self-problematizing, both internally and in the context of *Zarathustra* as a whole, not to mention the larger corpus generally, at every level and in every layer. Or there is the way in which Zarathustra's look of horror, and the hunchback's subsequent intervention, indicate a certain dissonance within the chapter, underlining that Zarathustra speaks "otherwise to his pupils than to himself" and thus that the discourse is still premature and exoteric and hence already radically compromised from the outset.[14] There is the way, too, in which the earlier chapter on the *Tarantulas* speaks of redemption from revenge as a "bridge" and a "rainbow," suggesting that the "bridge" itself may be only a "rainbow bridge" and the transition in some sense illusory.[15] Or there is the way in which subsequent chapters in *Zarathustra*, in particular the chapter on the "Vision and the Riddle" (which Heidegger himself had read intently in 1937), with its talk of confrontation and decapitation, will surely call into question any lingering notion of a standing or stable present along with any lingering notion of a unification or reconciliation of "fragments, riddles and dreadful accident."[16] And there is the way in which any reading of "Redemption" in *Zarathustra* must in any case take seriously Nietzsche's own most scrupulous critique of that same notion in the *Antichrist* and elsewhere.[17] and then there is, finally, the question of Heidegger's own very peculiar use of certain passages from the *Will to Power* in which Nietzsche allegedly celebrates the eternal stamp of Being upon becoming and in so doing brands himself eternally as the last metaphysician of the West.[18]

The turns and twists of Heidegger's trajectory, whatever they may be, are not now my concern. The issue is time. "High time," says Heidegger, to begin to think the nature of this time.[19] It is indeed late. Late for philosophy to begin to confront the "it was" of an all-too recent past. Late to be speaking of "redemption" and of the amor fati and of the ways in which such affirmation and such forgetting frees redemption from the specter of revenge.

Which leads us to consider whether Heidegger's very question may have been an ill-formed one. Might it not be that in asking about redemption *from* revenge we ask the wrong question? Is it not perhaps rather a question of thinking the redemption *of* revenge? Indeed, perhaps, of thinking redemption *as* revenge? Such that Nietzsche's own meditations on revenge, redemption, return might themselves need to be repeated, redeemed—and avenged?

III

Such is the task of reading the *Uses and Disadvantages of History*—a test which announces itself from the outset as being the voice of revenge,[20] a text painfully aware of its own historicizing tug, a text marked knowingly by nostalgia, by feverishness, by the very excesses it would condemn, a text full of reminiscence for a time beyond reminiscence (struggling to remember what it was like not to remember, turning memory against memory, history against history, knowledge against knowledge), a text forced to speak the language of "advantage" and "disadvantage," *Nützlichkeit, Nachteil,* the utilitarian calculus which it must simultaneously deconstruct—a conflicted enough text...

The second *Untimely Meditation,* no doubt, draws out the sense of the fetishized "it was" in its full political, ideological, even economic and institutional effects. In this text Nietzsche comes to elaborate precisely how an "inauthentic" relation to time and history can determine and distort our relation to perception, language, politics, culture, the body, sexuality itself. It is a text which shows how the inert pressure of the past, unassimilated and uninformed by the "vigour of the present,"[21] undischarged by the plasticity of the moment, can come to "paralyze" life at its most material moment, turning creators into spectators, latecomers into epigones, fighters into collaborators, and artists into the painted "men of culture" whom *Zarathustra* will describe so very well. Such a pressure defines the "spirit of gravity" in its most pervasive form.

It elaborates itself, physically, in the posture and gait of our bodies: the modern, mutilated bodies found strewn later throughout *Zarathustra*—dwarfs, cripples, eunuchs, hunchbacks, those who "hobble," stiff-necked, with small virtues, those who strut the "ticktock" of a small happiness,[22] those, in the *Genealogy,* who chant the falsetto chime of positivism[23]—stooped by the burden of the "facts," "limping"[24] in the twilight of the ages, puppet arms and legs jerked by the plenipotentiaries of the day,[25] impotent in promiscuity, sterile in lust, critical pens flowing prematurely in the ejaculations of a barren scholarship[26]—"eunuchs," says Nietzsche, before the "harem" of history.[27]

It elaborates itself, epistemologically, as the myth of objective scholarship: the neutral search for "facts," "causes," and "things in themselves"—the weary sigh of "if only" or "once upon a time"[28] ("Es war einmal": the narrative version of the "Es war") by which reason legitimates its own impotence and its collusion in the given. Repetition is reduced to that servile imitation which will later go by the name of pity. Truth is reduced to the adaptive ideology of *adaequatio* and identity. Such is the liberal myth of disinterested science—which can only mask, remarks Nietzsche astutely, a deeper form of repression.

It elaborates itself, institutionally, as the empty academic freedom which permits anything to be said because nothing may be done. Nietzsche remarks that the ascetic ideal of neutral science has reduced us all to the professional automata of "thinking-, writing- and speaking-machines":[29] machines described well in the *Future of our Educational Institutions;* machines Adorno will later come to call "culture industry"; machines which disturb the fertile time and space of spontaneous maturation and growth, the organic time of trees, blossoms, fruit (the time, for Nietzsche, of authentic culture); machines—and this is crucial—which are said to "think," "write," and "speak," but which, significantly enough, preempt the possibility of all "reading." ("Their blotting paper at once goes down even on the blackest writing, and across the most graceful design they smear their thick brush-strokes which are supposed to be regarded as corrections: and once again that is the end of that.")[30]

Such a pressure elaborates itself, economically, as the apparatus of modern science (and the police and the army are never, for Nietzsche, far off): plugged to the market, geared to the needs of the state economy, sundered by the divisions of labor, calibrated to maximum efficiency, harassed into accelerated production—"like a hen," remarks Nietzsche, "compelled to lay eggs too quickly.[31]

It elaborates itself, culturally, as the consumerist greed for commodities: the aestheticizing gaze of connoisseurship which turns us into "strolling spectators" through the gallery of history,[32] ingesting culture with an indifferent lust for "more and more." It is a greed so pressing that it will cram anything down—"je mehr desto besser"[33]— books, foreign languages, "the dust of bibliographic *Quisquilien*,"[34] undigested "stones of knowledge" which rumble in our belies,[35] leading only to oversaturation, dyspepsia, nausea, the endless insomnia of the night of Reason. Here the "artistic" drive to creation is exposed as the fetishism of sheer spectacle. An exaggerated moumentalist grandiosity relapses into the pettiness of mere "appreciation." An exaggerated antiquarian piety relapses into that indiscriminate reverence for the past which is ultimately, remarks Nietzsche, the greatest form of sacrilege.[36] An exaggerated exaltation of the "artist" relapses into (indeed exposes itself, almost dialectically, as) the philistine contempt for art. Creation collapses into consumption, art into aesthetics: everything summed up by Hegel's notion of the "death of art," everything Adorno will come to call by the name *Entkunstung*.

It elaborates itself, ideologically, as the belief in evolutionary progress—continuous, inevitable, irresistible, impenetrable. History becomes a stream in which we must "swim and drown":[37] a process culminating in the present, vindicating itself in the present, producing an apotheosis of the present—an "idolatry of the factual,"[38] a "tyranny of the actual,"[39] a naked admiration for "success."[40] It is an acquiescence in the "power of history"[41] which can only mask a deeper capitulation before the powers that be. It is a collusion in the given which can only rob the present of its potency, reducing the past to the role of mere exemplar, reducing the future to the quantitative accretion of infinitesimal reforms. ("He has only to go on living as he has lived, go on loving what he has loved, go on hating what he has hated, go on reading the newspapers he has read.")[42]

Such are some of the elaborations of the official, still unredeemed condition of metaphysical revenge in the face of a frozen "it was." In 1874, Nietzsche saw in advance the political consequences of such revenge.

IV

"Catastrophe—to have missed the opportunity, the critical opportunity."
—Benjamin, *Passagenwerk*

By 1940, the stakes will be high. For Benjamin, writing the *Theses on the Philosophy of History* in occupied Paris, in the full shock of the Stalin-Hitler pact, in the wake of the Moscow purge trials, after the collapse of the Popular Front, after the failure of the Left to mobilize proletariat resistance to fascism as it spreads throughout Western Europe—for Benjamin, in 1940, on the eve of his own untimely suicide, the stakes are extremely high.

Benjamin does not flinch from naming just what these stakes are. He spells out precisely how the historicist view of the past as the inert object of contemplative scrutiny—whether it is to be "grasped the way it really was"[43] (as in the positivist historicism of a Ranke), whether it is to be relived through empathic identification (as in the Romantic hermeneutics of *Einfühlung* [Schleiermacher] or *Nacherleben* [Dilthey], or perhaps even as in the mimetic catharsis of a Lukács),[44] whether it is seen to be amenable to an "eternal image,"[45] or whether, finally, it is just to be picked up indiscriminately like a "prostitute" (the inertly available "once upon a time" of historicism's "bordello")[46]—he spells out precisely how all such reductions of the past to an available, finished object can only strip the present of its potency and rob the future of its radical possibilities.

Benjamin describes precisely how such a representation of the past entails a belief in historical progress which has coopted an entire generation to the cause of fascism. It is evolutionary Marxism in its Social Democratic guise which is put to the most severe of all possible critiques. Benjamin insists that it was the belief in inevitable progress —a spinoff from the "casual chain" theory of history, historicism's consoling "rosary"[41]—that led to the most grievous capitulations on the Left. The faith that socialism need ultimately in any case triumph led to the various concessions culminating in the Soviet-German nonaggression pact. The belief in boundless progress led a generation to trade off present action for the sake of a "better" future. The Enlightenment belief in the triumphal unfolding of a "universal history" could only mask, by 1936, the blind particularisms of class, race, and nation, passing off in the name of an abstract "people" the narrow interests of a determinate rulership, passing off as a "Popular" Front the loaded neutralities of bourgeois hegemony. The belief in historical continuity (in time as an inert continuum, as a homogeneous flow of nowpoints) could only, argues Benjamin, reflect and ideologically justify what was, indeed, the merely factual continuity of accumulated power relations, thereby propping up the homogeneous order of an inherited status quo.

Memory itself is at issue. Whereas the "historicist" takes the past as inert, fixed, immutable—whether as a causal ground to be elaborated, or as a stable treasury to be plundered, or as an archaic residue to be transcended, or as evolutionary origin to be developed, or as a static model to be mimetically "reexperienced" (five versions of the "it was" in its most appeasing, quiescent form)—the "historical materialist" takes the past to be in a perpetual state of danger: charged with the needs of the present, revised by the exigencies of the moment, exposed as the place of barbarism, made present as the site of loss.

"Historical materialism" knows that the past, the "it was," "carries with it a secret index by which it is referred to redemption."[48] It knows as well that such redemption is "nourished by the image of enslaved ancestors rather than by the ideal of liberated grandchildren."[49] That it is animated and fueled by revenge as an act of memory rather than by the appeasement of a future promise. By the refusal to defer redemption because of the consciousness that redemption can only come, for the victims, far too late. Such memory and such refusal marks a revenge beyond retribution: a revenge which will never let itself be bought off by the lures of punishment and exchange. Such revenge refuses to trade off past misery for the abstract utopias of a future heaven; it releases memory from the punctuality of a reified time. This revenge releases time, therefore, from the metaphysics of exchangeability, and releases pastness from the empty passage of equivalent moments of a retributive account.

"Historical materialism" is that reminiscence which refigures repetition as the work of difference. As the memory of what cannot come back it refigures return as the intensity of pure loss—the singularity of death as such. Such repetition shatters the space of all imitation and identification, and thereby shatters every fantasy of compensation or adequation.

"Historical materialism" is the counter-memory which calls all accounting-memory into question. It opens the space of a future memory precisely by recapturing the past as the site of lapsed—because betrayed (and that can only mean, for the victims, eternally betrayed)—hope.

"Historical materialism" seizes *what was to have been the future* for generations now dead or silenced; it seizes the irreducible pastness of a future—the future as something lost and now "no longer"—and hence rethinks it without appeasement and without reprieve. Memory as such becomes the relentless revenge which knows no promise of fulfillment and will know no satisfaction in recompense.

"What was to have been the future." Note the strange tense of this formulation: a future radically imperfect because it will never have been rendered fully present; a future which persists precisely in and as its own failure *to have been*. It is a radically finite future which memorializes itself as the will-have-been of what was-not-to-be: a future whose only moment inscribes the missed moment of betrayed and relinquished hope. Its presence is thus just its forgone absence, its possibility just its impossibility: its self-disclosure just the gap left by its prior failure to appear.

Such a radically imperfect future marks the perfect inversion of the "Hegelian" future perfect. It is the inversion of the will-have-been of an ideal present projecting itself confidently toward the parousia of its proper reminiscence. History, for Hegel, concludes in the "temple of Mnemosyne":[50] where what-has-been [*gewesen*] is memorialized as essence [*Wesen*]:[51] where nothing essential, then, can truly be lost: where no revenge, therefore, will finally be thinkable, but simply because the accounts will have all been closed.

But it is precisely such a loss which Benjamin sets out to thematize: a loss which traces itself in the untimely movement of every materiality of all time. It is a loss which inscribes itself in the folds and detours of language. It traces itself in the creases of the body itself.

In his essay on Proust, Benjamin speaks of the irreducible lateness of experience as such, which materializes itself physically in the convolutions and doublings of syntax and in the wrinkles of old age. Aging itself is described by Benjamin as the cumulation of missed presents. It is constituted by the uncanny "too late" which marks the structure of lived time as such. Such a lateness disrupts the inevitability of every destiny, dislodges every claim to "mastery" (*Herrschaft*), disappropriates every comfort of being "at home":

> [Proust] is filled with the truth that none of us has time to live the true dramas of the existence that we are destined for. This is what ages us. Nothing else. The wrinkles and creases on our faces are the registration of the great passions, vices, insights that called on us—but we, the masters ["wir, die Herrschaft"], were not home.[52]

Memory assumes the involuntariness—"ungewolltes Eingedenken," Proust's "mémoire involontaire"—of a seizure without closure. Reminiscence becomes the recapitulation of what never did, in the first place, take place.[53] Time becomes the abyss of an insufficiency without fulfillment. Desire becomes the impatience which settles for neither nostalgia nor future balms.

Such a loss acquires a specific material density in Benjamin's reflections on technology. In his essay on surrealism, Benjamin speaks of the revolutionary energies latent in the experience of mechanical obsolescence itself: the charge induced, for an observer such as André Breton, by the sight of "outmoded" technological forms—the first factory buildings, the earliest photographs, the dresses fashionable only five years ago.[54] It is a charge, writes Benjamin, which converts "mournful railway journeys" into moments of "revolutionary experience," which converts the "destitution" of nostalgia into decisions of political action, which converts the empty exchangeability of what is perpetually out of date into a moment of radical rupture: the kind of rupture which is born only of irretrievable loss. In the self-obsolescing quality of technology itself—at the heart, thus, of the consumerist economy—there would seem to be a reminder of something escaping that economy. In the experience of time under industrial capitalism-time in its most homogenized, "metaphysical" manifestation, the time of pure accounting and exchange—is the experience of time "lost" in the Proustian sense. It is a loss which would seem to counteract every form of nostalgia and to fuel the desire for all revolutionary change.

Such a loss acquires a certain *historical* determinacy by 1940, when Benjamin writes his untimely *Theses*, in exile during the early days of the Occupation, at a moment when history has begun to speak, repeatedly, of a vanishing of definite hopes. It is a moment when the "it was" has already begun to institute itself as the uncanny recurrence of missed opportunities; in France alone, where Benjamin is writing, these have acquired specific date marks, and open up a series of reverberations without relent—1789, 1830, 1848, 1870, 1936—all the moments of failed revolution, all the turnings that did not quite turn.[55] The "Es war" is no longer "einmal" but enragingly manifold; and the revolutionary imperative of the present would seem to hinge precisely on the consciousness of its repeated frustration in the all-too recent past.

Such a loss has perhaps even more precise historic specificity for Adorno, who, outliving Benjamin, was to determine the issue of "out-living"—*überleben*—as the meaning of survival "after Auschwitz," the specific destiny of our time. When Adorno opens *Negative Dialectics* with the statement that "philosophy lives on because the moment to have realized it has been missed,"[56] he is referring of course to the specific lapse which marks reason's relapse: the special lateness we must learn to bear today. What has lapsed is thinking's final deadline, a deadline which is precisely a deathline: the historic line of judgment which has condemned philosophy, "after Auschwitz," to speak the guilt of its own failure to redeem. Philosophy "lives on" in the abject-ness of being too late for action, too late to undo; its "life" has become the afterlife, the overlife, the outlived, privileged life of a death that will no longer—despite Zarathustra—"come at the right time."

Zarathustra: "Many die too late, and a few die too early."[57] After Adorno we might rewrite this statement: "Few—the privileged few of philosophy—die too late, *because* many die too early."

Philosophy's own survival, its special kind of lateness, is, in Adorno, the prolonged, "outlived" life: the "overlife" which alone, today, can mirror and commemorate that other untimely death—the pre-mature death of all victims of history, the very deaths philosophy colluded in only recently through its own failure to engage. Its own untimely life doubles the untimely deaths of the oppressed of history: the last testimony left of an age in which "dying at the right time" has become impossible. An age in which—to quote Adorno—"das Leben lebt nicht."[58]

"Life does not live." Such death is the untimeliness that marks every time, shatters every moment of affirmation, limits every triumph of every will.

To think such untimeliness radically would be to think the very impossibility of all reconciliation. "Something higher," says Zarathus-tra.[59] Perhaps. In an age where reconciliation takes the appeasing form of officially sanctioned compensation; in an age where reconciliation can only appear—according to Adorno, in a sharp response to Lukács—"under extortion";[60] in such an age, which is to say, in our age, the only redemption possible is the redemption which comes too late for all redemption. But such is the structure of Messianic time itself, as described by Kafka:

The Messiah will come only when he is no longer necessary; he will come only on the day after his arrival; he will come, not on the last day, but on the day after.[61]

V

Redemption, thus conceived, would be the very opposite of the ascetic ideal: the opposite of "redemption" in its most reactive (Christian, Buddhist, Epicurean) guise, which Nietzsche dismisses, brusquely—in almost Marx's language—as a narcotic, a hypnotic, as the resentful phantasm of eternal compensation,[62] and which he compares more than once to the guilty projections of a hen imprisoned by the chalk line of responsibility.[63] In the *Will to Power*, Nietzsche attributes this phantasmatic projection to an elementary error in logic (the "seduction of language" is responsible)[64]—a confusion of "consequence" with "cause," of events with agents, the hypostasis of "grounds" for pure activity which unleashes a chain of retributive events.[65] In the *Antichrist*, Nietzsche goes on to determine this ascetic version of redemption psychologically, physiologically, in terms of a pathologically heightened sense of touch.[66] "Redemption" is the official doctrine preached by those ("psychological types") whose hypersensitivity to the given manifests itself as an incapacity for *resistance*. Reactive irritability becomes the conformism which is elsewhere the mark of pity: an intolerance to resistance (*Widerstand*), a warning against (*Widerraten*) resistance (*Widerstreben*), a resistance to resistance.

The instinctive exclusion of any antipathy, any hostility, any boundaries or divisions in man's feelings: the consequence of an extreme capacity for suffering and excitement which experiences any resistance [*Widerstreben*], even any compulsion to resist, as unendurable *displeasure* (that is, as *harmful*, as something against which the instinct of self-preservation *warns us* [*widerraten*]); and finds blessedness (pleasure) only in no longer offering any resistance ["Widerstand zu leisten"] to anybody....[67]

To think redemption beyond reconciliation would be to think the impossibility of this other—official—redemption. But it would be, then, to think the fragment beyond unity, the riddle beyond solution, the accident beyond necessity. It would be, indeed, to think the perpetual pastness of the "it was": beyond recuperation, beyond affirmation, beyond the eternal stamp of presence: a pastness without appeasement, a passage without harmony, the site of a repetition without recompense.

But to do so, then, would be to think a certain transvaluation of revenge. The will itself would face its limit: still gnashing, still lonely, still angry at its failure—at the limits of its power, at the limits of its own will. To sustain such a melancholy without the appeasing act of punishment—without the otherworldly solutions of the reactive, without the retributions of the weak—would be perhaps to think the very transvaluation of the will: beyond self-assertion and its opposite, beyond power and acquiescence, beyond affirmation and abnegation. Beyond Nietzsche and Schopenhauer alike—certainly a step beyond Heidegger's own Nietzsche. A step, perhaps, in the direction of Heidegger himself.

For this would be to think the very limits of the will to power. It would be to think the very spot at which the will splits from the ruses of power and becomes the locus of pure resistance. It would be to think the will as sheer counterwill, *Wille* as *Widerwille*. It would be, perhaps, to rethink Zarathustra's definition—certainly to rewrite Kaufmann's translation:

This, indeed this alone, is what *revenge* is: the will's ill will ["des Willens Widerwille"] against time and its "it was."[68]

"Des Willens Widerwille": but what would it be to think the will's own *Widerwille* nonmetaphysically? It would be to think *Widerwille* not as "ill will" or as "bad will"—not, as Hollingdale will render it, "antipathy"[69] or "repugnance"[70]—but rather as the counterwill which runs counter to the factual and hence ultimately to itself. Not retribution but resistance: a resistance to the given which is a resistance to the self: an anger beyond punishment, a vengeance beyond vengeance, a melancholy beyond lament.

A step beyond Nietzsche. The gay science yields to the "melancholy science" which Adorno has described so very well.[71] Such melancholy disrupts the harmony of every affirmation, displacing the master's triumph with the memory of those who, once slaves, will be remembered forever too late.

To think the *Wiederkunft* as the place of *Widerwille:* this is to think the "Wider" lodged within the "Wieder"—the "against" outstripping the conformity of every "again"—a resistance which opens the space of confrontation with every past and every present.

VI

A step beyond Nietzsche. Nietzsche himself began to speak of it. I'll stop here with two passages.

First, from the second *Untimely Meditation.* Nietzsche is speaking, as we have seen, of all the varieties of inauthentic memory, of all the ways in which a fetishistic sense of history will always politicize and institutionalize itself as an ideology of capitulation. He comes to speak of the special way in which success and "power" (*Macht*)—the brute "power of the acual," the "blind power of the factual"—have become idealized and idolized in the affirmation of the status quo. What is pernicious about historicism, insists Nietzsche, is the way in which it invariably falls into the hands of power so as to break the natural resistance of the will. Youth is compelled to rush into that premature "manhood" which keeps everyone and everything in its place.

What is striking here—surprising to read after passing through Heidegger's reading, but surprising to read, as well, after reading the *Will to Power*—is not only the way in which "power" itself is being problematized to a degree, I believe, unparalleled elsewhere in the corpus. Equally striking is the way in which Nietzsche comes to introduce a split between power and the will. It is a split which in turn would seem to split off the will from the affirmation of every present and indeed, finaly, even from itself. The operative word: *Widerwille.*

[The excesses of history] are employed ... against youth, so as to train them to that mature manhood of egoism which is striven for everywhere; they are employed so as to break the natural repugnance ["das natürliche Wilderwille"] of youth by a scientific-magical illumination of that manly-unmanly egoism which transfigures it. We know, indeed, what history can do when it gains a certain ascendancy, we know it only too well: it can cut off the finest instincts of youth, its fire, defiance, unselfishness [*Selbstvergessen*] and love, at its roots, damp down its sense of justice, suppress or regress its desire to mature slowly with the counter-desire to be ready, useful, fruitful as quickly as possible, cast morbid doubts on its honesty and boldness of feeling; indeed, it can even deprive youth of its fairest privilege, of its power to implant in itself the belief in a great idea and then let it grow to an even greater one.[72]

Second, from *Beyond Good and Evil*. An extraordinary aphorism in which language itself is revealed as the site of history's own special mode of memory, as the site of repetition and redoubling, as the site of silence and concealment, as the site of discord and even dissonance, as the site of danger and resistance. Again, the word: *Widerwille*.

One always hears in the writings of a hermit something of the echo [*Widerhall*] of the desert, something of the whisper and shy vigilance of solitude; in his strongest words, even in his cry, there still resounds a new and more dangerous kind of silence and concealment. He who has sat alone with his soul day and night, year in year out, in confidential discord and discourse... finds that his concepts themselves at last acquire a characteristic twilight-color, a smell of the depths and of must, something incommunicable and reluctant ["etwas Unmitteilsames und Widerwilliges"] which blows cold on every passerby.[73]

2

Translating, Repeating, Naming:
Foucault, Derrida, and The Genealogy of Morals

Gary Shapiro

Two cautions or warnings (at least) must be heeded in the attempt to do justice to Nietzsche's project of a genealogy of morals in the text that bears that name. While the *Genealogy* is often regarded as the most straightforward and continuous of Nietzsche's books, he tells us in *Ecce Homo* that its three essays are "perhaps *uncannier* than *anything else* written so far in regard to expression, intention, and the art of surprise."[1] If we should think ourselves successful in penetrating to these uncanny secrets and saying what Nietzsche's text means, once and for all, we would then have to read again its lapidary although parenthetical injunction that "only that which has no history can be defined." For since the work of Theodor Adorno and Max Horkeimer, Jürgen Habermas, Michel Foucault, Jacques Derrida, and Gilles Deleuze, genealogy has become a polemical word. When Nietzsche published the *Genealogy* in 1887, the main uses of the term arguably had to do with the ascertaining of actual family lineages to determine rights to titles, honors, and inheritances, as in the venerable *Almanach of Gotha*, and a careless librarian today might classify the book among those many middle-class popularizations which might all go under the title "Tracing Your Family Tree for Fun and Profit." But Foucault characterizes his *History of Sexuality* as a genealogy of the modern self, and Derrida describes a large part of his intellectual project as "repeating the genealogy of morals"; Nietzsche's practice and example are invoked in both cases.

How, then, might we proceed to assess the significance of Nietzsche's "genealogy" in relation both to its mundane cousins and to those who have been drawing on his inheritance? I propose only a partial, critical, and bifocal effort in that direction, consisting in a reading of a few paradigmatic readings of Nietzschean genealogy. Let me begin with the interpretation of Jürgen Habermas, who assimilates Nietzsche's project to the aristocratic attempt to demonstrate the superiority of the most ancient and archaic. According to Habermas, Nietzsche's rejection of all rational and critical criteria for assessing values leaves him no other option:

Once the critical sense of saying "No" is suspended and the procedure of negation is rendered impotent, Nietzsche goes back to the very dimension of the myth of origins that permits a distinction which affects all other dimensions: What is *older* is *earlier* in the generational chain and nearer to the origin. The *more primordial* is considered the more worthy of honor, the preferable, the more unspoiled, the purer: It is deemed better. *Derivation* and *descent* serve as the criteria of rank, in both the social and the logical senses.

In this manner, Nietzsche bases his critique of morality on *genealogy*. He traces the moral appraisal of value, which assigns a person or a mode of action a place within a rank ordering based on criteria of validity, back to the descent and hence to the social rank of the one making the moral judgment.[2]

This may be the genealogical scheme of values of the *Almanach of Gotha*, but it is not Nietzsche's. Despite his frequent bursts of admiration for the "blond beasts" (lions) of early cultures, Nietzsche's narrative never returns us to a point at which one single, pure form of morality obtains. Contrary both to the efforts of theological ethics and to the hypotheses of the English utilitarian historians of morality, *The Genealogy of Morals* insists that there is no single origin but only opposition and diversity no matter how far back we go. There are, always already, at least two languages of morality, the aristocratic language of "good and bad" and the slavish language of "good and evil." Where a Platonist would focus on the fact that "good" appears in both discourses and would search for its common meaning, Nietzsche notes that it is *only* the word shared by the two languages. One says "good" and happily designates its satisfaction with itself; the other reactively designates those who speak in such a way as "evil" and who define themselves as the opposites of the evil ones. Even within the aristocratic group, Nietzsche observes, there are again at least two varieties of the moral code "good and bad" which can be distinguished as the knightly and the priestly. Not myth, as Habermas would have it, but something much more like the structural linguistics or anthropology which the twentieth century has seen brought to bear on the inquiry into myth is at work here.

While Habermas seems to suppose that the rejection of the progressive and teleological enlightenment conception of history must entail a nostalgic valorization of the archaic, Michel Foucault's reading of Nietzsche and his own development of the genealogical project are vigorously committed to avoiding the temptations of both nostalgia and progress. Genealogy is the articulation of differences, of affiliations that never reduce to a system or totality and of the transformations of power/knowledge in their unplanned and unpredictable concatenations. Foucault's later writings, especially *Discipline and Punish* and *The History of Sexuality,* frequently acknowledge their indebtedness to Nietzsche with respect to all of these themes. Foucault would perhaps see his own distinctive contribution as the extension of the genealogical approach to the constitution of the human sciences and their associated disciplines and practices. In tracing out the "capillary" forms of power in these fields, Foucault exhibits that taste for the documentary, gray page of the legal text which, as Nietzsche indicates in his "preface" to the *Genealogy,* is the laborious side of the outrageous attempt to raise the question of the value of morality. These works might be called translations of the *Genealogy* into the worlds of the prison and surveillance, psychiatry and biopower. Foucault's commentators (for example, Hubert Dreyfus and Paul Rabinow) have assured us that these translations of the Nietzschean genealogy are clarified and to some extent grounded in his essay of 1971, "Nietzsche, Genealogy, History," which is both textual commentary on Nietzsche's book, the *Genealogy,* and a thematization of the principles that govern Foucault's later studies. I will direct some attention to this essay in order to suggest what is partial, specific, and limited in Foucault's appropriation of Nietzschean genealogy. Let me immediately register the qualification that I take the Foucauldian translations to be significant and deserving of the attention and even the imitations that they have generated.

You may recall that Foucault distinguishes two words, *Ursprung* and *Herkunft,* which play important roles in Nietzsche's text.[3] To be concerned with Ursprung, or origin, is to be a philosophical historian who would trace morality—or any other subject matter—back to an original principle that can be clarified and recuperated. The genealogist will, however, be concerned with the complex web of ancestry and affiliations that are called Herkunft, those alliances that form part of actual family trees, with all their gaps, incestuous transgressions, and odd combinations. (Incidentally, Wittgenstein's conception of "family resemblances" may stand in a certain Viennese line of Nietzsche's descent[4]). Here, Foucault tells us, the genealogist comes into his own: "Where the soul pretends unification or the self fabricates a coherent identity, the genealogist sets out to study the beginning— numberless beginnings whose faint traces and hints of color are readily seen by an historical eye."[5]

I want to concentrate on that decisive moment in Foucault's construction of the genealogical Nietzsche that appears in his reading of the distinction between *Ursprung* and *Herkunft* as determining the difference between the philosophical historian and the genealogist. Two possible points of view, two research programs, two types of inquirers are designated by the choice between these two words and concepts. If Nietzsche were to be misconstrued as one with a nostalgia for origins and an obsession with first principles, thn his praise, in the *Genealogy*, of "the blond beast" and the "artistic violence" of "noble races" would support something like the mysticism of racial purity for which the Nazis attempted to claim his authority. But Foucault tells us that the very beginning of Nietzsche's text, its "Preface," rules out such a reading: "One of the most significant texts with respect to the use of all these terms and to the variations in the use of *Ursprung* is the preface to the *Genealogy*. At the beginning of the text, its objective is defined as an examination of the origin of moral preconceptions and the term used is *Herkunft*. Then, Nietzsche proceeds by retracing his personal involvement with this question."[6] The point of *that* narrative, Foucault says, is to establish that even Nietzsche's analyses of morality ten years earlier operated within the orbit of *Herkunftshypothesen* rather than the quest for origins.

Now isn't it just a bit odd that Foucault wants to determine the nature of *this* Nietzschean text by attending to its *beginning*, as if one could expect the beginning to be transparent? What that beginning announces, so it seems, are the fundamental concepts of the genealogist and, even, the birth of the genealogist, his vocation toward a certain kind of scientific work. What will not be in question in Foucault's reading of the *Genealogy*, henceforth, is the identity and voice of the genealogist. But this search for a clear line, for a master speaker in Nietzsche's text, must give us some pause, first, because it apparently *exempts* this text from the very same genealogical, or differentiating, imperative that it *finds* in the text; and, second, because it does not completely read or translate everything that is to be found in the preface. In fact, Foucault starts not at the beginning of Nietzsche's beginning but with the second numbered paragraph of the "Preface." At the *very beginning* of the preface, that is, in its first lines, Nietzsche writes: "We are unknown to ourselves, we men of knowledge—and with good reason. We have never sought ourselves—how could it happen that we should ever *find* ourselves?"[7]

Might this not serve as a warning that the voice of the text, Nietzsche's voice, is not to be identified simply as that of the genealogist who understands his business? Perhaps it is a warning that no single voice animates the *Genealogy* and that this text must itself be read dialogically, as what Foucault calls in another context a "concerted carnival."[8] For shortly after the apparent confession of ignorance comes the bold sweep of the narrative to which Foucault directs our attention, the narrative in which Nietzsche explains the steps leading to his vocation. Yet these claims of dedication and discovery acquire an Oedipal tone in this context, suggesting a certain pride and self-assurance. This is a tragic voice. And it is not the only voice of the text, which alternates among a series of historical and fictional voices—those of the Oedipal scientist, the tragic dramatist, the buffoon of world history, the witnesses (both real and imaginary) whom Nietzsche summons to testify about the manufacture of ideals—and doubtless there are others.

We might have begun reading the *Genealogy* at its subtitle, "Eine Streitschrift" (a polemical text), which seems to tell us to what genre the book belongs. We might read this *agon* or *polemos* as directed not only toward others, like the philosophical historian, who are on the *outside* of the text; we should also read the battle, the dialogue the prosopopoeia and exchange that goes on within the text itself. If we were to pursue this internal differentiation of voices within Nietzsche's text further, we might begin by recognizing the stylistic affinities (in Nietzsche's strong sense of style) between this text and some of Dostoyevsky's, especially the latter's *Notes from Underground*, which Nietzsche read and remarked upon in the months preceding the writing of the *Genealogy*. These affinities go beyond thematic concerns with such oppositions as the man of *ressentiment* and the normal man or the claim that consciousness is an illness (aproductive, pregnant illness will be Nietzsche's restatement of the latter). We would also have to note what Mikhail Bakhtin has called the dialogical character of the Dostoyevskean text and its polyphonic structure.[9] Despite its external form of monologue, the *Notes* enacts an endless controversy and exchange between the narrator and his others, the "normal" men, with whom he sees himself in dialogue. Dostoyevsky's normal man speaks for the progress of science and the utopia of the "crystal palace"; in Nietzsche's *Genealogy* the voice who introduces the narative claims himself to be a scientist of sorts, but his scientific authority is called into question by the articulation of the polemic.

At one point Foucault seems to recognize a certain plurality in Nietzsche's text, for he notes that Nietzsche's challenge to origins is confined "to those occasions when he is truly a genealogist" (142), but he does not explain what the other occasions are. From this gene-alogist *qua* genealogist, Foucault draws a number of principles of reading. Let me cite just two of these principles, with the suggestion that each could be usefully employed in reading the *Genealogy* itself as a pluralized text:

1. To follow the complex course of descent is to maintain passing events in their proper dispersion.[10] (Then why not also the dispersion of voices in the text?)

2. The body is the inscribed surface of events (traced by language and dissolved by ideas), the locus of a dissociated self (adopting the illusion of substantialunity), and a volume in perpetual disintegration. Genealogy, as an analysis of descent is thus situated within the articulation of the body and history. Its task is to expose a body totally imprinted by history and the process of history's destruction of the body.[11]

Does not the metaphorics of inscription, volume, and imprinting call for an application of this principle to the body of the text and, in par-ticular to the inscribed textual body, the *Genealogy*, which would be the source of this principle? I mean to suggest not that Foucault has completely failed to see this side of the *Genealogy* but that he has tended to localize it, to confine it to the subject matter, assuming that such a subject matter can be isolated, rather than to see it as the actual multiplication of voices in the text. If he had done so, the gene-alogical studies that seem to be founded on this reading of Nietzsche might have been less in the mold of the new science, art, or discipline of genealogy. For part of the upshot of the pluralization of voices in the *Genealogy* is the calling into question of a number of postures of inquiry, including that of the dedicated genealogist who is, insofar as he would practice a normal science of genealogy, not very different from the philosophical historian whom Foucault criticizes and even ridicules.

Foucault's limitation of the pluralizing and differentiating movement in his genealogical projects has consequences that go beyond his reading of the Nietzschean text itself. Let me cite just one example from the second volume of *The History of Sexuality*. This part of Foucault's history is concerned with the formation of a sexual ethos in fourth-century Greece that would be responsive to the apparent contradiction between contemporary sexual practices and the prevailing norms of responsible citizenship. How can the love of boys not lead to the habituation of a generation of prospective citizens to patterns of submission and passivity that would be incompatible with their designated social roles? In the light of this question, Foucault undertakes a genealogy of the conception of the responsible self or subject that, as he sees it, is formed through the discourses and practices that propose solutions to this dilemma. These formations of power and knowledge he distinguished as: (1) dietetics (prudential advice concerning the use and abuse of pleasure); (2) economics (the principles of the household); (3) erotics (the wise conduct of love affairs); (4) and "true love" (the philosophical transvaluation of the love affair into the mutual pursuit of truth).

The crucial evidence for Foucault's analysis of this last discursive form comes from Plato, especially from the *Symposium* and *Phaedrus*. What is at first surprising about Foucault's reading of these Platonic texts is the degree to which he flattens them out into a form that seems drastically to understate their internal plurality and complexity. In reading these dialogues Foucault simply opposes the false speeches on love to the true speeches (Diotima's in the *Symposium*, Socrates' second in the *Phaedrus*). In describing what is going on in the dialogues, Foucault constantly, and more than accidentally, uses various forms of the locutions "Plato says" or "Plato thinks."[12] Plato discovers that the truth of love is the love of the truth, even though Plato never speaks in his own voice in the dialogues. Foucault ignores the fact that Diotima's speech is distanced from Plato by several degrees: it is reported by Socrates, and the dialogue as a whole is relayed to us through a series of less than completely reliable witnesses. Similarly, in the *Phaedrus*, Socrates' speech is part of a very complex thematics of love and discourse which raises questions about the self-sufficiency of the literary form in which it is embedded. This assimilation of the Platonic dialogues to the relatively linear development of a new ethics of love is at least as one-dimensional as the reading that would see them as nothing but preliminary versions of modern discussions of the universal and the particular.

Nietzsche, despite some of his raging against Plato, seems to have had a more genuinely genealogical view of the matter when he distinguished between the Socratic and plebeian theme and its Platonic, aristocratic reworking and sublimation, or when he remarked, in *The Birth of Tragedy*, that the Platonic dialogue was the vessel by which art survived the shipwreck of ancient culture.[13] As genealogical readers of Plato, Nietzsche's heirs are Roland Barthes, who reads the same dialogues as "fragments of a lover's discourse," or Jacques Derrida, who sees them as the polysemous ingredients of a Platonic pharmocopeia.[14] While some critics (Mark Poster, for example)[15] have suggested that Foucault's last series exhibits a decline in his powers, I would claim that his reading of Plato is continuous with his way of reading Nietzsche in the founding essay on genealogy. For example, in mapping Greek discourses on love and sex into the four categories—in ascending order—of dietetics, economics, erotics, and true love, Foucault seems to be under the sway of the "Platonic ladder" of the *Symposium* or perhaps of the divided line of the *Republic* itself. When the uncanny dimension of the text of the *Genealogy* is neglected, genealogy itself tends to degenerate into a mere method which circumscribes its subject matter all too neatly. After remarking on the uncanniness of the *Genealogy*, Nietzsche added, "Dionysus is, as is known, also the god of darkness." Could it be that Dionysus lies in wait for the normal genealogist at the heart of the labyrinth into which he has strayed?

Some years before this essay on Nietzsche that marks Foucault's later program, he and Jacques Derrida had an exchange concerning analogous issues in the reading and translation of Decartes. The questions developed in Foucault's *Histoire de la folie*, Derrida's "Cogito and the History of Madness," and Foucault's reply, "My Body, This Paper, This Fire" hinge on knowing how many voices are speaking in Descartes's *First Meditation*.[16] The crux of the dispute is the reading of the passage in which Descrates, or one of the voices of the *Meditations*, briefly entertains the possibility of doubting that he is sitting by the fire, only to elicit the reply that those with such doubts—who imagine that their heads are pumpkins or that they are made of glass —are mad and that he would be equally mad if he took them as a precedent for understanding his own case. For Foucault's representation of Descartes as juridically excluding the possibility of madness from the rational course of his meditations, it is important that there be one commanding voice that can be read as emblematic of the "great internment" of the mad in the seventeenth century. For Derrida, in contrast, it is crucial that we see a series of objections and replies within the text itself, so that the *Meditations*, far from excluding any possibility of madness, push this possibility to a hyperbolical extreme through the hypothesis that we are always dreaming or deceived by an evil demon. So the philosopher's voice would be always already juxtaposed to the voices of unreason, and his project would be one that proceeds whether or not he is mad. (Angloanalytic philosophers may want to take note of the fact that the translation of the *Meditations* by G. E. M. Anscombe and Peter Geach coincides in a general way with Derrida's reading of the text. Anscombe and Geach pluralize the text's voices by placing the objections concerning madness and dreaming in quotation marks.[17])

There are some resonances of this celebrated dispute concerning the reading of Descartes in the different readings or repetitions that Foucault and Derrida offer of the *Genealogy of Morals*. Unlike Foucault, Derrida does not explicitly devote an essay to the text. Instead he describes at least part of what he is doing in *Of Grammatology* as "repeating the genealogy of morals."[18] This self-description occurs at the end of the section "The Writing Lesson," which is devoted to interrogating Claude Lévi-Strauss's attempt to construct a series of distinctions between naturally good cultures without writing an exploitative Western societies that make use of writing. Moreover, this reference is rather oblique, for Derrida inscribes on his page not the title *The Genealogy of Morals*, in italics, but simply the phrase "genealogy of morals." On the other hand, there are reasons for taking seriously even such an indirect reference, for the reading of Lévi-Strauss has to do with the proper name and its possibilities of erasure or effacement. Some strategy of writing appears to be at work here in this partial effacement of a title or proper name of a text. Why should Derrida repeat the genealogy (or the *Genealogy*) in his analysis of Lévi-Strauss? In many ways Lévi-Strauss is a contemporary version of the normal scientist who appears in Nietzsche's *Genealogy* as infected by ressentiment, in whom the reaction against the other has turned into a dislike of himself or of a part of himself. As a spokesman for science, Lévi-Strauss is a universalist, a democrat suspicious of the ethnocentrism of the West.

"The critique of ethnocentrism," Derrida writes, "has most often the sole function of constituting the other as a model of original and natural goodness, of accusing and humiliating oneself, of exhibiting its being-unacceptable in an anti-ethnocentric mirror."[19] Lévi-Strauss is

one of those scientists, those knowers, who are unknown to themselves. He repeats the gesture of the English moralists (cited by
Nietzsche at the beginning of the *Genealogy*) insofar as he believes in
an original, natural morality that has been forgotten or effaced but
which is capable of retrieval or at least reconstruction through
memory. Here the place of historical memory is taken by the
experiment of the anthropologist who, by introducing writing to a
people previously innocent of it, is able to observe what he takes to be
its characteristic sudden infusion of violence and hierarchy into a
pacific, face-to-face society. Lévi-Strauss tells this story, or offers this
confession, in the chapter of *Tristes Tropiques* called "The Writing
Lesson." It is he, the guilty anthropologist, who explains how the
leader of the Nambikwara pretended to have learned the European's
art of writing in order to manipulate the others in his tribe with the
promise of rewards and the mysterious aura of an esoteric code.
Derrida's genealogical reading of this Rousseauian historical vignette
and confession focuses on the question of language; like the English
historians of morality, Lévi-Strauss has taken it to be much simpler
and more homogeneous than it actually is.

Let us recall the linguistic analysis, a kind of structural linguistics, of the first essay of Nietzsche's *Genealogy* in order to see the
analogous workings of Derrida's genealogy. Those English moralists,
Nietzsche says, want to know what good is; like Plato, they suppose
that it must have a single meaning. And while Plato sought that meaning through a kind of transcendental memory, the English seek it
through a historical reconstruction of original experiences of utility.
Yet there is no single language or discourse of the good that could
support either project. There are *at least two* languages of morals, one
that differentiates good from bad, another that differentiates good
from evil. In the good/bad discourse, the speaker first, and affirma-
tively, designates himself as good. Only as an afterthought, when his
attention is called to it, does he call the others (those who are not his
kind) the bad. In the good/evil discourse the starting point is the
characterization of the other (the master, the strong, or the noble) as
evil, because he is envied, because he is violent or negligent in his
dealings with us, the speakers of that language. "Good" is in each case
part of a system of differences; it is not at all clear that and how we
could translate it from one moral language to the other while preserving its sense. It already partakes of what Derrida calls the "proper
name effect" insofar as it both demands and resists translation. Naming oneself and naming the other involve initial acts of violence and
separation which are not well served by either Platonic or utilitarian

translations, for these assume incorrectly that there is only one voice, or one discourse, to translate.

Lévi-Strauss would like to think of the Nambikwara, the people without writing, as good in a Rousseauian sense of primal innocence. As such they must have a single language spontaneously and constantly animated by the intimacy of their daily life; their innocence can be read off from the fact that they have no writing, for writing would introduce a hierarchy of scribes and leaders, a differentiation that would disrupt an idyllic condition. One way in which Derrida *repeats* the genealogy of morals is to show that in Lévi-Strauss's own narrative we find the evidence of the Nambikwara's own writing. double coding, violence, and hierarchy which the narrator would like to depict as the property of the West. From Lévi-Strauss's text itself we learn that the Nambikwara language is spoken differently by men and women, who tend to view each other as distinct species. We also learn that the Nambikwara have secret proper names that must be disguised in most circumstances by substitutes. In this culture revealing the proper name to inappropriate others or at inappropriate times can set off a long chain of reprisals and retaliations. Similarly, Nietzsche had noticed that the spokesmen for an ethics of love often provide evidence of the desire for revenge (he cited Tertullian and Thomas Aquinas on the pleasures of the blessed in the torments that would be visited upon sinners). He also observed the periodic recurrence of epidemics of revenge and scapegoating among our supposedly innocent ancestors. But Lévi-Strauss would have us believe that violence arises among the Nambikwara only through the agency of the scientist who teaches writing or who transgresses the law of the tribe by provoking young girls to confess the secret names of their comrades and parents.

Science, intent on demonstrating these distinctions, will not hesitate to invoke the categorial apparatus of its own culture in order to protect the purity of the other culture that it studies. In arguing that the Nambikwara have no writing, Lévi-Strauss must account for their practice of "drawing lines," a practice for which they indeed have a word in their language. Lévi-Strauss's *translation* is of interest: "They called the act of writing *iekariakedjutu,* namely 'drawing lines,' which had an aesthetic interest for them."[20] But what is aesthetic value or interest? In Nietzsche's text we find a sketch of the genealogy of "aesthetics" that demonstrates its complicity with the culture of the eighteenth century, exemplified by the Kantian tripartition of knowing, willing, and an aesthetic experience devoid of knowledge and will.[21] "Aesthetics" is a very recent invention, a concept which is built on the exclusion of laughter, the festive, and the grotesque (we can now supplement Nietzsche's genealogy with that provided by Bakhtin at the beginning of his *Rabelais and His World*). Derrida asks, conerning Lévi-Strauss's translation and aestheticization of "drawing lines": "Is not ethnocentrism always betrayed by the haste with which it is satisfied by certain translations or certain domestic equivalents?"[22] And—this is Derrida's next question—does not the existence of a double system of names, and a system of marking, indicate that language is, even here, always already multiple and so characterized by the possibility of transgression, aggression, and violence that the guilty anthropologist would like to keep at a distance from these people? In this first repetition what is announced is the discovery of plurality and violence where an idealistic nostalgia had found only peace and unity.

Lévi-Strauss reveals elsewhere in his writing on the Nambikwara that they became adept at producing explanatory diagrams of such cultural matters as their kinship relations that were extremely useful to the party of anthropologists. Should we think of them, like Meno's slave boy, as being brought to discover a primal writing in the soul? Or as having been infected by the violence of the West? Or might we find Derrida to be the more insightful anthropologist here when he observes that "the birth of writing (in the colloquial sense) was nearly everywhere and most often linked to genealogical anxiety"?[23] This last suggestion has the virtue, like Nietzsche's critique of the Kantian-Schopenhauerian aesthetics of pure contemplation, of indicating the ties between art and life. We might also observe that from the time of the Homeric catalogues of heroes to the nineteenth-century Balzacian or Dickensian novel of marriage, property, inheritance and the discovery of unexpected blood relationships, writing—in the colloquial sense—has maintained its link to genealogical anxiety. It has often been observed that there is a certain homology or structural similarity between Hegel's philosophy of the development of absolute spirit and the *Bildungsroman* that traces the inevitable maturation and self-discovery of a young man thrown into an initially hostile world. But along with the *Bildungsroman* that typically ends with the hero's marriage and worldly success, such as *Wilhelm Meister's Apprenticeship*, we also have novels of incest, adultery, disrupted alliances, and unexpected affiliations, such as *Elective Affinities* or the fictions of Novalis, Kleist, Hugo, and Flaubert.

On another level, Derrida repeats the *Genealogy* in its critique or self-critique of science. The uncanniness of the *Genealogy* lies not only in its disruption of nostalgia and hope but in its demonstration of the impossibility of a certain kind of science. Science, when pushed to its limit, reflects upon itself and recognizes its indebtedness to the moral- ity of *ressentiment;* the scientist's dedication to the truth and his will- ingness to sacrifice himself for the truth are structurally identical with the asectic negation of one's self and one's present life for the sake of God. The scientist's final truth is one that he will never see, and its pursuit here and now requires the virtues of faith, hope, and charity: faith in the possibility that the truth will be attained, despite our present state of ignorance and error; hope that progress towards the truth will continue; charity as the willingness to abandon what- ever is one's own, one's own favored hypothesis for example, for the sake of truth as an ultimate goal. "We knowers" who pursue such a truth are unknown to ourselves insofar as we fail to see these gene- alogical affiliations of our activity with that sacrifice of self. But when science becomes historical and genealogical it will discover these affil- iations in a moment of tragic reversal and recognition. Science will become uncanny and undecidable, or, in Nietzsche's formulation: "The will to truth requires a critique—let us thus define our own task—the value of truth must for once be experimentally *called into question.* "[24]

Of Grammatology repeats or translates The Genealogy of Morals, then, not by proposing a new science—grammatology in the place of genealogy—but by reconsidering the project of several putative sci- ences which are shown to be impossible sciences. One of these is anthropology. Insofar as anthropology operates with a distinction between nature and culture, or between Rousseauian innocence and civilized evil, it founders on the impossibility of these distinctions themselves; in the very act of attempting to illustrate and maintain such distinctions, it provides the impetus to question and deconstruct them. But in a larger sense, *Of Grammatology* is concerned with the impossible science of grammatology, so that we might think of the entire text, and not only the chapter on Lévi-Strauss, as repeating Nietzsche's *Genealogy*. Since writing, thought seriously and essen- tially, is that which escapes presence, totalization, and the ideal of science that is indebted to these concepts, there can be no science of grammatology. But the experience or adventure of attempting to con- struct a grammatology will disclose the questionability of any science of language that would segregate or compartmentalize writing as well as the problematic project of scientificity itself.

Derrida asks a question of Lévi-Strauss that parallels Nietzsche's attempt to show that a consistent science must call itself into ques- tion: "If it is true, as I in fact believe, that writing cannot be thought of outside the horizon of intersubjective violence, is there anything, even science, that radically escapes it?" (127). To suppose otherwise is to place one's trust in "the presumed difference between language and power." At the end of what is arguably Lévi-Strauss's most philosophical work, *La pensée sauvage*, there is a very clear demonstration of the naiveté involved in such trust that is reminiscent of the positivist metanarratives of science that Nietzsche attacks through his *Genealogy*. In the rhetorically magnificent but ultimately unpersuasive coda to Lévi-Strauss's book, the claim is made that we are now witnessing the convergence of the most advanced contemporary science and the timeless patterns of savage or untamed mythical thinking. According to Lévi-Strauss, information theory can offer a universal account of both the codes and messages of "primitive" peoples at one end of the spectrum, based as they are on the holistic, macroscopic, and sensible qualities of the perceived environment, with the general, instrumentalized study of the production and reception of biological and physical "messages" at the other end that reveal themselves only with the help of the abstracting methods of the hypothetico-deductive sciences. With such a convergence, we hear: "The entire process of human knowledge assumes the character of a closed system. And we therefore remain faithful to the inspiration of the savage mind when we recognize that, by an encounter it alone could have foreseen, the scientific spirit in its most modern form will have contributed to legitimize the principles of savage thought and to re-establish it in its righful place."[25] This is utopian positivism. It is positivism because it takes the prevailing models in the sciences to be ultimately valid models. It is utopian because it supposes that we are on the verge of a total integration of various fields of knowledge, a "totalization" at least as extravagant as that practical, historical totalization espoused by the later Sartre, which Lévi-Strauss criticizes in the very same chapter. While rejecting Sartre's appeal to social and political history as modern myth, Lévi-Strauss seems to revert to the nineteenth-century scientistic version of this myth, unconsciously reviving the teleologies of Comte and Spencer. Nietzsche's genealogy of such science aims at showing that it must founder as soon as its concepts and methods of inquiry are turned back upon itself; at that point it discovers its own genealogy in a morality that its inquiries have rendered suspicious. Derrida, a few years before Foucault's programmatic essay on Nietzschean genealogy, makes a similar point in suggesting that the human sciences cannot innocently presume the distinction between power and knowledge that fuels the structuralist eschatology.

In this spirit we ought to read one of the multiple voices within the text of Nietzsche's *Genealogy*, the one at the end of its first essay that calls for a series of prize essays by philologists, historians, and philosophers on the question: *"What light does linguistics and especially the study of etymology, throw on the history of the evolution of the moral concepts?"*[26] One kind of answer is supplied by Nietzsche's first essay itself, with its analysis of the *gut/schlecht* moral system and the *gut/böse* moral system in terms of the social and ethnic differences of the ancient world; Foucault's genealogical study of the constitution of the *discourses* of psychiatry, punishment, and sexuality can be read as extensions of this linguistic genealogy. But the third essay of Nietzsche's *Genealogy* may be taken as pushing the question one step further by asking what consequences such investigations have for the sciences that pursue them. Can they remain above the battle or must they, as Nietzsche says, "submit to the law that they themselves have proposed" and, like all great things, "bring about their own destruction through an act of self-overcoming"?[27] Similarly, Heideggerean etymology is concerned not with unearthing an obscured presence through a new method of retrieval but with calling into question that very idea of an original presence and those historical sciences that invoke it. Derrida's repetition of the *Genealogy of Morals* is a repetition of the third essay and of its uncanny ramifications for the inquiry itself. Here we might pause and read Nietrzsche's question very slowly: "What light does linguistics and especially the study of etymology, throw on the *hstory* of the evolution of the moral concepts?" Why this apparent *repetition* of "history" and "evolution"? Must we not remember, especially if we are giving the close attention to language which Nietzsche demands and which is the theme of that question, that "history" is a double-barreled word, alternately designating either the subject matter studied or the activity of studying it?

   If we read the text *Of Grammatology* carefuly, we are constantly reminded that the *de*, the preposition, in its title, indicates a question rather than introducing a subject matter. It is not a "toward" in the Kantian sense of a *Prolegomena to Any Future Grammatology That Will Come Forward as a Science.* One learns in introductory language classes that prepositions are the most difficult words to translate in any language, and so far I have been operating here with conventional translations of the *de* in *De la Grammatologie* and *Zur* in *Zur Genealogie der Moral.* There has been some controversy among Nietzsche's translators about how this *Zur* might be rendered in English. Is it "On" in the sense of "concerning" or "about" or is it "toward"? "Toward" has been employed by those who favor a tentative reading of Nietzsche's text as a contribution toward something still in the making. But can one go toward that which can never be reached? Or should the title itself be read parodically? "On" is perhaps better in preserving an

ambiguity with regard to the question of whether a genealogy of
morals is possible, that is, whether we ought to take seriously the
scientific rhetoric with which Nietzsche, especially in his first essay,
attempts to situate his work in relation to historical and philological
science. Similarly, there is, in Derrida's repetition of the genealogy
while effacing its title, both a linguistic prudence and respect that
hesitates to violate this undecidablilty and a *mimesis* of that act of the
concealment of the proper name which has been identified as the
characteristic act of writing. So we might say that there is a motivated
absence of the very *name* Nietzsche in this part of the *Grammatology*
that repeats the genealogy. Derrida raises the question of how Lévi-
Strauss, while acknowledging Marx and Freud as his masters, can
write the idyllic scenario in which the anthropologist records his
nocturnal observation of the Nambikwara as a nonviolent people of
unsurpassed tenderness and intimacy. He can do so, Derrida tells us,
only because Rousseau has been substituted for Nietrzsche in Lévi-
Strauss's trinity of names (Marx, Rousseau, and Freud rather than
Marx, Nietzsche, and Freud).

Here we touch on the question of the genealogy of the text, a
philological question inseparable from the genealogy of morals. Genealogy has to do with seeking out the unsuspected ramifications of
proper names, whether present or absent. At the very beginning of
Derrida's reading of Lévi-Strauss, he suggests that "the metaphor that
would describe the genealogy of a text correctly is still *forbidden*."[28]
One might be tempted to say, for example, that "a text is nothing but a
system of roots," but to do so would be to contradict both the concept
of system and the pattern of the roots. To read Lévi-Strauss genealogically is to see the resonances of Rousseau. There is a sense in which
what we learn from genealogy is the inevitability of one's heritage, or
Herkunft, and the impossibility of attempting to make an absolute
beginning, or Ursprung. Not far removed from such efforts is the common assumption, which Lévi-Strauss makes in regard to Rousseau,
that one can determine and circumscribe precisely what use one will
make of one's intellectual roots, ignoring the complexities of their sub-
terranean system. This realization accounts for Nietzsche's warning
that "we are unknown to ourselves" and to his project of situating the
many voices of his text in relation to their roots in (for example) science, tragedy, history, and the novel. Derrida's effort to "repeat" the
genealogy of morals arises within this context. It is not a question of
whether the writer is consciously or fully aware of the Nietzschean

roots, still less of his being in command of the entire array of a manifold Herkunft. It is more a matter of the rigor and modesty of a confessed repetition and mimesis, one that makes no claims of origin-ality —that is, it makes no claim to restore the presence of an origin—and so would help us to think beyond the constant temptations of hope and nostalgia.

3

Nietzsche's Madman:
Perspectivism without Nihilism

Debra B. Bergoffen

Joyful Wisdom's story of the Madman presents us with a parable[1] of perspectivism. We have been loath to accept this present, however, for we fear that the thought that moves from perspectivism to pluralism will also arrive at relativism, anarchism, dogmatism, and nihilism. The question is twofold. (1) Can the thought of perspectivism be held in check? That is, can it be stopped before it hits nihilism? anarchism? dogmatism? (2) Does a philosophy of perspectivism necessarily undermine itself? That is, can a discipline committed to the pursuit of truth pursue the doctrine of perspectivism without self-contradiction?

This paper offers beginning answers to these questions by analyzing the meanings and implications of Nietzsche's doctrine of perspectivism. Using "The Madman" as its point of reference, it suggests that our traditional understanding of the relationship between perspectivism, relativism, and nihilism is the consequence of existing within a particular perspective, that of a centered subject in a metaphysically anchored world. It argues that Nietzsche's defense of the decentered perspective of perspectivism is not grounded in the claim that this is the true perspective but in the affirmation that decentered perspectivism is less repressive than the absolute perspective of the center. Nietzsche's argument necessarily appeals to the judgment which values a lifting of repression but does not, as we shall see, ask that we make this judgment unreflectively.

This chapter is ultimately grounded in an understanding of human subjectivity as desire. As desire, the human subject is the lack seeking to overcome itself as lack; the finitude seeking immortality; the limited in quest of the unlimited; the singular seeking the absolute. To understand desire as central to the human experience is not to suggest that humanity is teleologically oriented toward its object of fulfillment but rather to indicate that in naming our objects of desire we are attempting to fix what cannot be fixed in the hope of transcending the condition of our existence. That is, if to be human is to be desire, then no named object can arrest the dynamic of desire that is the human being. This notion of human subjectivity is indebted to Lacan not only in its insistence on the insatiability of the desire of the subject but also in its stand that (1) something becomes an object of desire when it takes the place of what by its very nature remains concealed from the subject[2] and (2) the notion \$ expresses the necessity that S be eclipsed at the precise point where the object a attains its greatest value.[3]

This grounding is neither arbitrary nor a matter of personal preference. It is more akin to the wager of Ricoeur's hermeneutic circle. The wager is that this understanding of subjectivity situates Nietzsche's philosophy in the full complexity of its problematic. For as I will attempt to argue in the pages that follow, Nietzsche understands Western culture's God as an articulation of the desire for the absolute, that is, as human subjectivity attempting to fulfill its being as desire by repressing the recognition of its being as desire. Rejecting this eclipse of the subject, \$, Nietzsche announces the death of God in the hope of initiating a new relationship between desire and its projected objects of satisfaction.

"The Madman" is best known for its declaration of the death of God. To suggest that it be understood as a parable of perspectivism is to assert that the way in which God's death is announced is indicative of the way in which perspective utterances are affirmed. The status of "The Madman" as a parable of perspectivism also lies in the relationship between the death of God and the destruction of the centered perspective which refuses to recognize its status as a perspective. Finally, "The Madman" may be read as a parable of perspectivism insofar as its teaching of the death of God releases the doctrine of perspectivism from its apparently nihilistic implications.

The Madman's question "Where is God gone?" and his response "We have killed him....there never was a greater event,—and on account of it all who are born after us belong to a higher history than any history hitherto"[4] are perspective utterances in two respects. First, they are historicized declarations. The appeal is not to logic but to history. We are not offered proofs for or against the existence of God but descriptions of a cultural context within which the question of God's reality has become critical. Second, they are utterances which refer us back to their speaker. The relationship between what is said and who is speaking is a point of focus. The question: "Where is God gone?" is neither abstract nor innocent, for the questioner is also the murderer. There is therefore a motive of the asking and a question that must be put to the questioner. That question is "Why do you, God's murderer, ask after His whereabouts?" To follow the Madman's discourse thus leads us from history (an attentiveness to context) to genealogy (an unmasking of desire).

Of the two paths opened up by the Madman's "Where is God gone?" "We have killed him," Nietzsche chooses to pursue only one here. Ignoring an inquiry into the motive of the murder, he focuses instead on the issue of repression. Why are the murderers ignorant of the murder? What motivates the refusal of the deed? In pursuing these issues, Nietzsche unveils his doctrine of perspectivism and distinguishes it from all previous perspectivisms, most notably its nihilistic counterpart, relativism.

To follow Nietzsche's thought, however, we must go behind it, that is, we must begin with the question prior to and presumed by the Madman's "Where is God gone?" This question is: Who is God? And we answer first traditionally (theologically): God is the absolute; second historically: God is Western culture's articulation of the absolute; and finally genealogically: God is Western culture's projection of its desire for the absolute. From the first and second perspectives, God is an affirmation of the absolute; from the third, God is an invitation to the absolute. The ways in which this invitation is played out and the ways in which this affirmation is challenged by the vicissitudes of history constitute the answer to the Madman's question "Where is God gone?"

The complexity of the answer to the question "Who is God?" reverberates in the answer to the question "Where is God gone?" As God is not a substance but a dialectic, the dialectic of the desire for the absolute as it projects its fulfillment, His whereabouts must be circumscribed within the dialectical process. To trace this process completely is beyond the scope of this chapter. To understand the distinction between the old and new doctrines of perspectivism, however, we need to identify the point at which God as the absolute came to be articulated as the absolute perspective. Thus the Renaissance emerges as our point of departure.

Were it not for the psychoanalytic category of inversion, it would be difficult to make sense of the Renaissance's ability to affirm the individual and the concrete historical, carriers of the categories of

finitude and limitation, as it exalts God, the infinite, unlimited absolute. For rather than recognizing the tension between these affirmations by establishing the wholly otherness of God, the Renaissance
represses the possibilities of alienation and empowers particularity by
aligning it with the absolute. Thus as Western culture's desire for the
absolute begins to confront the resistance of individuality and of historical limitation, it determines that these sources of resistance may
be overcome with the doctrine of the absolute perspective. Lacan suggests that there is something less than accidental in the fact that the
period in which the subject emerged as the critical point of reference
is also the period in which geometrical optics was an object of research. For as geometrical optics situates the subject in an absolute
overview, it hides the castrated subject, the subject as finite, as lack.[5]

Individuality and historicity are acknowledged as their meaning
is inverted. With the doctrine of the absolute perspective, the meaning
of the concrete and individual is transformed from that of finitude
and limitation to its opoosite. Descartes is critical here. Beginning
with the limitations of the singular cogito he reaches the infinite in
such a was as to transform finite subjectivity into the absolute point of
reference. With Descartes, reason emerges as the guarantor and
instantion of the congruence of the human and absolute perspective.

This philosophical move whereby the finite is transposed to the
absolute is echoed in Renaissance art. According to John Berger:

> "The convention of perspective which is unique to European art
> and which was first established in the early Renaissance centres
> everything on the eye of the beholder. It is like a beam from a
> lighthouse—only instead of light traveling outwards, appear-
> ances travel in. Perspective makes the single eye the center of the
> visible world.... The visible world is arranged for the spectator as
> the universe was once thought to be arranged for God."[6]

We have then a threefold congruence of forces. Science, philosophy, and art appear to be embarked in similar articulations of the
desire for the absolute. As noted by Lacan:

> "It is in Vignola and Alberti that we find the progressive inter-
> rogation of the geometral laws of perspective and it is around
> such research on perspective that is centered a privileged inter-
> est for the domain of vision—whose relation with the institution
> of the Cartesian subject, which is itself a sort of geometral point,
> a point of perspective, we cannot fail to see."[7]

With the Renaissance, the idea of a God-centered reality takes a new turn. The cogito's natural light of reason and the geometer-artist's single eye establishes the congruity of the human and the absolute perspective. Given this configuration of the fulfillment of the desire for absolute, the death of God cannot now refer to the end of the absolute as transcendent; it must instead refer to the end of the human presumption of absolute centeredness. The Renaissance move to secure absolute dimensions for the human perspective means that from now on, the fate of God will be tied to the success of this attempt.

Art historians are now content to recognize the absolute perspective of the Renaissance as a convention. Berger attributes this recognition to the invention of the movie camera. According to him, before the invention of the camera:

> Every drawing or painting that used perspective proposed to the spectator that he was the unique centre of the world. The camera—and more particularly the movie camera—demonstrated that there was no centre. The invention of the camera changed the way men saw.... this was immediately reflected in painting....For cubists the visible was no longer what confronted the single eye, but the totality of possible views taken from all points around the object (or person) being depicted.[8]

With the movie camera and cubism, the inversion whereby the individual is affirmed as its meaning is negated, is rejected. The individual perspective is indentified as a finite perspective—one among many rather than one that is the only one. This is not to say that the pursuit of the absolute perspective is abandoned, for with the movie camera and cubism a new strategy of pursuing the desire for the absolute emerges—the strategy of addition and multiplication. By substituting the multiplicity of perspectives for the convention of the absolute perspective, cubism enriches the imaginary and perceptual fields in order to apprehend that which is more fully. Thus though the absolute nature of the individual human perspective is denied, the possibility of the congruence of the absolute and human perspectives is maintained.[9] Through the many, the One may be made manifest. On this account, however revolutionary cubism may be as an artistic style, the cubist revolt is not an affirmation of radical pluralism and is not therefore a direct threat to the meaning of and desire for God. Though with cubism the individual human perspective is now recognized in its finite singularity as unable to provide an absolute vision, the possibility remains that the species perspective (the perspective captured by the partial visions of the totality of individuals) may transcend the particularity of the viewer. With this move, the thesis of angular, complementary vision is substituted for the thesis of the absolutely centered individual vision such that by situating oneself within the totality of the species, the desire for the absolute may still be articulated within the framework of the metaphysics of the absolute.[10]

The case in philosophy is quite different. That no consensus exists equivalent to the art community's recognition of the conventionality of the absolute perspective alerts us to the fact that something more is at stake when the issue is truth and reason rather than beauty, perception, and imagination. That God, the absolute, is identified as truth suggests that the recognition of existentially singular truths is a direct threat to the Renaissance reconciliation of the dialectic of desire and the recognition of subjectivity. While the artist can affirm the angularity of vision without negating the metaphysics of the absolute, the philosopher must choose to repress angularity or reject the metaphysics of the absolute. As the pressures of subjectivity continue to challenge the mechanisms of repression established in the Renaissance, the desire for the absolute risks being subverted by the demands of the existential. That is, under the pressure of the return of the repressed, the desire for the absolute must be renounced,[11] or inversion having lost its power, new strategies of articulating the desire must be sought.

In announcing the death of God, Nietzsche rejects the strategy of renunciation for the tactics of transvaluation. He insists on remaining within the dynamics of the dialectic. Anticipating the teachings of Freud and Lacan, Nietzsche recognizes the insistent and insatiable nature of the desire for the absolute as he argues against the reinstitution of the repression of subjectivity. Recognizing that the dialectic of desire cannot be given up, and insisting that the recognition of existential singularity should not be given up, Nietzsche uses the value of the recognition of subjectivity to displace the meaning of the desire for the absolute. Ultimately, he will propose the eternal recurrence as the object of this desire. At this point however (that is in "The Madman") Nietzsche asks us to recognize the nihilistic consequences of not acknowledging the death of God. He asks us to recognize the need to renounce God as the object of our desire for the absolute. Ultimately, he will demand that we transform our desire for the *one* into a desire for oneness, that we transform the desire for the singular to the desire for singularity. In his words: "Shall we not ourselves have to become gods?"[12]—that is, shall we not have to learn to desire ourselves as God has been said to desire Himself?

To learn this, however, requires an analysis of nihilism which distinguishes between nihilism as an experience of valuelessness and nihilism as a doctrine of devaluation. Such an analysis opens us to the possibility that the price of acknowledging God's death is an experience of nihilism which allows us to transcend nihilism. It allows us to see that confronting the abyss is not the ultimate but only the first experience of liberated subjectivity and that unrepressed subjectivity does not demand a renunciation of the desire for the absolute.

Though Nietzsche accepts the conventional definition of nihilism, that is, that it is that attitude or position which finds life devoid of meaning or which is unable to bestoe value on reality—he discovers that far from being a sometime threat, nihilism lies at the heart of Western culture.[13] He arrives at this conclusion by defining as nihilistic any thought which devalues the life of becoming, including all attempts to create a hierarchy of value based on the being-becoming dichotomy. Under this definition all Western metaphysics is nihilistic. This specification of the concept of nihilism with its consequent indictment of the Western intellectual tradition may be better understood if we see it as implicitly grounded in an analysis of the relationship between thinking, repression, and desire. According to this analysis:

1. All philosophical positions are the positions of particular philosophers.

2. As the position of a particular philosopher, a philosophical position reflects the humanness of the philosopher, that is, the individual's desire and finite perspective.

3. A philosophical position may either acknowledge or repress its relationship to the particularity of the human philosopher.

4. In acknowledging its relationship to a particular philosopher, a philosophy accepts the conditions of limitation and pluralism: limitation as a sign of the finite horizon of the philosophical position; pluralism as a recognition of other possible desire horizons from which other meanings may arise.

5. In repressing its relationship to a particular philosopher, a philosophical system refuses the possibility of pluralism. It does so by transposing the existential experience of limitation into a statement of uniqueness. The statement of uniqueness provides a bridge of repression between the singularity of the philosopher and the singularity of truth as absolute. As singularity is identified with the absolute, the desire for the absolute is fulfilled as the existential source of this desire is hidden.

From the perspective of this analysis, the notions of God, Truth, and Goodness which dominate Western philosophy identify it as functioning under the repression which denies the relationship between thought, desire, and horizon. The ultimate meaning of this repression is a refusal to value human life, human truth, and human meaning—in Nietzsche's word, nihilism.

Now, one would expect the death of God to resolve the issue of nihilism. For with God's death, the absolute centered perspective of repression is shattered, forcing the decentered human perspective to emerge as the foundation of meaning and value. But while it is true that Nietzsche believes that God's death has the *potential* to resolve the issue of nihilism, he identifies the first effect of the death of God as nihilism, for, with the death of God, one form of nihilism (the experience of valuelessness) replaces another (the devaluation of the human.)

The death of God represents the lifting of a repression and an unmasking of all those mechanisms which served to hide the relationship between thinker and thought. It is an affirmation of the thinker and the recognition of the desire of the thinker for the absolute. In a world which has been dominated by the thought of God, however, the thinker cannot be affirmed in this desire, for the desire is only valued insofar as it is experienced as fulfilled absolutely. We are thus left in an ironic situation. As long as the repression is successful, that is, as long as the God-centered perspective remains unchallenged, nihilism (the devaluation of the human) is masked and experienced as its opposite. Though the murder of God with its lifting of repression ought to be experienced as a liberation, it is in fact experienced nihilistically. The legacy of God must still be overcome. The noise of the gravediggers must be silenced and the need for consolation must be transcended. In Nietzsche's words:

> "Do we not hear the noise of the grave diggers who are burying God?...How shall we console ourselves the most murderous of all murderers?...Is not the magnitude of this deed too great for us?"[14]

The death of God is, therefore, the source of nihilism in a dual sense: (1) the value that was absolute is lost and (2) the idea that the non-absolute could be valued is rejected.

Thus while the death of God is the analogue of the technology of the camera, the philosophical activity comparable to cubism signals a wave of skepticism that threatens to undermine the culture. In Nietzsche's words:

who gave us the sponge to wipe away the whole horizon? What did we do when we loosened this earth from its sun? Whiter does it now move? . . . Is there still an above and below? Do we not stray as through infinite nothingness?[15]

The situation of God's death as Nietzsche describes it is both curious and complex. On the one hand, God has been murdered; on the other hand, those who are God's murderers are unaware of their deed and its implications. Only the Madman understands the meaning of what has occurred.

This prodigious event is still on its way and is traveling,—it has not yet reached men's ears. . . . This deed is as yet further from them than the furthest star,—*and yet they have done it*—.[16]

The key, I think, to deciphering the situation lies in Nietzsche's identification of the people in the marketplace as atheists. As Nietzsche says:

Have you ever heard of the madman who on a bright morning lighted a lantern and ran to the market place calling out unceasingly: 'I seek God! I seek God!'—As there were many people standing about who did not believe in God he caused a great deal of amusement.[17]

As an atheist is someone who rejects the reality of God, to accuse atheists of not knowing that God is dead would seem to make no sense at all unless the God rejected by the atheists is not the God who has been murdered. This seems to be Nietzsche's point. The atheist refuses to accept the reality of the God of religion without recognizing that the God of religion is necessary to guarantee the antiperspective principles of reason which ground science, morality, and Western culture as a whole. The atheist is someone who believes that God is irrelevant to the pursuit of truth and value, someone who accepts the reality of the absolute laws of nature and history while rejecting the reality of God. Nietzsche, however, insists that to understand the place of God in Western culture we must take the definitions of God literally. God is truth, power, and goodness. Without God, centered truth, secular and sacred, is impossible, power is diffused, and goodness lacks an absolute referent.

Sartre's distinction between idealist and materialist atheism is helpful here. According to Satre:

moving on from idealist atheism to materialist atheism was
difficult. It implied long drawn out work.... [Idealist atheism is]
the absence of an idea..., the idea if God. Whereas materialist
atheism is the world seen without God.[18]

The atheists in the marketplace are Sarte's idealist atheists. Confronted by the Madman, the materialist atheist, they fail to see the
connection between abandoning the idea of God and living in a world
abandoned by God.

That the death of God is acknowledged by the atheists in the
marketplace but not experienced by them nihilistically does not mean
that they have transcended the nihilism of the God perspective.
Indeed, Nietzsche suggests that just the opposite is the case. The atheist in the marketplace represents the power of repression, for while
God is rejected, the nihilistic principle of a transcendent truth remains. In response to the intensified resistances of recognized individuality and historical limitation, the desire for the absolute preserves the object of its desire by effecting a compromise. The nihilism
of religion is identified and rejected. The religious God is sacrificed so
that the dialectic of desire may enact its nihilistic movement in the
enlaged secular domain. Thus, the devaluating concept of an absolute
truth which transcends the human perspective remains under such
new names as natural law, or the doctrine of progress. Here, as before,
the desire to value the nonhuman is fulfilled, but the nihilism of the
desire is repressed, thus foreclosing the experience of nihilism.

A second strategy of repression available to the atheist is represented by the doctrine of historicism.[19] Here, though the loss of the
absolute perspective per se is acknowledged, the idea of an absolute
perspective persists. The historicist does not claim to know what the
absolute laws are and does not claim to be able to occupy that position
from which the absolute might be envisioned. In adopting a passive
attitude toward the facts, however, the historicist, like the cubist,
retains the hope of the absolute in suggesting that the absolute may be
grasped indirectly through the additive strategy of collecting all possible perspectives. Nihilism, the devaluation of the particular perspective per se, persists.

The experience of nihilism emerges only when the historicist project of acquiring all possible perspectives is undermined by the doctrine
of relativism. With relativism, the hope of approaching the absolute
directly or indirectly is abandoned. The death of God is finally

understood as the destruction of the absolute center. Multiple perspectives are no longer seen as complementary indicators of an absolute perspective but rather as instances of nontranscendable, incompatible human horizons. With relativism, the nihilism of the God hypothesis is unmasked, for it is now clear that, for a culture which posits the absolute perspective as the object of its desire for the absolute, the human is without value in itself.

It is important to insist, however, that the experience of nihilism which accompanies the discovery of relativism is not indicative of the fact that relativism per se is a nihilistic doctrine but rather indicates that relativism unmasks the nihilism of the God hypothesis. Relativism, the doctrine that the multiplicity of perspectives cannot be transcended, that human perspectives are perspectives in themselves, not perspectives (limited or otherwise) of something other than themselves, affirms the value of the human insofar as it insists that the particularity and multiplicity of the human condition is the source of meaning and value. Relativism is experienced as nihilism only when it is postulated against the horizon of the God hypothesis. Only then is the experience of human particularity an experience of valulessness. The essence of the experienced nihilism of relativism, then, is not the discovery of nontranscendable multiple perspectives but the inability to affirm the value of these human perspectives in the face of the desire for the lost absolute perspective.

The experienced nihilism of relativism reflects the power of the nihilistic expression of the desire for the absolute. Still unable to acknowledge the nihilism of the desire for the absolute perspective, the relativist experiences the loss of the absolute as nihilistic. Whereas before God's death the articulation of the desire for the absolute repressed the devaluation of humanity, now the loss of the absolute object of this desire is experienced as a negation of the value of the human. The experienced nihilism is a sign of the lifting of repression, however, insofar as the devaluation is revealed.

With the experience of nihilism, the hope of transcending nihilism emerges. The key to this hope is the recognition that the issue cannot be resolved by the discovery of a new *One* and will only be resolved when the desire for *The One* is renounced. As Nietzsche tells us:

> God is dead! We have killed him! How shall we console ourselves, the most murderous of all murderers? ... shall we not ourselves have to become Gods, merely to seem worthy of it? There never

was a greater event,—and on account of it, all who are born after us belong to a higher history hitherto![20]

With these words Nietzsche introduces us to his doctrine of perspectivism. Unlike the doctrine of relativism, to which it bears a superficial resemblance, the doctrine of perspectivism is not advanced against the background of a longing for the lost absolute. Thus the many perspectives are not treated as inferior substitutes for the desired one. The human is not all that is left. It is everything that is. Instead of measuring the truth of the human perspective against the truth of the absolute perspective in order to find it lacking, Nietzsche makes the human perspective the standard of measure. God, the singular perspective is dead, We—the many perspectives—shall have to become gods. The new history of which Nietzsche speaks is a history of polytheistic pluralism.

The substitution of the many for the one reflects more than a transference of power from the monotheistic divine to the pluralist human. Power is not simply diffused among the many possible perspectives, desire is refigured. To become gods we must affirm ourselves as individualized centers of meaning. For this affirmation to escape the nihilism of relativism, however, the recognition of the subjective source of meaning must express a configuration of the desire for the absolute which has abandoned the demand for absoluteness. Though he will wait for Zarathustra to develop this configuration more concretely, Nietzsche provides us with enough here to anticipate that the desire for the absolute will have to learn to speak the language of nonrepressed subjectivity. The doctrines of relativism and perspectivism speak the same words, but the desires spoken in their words differ. In relativism, nihilism is mourning its lost object. In perspectivism the desire for the absolute is affirming its subjectivity.[21] In issuing his doctrine of perspectivism, Nietzsche refuses the Renaissance conspiracy of philosophy, science, and art to define human subjectivity according to the criteria of geometrical relationships. He insists, in Lacan's words, that "the geometral dimension of vision does not exhaust... what the field of vision offers us as the original subjectifying relation."[22] It is important to understand here that in adopting the language of power (the will to power, the *Übermensch*) and rejecting the language of truth (there are no truths, no facts, only interpretations) Nietzsche is not returning to the crudest of relativisms, "might makes right." He is, rather, inaugurating the higher history of humanity by constructing a philosophy of perspectivism where the concept of the interpretive center[23] replaces the convention of absolute centeredness.

With the death of God and the doctrine of perspectivism, Nietzsche transforms the project of Western philosophy from the pursuit of truth to the exploration of meanings. Within the Western tradition the quest for truth is inevitably ensnared with the desire for the absolute's repression of subjectivity. As long as the project of philosophy is defined in terms of truth, where truth is understood to mean that which is so for all knowers at all times (the absolute perspective), a philosophy of perspectivism is self-contradictory. A noncontradictory philosophy of perspectivism is possible only if the nihilism of the quest for absolute truth is refused. This refusal constitutes a choice against the repression of subjectivity and resets the path of philosophy. The desire for the absolute must now be pursued in ways consistent with the recognition of the human ground of this desire.

The desire for the absolute must speak the desire of desire rather than the desire of fulfillment. It must value the lack and the movement of overcoming the lack rather than the lack overcome. Instead of being the bait that lures desire to renounce itself in the Being of the One, the desire for the absolute must express itself as that which unmasks all pretenders to the throne. Here the desire for the absolute shows itself as that which is beyond all reification, as that which exposes the limits of all claims of completion, as that which frees desire from its temptations to fix itself to a goal.

In resetting the task of philosophy from that of affirming the absolute to that of affirming the desire for the absolute, Nietzsche does not suggest that the dangers of repression are effaced. While more explicit about the ways in which the drive for truth corrupts the dynamics of desire than about the ways in which his philosophy of perspectivism opens us to the possibilities of anarchy and dogmaticism, Nietzsche says enough to suggest that desire's embrace of perspectivism is not without its dangers.

That the Madman expresses his desire of desire in utterances which declare that God is dead, that *we* have killed him, that *we* must learn to console ourselves, and that *we* shall have to become gods indicate I think, that the philosophy of perspectivism is neither a philosophy of dogmaticism nor anarchism. For in saying "we" rather than "I," the Madman establishes the communal context of the speech of perspectivism and suggests that the I who speaks is always situated vis à vis another. In speaking the we, the madman indicates that the dangers of the desire to be the absolute center are not exhausted in the hypotheses of God and Truth. The I, unhinged from its metaphysical groundings, may move to declare its decentered utterances absolute. Against this new conception of desire the madman contextualizes himself within the we that recognizes the otherness of the other.

The philosophy of perspectivism is a philosophy of pluralist contextuality. In replacing Kierkegaard's either/or with his own either ... or, Nietzsche rejects the logic of exclusive disjunction for a logic which affirms dejoined terms.[24] How the we can sustain the tensions of the inclusive disjunction is not yet clear. Indeed it might be suggested that this question of how to understand the we of perspectivism is one of the thorniest of Nietzsche's legacies. For while Nietzsche makes it clear that with the death of God such traditional groundings of the we as truth, absolute being, or essential nature are rendered impotent, he has not clarified the ways in which perspectivism provides grounds for shared contextuality.

I do not suggest that we are left without guidance. There are hints and scents of trails to follow. In following them we have identified at least two criteria of the we of perspectivism, limitation and pluralism. Also, from the fact that the necessary complementarity of perspectives is rejected, we may infer a third criterion conflict. A fourth criterion, communication/communicability, may be inferred from the actions of the Madman (and later Zarathustra), who goes to the marketplace to spread the news and who, upon failing to communicate the death of God directly by announcement, moves to indirect communication:

> It is further stated that the madman made his way to different churches on the same day and there intoned his *Requiem aeternam deco*. When led out and called to account he always gave the reply: "What are these churches now, if they are not the tombs and monuments of God?"[25]

Working with these criteria, we may propose that a philosophy of perspectivism speaks of the place from which meaning arises, the context within which meaning arises, and the place to which it is directed. It must remember that the I from which meaning emanates is a contextualized I in a dual sense: (1) its being as this particular I is possible only within the particualr historical horizon of its experience and (2) its meaning as this I must be spoken to and recognized by the other. Just as the philosophy of nihilism thrived on its forgetfulness of the existential source of meaning, the philosophy of perspectivism may repress the contextuality of meaning. In doing so it will fall prey to the temptation to interpret itself as the absolute (dogmatism) or the temptation to allow speech to become the absolute (anarchism).

The concept of the interpretive center is helpful here. The temptation to repress the we is grounded in the experience of myself as the center of meaning (an unavoidable, powerful experience) and in my desire to be, find, or refind the absolute (another powerful contingency of our existence). We need to be reminded that the existential experience of centeredness is not a justification for the assertion of absoluteness and that the configuration of the desire for the absolute as the absolute object is repressive. To recognize myself as an interpretive center is to allow the implications of the notion of interpretation to play off against the illusions of absoluteness fostered bvy the experience of centeredness and reinforced by the desire for the absolute. Further it forces one to reject the attempts of the I to dominate the we. As an interpretive center of meaning, my interpretations, since they cannot after the death of God refer to the thing in itself, must refer to the subject of the interpretation and the interpretations of the interpretive centers of others.

It is tempting to look for some philosophy of dialogue to ground the community of perspectivism. For dialogue, it seems, is capable of allowing for the conflict of perspectives and of providing the limitations necessary for avoiding dogmatism and anarchy. That is, it seems to be able to contain the plurality of perspectives without reducing them to a one and to constrain the plurality of perspectives from exploding into meaninglessness. The difficulties arise in the working out of such a philosophy. To be compatible with perspectivism and its new configuration of the desire for the absolute, it can neither invoke the notion of a transcendent grammar (the absolute perspective returning in new guise) nor preclude the possibility of the communication of otherness.

Again we are left with hints. The task the Madman tells us is to be like gods—gods, not God. Again, we find the I rejected for the we. But who are gods? What do they do? How do we become like them? From the Greeks we learn that gods play. From the Jews and Christians we learn that they create. From Nietzsche we learn that they affirm life. Moving beyond the either/or of the Greek and Judaeo-Christian alternative, Nietzsche teaches that to be like gods is to create in the spirit of playfulness. Following Zarathustra's story of the laughing death of the gods (or death of the laughing gods) and the birth of God,[26] we are tempted to suggest that ruminating on the conditions of the possibilities of laughter, creativity, and play may direct us toward fleshing out the configurations of the ways in which the desire for the absolute affirms itself in a philosophy and politics of perspectivism.

Part 2
Deconstruction

4

Language and Deconstruction:
Nietzsche, de Man, and Postmodernism

Maudemarie Clark

Paul de Man has provided an important basis for considering Nietzsche a postmodernist. According to de Man, Nietzsche's early works show us that truth cannot be "made present to man," that is, it cannot be pinned down or attained in a straightforward manner. The source of this problem, on de Man's account, is the rhetorical nature of language. Since all language is figural, it is incapable of expressing literal truth. These claims about truth and language clearly count as postmodern. In this essay I shall argue that they should not be considered Nietzschean.

I do not deny that there is some important sense in which Nietzsche should be considered postmodern. I do maintain that he should not be identified with the postmodern theses on language and truth that de Man attributes to him. Nietzsche may have held such views of truth and language in his very early works. If he was the first proponent of these postmodernist theses, however, he was also the first to see through them. I cannot hope to demonstrate this claim here. I will attempt to give it a degree of plausibility by challenging the postmodern theses that de Man attributes to Nietzsche. If successful, this argument will establish a basis for hoping that Nietzsche did see through them and will thereby undermine a major basis for considering him a postmodernist on language and truth.

My essay has four parts. The first section argues, with de Man, that *The Birth of Tragedy* involves serious contradictions. I concentrate on the problem created by section 18, in which Nietzsche classifies the Dionysian as a stage of illusion, on a par, as far as truth goes, with the Apollinian and the Socratic. This classification contradicts the main argument of *The Birth of Tragedy*, which depends on the association of Dionysus with truth. The best explanation for this contradiction provided by analytic or straightforward approaches is that we are faced here with "one of Nietzsche's careless mistakes, a slip on his part."[1] But it is difficult to believe that a "mistake" of this magnitude could be a mere slip. Something of deeper importance must be involved when a thinker of Nietzsche's stature is led into such a contradiction. De Man's deconstructive interpretation is attractive because it allows us to see a deeper significance in Nietzsche's "mistake." My second section explains de Man's interpretation to highlight its attractiveness and to show its dependence on the claim that the nature of language dictates the contradictions of Nietzsche's first work. According to de Man, language is such that we cannot say that we possess the truth without falling into contradiction. This view I will challenge in two ways. My third section argues against de Man's claim that the contradictions of Nietzsche's text are due to the nature of language, and it provides an alternative explanation of them. My fourth section offers an account of why de Man finds plausible Nietzsche's claim in "On Truth and Lie in the Extra-Moral Sense" that all language is metaphorical and why he should not (in effect, why Nietzsche was right not to publish the essay).

CONTRADICTIONS IN *THE BIRTH OF TRAGEDY*

In his first book, Nietzsche used the terms "Apollinian," "Dionysian," and "Socratic" to denote three different "redemptive strategies," that is, ways of overcoming the terror and horror of existence, of affirming life or finding it worth living.[2] For followers of Socrates, the belief that being is knowable, hence correctable, makes life affirmable. In the other two cases, art plays this redemptive role. Apollinian art throws a veil of beauty over the empirical world; it makes life seem worth living by transforming and glorifying individuals involved in it. Dionysian art, on the other hand, glorifies neither individuals nor any other aspect of the empirical world. It either bypasses the empirical world altogether (as in music) or destroys individuals (as in tragedy). Redemption is gained through identification with something that is more important than individuals, something that remains powerful while the individual is destroyed.

Walter Kaufmann's efforts to the contrary notwithstanding, it is difficult to resist the impression that Nietzsche values the artistic strategies more highly than the Socratic. While its stated aim is to explain the origin of tragedy, his book's philosophical aim is to establish the priority of aesthetic values: to show that art is of greater value than science and that aesthetic values are more important than "scholarly" ones. Again contrary to Kaufmann, the Dionysian seems to be the preferred of the aesthetic strategies. This impression is confirmed by Nietzsche's later comment about *The Birth of Tragedy*: "Indeed, what is Dionysian? This book contains an answer: one 'who knows' is talking, the initiate and disciple of his god" (*GT* V4).[3] Although Nietzsche presents Apollo as an equal partner in the origin of tragedy (the words, characters, and action are Apollinian), the feature he considers most important—the redemption that tragedy provides, the affirmation of life despite its horrors—is Dionysian.

When we ask for the basis of Nietzsche's apparent value hierarchy (his basis for valuing the Dionysian over the Apollinian and both of these over the Socratic), the answer seems to lie in the comparative truthfulness of the strategies. Dionysus represents redemption in full knowledge of the truth, and Apollo combines truth with illusion, whereas the Socratic mode of redemption is based completely on illusion. Nietzsche identifies Socrates as the god of the theoretical person who is motivated to search for truth by the "profound illusion that first saw the light of day in the person of Socrates: the unshakable faith that thought, using the thread of causality can penetrate the deepest abysses of being, and that thought is capable not only of knowing being but even of correcting it" (*GT* 15).[4] The illusion of the Socratic, Nietzsche makes clear a few sections later, has been exposed by "the extraordinary courage and wisdom of Kant and Schopenhauer," who have "diagnosed for the first time the illusory notion which pretends to be able to fathom the inner nature of things with the aid of causality" and who have "gained the victory over the optimism concealed in the nature of logic" (*GT* 18). Nietzsche regards the Socratic form of redemption as depending on a false belief, the belief that we can discover the ultimate truth about things through rational inquiry. His judgment as to the falsity of this belief (and the illusory nature of the Socratic) depends on his acceptance of the Schopenhauerian claim that the world accessible to us through sense experience and theory (ordinary, nonmystical modes of knowledge) is mere appearance, a distortion of reality as it is in itself.

In itself, according to Schopenhauer, the world is blind, striving will, involving no plurality or individuation. It appears to the subject of sense experience and theoretical knowledge as a world of individuals caught up in a network of spatial, temporal, and causal relations only because the subject of such knowledge is an instrument of will, and its object is therefore organized for it in terms of causal, temporal, and spatial structures which make possible willing guided by knowledge.[5] Socratic knowledge is illusory, then, in the sense that it presents the world to us only as it appears through the distorting veil of time, space, and causality.

Nietzsche also identifies Apollo with illusion—as "the ruler over the beautiful illusion of the inner world of phantasy" (*GT* 1), whose highest effect is the triumph over "an abysmal and terrifying view of the world and the keenest susceptibility to suffering through recourse to the most forceful and pleasant illusions" (*GT* 3). The Apollinian makes life appear justified by transforming and glorifying it, thus veiling or withdrawing from view the reality of empirical existence (*GT* 3). It nevertheless possesses a "higher truth" and "perfection" than "the incompletely intelligible everyday world" (*GT* 1). Nietzsche's basis is, once again, the acceptance (and transformation) of Schopenhauer's philosophy. Nietzsche considers the dream, the natural counterpart of Apollinian art, more real than empirical life because, as the mere appearance of a mere appearance, it is a "higher appeasement of the primordial desire for mere appearance" (*GT* 4), which is responsible for the existence of the empirical world.[6] The Apollinian attitude— that beauty or the transfiguration of life is more important than empirical reality—is in touch with the truth about the empirical world, that it is only appearance and not the reality the Socratic person takes it to be.

But only Dionysian art gives access to the ultimate truth, that is, to the world as it is in itself, the reality lying beyond the empirical world. As Nietzsche contrasts Apollo and Dionysus:

Apollo overcomes the suffering of the individual by the radiant glorification of the eternity of the phenomenon; here beauty triumphs over the suffering inherent in life; pain is obliterated by lies from the features of nature. In Dionysian art and its tragic symbolism the same nature cries to us in its true, undissembled voice: "Be as I am! Amid the ceaseless flux of phenomena, the eternally creative primordial mother, eternally impelling to existence, eternally finding satisfaction in this change of phenomena."

Dionysian art, too, wishes to convince us of the eternal joy of existence; only we are to seek this joy not in phenomena, but behind them. We are to recognize that all that comes into being must be ready for a sorrowful end; we are forced to look into the terrors of individual existence—yet we are not to become rigid with fear: a metaphysical comfort tears us momentarily from the hustle of the changing figures. We are really for a moment primordial being itself, feeling its raging desire for existence and joy in existence; the struggle, the pain, the destruction of phenomena now appear necessary to us in view of the excess of countless forms of existence which force and push one another into life, in view of the exuberant fertility of the universal will. [*GT* 16-17]

Nietzsche's basis for believing that Dionysian art puts us in touch with the true voice of nature is again found in Schopenhauer. In what Nietzsche calls Apollinian art, Schopenhauer believes the intellect is released from subservience to the will and therefore from the distorting influence of the forms of time, space, and causality. Art can therefore give us a truth inaccessible to science or theory: it can make present to us the eternal essences, the Platonic forms, of the world at the different levels of its articulation for the subject. But precisely because this process still takes place within the confines of the subject/object relation, we are given the world only as it appears to the subject, not as it is in itself. But if the subject/object relation is itself a distorting influence which reduces the object to the status of appearance, the only solution is the dissolution of that relation. And this is precisely how Nietzsche describes Dionysian experience: we become one with reality itself, which, following Schopenhauer, he calls "will." There is no longer any separation of subject and object to distort the truth. This interpretation is supported by Nietzsche's earlier claim (*GT* 5) that

all our knowledge of art is basically quite illusory, because as knowing beings we are not one and identical with that being which, as the sole author and spectator of this comedy of art, prepares a perpetual entertainment for itself. Only insofar as the genius in the act of artistic creation coalesces with this primordial artist of the world [Nietzsche's reinterpretation of Schopenhauer's will], does he know anything of the eternal essence of art; for in that state he is ... at once subject and object, at once poet, actor, and spectator.

Tragedy is also Apollinian but only by virtue of elements of illusion which act to veil, thereby making more bearable, the Dionysian truth. The truth revealed in tragedy—the horror of individual existence and the underlying oneness of all being—is identified solely with Dionysus. The tragic story is the attempt to put into words, to articulate in terms of individual characters and actions, the Dionysian vision of the chorus. But Dionysian wisdom is not adequately expressed by these Apollinian devices. Language itself is inadequate for disclosing the truth (*GT* 6, 17) and can at most point the way to the Dionysian experience in which truth is fully present.

Consider now the problematic passage from section 18:

It is an eternal phenomenon: the insatiable will always finds a way to detain its creatures in life and compel them to live on, by means of an illusion spread over things. One is chained by the Socratic love of knowledge and the delusion of being able thereby to heal the eternal wound of existence; another is ensnared by art's seductive veil of beauty fluttering before his eyes; still another by the metaphysical comfort that beneath the whirl of phenomena eternal life flows on indestructibly—to say nothing of the more vulgar and almost more powerful illusions which the will always has at hand. These three stages of illusion are only for the more nobly formed natures.

Nietzsche is apparently saying that the "metaphysical consolation" involved in the Dionysian experience of tragedy is just another illusion which seduces us to go on living. In that case, however, he loses his argument for the priority of aesthetic values.[7] If there is no access to a truth beyond the empirical, he cannot even consider art more truthful than theory on the grounds that it at least recognizes the illusoriness of empirical reality. But within the parameters of *The Birth of Tragedy*, only Dionysian experience can provide the required access to transcendent truth. How could Nietzsche fail to see that the classification of Dionysian experience as illusory undercuts his whole argument?

He also undermines his own argument in even more obvious ways. He proclaims the inadequacy of language for expressing the truth yet presents himself as offering us the truth—in language, of course. On the basis of a theory (Schopenhauer's or his own variation on it), he presents himself as knowing that only art, and not theory, can provide true knowledge. The straightforward or analytical response to such contradictions at the heart of *The Birth of Tragedy* is that they reveal the book's incoherence and explain why Nietzsche spent so much of his later work rejecting it. To the deconstructionist, on the other hand, it is by means of such contradictions that *The Birth of Tragedy* accomplishes its aim: namely, the deconstruction or subversion of its own logocentrism.

DE MAN'S ACCOUNT OF THE CONTRADICTIONS

I take "longocentrism," used by Derrida to denote the valuation of speech over writing, to have the wider meaning captured by John Searle: "roughly the concern with truth, rationality, logic and 'the word' that marks the Western philosophical tradition."[8] In other words, logocentrism involves a set of value priorities typical of Western philosophers and intellectuals: the value of truth over illusion, of science over art, of logic over rhetoric, of literal language over figurative, of the spoken over the written word. Since this is close to what Nietzsche means by the "Socratic," *The Birth of Tragedy* would seem to involve an argument against logocentrism. As a straightforward argument against the Socratic, however, it is self-contradictory in the ways that I have indicated. Indeed, all arguments against the Socratic or logocentric would seem to be self-defeating. How can one argue against the possibility of truth, the validity of logic, the importance of argument without presupposing that against which one is arguing? While the philosopher may smile at this point, assured that his values are immune to criticism, de Man claims that Nietzsche's text undermines these values from within by showing that logocentrism leads to self-contradiction.

Despite its apparent antilogocentrism, de Man places *The Birth of Tragedy* squarely in the logocentric tradition because it gives priority to voice (language as immediately present, or "speech") over language as representational or graphic ("writing") and because its value reversals are in the service of what de Man takes to be the core of logocentrism: "the claim that truth can be made present to man" (88).[9] This claim is put into question, according to de Man, by the conflict between Nietzsche's theory and rhetorical praxis—between the theory that truth is present only in Dionysian experience and the narrator's non-Dionysian presentation of this theory as the truth. Instead of yielding a mere cancellation or negation, this contradiction between theory and practice is supposed to leave a residue of meaning which can be translated into a statement having to do with the limits of textual authority (99): that is, the limits of its own access to truth. The text cannot make this statement—at least not without reducing itself to nonsense. The point seems to be that it can exhibit what it cannot sensibly assert. Since its own theory that truth is present in Dionysian experience can be expressed only by a rhetorical praxis inconsistent with that theory, we are here shown something about the limits of textual authority or access to truth which cannot simply be asserted in the text. It does surface in the text, de Man believes, in somewhat veiled form, in "enigmatic" statements which "cannot be integrated within the value-pattern of the main argument" (99). He interprets section 18 in this way. In classifying the Dionysian as a stage of illusion, Nietzsche in effect admits that the author who is speaking in the name of the god Dionysus does not possess the truth. If he had made this admission more directly, it would have been impossible for the text to unfold the "fallacy" (102) of claiming to possess truth.

One of the attractive features of de Man's interpretation is that it makes *The Birth of Tragedy* into a work of art. The text seems to aspire to a truth which de Man calls "referential": literal correspondence to an external reality. But when read in this referential mode, it contradicts itself, thereby subverting its own claim to such truth. In thereby showing what it cannot sensibly or literally say, it is like a work of literature, which may exhibit reality and truth to us, even though its sentences do not correspond in any literal way to external reality. For this reason de Man takes *The Birth of Tragedy* to support the view that literature is "the model of truth to which philosophy aspires" and that philosophy is an "endless reflection of its own destruction at the hands of literature" (115). On his interpretation, the central criticism of the *The Birth of Tragedy* can be answered: namely, if its point is that only art conveys truth, why did not Nietzsche create a work of art? The deconstructionist answer is that this is precisely what he so brilliantly did while at the same time subverting or deconstructing the dichotomy between art and theory.

Yet the question remains as to why a deconstructive interpretation of *The Birth of Tragedy* should be accepted. Granted that Nietzsche's theory and practice are at odds, why not interpret this problem, in traditional terms, as the sign of an inadequate theory of truth which Nietzsche tried to overcome? Rather than a case of logocentrism deconstructing itself, why is it not just a bad argument against logocentrism?

The best answer I can find in de Man's text is that the nature of language is such that logocentrism—particularly the claim to possess truth—always undermines itself. De Man believes that Nietzsche is "in the grip of a powerful assumption about language, an assumption that is bound to control his conceptual and rhetorical discourse whether the author is aware of it or not"(87), "bound to control all the movements of the work" (89). The assumption that all language is figural and cannot therefore express literal truth is made explicit and, according to de Man, is demonstrated deconstructively in Nietzsche's essay "Truth and Lie in the Extra-Moral Sense." If statements that contradict Nietzsche's logocentric claims follow directly from a demonstrable assumption about the nature of language, however, then language itself is such that logocentrism leads to its own contradiction, and de Man has every reason to interpret *The Birth of Tragedy* as an instance of this deconstructive pattern.

There are at least two ways to undermine de Man's interpretation: (1) to argue against the assumption that language is figural and therefore incapable of expressing truth, and (2) to deny that this assumption about language dictates the contradictions of section 18. I attempt the latter in my next section and the former in the final section below.

AN ALTERNATIVE ACCOUNT OF THE CONTRADICTIONS

De Man argues that Dionysian experience belongs either to "the domain of the text" (that is, is essentially linguistic) or to "nature." He rejects the second alternative on the grounds that the Dionysian would then be "forever and radically separated from any form of art," since no bridge connects nature to its representation (100).[10] Dionysian experience must therefore be essentially linguistic. But given the assumption that language cannot express the truth, it must also be illusory, as section 18 claims.

Unfortunately, de Man offers only an inadequate reason for denying that Dionysian experience could be nonlinguistic. Of course, art cannot state the truth present in ineffable experience. Nietzsche's reason for associating Dionysus with art, however, is not that such art states Dionysian truth but that it induces in us a certain state in which we are able to experience that truth, a state in which the subject/object relation which distorts the truth collapses. Nietzsche's denial that language can adequately capture the essence of things may require him to admit that "Dionysus" is an inadequate name for the experience in question, just as "will" is an inadequate name for the "in itself." But contrary to de Man (100-1), this notion does not rule out the possibility that the experience that we, however inadequately, call Dionysian does capture the essence of things, even if it cannot gain linguistic expression without distortion. The only assumption concerning language that would force Nietzsche to deny that Dionysian experience makes truth present is a denial that truth or experience can be ineffable or nonlinguistic. However reasonable this assumption may be, there is no evidence that Nietzsche is making this assumption or that de Man wants to attribute it to him. I therefore find no reason to believe that the admission of the illusory nature of the Dionysian is controlled by Nietzsche's assumptions about language.

What, then, does push Nietzsche to the self-contradiction of section 18? To support my answer to this question, it is helpful to consider another puzzling line which occurs a few lines after Nietzsche implies that the Dionysian is illusory: "All that we call culture is made up of such stimulants; and, according to the proportion of the ingredients, we have either a dominantly *Socratic* or *artistic* or *tragic* culture; or, if historical exemplifications are permitted, there is either an Alexandrian or a Hellenic or a Buddhistic culture" (*GT* 18). The implication that Buddhism exemplifies tragic culture has always been considered incomprehensible, since Nietzsche otherwise interprets tragedy as the highest means of affirming life and as a remedy against longing for the negation of the will which he associates with Buddhism (*GT* 7). Again, it seems implausible that this is merely a "slip": how could Nietzsche possibly equate Buddhism with the affirmation of life or forget that he was interpreting tragedy as affirming it? On the other hand, I see no way of accounting for it in terms of anything that Nietzsche believed about language.

I believe that we can account for both of the apparent lapses in section 18 as the surfacing of a conflict about the value of life to which the whole of *The Birth of Tragedy* gives expression and which infects the very concept of the Dionysian. In the later preface to the work, Nietzsche writes that he used the term "Dionysus" to name the "instinct that spoke in favor of life and discovered for itself a fundamentally opposite doctrine and valuation of life" from that of Christian morality (*GT*, V5). If Dionysus functioned as the god of the affirmation of life, however, he was also the god of truth. In itself, this is no problem. The greatest affirmation of life must be the one that admits the most truth, since one can affirm only as much life as one will admit to exist.[11] The problem is that Nietzsche regards as the truth not simply Schopenhauer's metaphysical doctrine of the world as will but, more important, the conclusion that Schopenhauer drew from it, that life is not worth living. Nietzsche translates this into the "terrible wisdom of Silenus" (*GT* 3-4) and Hamlet's "horrible truth" (*GT* 7). I propose that, in *The Birth of Tragedy*, Nietzsche is accepting this "truth" but is attempting to avoid the conclusion Schopenhauer drew from it: that the ascetic life is the highest life, that only negation of the will brings redemption. Nietzsche's alternative to asceticism is art—that "only as an *aesthetic phenomenon* is existence and life eternally justified" (*GT* 5). As de Man notes, this famous line is "an indictment of existence rather than a panegyric of art" (93). What he does not seem to realize is that this is sufficient to explain why the Dionysian must be identified with illusion: if life is not worth living, no art can redeem except through illusion. Given what Nietzsche takes the truth to be, Dionysus cannot represent both truth and the affirmation of life.

Section 18 lays bare the concept's contradictory nature. First we see what happens when one fully identifies Dionysus with the affirmation of life: it must be considered illusory—on a par, as far as truth goes, with the Apollinian and the Socratic. The other side then receives its due: that Dionysus represents the truth. In that case, it must be associated with the rejection of the value of life, with the negation of the will, as it is when Nietzsche equates the tragic, whose truth is Dionysian, with the Buddhist.

If this reasoning is correct, section 18 provides no evidence for an ironic or deconstructive reading of *The Birth of Tragedy*. Instead it gives evidence against the claim that de Man needs to defend such a reading, namely, that "all the movements of the work" are controlled by assumptions about language (89). Nietzsche's assumptions about values are more important than, and probably control, his assumptions about language. What surfaces in section 18 is the conflict between his acceptance of Schopenhauer's values and his desire to reject them (in the terms of the *Genealogy*, between the aestic ideal, which is responsible for both indictments of existence and metaphysics, and the life-affirming ethic that Nietzsche would later develop). The book's major contradictions are an expression of, and an unsuccessful attempt to resolve, this ambivalence. Assumptions about language provide no shortcut or special access to understanding the value commitments of a text, and the door is left open for believing that old-fashioned Socratic strategies—which always interpret contradiction as something to be overcome—provide the necessary and appropriate means for such understanding.

LANGUAGE AS METAPHOR

I hope now in a more direct way to raise difficulties for the belief (which Nietzsche clearly does accept in "Truth and Lie in the Extra-Moral Sense") that all language is metaphorical.

As in the case of "true" and "false," we seem to deprive "metaphor" of determinate meaning if we deny the possibility of its opposite. But a more specific reason exists for denying that all language could be metaphorical. Both the creation and the interpretation of metaphors seem dependent on the ability to use language nonmetaphorically. Suppose I say that a speaker was attempting to "cut through the argument with a rusty razor blade." I have made an assertion which could not possibly be true, since arguments do not take up space. Why would you be inclined to interpret my statement as a metaphor? Since you know what it means to cut through something with a razor blade (that is, the conditions under which it would be true to say that someone had done so), you know that my assertion cannot possibly be true and that I cannot possibly believe it is true (short of insanity, or a quite different interpretation of the assertion). You need not deny that I have made an assertion, that is, that I have put something forward as true. But you must assume that I have done so for reasons other than the usual ones people have for making assertions: for example, to express their own belief in them or to convince others of their truth. So you assume instead that I have deliberately asserted something blatantly false so that you will need to look beyond what has been asserted to the point of the utterance: in this case, to think of the analysis of an argument in an imaginative way, as similar in certain ways to trying to cut through a physical object with a rusty razor blade. But I could not use the words in question to make you notice or think of these similarities (that is, could not accomplish the aim of using the words metaphorically) unless both of us knew how to use the words literally: in ordinary assertions intended to express belief in what is asserted. And since I would not know how to use words literally unless I did so at least occasionally, it seems clear that I can use language metaphorically only if I use it literally as well.[12]

Why, then, do so many readers (especially, perhaps, those influenced by Derrida) believe that Nietzsche has demonstrated that all language is metaphorical (or, more generally, figural) and is therefore incapable of expressing literal truth? I will attempt only to account for de Man's (mistaken) belief to this effect. But I believe that my criticism of his position creates serious difficulties for anyone who accepts a similar view of language.

Why de Man takes all language to be figural—what this statement even means—is not entirely clear. He endorses the view, which he attributes to Nietzsche, that "the paradigmatic structure of language is rhetorical rather than representational or expressive of a referential, proper meaning" and insists that this marks "a full reversal of the established priorities which traditionally root the authority of language in its adequation to an extralinguistic referent or meaning, rather than in the intralinguistic resources of figure" (106). De Man would evidently consider language "literal" or "nonfigural" only if it received its "authority" from its adequation to something extralinguistic. But this could mean two quite different things. It could mean, as Socrates speculates in the *Cratylus*, that the literal meaning of a word derives from a natural or nonconventional relation between word and object (for example, that "bees" is the correct word to use of certain buzzing insects because the sound somehow corresponds to the insects' nature). On this interpretation, the figural character of language amounts to what Derrida, following Saussure, calls "the arbitrariness of signs," the fact that the use of a particular sound or inscription to mean what it does is arbitrary.[13] In that case, however, de Man uses "figural" in an idiosyncratic way and gives us no reason to think that language is figural in the ordinary sense. Furthermore, the arbitrariness thesis provides no plausible support for the claim that language is incapable of expressing literal truth. The arbitrariness of signs means that nothing intrinsic to signs can tell us what they mean or how they are used and thus that signs require interpretation. But as I shall argue, only the assumption that language can express truth makes interpretation possible.

We can avoid reducing de Man's denial of literal meaning to the arbitrariness thesis if we understand 'literal' as the kind of meaning or use that a word has in virtue of an extralinguistic object (for example, a physical object or a Fregean sense) with which it is matched by the rules or conventions of a particular language. On this interpretation, a denial of literal meaning rejects much more than the arbitrariness thesis. It also denies that linguistic rules are like strings that tie words to their proper objects. To deny this "string" picture of how words gain their meaning within a language certainly seems the point of de Man's repeated denial of "referential" meaning. His claim that all language is figural—which for de Man is equivalent to taking figure to be the paradigm for language (see p. 105)—then affirms a kind of holism with regard to meaning. The meaning (or "authority") of words comes not from a direct (linguistic) tie to objects but from relations to other words ("the intralinguistic resources of figure").

On this second interpretation, de Man's insistence on the figurality of language is curiously close to certain elements in the philosophy of Donald Davidson, in particular, the inscrutability of reference. Davidson argues for inscrutability as a heretofore unnoticed consequence of Quine's thesis of the indeterminacy of translation.[14] The inscrutability thesis tells us that there is no unique way to pick out what the singular terms of a language refer to or what the predicates are true of. When we interpret another person's speech, there will be different ways of assigning reference or tying words to objects that will prove equally correct, according to the behavioral (including verbal) evidence that we have for deciding on a correct interpretation. The behavioral evidence will allow you to interpret my phrase "that rabbit" as referring to a bird, for instance, as long as you presume a suitable permutation upon the predicate I use (for example "runs fast" might be interpreted as "runs fast or flies"). The unit of meaning is not the word but the sentence—or, better, the whole language. The meaning of individual words or singular terms is crucially determined by their relations to other words and ultimately by how the whole system functions. Thus to know the meaning of a word is to know how to use it in sentences. To know the meaning of a sentence is to know the circumstances under which the sentence would be true. Success in interpreting the speech of another person consists not in matching words or phrases to objects but in being able to match truths with truths and falsehoods with falsehoods. Therefore, as Wallace formulates it: "what good translation preserves is not a word's reference, but the pattern of its acceptable variations of reference relative to acceptable variations in the reference of other words."[15]

I find Davidson's holism quite convincing. Except for the part about truth, I also find it very similar to de Man's view of language. Like Davidson, de Man wants to deny the existence of an extralinguistic (Fregean) meaning which, for instance, "it is raining" and "es regnet" have in common. But de Man would have to admit that they "mean the same thing" in the sense that each correctly translates the other into a different language. His insistence on the "absence of a reliable referent" and the "loss of a primacy of meaning located within the referent" (47) requires only a denial that correct or good translation consists in preserving reference. Although de Man's point in the quoted phrases is made specifically about literature, he believes that literature only makes more explicit the rhetorical structure of all language. His affirmation of this rhetorical structure amounts to a denial that meaning has a "factual, referential foundation" (111) and a rejection of the "traditional priority" which locates meaning "in a referent conceived as an object." It therefore seems natural to read de Man's position in Davidsonian terms, especially when he defines "the medium or property of langauge" as "the possibility of substituting binary polarities ... without regard for the truth-value of the structure" (109). De Man seems to mean that the truth value of sentences, and therefore the structure as a whole, is independent of the referents assigned to the parts. If he agrees with Davidson on this point, however, de Man certainly places himself quite at odds with Davidson when he draws from the denial of referential foundations for meaning (the inscrutability of reference) a denial both of literal meaning and of truth itself.

I want to suggest that de Man's apparent assumption that inscrutability entails a denial of literal meaning stems from a confusion of literal meaning with literal (in the sense of word-for-word) translation. On the "string picture" of language, the paradigm of translation will be word for word. The translation of a sentence from one language to another will involve discovering the objects to which the words in one language are tied and then replacing those words with ones tied to the same objects in the second language. The necessary rejection of this understanding of the problem of translation makes it difficult to retain faith in the possibility of literal translation. Retaining the prejudice, however, that sentences have literal meaning only if literal (word-for-word) translation of them is possible will then seem to make the rejection of the "string picture" entail a concomitant denial of the very possibility of literal meaning. And if, as de Man gives repeated evidence of believing, literal meaning and truth stand or fall together, it will also entail a denial of the possibility of expressing truth linguistically.

Davidson would agree that truth and literal meaning stand or fall together. He would deny, however, that truth requires "referential" meaning (the scrutability of reference). Instead, Davidson argues precisely that a sentence can have exactly the same truth conditions even if we assume differences in the objects to which the individual words refer. Literal meaning and truth go together because knowing the literal meaning of a sentence consists in knowing the circumstances in which it would be true. But knowing this meaning has nothing to do with the possibility of word-for-word translation or with matching words to extra-linguistic objects in unique ways. This, in fact, constitutes Davidson's argument for the inscrutability of reference.

Unlike de Man, Davidson does not sever language from the world. De Man denies the conceivability of "the notion of a language entirely freed of referential constraint" because "any utterance can always be read as semantically motivated" (49). Yet he usually writes as if meaning belongs purely to the realm of syntax and has no semantical content—as if we have only language and no connection to the world. He claims that we can and must read sentences as "semantically motivated," that is, as relating to the world. But the nature of language subverts or deconstructs this semantic reading, forcing us to read sentences on another level, as related only to other bits of language. I suggest that de Man finds this view of language compelling because he thinks we can accept the inscrutability of reference only "at the expense of literal truth" (112). His view makes perfect sense if we assume that "the correspondence of sentences to reality is the resultant of the more basic relations which terms bear to pieces of reality,"[16] and we make the obvious identification of such correspondence with truth. But a denial of both reference and truth completely severs the connection between language and reality, confusing the human condition with one that exists only at the extreme limits of madness. Perhaps more to the point (since followers of de Man may not admit madness as an objection), the denial of both reference and truth leaves one without a basis for interpreting what anyone says or writes. If we accept the problematic nature of referential meaning—that is, of establishing meaning by matching words to objects—we can preserve the idea of meaningfulness and interpretation only by way of truth. That is, to consider a statement meaningful is to regard it as interpretable. But it makes sense to regard something as interpretable only if we believe that there is a basis for distinguishing between good and bad interpretations, between what counts as an interpretation and what counts as just another unrelated statement. Without reference to fall back on, only truth can provide this basis. If we cannot match words to objects, we must translate or interpret by matching sentences to their truth conditions. To give a correct interpretation or translation of an entire language would be to give the right truth conditions for all of its sentences. The problematic character of reference which de Man appreciates (and which Derrida, I believe, calls "différance") is therefore compatible with the assumption that truth exists and that it can be approached or expressed in a straightforward manner. It entails only that words are not tied to objects "except as these ties are dictated by the truth conditions of statements taken overall."[17] To reject the assumption that beliefs can be true in a straightforward sense, as Nietzsche does on de Man's interpretation, severs the connection between language and the world. This position can seem plausible only on the questionable assumption that reference constitutes the only source of semantical content, the only way of connecting language and the world.[18]

5

Nietzsche contra Nietzsche:
The Deconstruction of Zarathustra

Daniel W. Conway

Deconstruction presupposes the critic's insight into the contingency of the construction of authority. By exposing the empowering presuppositions of the author's discourse, deconstruction effectively discredits any claim to an epistemically privileged authority. But does deconstruction adequately provide for the author's *own* insight into the construction of textual authority? How does deconstruction (or any other self-conscious interpretative strategy) deal with a text whose textuality *presupposes* the kind of indeterminacy and self-referentiality upon which deconstruction operates?[1] These questions are especially central to an engagement with Nietzsche's most forbidding book, *Thus Spoke Zarathustra.* Rather than deny or ignore the contingency of his own textual authority, Nietzsche *anticipates* the deconstruction of *Zarathustra,* thus forging a deconstructive relation between himself and his readers.[2] By *accommodating* the deconstruction of his own authority, Nietzsche encourages/forces his readers similarly to acknowledge the contingent construction of their own claims to authority. A genuinely free and empowered agency, Nietzsche believes, involves the recognition that one's own claims to authority are just as partial, fragile, and contingent as those of anyone else. Underlying Nietzsche's self-compromising ideal is the conviction that partiality, fragility, and contingency do not in themselves constitute objections to one's specific claims to authority. In order to encourage his readers to reconstruct *Zarathustra* on their own (similarly contingent) authority, Nietzsche accommodates the deconstruction of his textual authority, thus providing his readers with an example of the ideal agency he recommends to them.

Zarathustra is notorious for its textual discontinuities, which philosophers have customarily attributed to Nietzsche's literary and/or emotional immaturity.[3] In light of the deflationary readings of *Zarathustra* that this strategy has produced, a deconstructive reading of the text becomes quite attractive.[4] In this essay, I focus primarily on the traditionally troublesome second part of the text, in which the reader encounters several glaring discontinuities. In what follows, I advance an interpretation of part 2 that accounts for these discontinuities within Nietzsche's general plan to accommodate a deconstruction of his own textual authority. My general strategy is to chart as related processes the devaluation of Zarathustra's model of self-understanding and the deconstruction of Nietzsche's textual authority, tracking the latter process to the former. By investigating the deconstructive relation between Nietzsche and his readers, I hope to suggest a reading of *Zarathustra* as Nietzsche's attempt to promote the freedom and empowerment of his readers.

At the close of part 1, Zarathustra takes leave of his disciples and bids them to enact in their own lives his teaching of the *Übermensch*. But before parting with his disciples, "He spoke thus and the tone of his voice had changed. 'Now I go alone, my disciples. You too go now, alone. Thus I want it. Verily, I counsel you go away and resist Zarathustra! And even better: be ashamed of him! Perhaps he deceived you.'" (190).[5] Zarathustra's unprecedented reversal is attributable to his suspicion that his pedagogy has failed to effect the desired change in his disciples. His evidence? As a farewell gift, they have presented him with a *staff*. Although at first "delighted with the staff," Zarathustra later later "weighed the staff in his hand, doubtfully" (190). By outfitting Zarathustra with a staff, his disciples have indicated that they view themselves as a flock and him as their shepherd, thus invoking a standard symbol of Christian redemption. Because Zarathustra's revolutionary teaching is supposed to liberate humankind from its perceived *need* for redemption,[6] his disciples' perception of him as their potential redeemer constitutes *prima facie* evidence of his failure to convey his teaching. Yet despite this evidence, Zarathustra concludes part 1 by hopefully invoking the mysterious vision of "the great noon, when man stands in the middle of his way between beast and *Übermensch*" (190). Having ostensibly led his auditors to the brink of *Übermenschlickheit*, Zarathustra retreats triumphantly to his mountain solitude.

The beginning of part 2 marks an abrupt end to Zarathustra's respite in solitude. While interpreting a disconcerting dream, he suddenly realizes that his teaching is now "in danger": "Verily, all-too-well do I understand the Sign and admonition of the dream.... My enemies have grown powerful and have distorted my teaching till those dearest to me must be ashamed of the gifts I gave them" (195). At first glance, the beginning of part 2 might therefore appear to herald a significant advance in Zarathustra's pedagogical project. Zarathustra vowed in part 1 to return only when all his auditors had denied him (190). He now ascertains that the anticipated apostasy is complete, and he prepares to resume his teaching: "I have lost my friends; the hour has come to seek my lost ones" (195). But we must be wary of Zarathustra's enthusiasm.[7] He is much more concerned to secure an outlet for his "impatient, overflowing love" than to promote the welfare of his disciples: "let all who suffer be my phusicians" (196). He seems largely unconcerned that his disciples have renounced him not from strength, as he had originally envisioned (190), but from weakness—a weakness he himself has fostered. He furthermore does not consider the possibility that his auditors may have denied him for good reason, as a charlatan whose teaching *ought* to be rejected. In light of Zarathustra's suspiciously selfish motives for resuming his pedagogy, his surprise upon waking from the dream appears largely disingenuous: did he not upon returning to solitude bid his disciples to "be ashamed of Zarathustra"? Why, then, is he *surprised* at his disciples' apparent apostasy? Was their presentation to him of a shepherd's staff not sufficient evidence of their rejection of his teaching? Furthermore, who are these heretofore unmentioned "enemies" on whom Zarathustra now blames the distortion of his teaching?

This discontinuity between the conclusion of part 1 and the beginning of part 2 is customarily attributed (when it is acknowledged at all) to the text's overall lack of a unified dramatic structure.[8] But Zarathustra's curious behavior at the beginning of part 2 is perfectly consistent with his (repressed) suspicions at the close of part 1. In order to preserve the integrity of his current model of self-understanding in the face of his palpable failure, Zarathustra succumbs here to self-deception. The textual discontinuity thus reflects a fundamental conflict within Zarathustra's own understanding of himself as the herald of the *Übermensch*. He consequently resumes his pedagogy in part 2 not because his earlier efforts were somehow inadequate (a hypothesis that he cannot yet seriously entertain) but because some mysterious "enemies" have sabotaged his teaching.[9] Throughout part 2, the distance separating Zarathustra from his "enemies" serves as a measure of his self-deception; only toward the end of part 2 does Zarathustra acknowledge that he is his own "enemy."

In order to account for the discontinuity between the close of part 1 and the beginning of part 2 we must therefore resist the temptation to identify Zarathustra strictly with Nietzsche.[10] To be sure, Zarathustra eventually "grows into" the role reserved for him as Nietzsche's "official" proxy and spokesman.[11] But in the first half of the book, Zarathustra serves as an example of an individual who finds it nearly impossible to treat his own authority as contingently constructed. This developmental account of the central character is warranted by the general dramatic structure of the book: Nietzsche envisions *Zarathustra* as a philosophical *Bildungsroman*, in which the central character gradually acquires self-knowledge as his experiences in the world collectively invalidate his original understanding of himself.[12] The *Bildungsroman* genre enables Nietzsche to unite symbiotically the structure and content of *Zarathustra;* as I have suggested, the deconstruction of Nietzsche's textual authority corresponds to the gradual devaluation of Zarathustra's original understanding of himself as the teacher of the *Übermensch.* Nietzsche's reliance on the *Bildungsroman* genre thus links his own fate inextricably to that of Zarathustra, with whom he entrusts the promulgation of his teaching.

In order to appreciate Zarathustra's need for self-deception in part 2, let us briefly review the original model of self-understanding under which he operates in the prologue. While ensconced in solitude, Zarathustra apparently witnessed an event of which he presumes humankind still ignorant: the death of God. Because God has served historically as the guarantor of all human value, we need no longer depend upon an external authority for our value. We are consequently free now to renounce the God-inspired view of ourselves as inherently sinful or deficient. Zarathustra thus ostensibly promotes Nietzsche's teaching of human *innocence:* although the death of God means that no redemption is forthcoming, *no redemption of the human condition is in order.* Mortality, contingency, and tragedy are *not* deficiencies of the human condition and therefore do not countenance an appeal to an external (or transcendent) guarantor of human value. Prompted by this insight into the death of God, Zarathustra departs his solitude in order to impart to mankind his vision of the *Übermensch,* an ideal of human freedom and power whose achievement represents the overcoming of the traditional Christian-Platonic appraisal of human nature as inherently deficient.

Having descended the mountain, Zarathustra confidently presents his revolutionary teaching to the crowd: "*I teach you the*
Übermensch. Man is something that shall be overcome. What have you
done to overcome him?" (124). By addressing his auditors in this
traditional, preacherly manner, Zarathustra assumes his auditors'
need for such a teaching and his own ability to promulgate it. In going
under,[13] Zarathustra thus presupposes the causal efficacy of his discourse to effect a transformation of his auditors' lives. His mission is to
supply his auditors with the knowledge that God is dead, which his
auditors need simply parlay into *Übermenschlichkeit* by dint of an act
of will. Zarathustra's preacherly manner furthermore indicates that
he has adopted the traditional posture of the Platonic teacher of
virtue, whose pedagogical authority rests on an allegedly privileged
states *vis-à-vis* his auditors. Zarathustra's uncritical adoption of a
pedagogical posture is crucial, for his understanding of himself as
teacher of the *Übermensch* ideal proves to be incompatible with the
teaching itself.[14] As a teacher of virtue, he views the construction of his
authority as neither contingent nor arbitrary. He consequently
exempts himself from his own teaching on the grounds that he has
already renounced his belief in the dead God; he is not a member of the
community to which he speaks. His knowledge of the death of God
apparently renders him sufficient unto himself, independent of his
fellow human beings. He therefore imparts his teaching to humankind
but requires nothing in return. Given Zarathustra's "privileged" status
as a teacher of virtue, his auditors cannot help but appear deficient
and obtuse to him. With respect to his auditors, then, Zarathustra
commands the privilege of *autarky* and can only *give* to others.

In his opening speech of the prologue, Zarathustra anthropo-
morphically likened the sun to himself, declaring their common need
for audience or community: "Behold, I am weary of my wisdom, like a
bee that has gathered too much honey; I need hands outstretched to
receive it.... For that I must descend to the depths, as you do in the
evening when you go behind the sea and still bring light to the underworld, you overrich star. Like you, I must *go under*—go down as is said
by man, to whom I want to descend" (122). Having since adopted the
posture of the Platonic teacher of virtue, Zarathustra now cosmomor-
phizes himself and assumes for himself the sun's privilege of autarky.
In assuming that he has become his own "sun," independent of his
"deficient" auditors, Zarathustra betrays a fundamental *mis*understanding of his own teaching: although the death of God frees us from
our dependence on an external guarantor of value, we are still
dependent for our well-being on some form of community, in which

agents give and receive reciprocally. Zarathustra admitted as much when he acknowledged his need for "hands outstretched to receive [his wisdom]" (122), but his initial confrontation with his "deficient" auditors led him to deny any dependence on them. Zarathustra's autarkic model of self-understanding is therefore incompatible with his vision of the *Übermensch*. Because he speaks from the privileged perspective he means to preclude, he rejects his teaching even as he utters it. This discordance manifests itself as an asymmetry between *what* he teaches and *how* he teaches it: Zarathustra *says* he comes to bury God, but his *manner* praises Him instead.

Zarathustra's fundamental methodological error, to which he is recidivistically prone, is to exempt himself from the categories in terms of which he understands his auditors. Fully prepared to expose the contingently Christian and ascetic construction of his auditors' authority, he refuses to view his own authority as similarly constructed. He therefore unwittingly reproduces at another level the very presuppositions of which he seeks to disabuse his auditors, thus presenting the *Übermensch* as the redeemer of his auditors' need for redemption. By treating his auditors' ignorance of their own sufficiency as *itself* a deficiency, Zarathustra unwittingly reinforces the Christian construction of "original sin" that he ostensibly seeks to subvert. Rather than liberate his auditors, Zarathustra transfers their relation of dependence from God to himself.[15]

The failure of Zarathustra's pedagogy in part 1 attests to the incoherence of his enterprise. Handicapped by his traditional presentation of a revolutionary teaching, he was unable to attract any receptive auditors. Nietzsche therefore devotes part 2 of *Zarathustra* to a standard feature of the *Bildungsroman* genre: rather than abandon his original preconceptions about the world in the face of contrary experience, the novitiate dismisses his initial experiences as aberrant and sets out in search of the "real" world, in which his experiences are consonant with his preconceptions. Dissatisfied with his reception thus far, Zarathustra resolves in part 2 to discover an audience untainted by the receptive deficiencies that thwarted his pedagogy in part 1. Rather than return to his "lost ones," as he promised upon interpreting his dream (195), Zarathustra departs the town of the Motley Cow in search of an audience to which he can impart his vision of the *Übermensch*.

Zarathustra's "solution" to his pedagogical problems is crucial to an understanding of his self-deception: "Like a cry and a shout of joy I want to sweep over wide seas, till I find the Blessed Isles where my friends are dwelling. And my enemies among them! How I now love all to whom I may speak! My enemies too are part of my bliss" (196). Most of the speeches of part 2 ostensibly take place on the Blessed Isles,[16] a utopian community "discovered" by Zarathustra, where receptive auditors anxiously await the arrival of a liberating teacher. Here he need no longer concern himself with modifying his pedagogy to accommodate deficient auditors. Yet Zarathustra's effortless emigration to the Blessed Isles in part 2 may strike the reader as a surprisingly facile solution to his earlier pedagogical difficulties.[17] Why has he never before mentioned these idyllic Blessed Isles if in fact his friends and enemies blissfully dwell there together? Nietzsche's deployment of an image of detachment and isolation (specifically, an island) only reinforces the suspicion that Zarathustra's "discovery" of a receptive audience represents a self-deceived retreat from the failures of his pedagogy; the allusion to the "Isles of the Blest" of Greek mythology further suggests that Zarathustra has engineered an afterworldly redemption of his pedagogical struggles. As we shall see, Zarathustra has in fact "invented" the conditions of his own pedagogical success.[18]

In many respects, the text of part 2 resembles that of part 1: under the aegis of his sun-inspired autarky, Zarathustra continues to promote the *Übermensch* ideal to virtually anonymous auditors. The text thus reflects Zarathustra's own perspective on his enterprise and proceeds as if his pedagogy were highly successful. But in order to accommodate the internal tension occasioned by Zarathustra's self-deception, Nietzsche now begins to chronicle Zarathustra's misgivings about his career as the teacher of the *Übermensch*. By informing the text of part 2 with several radical discontinuities, Nietzsche inaugurates a subtext in which Zarathustra honestly surveys the evidence mounting against his current model of self-understanding.[19] Within this subtext Zarathustra's *Bildungsgang* continues unimpaired by self-deception. The dominant text, which derives its authority solely from Zarathustra's own, remains stubbornly Apollonian; under the spell of the coming "great noon," Zarathustra continues to operate under his autarkic model of self-understanding. The subtext, however, comprises a Dionysian attack on Zarathustra's model of self-understanding. The interplay of Apollonian text and Dionysian subtext consequently parallels the tension inherent to Zarathustra's pedagogical project.

The eruptions of this subtext challenge Zarathustra's model of self-understanding by providing *internal* evidence against it: Zarathustra's subtextual forays gainsay his pretentions to autarky and thus expose the incoherence of his enterprise. As we have seen, the authority of Nietzsche's text derives entirely from Zarathustra's own authority as an autarkic agent. In challenging Zarathustra's autarkic model of self-understanding, the eruptions of the subtext thus also challenge the authority of the text itself. The emergence of this subtext consequently serves to catalyze a deconstruction of *Zarathustra;* the dramatic structure of the text mirrors the internal structure of Zarathustra's enterprise. By thus orchestrating the eruptions of the subtext, Nietzsche both anticipates and accommodates the deconstruction of his own textual authority. He is entirely reliant upon Zarathustra to promulgate his teaching, and Zarathustra's *Untergang* is destined inexorably for "demise."

To designate the occasional eruptions of this subtext, Nietzsche employs Dionysian images as signposts. Throughout part 2 we encounter intermittent chapters staged amid the imagery of dream, night, tomb, intoxication, song, dithyramb, underworld, and shadow. For example, Zarathustra's alarm at the beginning of part 2 is triggered by a *dream* in which his own reflection in a child's mirror reveals a devil's visage. Nietzsche's title for this inaugural chapter of part 2—"The Child with the Mirror"—suggests that this subtext is related to the text as a *mirror* that reflects the failures of Zarathustra's pedagogical career. Because Zarathustra enacts the reflections in this mirror, however, he does not enjoy the critical distance that informs our "privileged" standpoint; his own appraisal of the mirror's reflections is prejudiced by his autarkic model of self-understanding. We have already seen him interpret his initial dream as an endorsement of his pedagogy rather than as a challenge to it. Zarathustra's continued susceptibility to self-deception thus not only generates the subtext but also mitigates its potential utility for him as a mirror.

At the beginning ot part 2, Zarathustra's interpretation of his dream persuades him to go under once again: "New ways I go, a new speech comes to me; weary I grow, like all creators, of the old tongues" (196). This "new speech" largely comprises a series of fulminations against the obtuse auditors in the town of the Motley Cow, to whom he originally presented his teaching before emigrating to the Blessed Isles. Here Zarathustra gloats over his good fortune, for on the Blessed Isles he need no longer associate with the "rabble" to whom he initially tried to speak: "Oh, I found it here my brothers! Here, in the highest spheres, the fount of pleasure wells up for me! And here is a life of which the rabble does not drink." (210). Zarathustra's "discovery" of the Blessed Isles furthermore vindicates his claim to an autarkic privilege. He is now certain that his pedagogical failures in part 1 are wholly attributable to the deficiencies of his original auditors. Zarathustra thus celebrates his arrival on the Blessed Isles by lampooning those whom he left behind: the pitying, the priests, the virtuous, the rabble, the preachers of equality (that is, the tarantulas), and the famous wise men (chapters 3-8).

But Zarathustra's celebration comes to an abrupt end in chapter 9 of part 2, as the Dionysian subtext interrupts the course of the text.[20] From the very outset of his pedagogical career, when he brazenly likened the sun to himself, Zarathustra has identified himself exclusively with light, with giving, with the redemptive "Great Noon." He has consequently denied his need for (and susceptibility to) any additional *Bildung*. The text has been illuminated thus far by Zarathustra's own solar radiance. But in *The Night Song*, which Nietzsche describes as Zarathustra's "immortal lament at being condemned by the overabundance of light and power, by his sun nature, not to love,"[21] the Dionysian subtext challenges Zarathustra's claim to an autarkic privilege by temporarily eclipsing the Apollonian daylight of the text. Submerged now in the darkness of the subtext, Zarathustra acknowledges that he longs also to receive: "Light am I; ah, that I were night! But this is my loneliness that I am girt with light. Ah, that I were dark and nocturnal!... But I live in my own light; I drink back into myself the flames that break out of me. I do not know the happiness of those who receive" (217-218).[22] Zarathustra's yearning in *The Night Song* "to receive light" implies that autarky is an unacceptable (and illusory) alternative to membership in a reciprocal community.[23] Here he acknowledges that a coherent model of self-understanding must be predicated on the recognition of others as "suns" in their own right: "Many suns revolve in the void: to all that is dark they speak with their light—to me they are silent" (218). Zarathustra consequently longs to renounce his autarkic "privilege" and take his place *within* the community to which he speaks: "And even you would I bless, you little sparkling stars and glowworms up there, and be overjoyed with your gifts of light" (218). Zarathustra's *Night Song* finally questions whether his teaching can be imparted at all under the aegis of an autarkic model of self-understanding: "They take from me, but do I touch their souls? There is a cleft between giving and receiving; and the narrowest cleft is the last to be bridged" (218). This "cleft between giving and receiving" corresponds to the original asymmetry between Zarathustra's untimely teaching and his traditional model of self-understanding. Zarathustra admits here that his autarkic posture has compromised his pedagogical project: "My happiness in giving died in giving; my virtue tired of itself in its overflow" (218). *The Night*

Song thus comprises Zarathustra's first consideration—albeit a subtextual one—of the possibility that *he* is responsible for the failure of
his pedagogy.

The doubts expressed by Zarathustra in *The Night Song* are
amplified in the final song of the subtextual eruption, *The Tomb Song.*
Here Zarathustra leaves the Blessed Isles, crossing the sea to the Isle
of Tombs (222); Nietzsche thus implies that Zarathustra's model of
self-understanding has thrust him once again into the unwanted role
of "gravedigger."[24] Freed from the self-deception indigenous to the
Blessed Isles, Zarathustra here reflects subtextually on his pedagogical failures—an exercise he cannot yet perform in the light of day, lest
his enterprise come to an end. Fully expecting an immediate and universal reception of his teaching, Zarathustra has come to loathe his
original auditors for their apparent recalcitrance and ingratitude. He
consequently accuses his "enemies" of misleading him with an unreal-
istic exception of pedagogical success: "Thus spoke my purity once in a
fair hour: 'All beings shall be divine to me.' Then you assaulted me with
filthy ghosts; alas, where has this fair hour fled now? . . . All nausea I
once vowed to renounce: then you changed those near and nearest me
into putrid boils. Alas, where did my noblest vow flee then?" (223).
Zarathustra subsequently discloses that his experiences in the world
have in fact sullied the innocence of his solitude: "You have taken from
me the irretrievable: thus I speak to you my enemies. For you murdered the visions and dearest wonders of my youth. . . . you have cut
short my eternal bliss, as a tone that breaks off in a cold night" (223).
Zarathustra's loss of innocence attests to the incoherence of his enterprise. He goes under to promote an ideal of human sufficiency, yet as
an autarkic agent, he cannot help but deem his auditors deficient. On
the subtextual level, then, Zarathustra's *Untergang* engenders an
absurdum practicum: his claim to an autarkic privilege *guarantees*
the failure of his pedagogy. *The Tomb Song* thus portends the eclipse of
Zarathustra's sun-inspired autarky.[25]

But the sentiments expressed in these songs do not yet mirror
Zarathustra's "daylight" appraisal of his destiny as the teacher of the
Übermensch. Despite the eruption of the Dionysian subtext, Zarathustra remains committed to his autarkic model of self-understanding.
His strength of will enables him to "endure" and "overcome" these subtextual distractions (224–25). Immediately following *The Tomb Song.*
Zarathustra ignores these "irrational" songs and takes solace in the
potential receptivity of his current auditors, those individuals who
allededly overcome themselves.[26]

Zarathustra turns hopefully to his new auditors, who he assumes have eagerly internalized his teaching of the *Übermensch;* evidence of pedagogical success on the Blessed Isles would presumably dispel the doubts raised by these songs. Nietzsche devotes chapters 13–17 of the text of part 2 to a narrative tour in which Zarathustra surveys the gamut of his auditors on the Blessed Isles. Zarathustra displays for the reader various individuals who are renowned on the Blessed Isles for their feats of self-overcoming: the ascetics of the spirit, the hypercritical men of today, foundationalists (that is, disinterested perceivers), scholars, and poets (chapters 13–17). But to his dismay, Zarathustra soon discovers that his emigration to the Blessed Isles has degenerated into a *via negativa.* Although each candidate is admittedly virtuous in some important regard, all nevertheless remain "fragmentary" in their common failure to renounce their God-inspired commitment to the deficiency of human nature.[27] The virtue specialists who inhabit the Blessed Isles are nothing more than "inverse cripples" (250) who compensate for their perceived deficiencies by cultivating one virtue to the exclusion of all others. Zarathustra is consequently forced to conclude this *via negativa* by admitting that his pedagogy has produced no *Übermensch*—even on the Blessed Isles. In fact, his disciples on the Blessed Isles are virtually indistinguishable from his previous auditors in the town of the Motley Cow, whom he thought he had left behind. The ridicule that he heaped upon his former disciples (chapters 3–8) thus reverberates mockingly, as a dismissal of his current auditors as well. Yet Zarathustra still fails to acknowledge that his *via negativa* is ultimately self-consuming in scope.

At this critical juncture, the Dionysian subtext once again interrupts the course of the text, in the chapters "On Great Events" and "The Soothsayer." In the former chapter, Zarathustra's "shadow" offers the following warning: "It is time! It is high time" (245).[28] But Zarathustrais as yet unable to decipher this parabolic message, requiring, it would seem, a more straightforward clue that "it is high time" to abandon his current model of self-understanding.[29] Nor does Zarathustra recognize his shadow's "descent to hell" (242) as a portent of his own imminent *Untergang* (that is, "demise"), for he does not yet view these subtextual eruptions as accurate reflections of his own inadequacies.

But in the latter chapter, the darkness prefigured in *The Night Song* and *The Tomb Song* finally descends: here the righ nocturnal imagery of Zarathustra's nightmare embellishes the failure of his pedagogy. The soothsayer's prophecy that "the best grew weary of their works" echoes Zarathustra's confession in *The Night Song* that he no longer derives joy from his teaching. The ripe, sweet figs that earlier (197) symbolized Zarathustra's teachings have now turned "rotten and brown." The soothsayer's prophecy moreover likens Zarathustra's teaching to an ambiguous Promethean gift: "and if fire should descend on us, we should turn to ashes; indeed, we have wearied the fire itself." Finally, Zarathustra's own fluid metaphor for his "new speech" in part 2 (196) is here distorted into a portent of death: "All our wells have dried up; even the sea has withdrawn." The soothsayer finally concludes his prophecy by suggesting that Zarathustra's teaching has in fact precipitated the advent of nihilism: "Verily, we have become too weary even to die. We are still waking and living on—in tombs" (245). As Zarathustra's subsequent nightmare confirms by casting him in the role of "night watchman and guardian of tombs" (246), the "deadly doctrine" that the soothsayer describes is Zarathustra's own teaching. Despite his apparent efforts to liberate humankind from the shadow of the dead God, his teaching has nevertheless been internalized as the paralyzing doctrine that "All is empty, all is the same, all has been!" (245).[30] Zarathustra consequently dreams of himself as a servant "in the castle of Death" (246).

Upon hearing Zarathustra's account of the nightmare, his favorite disciple eagerly volunteers an interpretation. Interestingly enough, the youth diagnoses the awful dream as yet another endorsement of the *success* of Zarathustra's pedagogy: "Are you not yourself the wind with the shrill whistling that tears open the gates of the castles of death? Are you not yourself the coffin full of colorful sarcasms and the angelic grimaces of life?" (247). Zarathustra's *Bildungsgang* in part 2 thus comes full circle: for him to witness his favorite disciple's interpretation of the dream is like looking into a mirror—a child's mirror—for the second time. And once again, his "devilish" reflection has been interpreted charitably. This time around, however, owing perhaps to the therapeutic eruptions of the subtext, Zarathustra is able to distance himself from his own enterprise; his newly acquired *Bildung* renders him suspicious of his disciple's Zarathustresque interpretation of the nightmare. Nietzsche's imagery here suggests that the youth's interpretation of the nightmare has initiated the dissolution of Zarathustra's self-deception.[31]

This spell of self-deception if finally shattered in the chapter "On Redemption," which begins as Zarathustra crosses over a great bridge (249). As he earlier did on the subtextual level (222), Nietzsche signals the end of Zarathustra's self-deception on the textual level by means of the latter's departure from the Blessed Isles. On the other side of the bridge, a hunchback informs Zarathustra that "one thing is still needed" before he and his fellow cripples can "believe in [Zarathustra's] doctrine": Zarathustra must first "heal the blind and make the lame walk" (249). Once again, Zarathustra's failure as the teacher of the *Übermensch* is manifest, for these auditors perceive him as a potential redeemer of human deficiencies, just as at the close of part 1.[32]

Zarathustra consequently takes this opportunity to clarify his teaching one final time. As a Platonic teacher of virtue, he believes that he need only inform his auditors of the death of God; they in turn will transform themselves into *Übermenschen* by dint of an act of will. At the beginning of part 2, Zarathustra proclaimed that "willing liberates: that is the true teaching of will and liberty—thus Zarathustra teaches it" (199). He later responded to the subtextual challenge of *The Tomb Song* by reaffirming his faith in human creativity: "Indeed, in me there is something invulnerable and unbearable, something that explodes rock: that is *my will*.... You are still the shatterer of all tombs. Hail to thee, my will!" (224–25). But in the aftermath of his soothsayer-induced nightmare, Zarathustra is obliged to revise his teaching significantly: "Will—that is the name of the liberator and joy-bringer; thus I taught you, my friends. But now learn this too: the will itself is still a prisoner" (251). Within the context of the nightmare, we recall, Zarathustra was able to open all gates save a single one (247); his "watchman's keys" symbolize the creative "Yea-sayings" of the will and the open gates his successful self-overcomings. As Zarathustra discloses in his speech "On Redemption," the single unyielding gate symbolizes the *past:* "Powerless against all that has been done, he is an angry spectator of all that is past. The will cannot will backwards; and that he cannot break time and time's covetousness, that is the will's loneliest melancholy" (251). As Zarathustra himself now realizes, his teaching is much more complicated than he initially thought when he straightforwardly presented it to the crowd. Although the will cannot objectively *change* the past, for example, alter the Christian-Platonic heritage of self-depreciation that defines us as historical agents, a form of redemption is nevertheless possible: "All 'it was' is a fragment, a riddle, a dreadful accident... until the creative will says to it 'But thus I will it; thus shall I will it'" (253). But the redemption of the will from its "revenge against the past," a feat that would require "something higher than any reconciliation" (253), is among the darkest of Zarathustra's teachings. Zarathustra himself asks, "how shall this be brought about? Who could teach [the will] also to will backwards?" (253).

The subsequent aposiopesis in Zarathustra's speech signals an epiphantic moment of realization: the will that could say to the past "But thus I willed it" is *not* the will that Zarathustra reveres. The redemption Zarathustra seeks involves a *liberation* from his past, and his own strategy for "willing backwards" calls for the advent of a redemptive *Übermensch:* "When my eyes flee from the now to the past, they always find the same: fragments and limbs and dreadful accidents—but no human beings. The now and the past on earth—alas, my friends, that is what *I* find most unendurable; and I should not know how to live if I were not also a seer of that which must come" (251). Zarathustra thus realizes that he too envisions the *Übermensch* as a redeemer—albeit of our need for redemption. Although he ostensibly promotes the sufficiency of the human condition, he wants no part of a destiny that requires him to engage in a potentially interminable exchange with "fragments" and "cripples."

Zarathustra's predicament at the close of part 2 is succinctly represented in his final exchange with the hunchback, who apprises Zarathustra of the asymmetry between his words and manner: "But why does Zarathustra speak otherwise to his pupils than to himself?" (254). That is, why does Zarathustra say one thing but teach another? Despite his pretensions to autarky, Zarathustra's primary goal all along has been to discern in his disciples a sign that they have internalized his teaching; he longs, as the *Night Song* confirmed, also to receive from them, and the failure of his pedagogy is attributable to his unacknowledged need for them *not* to internalize his teaching. Throughout part 2, Zarathustra has sought in vain to witness his teaching reflected in his auditors, discovering only "fragments" and "cripples." But we now see that Zarathustra has pursued the wrong evidence all along. Fully convinced of the efficacy of his discourse, he sought in his disciples only a reflection of his "official" teaching. In fact, whenever the subtext afforded him a contrary mirror image, he simply reassimilated his reflection. Now that his self-deception has been exposed, however, Zarathustra realizes that he has effectively advanced two separate, incompatible ideals of *Übermenschlichkeit.* The "official" Nietzschean teaching that Zarathustra failed to promulgate comprises two tenets: the death of God and the innocence of the human condition. The inadvertent teaching that Zarathustra successfully promulgated comprises only the former tenet and thus encourages his auditors to welcome a new redeemer of their human deficiencies. In this light, his pedagogy has been ironically successful after all: his disciples have in fact replicated his manner perfectly and have afforded him a reflection of his inadvertent teaching. Like him, they not only view the *Übermensch* as a potential redeemer of human deficiencies but also view themselves as needing external redemption.[33] Zarathustra thus finally realizes that *he* is the enemy responsible for the distortion of his teaching. Because he refused to acknowledge his dependence on his auditors for their recognition of him as a teacher of virtue, Zarathustra unwittingly sabotaged his teaching; in order to secure their recognition, he was obliged to set himself up as the successor god, as the anti-*Übermensch*. After all, did *his* reflection in the child's mirror not reveal "a devil's grimace and scornful laughter"? (195).[34]

The climax of Zarathustra's crisis occurs, appropriately enough, in the ambiguous midnight/noon midpoint of the text, "The Stillest Hour."[35] At this juncture, the solar radiance of Zarathustra's autarky is rudely eclipsed, as the Dionysian subtext finally supplants the text of part 2. The deconstruction of the text is now complete. Zarathustra's mode of self-understanding, the source of authority for both Zarathustra and Nietzsche, has devalued itself. Here Zarathustra finally accepts the verdict originally pronounced in *The Tomb Song:* "As yet my words have not moved mountains, and what I said did not reach men. Indeed, I have gone to men, but as yet I have not arrived" (258). Zarathustra therefore concludes that "it is beyond [his] strength" (257) to impart a teaching he neither embodies nor esteems.[36] The *Bildungsgang* of part 2 thus delivers a tragic conclusion: Zarathustra is unable to convince even *himself* of the merit of his own teaching. He knows that God is dead, but he is powerless to inform his own practices with this knowledge. Zarathustra's pronouncement of the death of God therefore signals only an interregnum period until a successor arrives; as we have seen, Zarathustra both assumes and denies the role of successor god. In the meantime, Zarathustra and his auditors, deprived of the guarantor of their value, now deem themselves irremediably deficient. As the soothsayer prophesied, Zarathustra's revolutionary teaching of liberation has degenerated into an enervating damnation: "All is empty, all is the same, all has been!" (245).

We must bear in mind, however, that the deconstruction of *Zarathustra* marks the midpoint of the book and not its conclusion. To view the deconstruction of Nietzsche's textual authority as a purely negative result would therefore be mistaken or at any rate premature. I believe that Nietzsche anticipated the deconstruction of his textual authority and fashioned *Zarathustra* to accommodate the contingency and fragility of his authority. As we have seen, Nietzsche promotes an ideal of human sufficiency that is predicated on the innocence of the human condition; for Nietzsche, the mortality, contingency, and tragedy of the human condition do not detract from its value. But by promoting this ideal through a literary medium, Nietzsche risks exerting on his readers a dangerously formative influence such that they might come to regard *him* as the new guarantor of their value. In order to allay his greatest fear as a philosopher—that he might be involuntarily conscripted as the new redeemer—Nietzsche welcomes the deconstruction of his own textual authority, thus pre-emptively sabotaging his potential candidacy for the position of interim God. Zarathustra's unwitting complicity in the Christian-Platonic moral tradition is designed to obviate a similar fate for Nietzsche. Appropriating for his own purposes a familiar myth, Nietzsche sacrifices his own "son/sun"—not to redeem humankind but to free humankind from its perceived need for redemption. Of course, some readers will still revere Nietzsche's authority even in the wake of Zarathustra's dismal failure and "demise"; such readers lie ultimately beyond Nietzsche's authorial control.[37]

Having accommodated the deconstruction of his textual authority, Nietzsche in parts 3-4 encourages his readers to reconstruct *Zarathustra* on the strength of their own authority, whose construction he has shown by implication to be similarly contingent; only in this way can he promote the sufficiency of his readers without appealing to a privileged standpoint. Parts 3-4 of the text chronicle Zarathustra's gradual convalescence from his midbook crisis, a convalescence that corresponds to a reconstruction of the authority of the text independently of Nietzsche's authority.

Part 3 comprises a series of comic failures. Apprised of his own failure to embrace the *Übermensch* ideal, Zarathustra resolves to impart this teaching to *himself* before resuming his public pedagogy: "Thus I am in the middle of my work, going to my children and returning from them: for his children's sake Zarathustra must perfect himself" (273). Zarathustra unwittingly reproduces in this autodidactic enterprise the same presuppositions that invalidated his original pedagogical project. Still convinced of the causal efficacy of his discourse, he comically seeks to provide himself with the knowledge whereby he might willfully transform himself. Because he unwittingly resumes an autarkic posture, the incipient reconstruction of the text of part 3 is interrupted on two occasions by the emergence of the subtext: the chapters "The Vision and the Riddle" and "On the Three Evils" both reflect the incoherence of Zarathustra's autodidactic enterprise. Only in "The Convalescent," following the final eruption of the Dionysian subtext, does Zarathustra finally renounce his claim to an autarkic privilege, thus setting the stage for part 4, in which he coherently, if not successfully, promotes the *Übermensch* ideal.[38].

In part 4, the text proceeds without subtextual interruption, for Zarathustra has finally abandoned the autarkic posture that undermined his pedagogy and precipitated his self-deception. Yet how can Zarathustra continue his pedagogy if he does not assume his customary posture as Platonic teacher of virtue? This concern is only exacerbated as part 4 begins, for the supposedly transfigured Zarathustra exhibits no interest whatsoever in teaching.[39] Perhaps his rejection of an autarkic privilege requires him to abandon his pedagogical project as well; after all, Zarathustra seems content in the opening scene of part 4 to spend his time *fishing*.[40]

But as Zarathustra confides upon scaling a nearby mountain, his apparent indifference to his teaching is a "mere cunning" (351) designed to appease his anxious animal companions. He now likens himself to a fisher of men,[41] insofar as he now views his audience "as an abysmal, rich sea—a sea full of colorful fish and crabs, which even gods might covet, that for their sakes they would wish to become fishermen and net throwers: so rich is the world in queer things, great and small. Especially the human world, the human sea: *that* is where I now cast my golden fishing rod and say: Open up, you human abyss!" (351). In parts 1–2, we recall, Zarathustra was primarily interested in becoming empty, with *giving* to humankind; here in part 4 however, he also longs to *receive* from his auditors, to draw them to himself. Zarathustra now consciously embraces the ideal of reciprocal community that was originally suggested in *The Night Song*. In exchanging his autarkic privilege for a "golden fishing rod," Zarathustra has not retired after all from the promotion of virtue but has instead corrected the error that thwarted his earlier attempts at pedagogy. Rather than risk inadvertently setting himself up as the new redeemer, Zarathustra no longer predicates his teaching on the priviledged authority of the teacher of virtue. In order to avoid another "demise," Zarathustra now refuses to go under: "Thus men may now come *up* to me; for I am still waiting for the sign that the time has come for my descent. I still do not myself go under, as I must under the eyes of men" (351).

But if Zarathustra refuses to go under, then in what sense does he promote the virtue of others at all? Why would anyone voluntarily come to *him* in search of moral advice and edification—especially now that he has relinquished his claim to a privileged authority? Anticipating this objection, Zarathustra acknowledges that his fishing expedition *is* foolish, yet he defends it nonetheless, as an improvement upon his former "solemnity" (*Feierlichkeit*): "Has a man ever caught fish on high mountains? And even though what I want and do up here be folly, it is still better than if I became solemn down there from waiting... [like] an impatient one who shouts down into the valleys, 'Listen or I shall whip you with the scourge of God!'" (351). In the absence of receptive auditors, Zarathustra originally viewed his promotion of *Übermenschlichkeit* as self-sacrificial; as he confessed in

"On Redemption," he could endure "the now and the past" only by anticipating the advent of a redemptive *Übermensch*. His unconditional gift for humankind, which he had originally likened to a surfeit of honey (122), has consequently degenerated into a "honey sacrifice" (*Honig-Opfer*). Zarathustra therefore renounces his initial model of self-understanding; one cannot consistently maintain, as he did, that one's gift for mankind is both unconditional *and* sacrificial.

In contrast to the "honey sacrifice" that culminated in his "demise," Zarathustra now recommends a new metaphor for his teaching: "Why sacrifice? I *squander* [*verschwende*] what is given me, I—a squanderer with a thousand hands; how could I call that sacrificing?" (350, emphasis added). Here Zarathustra overcomes the internal incoherence that compromised his initial efforts to promote the *Übermensch* ideal: like the bee, he too squanders his "honey." He consequently imposes no conditions whatsoever on his teaching—he does not even require anyone to *listen* to him: "That is why I wait here, cunning and mocking on high mountains, neither impatient nor patient... For my destiny... does not hurry and press me, and it leaves me time for justs and sarcasms, so that I could climb this mountain today to catch fish." (351). As a squanderer, Zarathustra now embraces the folly endemic to his enterprise: he *is* foolish to fish on high mountains. Yet his conscious folly is "useful" to him as his unwitting folly was not (350). First of all, by acknowledging the folly of his enterprise, Zarathustra obviates the solemnity that earlier consumed him. Although he seriously pursues his promotion of virtue, he no longer justifies himself solely in terms of pedagogical success. Second, Zarathustra enjoys greater pedagogical freedom as a self-conscious fool: "Up here *I may speak more freely* than before hermits' caves and hermits' domestic animals" (350, emphasis added). The self-conscious fool can actually exploit the folly of his enterprise to his own advantage. Since "no one" takes seriously the teaching of a fool, Zarathustra is free to articulate to "everyone" an alternative moral ideal. Zarathustra's advantage as a squanderer thus resembles Nietzsche's own: having accommodated the deconstruction of his own authority, Nietzsche is now free to promote the sufficiency of others without simultaneously exerting on them an unduly formative influence.

Yet even as a squanderer, Zarathustra must present his teaching as in some sense authoritative; the same holds for Nietzsche as well if he is to contribute at all to the well-being of his readers. Zarathustra must now confront the problem of audience that he has habitually ignored: why should anyone come up to him at all? Here Zarathustra reveals that he tempts his prospective auditors with some extraordinary "bait"; "With my best bait I shall today lure the queerest human fish. My *happiness* I cast out far and wide ... to see if many human fish might not learn to wriggle and wiggle from my happiness, until, biting at my sharp, hidden hooks, they must come up to *my* height" (351, emphasis added). In part 4, Zarathustra has actually turned his initial problem of self-reference to his own advantage: he is now both fisherman *and* bait. Earlier in his pedagogical career, Zarathustra failed because he could do no more for his auditors than gesture darkly toward an uninstantiated ideal that he inconsistently described to them; as we recall, he too fell short of the prescribed ideal. At the midpoint of the text it became clear that if Zarathustra's auditors are to renounce their belief in God as the guarantor of human value, then simply to teach or to herald the *Übermensch*, as Zarathustra had done in parts 1-2, is inadequate. Rather than attempt to promote this ideal discursively, as he did in parts 1-2, Zarathustra now submits his own life as a concrete exemplification of it.[42] In part 4, Zarathustra has in fact *become* the *Übermensch*, but *not* the *Übermensch* he originally heralded and inadvertently taught.[43] The *Übermensch* is not he who transcends the human but he who embraces the human as it is: mortal, contingent, and tragic. As the *Übermensch*, Zarathustra no longer views the folly of his enterprise as an objection to it, for his teaching of virtue is now inseparable from his practical exemplification of virtue.

Zarathustra stakes his claim to authority by virtue of the freedom, power, and happiness evident in his own life. As an actual exemplar of *Übermenschlichkeit*, he claims for himself "only" the authority of his own limited perspective; as he reminds the "higher men" who seize his "bait," "I am a law only for my kind *[das Meinen]*, I am no law for all" (397). Yet in emphasizing his role as an *exemplar* of Nietzsche's ideal, Zarathustra does not necessarily forfeit his authority as a *teacher*, for his life now constitutes a kind of teaching that others can acquire through imitation and emulation. Zarathustra's newly won authority is secured not *internally*, by appeal to a priviledged standpoint, but *externally*, by appeal to the consensus of those "queen human fish" who voluntarily seek to cultivate the virtue he exemplifies as their own. Zarathustra's pedagogical authority now lies beyond his control and Nietzsche's as well.[44]

Zarathustra's exemplification of *Übermenschlichkeit* thus transfers the onus of authority from his discourse to his practices in the world. Here Nietzsche's insight echoes that of Plato and Aristotle: to be a virtuous exemplar *is* to promote the virtue of others. By exemplifying the ideal that Nietzsche recommends, Zarathustra completes Nietzsche's teaching while minimizing the chances that Nietzsche might become yet another redeemer or god.[45] To reinforce the dependence of "his" ideal on the authority of his readers, Nietzsche officially resigns his remaining narrative authority toward the end of the book[46] and bequeaths to us Zarathustra, an admittedly fictional character whose own authority as a teacher extends no further than we voluntarily allow. By means of this "anonymous" reconstruction of the text, Nietzsche encourages/forces his readers to rely on their own limited, contingently constructed authority; "his" ideal must actually become their own, to the extent that his own authority is ultimately irrelevant. Nietzsche thus provides for the reconstruction of *Zarathustra* on the authority of his readers, as they progress toward *Übermenschlichkeit.*

6

De Man Missing Nietzsche:
Hinzugedichtet *Revisited*

Richard H. Weisberg

A struggle rages for Nietzsche's soul, and despite Richard Rorty's pragmatic parry,[1] the struggle involves epistemology as much as hermeneutics. Paul de Man, in his still absorbing 1975 article "Action and Identity in Nietzsche," put it best and earliest: "The question of the relationship between philosophical and literary discourse is linked, in Nietzsche, to his critique of the main concepts underlying Western metaphysics."[2] And since de Man, in his *Allegories of Reading*, never assumes away a Nietzschean epistemology—indeed states that "the 'history' of Nietzsche's work as a whole remains that of a narrative moving from false to true, from blindness to insight"[3]—we must persevere to understand wherein lies Nietzsche's true radicalism and in what realms he restrained himself from iconoclasm.

As in other profound respects, to which we shall return later, de Man's blindnesses here may be more important than his insights. For, having established, in the part of the *Allegories* just cited, that the Nietzschean oeuvre strives toward truth, de Man almost immediately undoes that good by producing a grotesque misreading of a central passage about what might be called "truth doing" in Nietzsche. So intent seems de Man on "proving" that Nietzsche's attack on logic and rationality indicates an aversion to all certainties (rather than merely a dislike for modern, Western systems of logic) that he proceeds almost deliberately to distort the very different atmosphere of Nietzsche's late masterpieces. It is to de Man's facially deficient analysis of the word *hinzugedichtet* in I.13 of the *Genealogy of Morals* that we shall return after stating the case more generally for "certain truths" (including, of course, hermeneutic truths) in Nietzsche. Not all readers, by any means, have even accepted what de Man takes as axiomatic: for all his iconoclasm and irrationalism, Nietzsche is still, after all, a seeker after truth.[3]

The struggle in this ultimate regard has often taken on the coloration of a "war," to use Nietzsche's own metaphor about earlier struggles over texts and truths.[4] Almost all camps willing to heed Nietzsche's own call to "ruminate"[5] his texts carefully recognize the force of his rhetoric in the service of deeply felt insights about Western metaphysics, insights that rise to the level of belief and even moral system. A leading "perspectivist" Nietzschean, Alexander Nehamas, sees as his camp's "first problem that Nietzsche . . . holds a number of positions which he seems to accept in all seriousness. Does he, or does he not, then, think that his views on the self, on morality, or on history, many of which are themselves at least apparently paradoxical, are true? If he does, how can this possibly be consistent with his view that all views are only interpretations? If he does not—that is, if he does not think that his views are true—why does he make the effort to present them in the first place?"[6] Nehamas's somewhat wide-eyed amazement makes him seem to be stating a paradox: how can we place infinite perspectivism and limitless interpretability of all things in the mouth of one who not only espoused truths good for him alone (*pace* Derrida)[7] but who dearly wished his reader to espouse them, too, "denn es gibt solche Wahrheiten"?[8]

In Europe, intelligent and passionate partisans have staked out positions more extreme than those taken by many American Nietzscheans. Sarah Kofman, in her comprehensive but yet more often misguided work *Nietzsche et la métaphore*, criticizes Jean Granier's book[9] for its traditional epistemological assertions about Nietzsche's hermeneutics: "If it were that way," she says, "this regorous philology would attain to the essence of being (l'essence de l'être) and Nietzschean philosophy would be an ontology which we could scarcely distinguish from the deconstructed dogmatic philosophy. As M. Heidegger says, Nietzscheanism would thus be nothing but an inverted platonism."[10]

Putting aside the allusion to Heidegger who, as Gillian Rose has most recently demonstrated,[11] misapprehended Nietzsche in many vital ways, Kofman's statement must assume its own logic. Few readers of Nietzsche's last great works would find a problem in both affirming a Nietzschean belief in truth and asserting that he completely undercuts the bases of Western metaphysics. Nietzsche's

mature aim may have been less to destroy epistemology than to annihilate the way in which people have been seeking knowledge for 2000
years. As he states trenchantly in the thirty-fifth aphorism of *Beyond
Good and Evil,* "The search for truth . . . if people seek it out too hu-
manely—'il ne cherche le vrai que pour faire du bien'—I bet they will
find nothing (Cowan, 42).[12] As always in Nietzsche, the attack is on our
manner of truth seeking, not on truth seeking itself.

The Europeans' debate has been advanced recently by findings
of Hendrik Birus, who perceives in Nietzsche a philological, if not quite
an epistemological, conservative.[13] Birus quite methodically and con-
vincingly gathers from among the many statements Nietzsche made
on the subject perhaps the strongest proofs that Nietzsche believed in
the text above the reader and thought that false readings were both
identifiable and closely related to moral slavishness and ressentiment.
Birus strives to answer Sarah Kofman's view that "chez Nietzsche l'in-
terprétation n'est pas le commentaire d'un texte préalable; ce qui
préexiste à l'interpretation n'est pas du texte mais du chaos."[14] (Here
Kofman reflects but does not go as far as Derrida, who, in a passage in
Spurs (at p. 107), manages to determine that Nietzsche "disqualifie le
projet hermeneutique postulant le sens vrai d'un texte."[15] Kofman, we
should recall, is herself at this point talking less about literary texts
than about concepts and events such as the French Revolution. Nonetheless, her work strongly implies what Derrida makes overt—that
texts exist only as interpretations.) Birus, having already mustered a
host of fully matured Nietzschean aphorisms to the contrary, observes: "In spite of all indissoluble incongruence between the work and
its interpreter there is a *text,* to which all—however subjectively motivated—interpretations refer. There is no abysmal *chaos* here, into
which meaning must be arbitrarily and randomly projected."[16]

Birus's confidence that the text trumps an otherwise chaotic situation and imposes itself, willy-nilly, on the reader has a firmer basis
than Birus's apparent intercultural ignorance of Stanley Fish's famous
titular question.[17] After all, we have just seen reiterated the Nietzsche
of *Human, All-too-Human:* "The worst readers. The worst readers are
those who act like plundering soldiers. They take out some things that
they might use, cover the rest with filth and confusion and defame the
whole,"[18] a typically *strong* Nietzschean statement matching hermeneutics and morals and patently implying the independent existence
of an entity outside the reader. Moreover, this pithy aphorism's substance is repeated often in Nietzsche—who even believed in a truthful
reading of his own *Genealogy,* an event he did not expect for many
generations—and outweighs (as Birus shows) the one or two statements used for the opposite proposition by the other camp. One of

these has been brought up by a distinguished law professor and reader of the U.S. Constitution, with whom I am now engaged in what is politely called "dialogue" these days (a very non-Nietzschean description) and who has seized to justify the complete control of reader over text the following words from the second essay of the *Genealogy:* "Everything that exists, no matter what its origin, is periodically reinterpreted by those in power in terms of fresh intentions;... all processes in the organic world are processes of outstripping and overcoming,... in turn, all outstripping and overcoming means reinterpretation, rearrangement, in the course of which the earlier meaning and purpose are necessarily either obscured or lost."[19] In another context[20] I note first that this aphorism has nothing to do with interpretation—for Nietzsche, as we shall show, text, precisely because of its materiality, is privileged over concept (it becomes *matter*, upon which the will to power can have no effect)—and second that the aphorism is set in an essay bemoaning the contemporary reintrepretation of the concept of justice (in terms of *ressentiment*). Nietzsche treats a favorite theme here—the fallacious behavior of interpreters in trying to understand a phenomenon's origin by looking at its present uses. (This point is very effectively discussed by Kofman even as she misreads justice as an inverted Nietzschean metaphor rather than as a strong, text-based concept.) Indeed, Nietzsche has just advised (in the central and hermeneutically conservative aphorism on justice as text (II, 11) that immediately precedes this aphorism but that is always avoided completely by commentators such as Kofman in discussions negating a Nietzschean belief in justice)[21] that we continue to think about justice in terms of the production by noble individuals of a text, a long-lasting code to which all can refer when, as is inevitable, ressentient interpreters seek to pervert its meaning. The chosen text winds up implying the converse of its chooser's claim, but this Nietzsche himself would have predicted.

Yet Birus, at least for his purposes in the *Texte* article, does not really explain *why* any reader capable of imposing a view on another set of readers would abstain from doing so even at the expense of the philological conventions Nietzsche valued so highly. As de Man shows of the Heidegger who fully distorts these conventions for a brilliant reading of Hölderlin, in an epistemologically free universe, all bets are off.[22] But de Man, as always, is very careful: the stakes justifying the cessation of traditional interpretive principles must be high, and the reader must be approaching Dasein; at these moments, the phenomenon is elsewhere described by de Man in words from Nietzsche that sound very different from what we would expect:[23] "To be able to read the text as text without the interference of an interpretation is the latest-developed form of 'inner experience'—perhaps one that is hardly possible" (Will to Power, aphorism). We shall reconsider this passage from *The Will to Power* again, noting its avoidance of metaphor and its strong leaning toward openness to text.

The questions left unanswered both by Birus and by this last aphorism help us to bridge the gap between Nietzsche's hermeneutics and his epistemology. First, why choose to be controlled by a text? And second, what is the mechanism of this control, the path to understanding the "text as text"?

Our inquiry begins in the very heart of that centennial text *Beyond Good and Evil.* Throughout this treatise on moral philosophy, Nietzsche both practices and conceptualizes literary criticism. In an early aphorism, he reiterates his love of the heroic Old Testament while at the same time identifying as the greatest hermeneutic sinners of our era those who placed that text side by side with the New Testament and gave them the same name, "the Bible" (aphorism 52; Cowan, 59–60). (Again, as Birus further indicates through the powerful critique launched in *Dawn of Day* against the church's perverse reading of the Old Testament, Nietzsche equates misreadings with moral infirmity.) In a closing section of *Beyond Good and Evil,* he compares modern French fiction with its German equivalents (aphorism 254; Cowan, 191). Our text here comes at the midpoint of *Beyond Good and Evil,* at aphorism 188 (Cowan, 94–6):

Every morality is, as opposed to *laisser aller*, a piece of tyranny against nature, and also against "reason"; this is, however, not an objection to it, as one would have to have somehow decreed as a morality that all tyranny and irrationality be prohibited. The essential and priceless aspect of each morality is that it is an abiding constraint ["ein langer Zwang"]: in order to understand stoicism or Port Royal or Puritanism, we must recall the constraint by which each language reaches strength and freedom, the constraint of metre, the tyranny of rhyme and rhythmics. How much trouble have the poets and speakers of each people taken!—including several contemporary prose-writers, in whose ear an unremitting conscience dwells—"for the sake of a folly," as the utilitarian fools say, thinking it makes them seem so clever,— 'as subject to arbitrary laws ["Willkur-Gesetzer"]'. as the anarchists say, who thus imagine themselves free, even freethinking. The peculiar fact is, however, that everything of freedom, finesse, boldness, dance and masterful certainty that we can find, or ever have found on earth, whether in the domain of thinking itself, or of ruling, or of thinking or persuading, in the arts as well as in moral conduct [*Sittlichkeiten*], has been able to develop the "tyranny of such arbitrary laws"; and in all seriousness the probability is not small that this precisely is "nature" and "natural"— and not laisser aller! Every artist knows how far his most "natural" condition is from letting himself go, the free ordering, composing, arranging, fashioning in the moments of "inspiration,"—and how strongly and finely he obeys the thousandfold laws that mock any reduction to concept precisely because of their rigor and certainty [!] (even the firmest concept, compared to them, has something murky, multifarious and ambiguous about it). The most important thing, "in heaven and on earth," it seems, is, to say it again, a long obedience to *one* constraint ["in *einer* Richtung"]: from this has always come in the long run something that makes life on earth worthwhile, such as virtue, art, music, dance, reason, spirituality, something transfiguring, refined, mad and devine.

The passage is complex and full of Nietzschean reversals. For example, Nietzsche proceeds to include Christianity as one possible "abiding constraint" even though, of course, he detests the substance of the religion. All the more daring does the conclusion seem that "'You must obey, no matter whom, and for a long time; if not, you perish and lose any self-respect.' This seems to me to be Nature's moral imperative, one that is surely neither 'categorical', as old Kant might have wanted (thus its 'if not') nor directed to any individual (what does she care for individuals!), but rather to peoples, races, epochs, ranks, but above all to the whole animal man, to mankind." The discussion in aphorism 188 is, of course, beyond good and evil. People may choose to obey, over a very long period of time, certain systems that exhaust them and rob their wills to power of vitalistic force. On the other hand, other long standing cultural constraints are warmly endorsed later in *Beyond Good and Evil*, precisely because of their inclination to change "as slowly as possible" (the Jews and the Russians, aphorism 251; Cowan 185).

What emerges is a fairly typical Nietzschean hierarchy of human responses, in which constraint is deemed a natural urge within the healthy will to power. As an urge, constraint is privileged above some merely cognitive, philosophical, or idealized concept, for as Kofman and others have well observed, concepts in Nietzsche are usually metaphoric and are certainly open to a greater degree of interpretive manipulation than are naturalistic phenomena (125–29, K). These latter are not subject to shifts in fashion. So we are *always*—if we are creatively exercising our will to power—seeking some constraint. In a godless age, we will seek something else to obey; perhaps our credo will be a denial of all truth, but this is nothing more than another systemic *Zwang*, as likely to bind us as any traditional belief.

The naturalistic urge to be bound (associated here by Nietzsche with the most creative, the most artistic of enterprises) obviously has ramifications for the will to power, but we must seek these out from earlier aphorisms in *Beyond Good and Evil*, notably the important triad, numbers 34–36. In the last of these, Nietzsche points out that the will to power "can only act on other wills and not upon matter, not on 'nerves', for instance." ["'Wille' kann natürlich nur auf 'Wille' wirken—und nicht auf 'Stoffe' (nicht auf 'Nerven' zum Beispiel)"]. Again, the natural order is privileged, but the term *Stoffe* renders more general the hierarchical elevation of material objects that exist above, say, concepts or ideals. (As Allan Megill recently reminds us[24], even the famous 1873 essay "On Truth and Lie in an Extra-Moral Sense" deals mostly with cognitive conceptualizations and *not* with textual interpretation.) The strong declaration of number 188 becomes clarified here on the phenomenological plane: the material world has claims upon us that outstrip the claims of concepts. Upon the latter, we may be expected to unleash our own wills, to indulge in laisser-aller or metaphoric revaluations; upon matter, however, we not only will fail to succeed but also risk antinatural nihilism by attempting to change what is there. (Thus, at the end of the passage deconstructed in *Spurs* by Derrida, Nietzsche states, in Derrida's translation: "Je veux dire que le monde abonde de belles choses, mais n'en est pas moins pauvre, en beaux instants et en belles révélations de pareiles choses.")[25]

In the natural predilection for obedience, matter (and not other wills to power) offers the noblest form of constraint. (There is something of this approach in the famous third chapter of part 1 of Dostoevski's *Notes from Underground*, in which the ressentient narrator fruitlessly fights against such constraints.) As nature stands to concept, so matter stands to the will to power. (Kofman may err, therefore, in equating every appearance outside the will with *concept*, or with other wills, thereby concluding that everything is interpretable and infinitely changeable.[26] Nietzsche straightforwardly *names* the best and the worst of potential constraints. The most noble is material and the least—the one most likely to lead to ressentiment—is intersubjective, tied to another's will to power. The moral inversion in Western values, as Nietzsche shows throughout the *Genealogy of*

Morals, in fact began when the other was posited, externalized, and made the restraining guide for a thereafter reactive, dualistic, and matter-denying subject, the man of ressentiment himself.

Instead, matter, the world of appearances, stands ready to seize and be seized by people not as yet infected with the intersubjective fascinations typical of ressentiment. Hence the oft-quoted but easily misinterpreted comment in aphorism 34: "It is no more than a moral prejudice that truth is worth more than semblance" ("dass Wahrheit mehr wert ist als Schein").

The word here is the oft-used Nietzschean term of approbation —*Schein*—the way in which *"Stoff"* shows itself to people. (There are similar passages in *Ecce Homo*, at the foreword and aphorism 3, first essay, as well as elsewhere in the late Nietzsche.) For Nietzsche believes in a graspable (although not necessarily an articulable) reality; he attacks those idealisms that have falsely inverted reality and appearance. What people teach us to believe is often mere "fabrication"; the Schein, which we teach ourselves to disbelieve or disregard, is in fact reality itself.

Literary texts, by their materiality, are part of the world of semblance—of Schein—to which we might naturally be bound. While they are not the highest form of Nietzschean Stoff, they are clearly privileged—by their materiality—above system, history, and especially concept.[27] In approaching a text, we are not confronting another will to power (at least not if we are approaching it as matter); reading does not imply the false dualities of author-reader, object-subject. Engagement with a text requires the same clear-eyed and nonnihilistic openness to the world, to Schein, that "die vornehme Art Mensch" brings to all his or her engagements with the world of matter. "To be able to see the text as text"—not as metaphor but as identity—would be the ideal, the first step toward understanding and, eventually, if naturally provoked by the relationship of will to text, toward obedience.

And this point leads me to the second unanswered question in Hendrik Birus's reply to Sarah Kofman: if there are reasons, beyond Nietzsche's training in and love for literature, to underscore his repetitive request that we understand texts on their own terms, how does the always subjectivist will to power manage to do so? As little in this domain as elsewhere is Nietzsche a positivist. The vast preponderance of texts are likely to remain mute for most potential readers.

Indeed, as to matter generally, so also to literary texts, the individual admittedly brings his or her senses to the task of engaging Schein. "Only from the senses," says Nietzsche in *Beyond Good and Evil* 134, playing again with the word *Schein*, "Only from the senses comes all clear consciousness, all self-evidence of truth ["Augenschein der Wahrheit"]." Thinking may attract us to reading certain texts, but only thinking along Nietzschean lines. Aphorism 36 has already taught us, after all, that "thinking is nothing more than the interaction of our drives." Such rhetoric, all too often considered demeaning of our cognitive apparatus when it in fact ennobles the other sides to our will to power, helps explain the paucity of texts a Nietzschean is likely to approach. For the nondecadent will to power, we are taught throughout *Ecce Homo*, [28] says no to much more than it affirms, says no *early* in the sensory experience of the given matter, and generally *"react[s] as seldom as possible*... withdrawing from situations and relationships in which one would be condemned as it were to suspend one's freedom" (*EH*, "Clever", no. 81; Hollingdale, 63-4; italics in original).

This rejection of many things is not nihilism but "the first imperative of prudence." We are not, like the Christians, denying the world or trying to distort it but only "passing"—to use Dostoevski's verb (*pasovat'*) about the "natural man" in the famous third chapter of *Notes from Underground*. Nietzsche himself, of course, only allowed a "small number of books" to act as long-lasting constraints on his development (*EH*, Clever," no. 3; Hollingdale, 57).

Saying "yes" to a text need happen rarely. As Nietzsche observes still later in *Ecce Homo*, "Early in the morning at the break of day, in all the freshness and dawn of one's strength, to read a *book*—I call that vicious" ("Clever," no. 8; Hollingdale, 64). There are higher, more ecstatic, modes of interaction with the material world. But when, in a manner less freely chosen perhaps than influenced by our early sense experiences (*Jenseits*, no. 268), we do decide to engage a text, the healthy will to power must move beyond sense to method.

Across Nietzsche's writings, the hermeneutic strategy gleams. In number 52 of "The Anti-Christ," as Nietzsche strikes a recurrent note in criticizing the Christian theologians for their distortion of the Old Testament, and hence for their ineptitude as interpreters, he observes: "Philology is to be understood here in the very broad sense as the art of reading well—of being able to read off a fact *without falsifying it by interpretation, without* losing caution, patience, or subtlety in the desire for understanding. Philology as *ephexis* [constraint] in interpretation."[29]

In the preface to the *Genealogy* itself, Nietzsche advises us as to the proper engagement with the rest of that remarkable work:

An aphorism, properly stamped and molded, has not been "deciphered" when it has simply been read; rather one then has to begin its *exegesis* [*Auslegung*], for which is required an art of exegesis....[30] To be sure, one thing is necessary above all if one is to practice reading as an *art* in this way, something that has been unlearned most thoroughly these days—and therefore it will be some time before my writings are *"readable"*—something for which one has almost to be a cow and in any case *not* a modern man: *rumination* ["das Wiederkäuen"]. [Preface, no. 8]

The Nietzschean reader, engaging the texts as Stoff—and not as a contest of wills with its author or its other readers—and having said "yes" to a relatively small number of will-enriching texts, avoids the human, all-too-easy urge to conquer them. He or she "ruminates," remaining alive to every nuance of language and to every structural mechanism that he or she has been trained to recognize. Somewhat along the lines Paul de Man has postulated in the rhetoric essays of the *Allegories*,[31] a reader emphasizes the various patterns of wordplay and, like de Man with the Nietzschean passages he analyzes there, does not hesitate to bring in other works by the same author. The Nietzschean reader follows the master's example in remaining sensitive to the cultural patterns that influence any given writer. (For Nietzsche, to take a central example, ressentiment so permeated nineteenth-century Europe that its reactive venom was perceived as extending to many fictional works.[32]) Nor is the reader of this kind indifferent to the author's biography, but there is something short of any fascination that would risk intersubjective pathology.

The author's statements about the meaning of his or her fictional works would be of less interest than the cultural influences consciously or unconsciously felt that we have just discussed, but of special significance would be the author's views on hermeneutics or the *path* to literary meanings. Thus in reading texts, an author's established *skepticism* about words as an effective meaning of communication would be of notable value in understanding the way to approach such texts.

Indeed, the intense skepticism that Nietzsche himself constantly expresses about verbal communication undoubtedly sets the Nietzschean reader apart from more traditional exegetes. Within the hierarchy of offers made to us by the material world, the Nietzschean sees written texts as less ennobling than many other experiences. (But I cannot follow Derrida in positing any primacy for *spoken* verbal communication—quite the contrary, for the reasons already indicated above.) The 1887 Nietzsche preferred taking walks to either reading or speaking. Throughout his life, even in rejecting Wagner, he saw music (not literature) as the pathway to Dionysian truth.

Here we must return to de Man and his bizarre reading of the word "hinzugedichtet" in the first essay (aphorism 13) of the *Genealogy*. It seems to have become existentially vital for de Man to undermine the forceful privilgeing in that text of action over speech, and of certain categories over others, of speech acts themselves. De Man, we might recall, is in the process of using one posthumous fragment to suggest that Nietzsche believed in the constant availability of X and not-X as "true at the same time, and hence disbelieved in any truth categories.[33]

Now the thing that any reader of the *Genealogy* must observe is that there is a constant allusion to truth (not just "meine Wahrheiten," as Derrida disingenuously insists in *Spurs*, but "solche Wahrheiten," as Nietzsche insists "do exist")[34] throughout that text, and there is—as in all the late masterpieces—an insistence that the forces of negativity must be stopped before false versions of events, texts, concepts, and so forth are permitted to prevail. De Man, indeed, has just admitted, by recalling the powerful concept of ressentiment and the havoc it has wrought upon Western culture, that the *Genealogy* does prefer "active forms of language over passive or merely reactives ones."[35] Yet, as though by magic, de Man proceeds to undo the even more pervasive Nietzschean celebration of action over *all* speech acts! The truthful in Nietzsche is, as we have seen, material (however false the naming process can be during resentful interpretive periods), and the highest form of truth is the noble *act* itself, prior to the naming of that act,[36] but de Man proceeds as follows, quoting first from the *Genealogy:*

There is no 'being' behind doing, effecting, becoming: the 'doer' is merely a fiction added to the deed—the deed is everything ["Es gibt kein 'Sein' hinter dem Tun, Wirken, Werden; 'der Tater' ist zum Tun bloss hinzugedichtet—das Tun ist alles." Now de Man's voice:] The use of the term "hinzugedichtet" (added by poetic invention), as well as the context, indicate that action here is conceived in close connection with linguistic acts of writing, reading, and interpretation, and not within a polarity that opposes language, as speech or as writing, to action.[37]

De Man shortly elaborates on his startling interpolation: "Non-verbal acts, if such a thing were to be conceivable, are of no concern to [Nietzsche], since no act can ever be separated from the attempt at understanding, from the interpretation, that necessarily accompanies it and falsifies it."[38]

Proving his own assertion in the process, de Man here deliberately "accompanies" and "falsifies" the Nietzschean text—but Nietzsche would be the first to assert that he cannot thereby change it! The text, like an act or any other anterior phenomenon, retains its integrity despite the falsifying exegesis. For the hinzugedichtet passage, and its "context" (de Man's word), explicitly isolate the deed (or act) from subsequent attempts to describe it. These latter need not occur in order to establish the existence of the act, and Nietzsche nowhere posits such a claim. After-the-fact interpretations often occur, of course—the naming itself of the event is the first of these and is subject to truer or more devious accounts in and of itself. (See especially here, again, II.11 of the *Genealogy.*) But these are always poetic diminutions of the original material thing—the act itself. *Hinzugedichtet*, after all, is itself a pejorative term.

Indeed, aphorism 13 in its fullness resumes Nietzsche's inquiry into resentful falsifications of prior phenomena. He characteristically debunks the pathetic attempts of the resentful to square reality with their own weak place in it. But as to a "postmodern" analyst going haywire over a text or a historical event (the Holocaust, for example),[39] the original deed remains indifferent to verbal meanderings—pristine, blissfully unaltered by any post hoc linguistic distortion:[40]

There is nothing very odd about lambs disliking birds of prey, but this is no reason for holding it against large birds of prey that they carry off lambs. And when the lambs whisper among themselves, "These birds of prey are evil, and does not this give us a right to say that whatever is the opposite of a bird of prey must be good?" there is nothing intrinsically wrong with such an argument—though the birds of prey will look somewhat quizzically and say: "We have nothing against these good lambs; in fact, we love them; nothing tastes better than a tender lamb." To expect that strength will not manifest itself as strength, as the desire to overcome, to appropriate, to have enemies, obstacles, and triumphs, is every bit as absurd as to expect that weakness will manifest itself as strength. A quantum of strength is equivalent to a quantum of urge, will, activity, and it is only the snare of language ["unter der Verführung der Sprache"] (of the arch-fallacies of reason petrified in language), presenting all activity as conditioned by an agent—the "subject"—that blinds us to this fact.

Language distorts, especially contemporary language (scientific, literary, or philosophical), for that language is in the hands of the resentful. Yet Nietzsche never despairs that—however long it may take—the original phenomenon will eventually be grasped, or better, *named* more accurately.

It is almost impossible, then, except through the most empathetic eyes, to understand de Man's assertion that, "even in the *Genealogy*, the pure act that is said to be all there is, is conceived as verbal."[41] De Man strives to open up the very world of endless verbal distortion that Nietzsche brilliantly forecloses. We live in a world of actions and of material realities; we distort that world at our peril (for the truth both survives our distortions and will someday emerge through more accurate readings of it), but we have no right to raise to a level of *theoretical* veracity our own all-too-human weaknesses. Control over text, history, ourself—like the temporarily articulate lambs and their version of birds of prey—always inheres in the thing itself and eventually reverts to the truthful narrator of that thing.

Although the privileging of act over language must first be understood, it seems to me that de Man also misses Nietzsche when he attempts to dissolve distinctions as among speech acts. Nietzsche does seem to privilege performative (or persuasive) over figurative (or literary) speech acts. His harshest scorn as a philologist is directed less at literary critics (even for misreadings of his own late works, which, after all, he felt had a "legislative" function)[42] than at those politicians or priests who had distorted written, normative *codes* of conduct. His scorn, of course, directly compares to his admiration of such texts. Thus in *Genealogy* II.11—mentioned early in this chapter as a centrally important aphorism on the notion of justice—Nietzsche advises the codification by active individuals of a code of justice to which all but ressentient interpreters would thereafter refer in an "impersonal" manner to dictate questions of "right" and "wrong."

Just such a performative speech act—just such a code—is the Old Testament, and Nietzsche's hermeneutic wrath extends most forcefully and frequently to interpretive perversions of that text. Thus in aphorism 84 of *Dawn of Day:*

However much the Jewish scholars protested, everywhere in the Old Testament there were supposed to be references to Christ and only to Christ and particularly his cross. Wherever any piece of wood, a switch, a ladder, a twig, a tree, a willow or a staff is mentioned, this was supposed to indicate a prophecy of the wood of the cross; even the erection of the one-horned beast and the brazen serpent, even Moses spreading his arms in prayer, even the spits on which the Passover lamb was roasted—all are allusions to the cross and as it were preludes to it! Has anyone who asserted this ever believed it? Consider that the church did not even shrink from enriching the text of the Septuagint (e.g. in Psalm 96, verse 10) so as afterwards to employ the smuggled-in passage in the sense of Christian prophecy. For they were conducting a war and paid more heed to their opponents than to the need to stay honest. (Degruyter, V/1, 76)

For many readers, the basic message of textual reverence will be hard to discover amid the iconoclastic thorns of passages such as these. But Nietzsche, as we have been suggesting, deliberately integrates his hermeneutics with his epistemology. Thus "rumination" upon this aphorism pushes the reader to perceive that textual distortions became institutionally acceptable at the same time and for the same reasons that other moral distortions came to systematic dominance. One of these inversions may well have been the metaphorizing of—the claim of substitution of spirit for—law. But this is indeed *Stoffe* for another occasion.

Part 3
Reading, Writing, and Rhetoric

7

The Dance from Mouth to Hand
(Speaking Zarathustra's Write Foot ForeWord)

Graham Parkes

> The feelings move inwardly, and are embodied in words. When words are insufficient for them, recourse is had to sighs and exclamations. When sighs and exclamations are insufficient for them, recourse is had to the prolonged utterances of song. When those prolonged utterances of song are insufficient for them, unconsciously the hands begin to move and the feet to dance.
>
> —Great Preface to the *Book of Songs*

Thus Spoke Zarathustra: the title prepares the reader for the presentation of speech—and indeed few philosophical texts since Plato's dialogues have been as filled with *logoi*, with talk and speeches. In this, Nietzsche's favorite and greatest book, there appears to be little concern with writing; the author rather presents a preponderance of direct speech (even if appropriate punctuation does not always announce it). Such a lack of self-reflectiveness is hardly a hallmark of the postmodern, and one would be inclined to view an author who speaks so much through the first person of his protagonist as firmly ensconced in the "logocentric" tradition. It should strike us as stranger than it apparently does that the finest work of this author—protodeconstructionist and putative precursor of the postmodern—should be a play of *speeches*, consisting largely of first- rather than third-person narrative. Particularly puzzling here would be Nietzsche's closeness to Plato, grand father apparent of logocentrism, who in the persona of Socrates tends to denigrate writing in favor of speaking— insofar as in writing *Zarathustra* Nietzsche speaks through the mask of a loquacious protagonist who yet speaks of writing only rarely, then in a mostly pejorative tone, and apparently never himself applies pointed implement to plane surface. Can it be that Nietzsche at the apogee of his writing career reverts to a conservative stance in the mainstream of logocentrism, or is there more reflexivity there after all, more about writing than at first meets the eye—a dance between the lines which subverts the tradition and ironizes the figure of Socrates, that most eloquent of speakers who, above all, "does not write"?[1]

Let us begin by eavesdropping on the Prologue. Zarathustra has just finished delivering the second part of his first speech to the people in the marketplace.

"There they stand," he said to his heart, "there they laugh: they do not understand me, I am not the mouth for these ears. Must one first shatter their ears before they learn to hear with their eyes?"[2]

The audience stands there, unmoved, it appears, by his speech. They fail to understand him perhaps precisely because they are just standing there—rather than responding more dynamically to his speaking. Why should they learn to "hear with their eyes"? Possibly because (as we have just learned from the old saint in the forest) Zarathustra "walks like a dancer," and so might speak with body and limbs, inviting his audience to look at him and follow the text inscribed by his moving gestures. It is, however, in the more literal act of reading (and not only of reading a musical score) that we most hear with the eyes, and this consideration prompts the question of whether Zarathustra is not after all a *writer* as well as—even prior to—being a speaker. To entertain this possibility requires tracing the chains of significations in the text which link the images of speech, song, laughter, flight, and dance with the idea of writing. As the speaking voice begins to break, it splits into song and laughter, one branch losing verbal signification as the other assumes melody and then takes off into flight, before both settle down to the silent intermediation of the dance.

SPEECHES AND SUPPLEMENTS

It is instructive to compare Zarathustra as a speaker with Socrates.[3] Like his loquacious predecessor, Zarathustra loves dialogue but is fonder still of monologue and diatribe, favoring enigmatic riddling over dialectical questioning. While Socrates would on occasion listen to the admonitions of his inner *daimon*, his speeches are addressed primarily to his fellow interlocutors, with the occasional prayer to some deity or other. Zarathustra's audience is far more heterogeneous, comprising a multitude of figures both inner and outer. This most verbal of protagonists is prepared to address anyone and anything under (and including) the sun—and especially a host of aspects of himself. He outdoes Odysseus in conversing with his heart, his life, his shadow, his conscience, his happiness, his fate, his loneliness, his stillest hour, his wild wisdom—and above all, with his soul. Like Socrates, whose fondness for talks takes him to the point of being "sick with the love of speeches" (*Phaedrus* 228b-c), Zarathustra is made ill—almost fatally so—by a speech, by his own speech which he was unable to speak: the failed announcement of the thought of the eternal recurrence of the same, a thought that rendered him a convalescent ("Der Genesende") and to which we shall, appropriately, return. And as well as speaking, there is in *Zarathustra* much singing and laughing—and a remarkable variety of characterizations of other modes of vocal utterance.[4]

Socrates' love of speeches is accompanied by a lack of interest in written discourse: he himself did not write and appears to look down on the practice. ("The cleanest thinker in the West," Heidegger calls him, "one who wrote nothing.") Socrates understands both speaking and writing as the sowing of seed, seeing speaking, in the form of dialectic, as the responsible and fruitful kind of husbandry, in contrast to writing as frivolous and sterile dissemination.[5] It looks at first as if Zarathustra may be a sensible sower in Socrates' sense, given his penchant for delivering speeches. Just as Socrates speaks in the *Phaedrus* of the orator's "reaping a harvest from his speaking" (260c-d), so in Zarathustra's *Vorrede* ("Fore-Speech") the speaker says: "Companions the creator seeks, and fellow harvesters: for everything in him stands ripe for the harvest" (prologue sec. 9). Part 1 of the book, the only one of the four to bear a title—"Zarathustra's Speeches" —begins with "Zarathustra's Prologue" in ten parts and is followed by twenty-two sections which consist almost entirely of speeches in the first person.[6] Part 2 opens with the protagonist's withdrawing up to his mountain retreat and "waiting like a sower who has scattered his seed" (II.1), and one may assume that this simile refers to his myriad speaking engagements, his sowing of spoken words upon the (generally stony) ground of his listeners' souls. He tackles his task in this field with a brutal zeal. "Like the boar's snout," he says to those who are virtuous, "my words will tear open the ground of your souls; ploughshare you shall call me."[7]

The apparent insignificance of writing in *Zarathustra* seems to bring its protagonist even closer to Socrates when we consider that in all his many speeches Zarathustra never once speaks of himself as doing any kind of writing. His references to the activity tend to be oblique and nowhere explicitly say that he himself practices it, leaving the reader with the impression that he may be following Socrates in leaving the writing to his disciples or fellow creators. There was certainly no danger of the work's being entitled *Thus Wrote Zarathustra*, since writing is mentioned only twenty times in the whole book, a third of these references being pejorative.[8] The only written texts we hear of are some "old books" and "history books" (III.12, IV.12), these mentioned very casually in passing, and a couple of contemptuous references to newspapers (I.11, III.7). Apart from a single, derisive mention of ink and of pens,[9] there is no talk of writing instruments— no stylus, quill, or calamus—nor of paper, parchment, writing tablets, or printing of any kind; and the only other fluid writing medium mentioned (in the speech "On Reading and Writing") is blood.

The lack of talk about written texts appears as a significant absence and may prompt the question whether there is not some kind of "writing block" at work here. Nietzsche chooses for his protagonist, after all, the founder of one of the most ancient living religions, who lived in an epoch when "writing and the book have a sacred character, are in the hands of a priestly caste, and become the medium of religious ideas."[10] Four of the five *Gathas* to be found in the *Yasna* section of the Avesta, the collection of sacred texts that form the basis of Zoroastrianism, are thought to have been written by the historical Zarathushtra.[11] Perhaps it was the paramount importance of epistles and scriptures in the Judaeo-Christian tradition that prompted Nietzsche to portray his protagonist as being so uninterested in writing. He may have been especially concerned to distance his mouthpiece from the writers in the New Testament (a text the great majority of whose books consist of letters) and from St. Paul in particular, that prolific scribe for whom Nietzsche had a peculiar distaste.

In reading *Zarathustra* it is generally instructive to examine the initial introduction of any image or theme, and in the case of writing the first mention alludes to an important episode in the Old Testament. In fact, it is remarkable that of the few references to it in *Zarathustra* almost a third concern writing on *tablets*—a major element in the story of Moses in the Book of Exodus. The first mention occurs in the context of Zarathustra's hoping to find cocreators who will "write new values on new tablets" (prologue sec. 9). The "values" here are the moral laws and commandments that peoples give themselves through valuing, or assigning praise and blame, even though they may claim that such valuations "fall to them as a voice from Heaven" (I.15). Tablets appear again in this speech "On the Thousand and One Goals," together with the first published mention of the will to power:

> A tablet of the good hangs over every people. See, it is the tablet of their overcomings; see, it is the voice of their will to power.

If the voicing of such important things is to last, it must be inscribed, and one of the most durable mediums for the inscriptions of laws and the like has traditionally been stone. Bulking heavy, stone is hard to move and difficult to lose; being hard, inscriptions in it are not easily effaced.

In the Book of Exodus, God summons Moses up to the mountaintop in order to give him the two tablets of stone on which He has written "a law, and commandments" (*Exodus* 24:14). There is no need to call Zarathustra up to the mountain because he lives there already, and in fact he later calls upon his "brothers" to help carry new tablets "down into the valleys" (III.12, sec. 4). There being no God in *Zarathustra* to inscribe the tablets, the protagonist seems—in the light of his own inclination toward divinity—strangely coy about doing the writing himself: he looks forward to having as a cocreator "one who will write for me my will on my tablets" (III.3). His role here would be analogous to God's in *Exodus*, who, after Moses has broken the tablets, has him transcribe the Ten Commandments onto new tablets at his divine dictation (*Exodus* 34:27–8).

The significance of the breaking of the tablets is different in the two stories. Moses comes down from the mountain with the tablets, and is prompted to break them by the sight of the people dancing (!) around Aaron's golden calf (*Exodus* 32:19). For Zarathustra, a dancer in the style of Dionysus or Shiva, a creator must first be a destroyer, and so he calls upon his brothers to help him break the old tablets, and speaks of writing "anew upon new tablets."[12] Zarathustra's speeches "On Old and New Tablets" are set in the scene of his sitting amidst "old, broken tablets . . . and also new, half inscribed tablets" (III.12, sec. 1). Whereas Moses breaks the tablets because their commandments are not being obeyed, Zarathustra breaks them because universal commandments ought not to be obeyed. But there is still no sign that Zarathustra is himself a writer, and indeed every indication that he would prefer to surround himself with amanuenses.[13]

"ON READING AND WRITING"

The only speech explicitly concerned—nominally, at least—with the
topic of writing begins:

> Of all that has been written I love only that which one writes with
> one's own blood. Write with blood: and you will learn that blood is
> spirit.[14]

Through the medium of fluid laid down on a plain plane surface by
means of an intermittent flow, the word is brought to stand, to endure
beyond the moment of its being spoken—and beyond the speaker's
death.[15] But there is a price to pay: the writer who (like the author of
Zarathustra) writes with blood is thereby depleted, drained,
weakened, diminished, having expended the very stuff of life.

> Whoever writes in blood and sayings [*Sprüchen*] does not want
> to be read, but rather learned by heart.

An author who writes in "sayings," or aphorisms, sounds (especially in
German, where *Sprüche* are literally "speakings") like an unusually
reluctant writer—as if he wants not to be read but learned by heart, so
that he will not need to be read (again). He is also reminiscent of the
Socrates of the *Phaedrus*, who through the persona of King Thamus
expresses a mistrust of writing because it diminishes one's ability to
learn by heart (275a). And yet it is hard to imagine spirit's being hap-
pier *speaking;* could it still be spirit without *writing?* "In the mountains the shortest way is from peak to peak; but for that you must have
long legs. Sayings should be peaks: and those to whom they are
addressed great and tall." *Sprüche* are like peaks insofar as they are
difficult to reach and are supported by an enormous mass of material,
which provides a vast amount of work for the archaeologist of meaning. "And the lover of knowledge shall learn to *build* with mountains!"
says Zarathustra later; "that the spirit moves mountains is nothing"
(II.8). In order to build peaks, one must dig deep; Zarathustra tells of
his learning that the highest mountains came from deep beneath the
oceans: "The evidence," he says, "is written in their stone and the walls
of their peaks" (III.1).

　　　There is a danger, however, that such hard labor in the profound
depths will make the descender too gloomy and ponderous: back in
"On Reading and Writing," we are reminded of the necessity to retain a
sense of humor and be able to "laugh over . . . what is black and heavy."

Because the enemy is "the spirit of gravity—"through [whom] all things fall"—Zarathustra can "only believe in a god who could dance." Belief leads to identification, as Zarathustra's laughter makes him feel light, and take off, so that "now a god dances through [him]."

The remarkable thing about this speech is how quickly it drops the theme announced in its title—reading and writing: neither topic is mentioned after the first fifteen lines. Instead the imagery turns to laughter, and then moves through lightness into height and flight before culminating in the dance.[16] There is in the text another path (to be explored shortly) complementary to this one, which leads from speaking to the dance by proceeding through song and the image of the bird and again by way of flight. But flying means an excess of lightness for Zarathustra, for whom "the sense of the earth" is paramount; there must be contact—even if not continuous—with the earth and the "unground" of the abyss.

The suspicion, prompted by the diminishing incidence of direct speeches mentioned earlier, that there is a movement afoot *away* from the "speaking" alluded to in the book's title is reinforced by the difficulty Zarathustra experiences—strange in one so easy with his speeches—in enunciating the book's central idea, the thought of recurrence. Why does speaking the thought threaten to break the "advocate [*Fürsprecher*, "for-speaker"] of the circle"? How does it almost kill the spokesman of suffering and life? One can learn from lending an ear, preferably one cocked for the sound of doves' feet, to the progression ("one has perhaps to count the whole of *Zarathustra* as music") through which the protagonist's vocal cords prove unequal to the task of giving voice to the idea of eternal return.

THE UNSPEAKABLE THOUGHT

The first intimation of the thought of recurrence comes when a voice speaks clearly to Zarathustra: "It's time!" (II.18). The next time he comes close to the thought he is struck dumb by it: on asking how it might be possible to teach the will to will backward, Zarathustra is shocked into a horrified silence (II.20). And when he finally recovers, the first thing he does, significantly, is to laugh. Later still, his "silent hour," his "terrible mistress," speaks to him—but, strangely, "without voice": "*You know it, Zarathustra?*... but you don't speak it!" (II.22). "It" is his abysmal thought, the greatest heavyweight: "What's getting you down, Zarathustra? Speak your word and break!" Ten times his stillest hour speaks to him, every time "without voice," and immediately before and after the last time, she laughs. But the thought is hard to enunciate and even harder to speak to, for he replies: "I lack the lion's voice for any commanding."

Zarathustra's first major engagement with the thought, in "On the Vision and the Enigma," culminates in the spectacle of the young shepherd who has fallen asleep on the ground and is choking because "a black, heavy snake" has crawled into his mouth and bitten fast there.[17] The idea of recurrence in its passive-nihilistic aspect goes for the throat and renders speaking impossible. Zarathustra's emotions at the scene scream to the shepherd to bite the snake's head off; the young man does so and then spits out the head and leaps to his feet. His first act then is not to utter a word but rather to laugh—"a laughter that was no human laughter." (Something *übermenschliches*, then: the laughter of the "overhuman.")

Whereas, in song, speech conforms to melody and may thereby lose some articulation into phonemes, laughter is vocal utterance without words, rhythmic voicings released semiconvulsively, devoid of verbal meaning. The text of *Zarathustra* reverberates with a remarkable amount of laughter (an average of one mention every three pages). In "On Reading and Writing" it generates the lightness and elevation that help one overcome the spirit of gravity (not to mention write well), and it is particularly liberating in Zarathustra's reappropriation of his childhood and his confrontation with death in "On Great Events" and "The Soothsayer" (II.18, 19). There it is associated with the spontaneity of the child, which derives in part, presumably, from the child's not yet having acquired language. But the most talk of laughter comes in part 4, where Zarathustra does his best to enlighten the higher humans by teaching them to laugh—first and foremost at themselves (see especially IV.13, sec. 20). Laughter affords distance and the lightness that is the antidote to the spirit of gravity, in thrall to which one takes oneself too seriously.

Eventually Zarathustra finds the lion's voice to awaken his thought and call it forth. But when the abysmal thought begins to speak, the "advocate of life" collapses and lies for seven days "like one dead" (III.13). On regaining consciousness, he responds to the exhortations of his serpent and eagle to go outside and recuperate by saying:

> Oh my animals... keep on chattering and let me listen!
> How charming it is to have words and tones: aren't words and tones rainbows and seeming bridges [*Schein-Brücken*] between what is eternally separated?...
> It's a beautiful foolishness, speaking: with it human beings dance over all things.

How charming all talking and lying with tones is! With tones our love dances on colored rainbows.[18]

Zarathustra's ironical tone in speaking about tones here echoes his ambivalence concerning the "beautiful foolishness" of the dance that is speaking. Deeper than a simple condemnation of a certain kind of chattering (of what Heidegger calls *Gerede* in *Sein und Zeit*, for example), these remarks of Zarathustra's reflect his growing awareness of the limitations of all spoken utterance. There is a crucial difference between this kind of tone-dance and the dance in which one speaks "the image of the highest things" (II.11), and between these rainbows, which are only "seeming-bridges," and the rainbow that signifies the overhuman, the steps to which Zarathustra has said he will demonstrate (prologue sec. 9; I.11). The animals respond to this speech deprecating speech by encouraging Zarathustra to give up speeches in favor of song.

FROM SONG TO DANCE

In the book's first part, "The Speeches of Zarathustra," not a single note is sung. In part 2 we hear three songs in succession: the Night-Song, the Dance-Song, and the Grave-Song. Part 3 brings a song not announced as such, "On the Mount of Olives" (which ends "Thus sang Zarathustra"), and culminates in the Other Dance-Song and the Yes-and Amen-Song. The fourth part contains the Song of Melancholy and "Among Daughters of the Desert" and reaches its climax in the Nightwanderer-Song (or Drunken Song). After this last—"good songs want to resound well; after good songs one should remain silent long"—comes just one more chapter: "The Sign."[19]

As Zarathustra begins to talk about "the eternal recurrence of the smallest," the eagle and serpent sense the danger of his speech—that it may, as his stillest hour had warned, "break" him—and interrupt it:

"Speak no farther, you convalescent!... but go out .... to the song-birds, so that you can learn from them how to *sing*!...
Sing and overflow, oh Zarathustra, heal your soul with new songs" (III.13).

They suggest that he fashion "a new lyre" for these songs. Zarathustra sees the wisdom in this but reproaches his animals for making a hurdy-gurdy song (*Leier-Lied*) of his ideas—the *Leier* being presumably too Apollonian an instrument for such a Dionysian thought.

In the next chapter, Zarathustra appears to be following the animals' advice: "so you will have to *sing*," he says to his soul (III.14), and at the culmination of the final song of part 3, "bird-wisdom" chimes in:

> "Sing! speak no more!
> Aren't all words made for those who are heavy? Don't all
> words lie to one who is light! Sing! speak no more!" (III.16).

These utterances further the progression from speech, through the images of song and bird, to lightness and flight. By the time "Midday" comes, however, things have quieted down, and everything has to submit to the command "Still!" "Do not sing, grass-wings," Zarathustra now says to his soul, "Don't even whisper! Because look—still! the old midday is sleeping."[20] The tensions of soul and world cannot be resolved, nor can the dropoff into the well of eternity be consummated; midday cannot unite with midnight (as it must in the Nightwanderer-Song shortly thereafter) if any sound uttered—however sibilantly or melodically—disturbs the stillness. The last move is to fall silent.

When in "The Yes- and Amen-Song" Zarathustra sings his A[lpha] and O[mega]—"That everything heavy become light, that all body become dancer and all spirit bird" (III.16)—the themes of song and flight and lightness as manifest in laughter begin to coalesce in the image of the dance. While some of the apostates of whom Zarathustra spoke earlier "once lifted their legs like dancers [as] the laughter in [his] wisdom waved to them" (III.8), and what is preventing the higher humans from doing the dance that would transpose them into the realm of the overhuman is their inability to laugh, what they need is someone to "make [them]" laugh again...a dancer and a wind" (IV.11). At the climax of his lengthy speech "On the Higher Human," Zarathustra invokes the flight of birds and the lightening of feet so as to join the themes of dancing laughter and the laughing dance (IV.13, secs. 15-20)

As mentioned earlier, however, flying is for Zarathustra only a stage on the way, being too little dependent on the earth to be the ultimate *methodos* of the overhuman. Rather than stay with the advice of his animals to emulate the birds in song and flight, he must follow the middle course between his eagle who soars and his serpent condemned to crawl: one may only overcome the spirit of gravity while still retaining a sense of the earth by undertaking to *dance*. It is made clear as early as the Prologue that the dance is crucial: just after the old saint compliments Zarathustra for walking "like a dancer," there appears the proto-image of the overhuman in the form of the *Seiltänzer*, the rope-dancer (though the more pedestrian English translations have him only *walking* the tightrope). After the Death of the One Christian God, the archetype of the spirit of gravity who represents all absolute value, there is no ground on which to take a firm stand: our feet are faced with the abyss. An appropriate response is then to dance, to cultivate a lightness of foot that will obviate becoming stuck in any single perspective.

Zarathustra makes it clear early on that he wants ultimately to speak with his hands, arms, legs, and feet rather than with his vocal cords:

> "Only in the dance do I know how to speak to the image [*Gleichnis*] of the highest things:—and now my highest image stayed unspoken in my limbs" (II,11).

Later, he says that he wants man and woman to be "able to dance with head and legs" (III.12, sec. 23), and in admonishing the higher humans to raise their hearts and legs to dance, he adds: "And better still: stand on your heads!" (IV.13, sec. 19). Now, while this may be a posture from which one can better appreciate Nietzsche's inversion of traditional values, and while the head contains the organs of balance in the inner ear which allow one to maintain some kind of *Gleichgewicht* between the opposite values that have been set swaying by the concomitant loss of ground, the idea of dancing with one's head remains somewhat disconcerting. It becomes less so when viewed in the broader context of connections between feet, hands, and head which forms the background imagery for the activity of writing.

THE WRITE STEPS

The passages, discussed earlier, concerning writing on tablets made no mention of the implements employed. One might expect a chisel to be necessary, but there is no mention in the text of any suitably sharp instrument (*Zarathustra* seems to lack what Derrida would call a *style*). Hammers, however, are mentioned twice. Just as the thought of recurrence is sleeping in Zarathustra's abyss and requires the lion's voice to waken it, so the image of the overhuman "sleeps in the stone" of his fellow human beings and has to be liberated from its prison by the cruelty of Zarathustra's raging hammer. His will—itself capable of splitting rock (II.11)—drives him again and again toward human beings "like a hammer toward stone" (II.2). "You only know the spirit's sparks," he says to the famous wise men, "but you don't see the anvil that it is, nor the cruelty of its hammer" (II.8). We must beware, however, of thinking of the image (*Bild*) of the overhuman as something set in stone, as a statue (*Standbild*). The overhuman as (rope)-dancer is always "a dangerous on-the-way"(prologue sec. 4); and

> whoever comes close to his goal dances.
> And truly, I did not become a statue, I am not still standing there, stiff, solid, like stone, a pillar (IV.13, sec. 17).

The concrete image Zarathustra presents is far from static, the same for all; it is rather something moving and vital, capable of supporting a variety of perspectives and sustaining changing interpretations. The integrity of the ideal he is attempting to embody is fluid like the dynamics of music, a choreography of tones.

We encounter the hammer again on the final page of the last work that Nietzsche himself published. Above the concluding section of *Twilight of the Idols*, the entire page of which is emphasized typographically, stands the legend "The Hammer Speaks."[21] This speaking may become more intelligible if we consider the hammer's employment in chiseling and, by way of the role of striking in printing, its implication in writing. And the subtitle of the book—"How one philosophizes with a hammer"—can be amplified by reflecting that the foreword's explanation of the appropriate *mode d'emploi* is that one uses it to sound out idols, as with a tuning fork (the first syllable of *Stimmgabel* connotes "voice" as well as "tuning") which may then proclaim their hollowness. But what does the section entitled "The Hammer Speaks"—itself a transcription of section 29 of "On Old and New Tablets' in *Zarathustra*—say? It begins with the kitchen coal's asking the diamond: "Why so hard?" Zarathustra asks in return:

> Why so soft? Oh my brothers...
> And if your hardness does not want to flash and separate and cut: how could you expect to accompany me—in creating?
> For creators are hard. And what bliss it must be, to impress your hand upon millennia as on wax—
> —Bliss, to write upon the will of millennia as on bronze— harder than bronze, nobler than bronze. Only the most noble is hard.

To be Zarathustra's brother one must be like the lightning that flashes forth from the "dark cloud of the human" and licks the underhuman with its tongue (prologue secs. 3-4). While this tongue may not speak—though the lightning laughs (III. 16, secs. 1, 3)—it is sharp and cutting nonetheless. It is an incisive will that can "impress [itself] on millennia as on wax," but to write on "the will of millennia as on bronze" one must be harder even than bronze—hard as a diamond. The coal burns and provides light and heat, but whereas its traces soon dissipate, those of the less overtly spectacular diamond can endure. The diamond flashes forth again in Zarathustra's lyrical conversation with his soul ("On the Great Yearning"), where he speaks of its longing as "the urge of the vine for the vintager [who] waits with his diamond knife" (III.14). One wonders whether this diamond knife may be the sharp implement for writing that has seemed to be somehow absent.

In the prologue, just after expressing his desire for co-creators to write new values on new tablets, Zarathustra had said:

> Companions the creator seeks, and fellow harvesters: for everything in him stands ripe for the harvest. But he is lacking the hundred sickles (sec. 9).

Writing may then be seen as a process of "self-harvesting" on the part of the author: hard work, exhausting, requiring sharp implements that do violence to the living growth of the soul. By part 3, Zarathustra appears to have outgrown the need for fellow harvesters but now sees his own offspring, the children who are trees, as ones who will become his companions and such as will "write [his] will on [his] tablets" (just what a generation or two of Nietzsche scholars have done—and may continue to do, for generations, the seeds having been sown). And when in the penultimate chapter of the book, in the Nightwander-Song, Zarathustra addresses his soul as a vine and asks:

> You vine! What, do you praise me? But I cut you! I am cruel, you are bleeding: what does your praise want with my drunken cruelty?[22]

is he not apologizing to his soul for having taught her, through writing with her blood, that "blood is spirit"—*Geist*, the intoxicating spirit of the vine, the sign of Dionysian "life that itself cuts into life" (II.8)?

A final passage from *Twilight of the Idols* reinforces the connection alluded to earlier between dance and the head and at the same time makes explicit the link between writing and dancing:

To learn *thinking:*...logic as ...*handwork*...thinking
wants to be learned, as dancing wants to be learned, *as* a kind of
dancing..., to be able to dance with the feet, with concepts, with
words; do I still have to tell you that one must also be able to
dance with the *pen*—that one must learn to *write?*[23]

Thinking as handwork, craft (*Handwerk:* an anticipation of
Heidegger's understanding of *Denken*), as well as headwork; light
footwork too, it turned out in *Zarathustra*, requiring an ear to the
ground. Listen to Zarathustra's response to the laughing glance of his
life toward his itching foot in "The Other Dance-Song":

"My heels twitched, my toes listened to understand you: for
the dancer has his ear—in his toes?...
I dance after you, I follow your tiny trace. Where are you?
Give me your hand! Or only a finger!" (III.15).

It is light and easy to dance over all things with speaking, but more
difficult to let words fall, following the musical notes of life, so that
they themselves leave vital traces that will outlast the author's death.
This requires that one overcome the spirit of gravity, "through whom
all things fall," that spirit which brings the longest life down and forces
the highest soul to go under—unless in the dance of writing one can
set down with feather-light hand a trace of life. If Zarathustra can get
hold of life by the hand, if he can channel her flow through his fingers,
he may be able to outdo the God of *Exodus*, who inscribes commandments on stone tablets with his fingers alone (31:18). In pressing one's
hand on millennia as on wax, one can avoid heavy-handedness by
lifing up one's legs. For writing, like dancing, is for Zarathustra a divine
affair that requires an inversion of the natural attitude; and a
standing on the head, ear close to the ground, will at least keep one's
feet pointed toward heaven—that "dance floor for divine accidents"
(III.4).

Now I am light, now I am flying, now I see myself beneath
myself, now a god dances through me.
Thus spoke Zarathustra.

Now he is writing.

FOOTNOTE AFTERWORD

Apart from any source it may have in divine inspiration, what do we learn about writing from Nietzsche's assimilation of it to dancing?

That it is an activity involving the whole body, rather than just head and hand; that it involves a response to the counterpart of the music, a listening through the feet, which are in touch with the earth; that it demands a flexibility that responds dynamically to the ever-changing conditions of becoming, alternating lightness and gravity; that it requires training, exercise, discipline, and a balance between control and inspiration which makes hard work look like effortless play; that a writer must learn to listen, hear, and record with such careful attention that the traces are animated and thus live and move after having been laid down; that the true text may be inscribed behind or beyond the page by means of a "writing in water" that is more fruitful than the one derided by Socrates in the *Phaedrus*, a counterpart to inscription in bronze which sets down in the river of time vital signs, capable of generating continual reinterpretation and bearing fruit in successive understandings.

ENDNOTE

The talk of the writer's relation to life prompts a biographical note on which to end. In attempting to understand Nietzsche's reluctance to speak directly of writing in his most literary and self-reflective work, the author's apparently apotropaic aversion to the very mention of the tools of his trade, and his hiding behind the mask of one who appears not to write, one might recall that when he was working on *Zarathustra* Nietzsche came to the realization that he was condemned from then on to be a writer in solitude, that he would never be able to speak like his alter ego, Zarathustra. He realized that from then on his relationships with those dear to him would for the most part be conducted at a distance, not in the living presence of face-to-face dialogue but through a medium conditioned by absence, by letters and the written word.

8

Reading as a Philosophical Strategy:
Nietzsche's The Gay Science

Clayton Koelb

There is a prima facie case to be made for Nietzsche's early and abiding interest in the rhetorical aspect of all discourse. Much of that case has already been made by Paul de Man in *Allegories of Reading* and has become widely known and frequently discussed. Because of de Man and others associated with the "new Nietzsche," who come mainly from France, many readers are now familiar with the formerly obscure little fragment "On Truth and Lie in an Extra-moral Sense" ("Über Wahrheit und Lüge im aussermoralischen Sinn") and its relation to Nietzsche's lecture notes on rhetoric made in the early 1870s. These documents give us a clear sense of Nietzsche's transition from philology to philosophy in the period from 1868 to 1876, when he was in effect working as both philosopher and professional philologist at the same time. Consideration of classical rhetoric as expounded by scholars such as Richard Volkmann and Gustav Gerber provided Nietzsche with important materials from which could be built a bridge between the study of language and the reexamination of some of philosophy's fundamental questions.

Section 3 of the lecture notes deals specifically with "The Relation of the Rhetorical to Language" and introduces the important notion that rhetoric cannot be identified with an aritifical and unnatural supplement to "natural" language. What we call rhetoric, Nietzsche argues, is only a further development of a process already at work in all language:

> There is obviously no unrhetorical "naturalness" of language to which one could appeal; the language itself is the result of audible rhetorical arts. The power to discover and to make operative that which works and impresses, with respect to each thing, a power which Aristotle calls rhetoric, is, at the same time, the essence of language; the latter is based just as little as rhetoric is upon that which is true, upon the essence of things ... The *tropes*, the non-literal significations, are considered to be the most artistic means of rhetoric. But, with respect to their meanings, all words are tropes in themselves, and from the beginning.[1]

There is an obvious but important similarity between these notions and the position taken in "On Truth and Lie" about the nature of truth:

> What therefore is truth? A mobile army of metaphors, metonymies, anthropomorphisms: in short a sum of human relations which became poetically and rhetorically intesified, metamorphosed, adorned, and after long usage seems to a nation fixed, canonic, and binding; truths are illusions of which one has forgotten that they *are* illusions; worn-out metaphors which have become powerless to affect the senses; coins which have their obverse effaced and are no longer of account as coins but merely as metal.[2].

These sentiments are well known and might seem to require little additional comment. It is worth noting, however, that Nietzsche makes sure that his own language here is itself highly rhetorical: the worn-out nature of the metaphors-become-truths is to be explained only metaphorically, by recourse to a figure which acts out the literal meaning of "worn-out." The text makes an effort to set forth the worn-out nature of the figurative expression "worn-out" by (paradoxically) revivifying it, by making its effaced literal import evident again. The illustrative image, in addition, pictures a process only rhetorically analogous to the one under dicussion. From the standpoint of logic, the image of the coin depicts an action that tends in the opposite direction: instead of the tenor's effacing the vehicle, as in the metaphor "worn-out" and other worn-out metaphors, the vehicle of the coin is revealed by the effacement of its tenor. But rhetoric overwhelms logic by means of the play on the word *Bild*, which refers on the one hand to the "picture" stamped on the coin and on the other to the character of the trope as "image." Nietzsche tells us that these "coins" (worn-out metaphors) have "lost their quality as image," or in other words that they function no longer as representations but as things.

The rhetorical quality of this discourse about rhetoric is not merely witty and clever; it is a way of coming to terms with the consequences of the argument Nietzsche is making. Supposing that Nietzsche accpets his own conclusion that all discourse is metaphorical and that all truth is simply an unacknowledged catachresis, two principal reactions seem possible for the philosopher determined to pursue the truth. On the one hand, one might try to develop ways to circumvent language altogether and thus avoid its contaminating metaphoricity, or on the other hand, one might decide to join the forces one cannot beat and look to the resources of language itself for strategies by which one might subvert our tendency to accept as truth "the obligation to lie according to a fixed convention, to lie gregariously in a style binding for all."[3] Nietzsche's reaction is never the former; often it is recognizably the latter; at other times, however, he appears to act as if he did not accept the conclusion of "On Truth and Lie," to write as if language were a perfectly transparent medium, and to assume the pose of an authority untroubled by the rhetorical nature of his own discourse. Even the essay "On Truth and Lie" itself adopts this pose and even in the passage under discussion. It appears to be telling us the real truth about the truth (that it is a mobile army of metaphors) from a perspective that is somehow privileged. But that perspective undermines itself by relying so overtly on the process of figuration to make its point. Self-deconstructing propositions of this type are to be found relatively frequently in Nietzsche's writing and contribute importantly to his reputation as a literary writer.

The self-deconstructing Nietzsche is a figure that has already become familiar in one form or another over the past decade, and it is not my intention to paint that portrait again. While self-deconstruction is an important feature of Nietzsche's rhetorical style, it is not the aspect on which I want to focus attention now. I prefer to draw out a slightly different implication of the position taken in the lecture notes on rhetoric and in "On Truth and Lie" that focuses attention on its inventive rather than its subversive function in Nietzsche's philosophical project. That is what one might call, following Gregory Ulmer's extension of Derrida's term, the "grammatological" rather than the deconstructive turn in Nietzsche.[4] If indeed all language (and thus all truth) is figurative and therefore subject to deconstruction, it offers the possibility of becoming an almost endlessly fertile source for philosophical thinking. If there is no distinction to be made between the figurative nature of even the most ordinary language and truth, then one way to think about "truth" in fresh ways would be to "let language do some thinking for us"[5] by interrogating the figures themselves.

Interrogating them, however, would not mean attempting to discriminate between their "true" and "false" significations. Since all significations are the result of troping, according to "On Truth and Lie," there is no way to carry out such a discrimination. It would have to mean accepting both the literal and figurative meanings as belonging to the same order—both, of course, figurative. While one point of view would see this leveling as destroying the value of both, Nietzsche often works on the assumption that all available meanings are equally useful. From this assumption comes a strategy for writing (in this case, writing a kind of philosophy) that derives from reading. The writer reads an already deconstructed language and from that reading forms a new discourse that actualizes both the literal and the figurative, both the assertion and its subversion. The discovery that all truth is nothing but figuration ceases to be an alarming or paralyzing problem for the philosopher; on the contrary, it opens up new space for investigation. Rhetoric, since Plato the thing that philosophy has sought to purge from its midst, becomes the wellspring of philosophy.

Before pursuing this line any farther, I have to grant that Nietzsche seems to retain no small dose of ambivalence about a philosophy founded on rhetoric. This is evident enough in the direction taken by the argument in "On Truth and Lie," where words like "dissimulation" (*Verstellung*) and "deception" (*Täuschung*) figure prominently. He even asks, rhetorically, whether language is "the adequate expression of all realities."[6] The implication of such a vocabulary is that there exists some bedrock of reality which the metaphorical nature of speech hides from us. But does this bedrock of reality actually exist? There is no consistent answer to this question to be found in Nietzsche's writings. In the following sentence from "On Truth or Lie," for example, it is impossible to determine the author's opinion on the subject under discussion: "The 'Thing-in-itself' (it is just this which would be the pure ineffective truth) is also quite incomprehensible to the creator of language and not worth making any great endeavor to obtain."[7] We simply cannot tell whether the "creator of language" (*Sprachbildner*) has taken a proper or improper perspective in Nietzsche's eyes. Is the *Ding-an-sich* incomprehensible to the creator of language because of the shallowness of his own perception or because of the inconsequence of the notion of a Ding-an-sich, a truth which is "ineffective" (*folgenlos*)? There are explicit statements scattered through Nietzsche's works to support both views.

I do not propose to try to settle this perhaps unsettlable question. My interest in any case lies less with the issue of Nietzsche's "realism," if that is how one would want to put it, than with the way in which his assumptions about the pervasive and unavoidable metaphoricity of language, ambivalent though they were, became fruitful in his philosophical praxis. One thing we can say for certain is that the notions advanced in "On Truth and Lie" did not precipitate a paralyzing crisis in Nietzsche's own project of writing. He did not feel that his discourse was so contaminated by dissimulation and deception that there was no point in engaging in it. On the contrary, he wrote away with considerable zeal and with an apparent faith that writing was still very worthwhile, even at times "truthful." In aphorism 381 of *The Gay Science*, for example, Nietzsche excuses the brevity of his aphoristic style by claiming that "there are truths that are singularly shy and ticklish and cannot be caught except suddenly— that must be *surprised* or left alone."[8] The implication is that Nietzsche has indeed surprised some of these shy "truths" (*Wahrheiten*) in the lightning flash of his writing.

It is fair enough, then, to say that Nietzsche's reaction to the conclusions reached through his study of rhetoric was not to shun rhetoric but to immerse himself in it. Nowhere is that decision more evident than in *The Gay Science* (1882), a work which in several ways announces itself as the marriage of philosophy and poetry. The epigraph to the first edition, slightly misquoted from Emerson, emphasizes the close relationship between the poet (*Dichter*) and the philosopher (*Weiser*). Emerson had included the saint in this brotherhood, but Nietzsche quietly deletes him.[9] The confrontation of gaiety with science in the title not only suggests the importation of a lighter tone into philosophy but also refers quite directly to the "gaya scienza" of poetry itself. Nietzsche's book is to be both a work of *Wissenschaft*, as philosophy was supposed to be, and an example of the art of poetry. The book begins with a section in rhymes and, in the second edition, ends with another. It is an enterprise in which both joy and science are founded upon serious attention to language.

Nietzsche thought paying attention to language was worthwhile as part of the process of thinking. In the notes from the fall of 1881, for example, he writes down a number of wordplays or puns (*Wortspiele*) for possible use later.[10] It is characteristic of Nietzsche that he would do so, but certainly not characteristic for the mainstream of philosophy in the nineteenth century (or—with the exception of those following in the Nietzschean tradition, such as Heidegger and Derrida—of the twentieth century either). Nietzsche has the kind of verbal imagination that sees, in the accidental, the interplay of signifiers, the impetus for thought. The shared syllable of *ridiculosus* and *cultura* suggests to him a shared quality, and he notes the possibility of the "*Ridicultur* eines Menschen." He might have seen in this portmanteau word the occasion for satire directed against those whose notion of culture is so philistine as to be ridiculous, or he might have been thinking more positively of the potential for culture to emerge out of things that are laughable (such as the word *Ridicultur* itself). Whichever way Nietzsche might have thought to use the joke, it clearly belongs to the same project as the set of notes in which it is embedded.

The rhymes which open *The Gay Science* show Nietzsche attempting publicly to demonstrate the integration of a form of rhetorical or poetic invention into his philosophical discourse. He starts right off by using wordplay to explain the nature of his enterprise. The first piece of verse, "Invitation" (*Einladung*), plays on the two possible readings of *sieben*, one as the number "seven," the other as a deprecatory prefix:

> Wagt's mit meiner Kost, ihr Esser!
> Morgen schmeckt sie euch schon besser
> Und schon übermorgen gut!
> Wollt ihr dann noch mehr,—so machen
> Meine alten sieben Sachen
> Mir zu sieben neuen Muth.[11]

Interestingly enough, this wordplay seems to repeat the sense of the Ridicultur joke in the notes. The locution *Siebensachen* refers to one's belongings in a belittling fashion: they are "odds and ends" or "trifles," as for example in Goethe's little poem comparing the "works of the masters" with his own poor Siebensachen. The *sieben* barely hangs onto its character as a number in this locution; the issue is not, after all, how many *Sachen* there are but rather the perception that they are of no account. *Sieben* acts to put these things in their place by suggesting that they are few and paltry. The very same word, though, when used in the next line, works in just the opposite direction. It refers to an operation that adds rather than reduces value. By looking again at those Siebensachen, the reader (even when the reader is the author) can rediscover the augmentative power of the number seven embedded in the old text. Seven, after all, is a number of mystical power often associated with increase in the Bible and other canonical texts. The reader's stock of ideas increases in the very recognition of this possibility, and like Nietzsche, he or she is quickly in possession of fresh *Muth* (that is, "spirit" or "courage") for generating more and more ideas. One might even get "culture" out of this ridiculous stuff.

The notion of adding acts here as a metaphor for the results of reading (and rereading), as does eating or tasting earlier in the verse. The point of the poem is that what at first seems valueless can become valuable upon rereading. That is what the reader of *The Gay Science* is supposed to discover about this book, just as Nietzsche has discovered it about the word *sieben*. Nietzsche, though by no means a great poet, is an extremely skillful rhetorician. He not only preaches his point; he practices it in such a way as to drive home the doctrine being preached. We are not simply told that creative acts of interpretation can turn trifles into treasures; we are shown how the German language encourages just such a transformation of sieben. Even if the reader at first considers the book before him to be "indigestible" (one of Nietzsche's favorite metaphors), repeated reading will be able to make something of it. But the obligation and the responsibilty rest, as they have since Plato, with the reader.[12] The author cannot do the job for him.

This point is stressed in the twenty-third poem in the group, "Interpretation":

> Leg ich mich aus, so leg ich mich hinein:
> Ich kann nicht selbst mein Interprete sein.
> Doch wer nun steigt auf seiner eignen Bahn,
> Trägt auch mein Bild zu hellerm Licht hinan.[13].

The equation between "sich auslegen" (interpret oneself) and "sich hineinlegen" (get oneself into trouble) is another paradoxical word-play. Since *ein* ("in") and *aus* ("out") are semantic opposites, the assertion that "sich hineinlegen" and "sich auslegen" are parts of the same process might come as a surprise, but since the locutions are so similar phonologically (the parallel structure "Leg ich mich ... leg ich mich" emphasizes this point), the author's surprising conclusion seems justified. If self-interpretation on the part of the author can only get him into trouble, then, he must count on the reader to do the work of interpreting, even if that reader has no particular interest in advancing Nietzsche's project. It is interesting to compare this text with a slightly earlier version written in February 1882 and found in the *Nachlass* (11 [336]). The first line is the same, but the last three go in a somewhat different direction: "So mög ein Freund mein Interprete sein. / Und wenn er steigt auf seiner eignen Bahn, / Trägt er des Freundes Bild mit sich hinan."[14] In this version, written with a specific person in mind, Nietzsche presupposes that the interpreting other will be well disposed toward him. The relation between reader and author is that of friend and friend. This supposition is dropped from the published version. The context of the other poems of "Scherz, List, und Rache" makes clear that Nietzsche does not expect an audience necessarily friendly to him or to his project, especially since the material presented is not always easy to take. Poem 54, for example, admits that *The Gay Science* will need a reader with strong teeth and a strong stomach ("ein gut Gebiss und einen guten Magen") to consume what Nietzsche has to offer.

Even the unsympathetic reader, the one whom Nietzsche himself has put off with his "hardness" (*Härte*) and willingness to step on others to reach the heights (poem 26), will be a better interpreter of Nietzsche than Nietzsche himself. There is a certain charming modesty about this, but we quickly realize that there is in fact not the slightest trace of self-deprecation in what Nietzsche is proposing. The protagonist of the poem may not be the author himself, but it does turn out to be his image (*Bild*). The goal of interpretation is to place the author's image (in both senses of "picture" and "trope") in a clearer light, and it is proposed that the reader is better equipped for that task than the author—even indeed when the reader is climbing along "his own way" and not necessarily Nietzsche's. Read my metaphors in whatever way you will, Nietzsche seems to be saying, as long as you keep reading them. That which is closest to me, my image, will emerge clearly in the process.

This notion that the reader can do the author's business while in fact attending strictly to his own is a particularly postmodern concept that goes somewhat, but not entirely, against the grain of the traditional imagery of reading invoked by Nietzsche himself in his "Invitation." The idea is traditional in that it still assumes that the reader's role is to take over from the author a burden the author is no longer in a position to assume, but it departs from the tradition in supposing that readerly independence, not subservience, will facilitate the transfer of the burden. In the Platonic formulation of the principal Western orthodoxy of reading, the author is understood as the parent of the text ("pater logou"), both progenitor of and absolute authority over his offspring; the reader is a kind of foster parent responsible to the wishes and intentions of the "father of the discourse," subservient to him in all matters pertaining to the welfare of the precious child. The goal of this fostering care could properly be described by Nietzsche's words, to carry the "image" of the author into the clear light of productive interpretation. This very traditional goal, however, is paradoxically alleged by Nietzsche to be most likely of attainment when the reader steadfastly pursues his own path without worrying about what path the author might have chosen.

This same idea is presented in the seventh poem, "Vademecum—Vadetecum":

> Es lockt dich meine Art und Sprach,
> Du folgest mir, du gehst mir nach?
> Geh nur dir selber treulich nach:—
> So folgst du mir—gemach! gemach![15]

The poem is concerned with *folgen* and *nachgehen* in their figurative senses of "comply with" and "inquire into" and thus once again with the issue of interpretation. Again the assertion is made that the proper method of inquiry into Nietzsche's writing is faithful investigation of the reader's self and that this act of self-examination will be the best way to imitate and obey (*folgen*) Nietzsche himself. This advice is at once both surprising and expected. It is very traditional in that it takes the Socratic position that the beginning of wisdom is self-knowledge, that to "follow" the philosopher is not so much to learn his doctrines as to obey the Delphic injunction to "know thyself." It is unexpected—and deliberately so—at the beginning of a volume so full of advice, warnings, precepts, and other forms of guidance. Nietzsche acknowledges that he is offering here a kind of guidebook, a vademecum for the philosophically inclined, but in the moment of acknowledging it he turns it against itself. The advice he gives here is that the best way of taking his advice is not to take anyone's advice but your own. Nietzsche evidently loved the logical involution implied by this game.

The gesture made by the text's rhetoric once again authorizes radical reinterpretation as the most valid mode of reading. We can read "vademecum" as "vadetecum" and vice versa, just as we could read "sich auslegen" as "sich hineinlegen" in poem 25. Nietzsche is showing us a method for rhetorical reading but at the same time is urging that we must ourselves take up this tool and not simply wait for Nietzsche to do it for us. It is Nietzsche's version of the traditional invitation "Tolle, lege" but with the notion of "reading" substantially revised.

Nietzsche is prepared to defend the value of incessant rereading even in the extreme case of rereading his own earlier readings. The thirty-sixth poem, "Juvenalia" (*Jugendschriften*) exemplifies the process:

> Meiner Weisheit A und O
> Klang mir hier: was hört' ich doch!
> Jetzo klingt mir's nicht mehr so,
> Nur das ew'ge Ah! und Oh!
> Meiner Jugend hör ich noch.[16]

The commonplace German expression "das A und das O" ("the alpha and the omega") is regularly used to mean the sum total of something, even the "be-all and end-all." The clear implication of the poem is that the author did at one time think the sum total of his wisdom to be something grand, all-inclusive, and definitive. That interpretation comes under scrutiny when a now somewhat older Nietzsche looks back at his early writing and finds it "nicht mehr so," no longer what he once thought it was. The text is the same, but its meaning has radically changed. That change is cleverly exemplified in the rereading of the poem's own initial text, the phrase "A und O," now revealed as the semiarticulate cries of one whose feelings are more powerful than his means to express them. The transformation of "A und O" into "Ah! und Oh!" involves a dramatic change of signification with no change at all in the (oral) signifier. The change in the graphic signifier (the addition of -*h!*) is the mark of an alteration in perspective that both does and does not change the nature of the material interpreted. One could argue equally persuasively that there is no difference between the signifiers *A* and *Ah!*, *O* and *Oh!*, and that there is a huge difference; that is, one could take the point of view of a phonologically oriented linguist such as Saussure, or a graphically oriented grammatologist such as Derrida. The crucial thing here—which a Saussurian would be as quick to see as a Derridean—is the interplay of sameness and difference, in which the phonological samesness stands as a figure for a persisting, invariable text and graphic difference for the highly mutable act of reading.

The referential malleability of particular instances of discourse stands everywhere in these poems as a figure for the metaphoricity, and thus infinite interpretability, of all language, even of the whole world. Aphorism 374 in the body of the book (*Our new "infinite"*) makes explicit the presupposition inherent in the poems of "Scherz, List, und Rache":

> How far the perspective character of existence extends or indeed whether existence has any other character than this; whether existence without interpretation, without "sense," does not become "nonsense"; whether, on the other hand, all existence is not essentially actively engaged in *interpretation*—that cannot be decided even by the most industrious and most scrupulously conscientious analysis and self-examination of the intellect...Rather has the world become "infinite" for us all over again, inasmuch as we cannot reject the possibility that *it may include infinite interpretations*.[17]

The world (Nietzsche uses *Welt* and *Dasein* interchangeably here) is analogized to a text of a certain sort. This is not the "book of the world" of the church fathers, a text whose form and meaning are ordained by God and whose legibility is guaranteed by God's perfection; this book is constantly reading itself and in that self-reading is making interpretive changes such as that from *A* to *Ah!*. The world, moreover, often reads itself in ways that testify to the absence of any guiding divine perfection: "Alas, too many *ungodly* possibilities of interpretation are included in the unknown, too much deviltry, stupidity, and follishness of interpretation—even our own human, all too human folly, which we know." [18]

But the poems of "Scherz, List, und Rache" demonstrate in their own way that even interpretation that is devilish or foolish has its uses. Nietzsche warns of his own deviltry in poem 9, "My Roses," in which he observes that, while his "happiness" (presumably the happiness of engaging in the gay science) wants to bring happiness to others ("es will beglücken"), it also has a special fondness for teasing (*Necken*) and malicious tricks (*Tücken*). Those who want to pick the roses of this philosopher will often prick their fingers on his thorns. Teasing and trickery are part of a method which retains the traditional aim of philosophy, to get to the bottom of things ("den

Grund") but does not suppose that it can achieve that aim by means of research (*Forschung*):

> Ein Forscher ich? Oh spart diess Wort!—
> Ich bin nur *schwer*—so manche Pfund'!
> Ich Falle, falle immerfort
> Und endlich auf den Grund![19]

Walter Kaufmann makes a noble try at translating Nietzsche's wordplay by rendering the title "Der Gründliche" as "The Thorough Who Get to the Bottom of Things," but even this laudable effort actually obscures the rhetoric of the original. The point of the poem (no. 44) is that one can be *gründlich* in the sense of getting to the bottom of things *without* being gründlich in the sense of thorough or rigorous—without, that is, being a *Forscher*. The title is revealed by the poem to be readable as both ironic and not ironic, since the denial of Gründlichkeit as a method is shown to in no way to prevent achievement of the *Grund*, the bottom of things.

The method proposed as Nietzsche's alternative to Forschung is cast in terms which will become very familiar to readers of *The Gay Science* and *Zarathustra* but is presented here with an almost dismissive comic casualness. The author proclaims that he is not thorough, he is merely *schwer* ("heavy" or "difficult" or "indigestible") and therefore keeps falling (or declining) until he reaches the ground. What makes him heavy and difficult is that he is full of *Pfunde*, but these "pounds" are things that add rhetorical weight, rhetorical Pfunde that are barely distinguishable from *Funde* ("discoveries"). The paronomasia Pfund'/Fund' is called for by the figurative context, since discoveries are far more likely than pounds to make a philosopher *schwer*. It is certainly this sort of intellectual "weightiness" that is at issue when the same vocabulary returns in a more sober guise much later in the book. Aphorism 341, the famous passage which Nietzsche considered the first announcement of the basic idea of *Zarathustra*, eternal recurrence, bears the title "Das grösste Schwergewicht," again stressing the importance of being "weighty." And Aphorism 342, a passage almost identical to the opening section of *Zarathustra*, plays repeatedly on the term *untergehen*, a synonyn of *fallen*. We can be sure that Nietzsche was very serious about *Schwergewicht* and *untergehen*, even if we harbor doubts about the seriousness of *schwer* and *fallen* in the poem "Der Gründliche." This is the devilish, foolish, unthorough method in operation, of course. That which is introduced as a teasing joke opens the way to something important: one falls, as it were, to the bottom of things by making jokes that are heavy and difficult. The process of falling to the philosophical ground is illustrated with particular consistency in the poems of "Scherz, List, und Rache" but is an important strategy in all of Nietzsche's writing. It is essentially a strategy of rhetorical reading, and it is plainly visible in a number of aphorisms in the main body of *The Gay Science*. Here the prose format makes no special pretension to literariness, but what we might regard as literary methods (because they are rhetorical) can be found as readily as in the rhymes. Nietzsche proceeds as if everyday language were a joyous *Wissenschaft* the power of which can be unlocked by an innovative act of reading. That is his method in *The Genealogy of Morals*, where he discovers *in language* the repressed relation between concepts of good and evil and facts of power, and this is his method in numerous aphorisms in *The Gay Science*, where wordplay and other forms of rhetorical reading play a significant role. His rumination on the role of deception in art (no. 361), a passage that could have served as a program for Thomas Mann's entire literary career, concludes with a typically rhetorical, if somewhat misogynistic, discussion of the artistic nature of women. Women are actresses even in the act of love, he claims. One discovers "that they pretend even when they—give themselves" ("dass sie 'sich geben,' selbst noch, wenn sie—sich geben"). Nietzsche finds a way to actualize both the figurative and literal meanings of "sich geben" at once and to make that actualization the basis for an earnest discussion of a problem he considers to be philosophically important. The very same procedure is at work in no. 383, the last aphorism of the volume, in which he plays on the two senses of the word *Grillen* ("moping" and "crickets"): "Who will sing a song for us, a morning song, so sunny, so light, so fledged that it will *not* chase away the blues [*Grillen*] but invite them instead to join in the singing and dancing?"[20] The blues are also a form of singing, as Kaufmann's translation cleverly reminds us.

This pun on *Grillen* appears in the context of a discussion of "the virtues of the right reader ['des rechten Lesens']—what forgotten and unknown virtues they are!"[21] Right reading turns out to be exactly what our discussion of Nietzsche's rhetorical practice would lead us to think it is: a playful but radical rereading of the familiar. Nietzsche puts it as directly as could be at the end of number 382.:

Another ideal runs ahead of us...: the ideal of a spirit who plays naively—that is, not deliberately but from overflowing power and abundance—with all that was hitherto called holy, good, untouchable, divine...; the ideal of a human, superhuman well-being and benevolence that will often appear *inhuman*—for example, when it confronts all earthly seriousness so far, all

solemnity in gesture, word, tone, eye, morality, and task so far, as
if it were their most incarnate and involuntary parody—and in
spite of all this, it is perhaps only with him that *great seriousness*
really begins, that the real question mark is posed for the first
time.[22]

The fundamental Nietzschean project that he came to call the
"transvaluation" or "revaluation of all values" ("Umwertung aller
Werte") has as its other name "das rechte Lesen," right reading, and it
is less a doctrine than a practice. While orthodox thinkers—or even
some unorthodox ones such as Harold Bloom—might want to label
this practice *mis*reading, Nietzsche is explicit in calling it right,
correct, proper. It is a right and proper practice particularly because
it refuses to exclude the naively playful as a necessary part of
seriousness. The playful and the serious, the sad and the joyful, the
blues and the crickets, all belong together. The kind of philosophy
Nietzsche seeks is one which "die Grillen *nicht* verscheucht," that is,
does not banish the blues, nor the crickets, nor caprices and whims
(another figurative meaning of *Grillen*). These Grillen, one imagines,
are most likely to be found among the roses mentioned in "Scherz, List,
und Rache," those plants so full of tricks and teases, songs and
caprices—the roses that stand as a figure for the aphorisms of *The
Gay Science.*

Nietzsche's practice in *The Gay Science* has been very much in
accord with the advice given in number 383 by the "spirits of my own
book," as he calls them. He frequently calls upon the "Grillen" of the
verbal imagination to stimulate his philosophical invention.[23] He is not
embarrassed to resort openly to some of the least revered forms of
rhetorical whimsy, such as paronomasia. The pun on "Pfund'/Fund'"
in "Der Gründliche" is a taste of things to come, as for example in
number 310, which explicitly takes off from the phonological similarity of "Wille und Welle" ("will and wave"). Though not in verse, this
aphorism is really in many ways more of a poem than any of the
rhymes of "Scherz, List, und Rache." (One might recall also no. 22,
"L'ordre du jour pour le roi," which is also essentially poetic in its mode
of presentation.) It has a poetic quality because it presents and
elaborates an image asking for interpretation rather than proposing a
set of observations or opinions. But the image it presents—this
elaborate personification of breakers on a beach—is given *as a
reading* of the equation suggested by the paronomasia, the similarity
of will and wave, and thus defines sharply the parameters of
permissible interpretation. Everything that is said about the waves is

to be understood as somehow applicable to the will: "Thus live waves—thus live we who will—more I shall not say."[24]

Exactly this same paronomastic fancy shows itself elsewhere, as in number 371 ("We incomprehensible ones"), which depends on the interplay of *verwechseln*, *wechseln*, and *wachsen*: those who are incomprehensible are "misidentified" (*verwechselt*) precisely because "we ourselves keep growing [*wachsen*], keep changing [*wechseln*], we shed our old bark, we shed our skins every spring."[25] The phonological relationship between the German words for "misidentify," and "change," and "grow" is not exploited here because of any supposedly genuine connection between language and something we might want to call reality; it is on the contrary an explicitly rhetorical device, a trick, a caprice. It is a way of acknowledging that Nietzsche's "truth"is no more exempt from contamination by metaphor than anyone else's. Furthermore, it announces that Nietzsche's method of philosophical discovery is a form of rhetorical *inventio* that is quite content to plunder the storehouse of available signifiers for all the ideas it will yield up.

The authorial persona reads the mother tongue as if he were a Cratylist and believed in some deep and essential connection between signifier and signified; as if, that is, the phonological similarity between *Wille* and *Welle* or *wachsen* and *wechseln* reflected a similarity existing at some "deeper" level. But the Cratylism of such passages must be understood as nothing more than a heuristic device, since we know from numerous declarations on the subject ("On Truth and Lie" among them) that Nietzsche was as skeptical as could be about language as a repository of truth. The truth that Nietzsche proposes to have found here is one of his own manufacture, reached by attending scrupulously to the *surface* of the linguistic sign. He embraces the relationships among signifiers, not because he believes they reflect the relationships obtaining among things-in-themselves, but because that is all he has to work with. Nietzsche is filled with what he calls the "consciousness of appearance" (no. 54):

Appearance is for me that which lives and is effective and goes so far in its self-mocking that it makes me feel that this is appearance and will-o'-the-wisp and a dance of spirits and nothing more—that among all these dreamers, I, too, who "know," am dancing my dance; that the knower is a means for prolonging the earthly dance and thus belongs to the masters of ceremony of existence; and that the sublime consistence and interrelatedness of all knowledge perhaps is and will be the highest means to *preserve* the universality of dreaming and the mutual comprehension of all dreamers and thus also the *continuation of the dream.*[26]

Fancies like the elaborate discourse on Wille/Welle can only be understood as belonging to the dance of a "knower" engaged in preserving the universality of dreaming. It is one of Nietzsche's ways to be, like the Greeks, "superficial—*out of profundity*" ("oberflächlich—*aus Tiefe*").[27]

Nietzsche's inclination toward superficiality, his interest in exploiting the resources of language understood as surface, is matched by an equally strong urge toward depth. Being one of the "masters of ceremony of existence" requires something other than the kind of thoughtless assurance that goes with superficiality as we normally understand it. To be superficial out of profundity means to engage with the great sea of signifiers and to read it actively. You cannot be superficial in Nietzsche's sense by letting others read for you, by quietly accepting conventional interpretations as self-evidently correct. To let convention stand as truth—that is the surest way to be superficial out of superficiality. The great virtue of the artist/philosopher Nietzsche values so highly is that he is always active, always making his own readings, even rereading in a different way that which he had read before.

"Right reading" is thus an at whereby a particular human will engages the great, endlessly figurative body of language and makes his own sense of it. "The will to power *interprets*," and as Stanley Corngold observes, the Nietzschean self is nowhere more clearly in evidence than in its efforts at reading, including especially its attempts to read the self.[28] The interaction between language, a system of tropes received essentially fully formed and belonging to the community, and the will, the individual human self that is for Nietzsche not only *a* "generative concept"[29] but *the* generative concept par excellence. Everything of intellectual value arises out of this interaction, including that most fundamental of pholosophical goods, knowledge. We see Nietzsche working on precisely this problem—in a typically rhetorical way—in aphorism number 355 of *The Gay Science*, where he seeks to explain "the origin of our concept of 'knowledge'":

I take this explanation from the street. I heard one of the common people say, "he knew me right away." Then I asked myself: What is it that the common people take for knowledge?

What do they want when they want "knowledge"? Nothing more than this: Something strange is reduced to something familiar. And we philosophers—have we really meant *more* than this when we have spoken of knowledge?[30]

How much this passage depends on the process of reading the German language is in part revealed by the text's lack of any point in the English translation. Kaufmann was forced to employ a series of footnotes to alert the reader to the play on various expressions formed out of the verb *kennen*, but to a reader with no German the crux of the matter would still remain mysterious. That crux is of course that what is known (*Erkenntnis*) is, for a German-speaker, only a variation on what is familiar ("das Bekannte"). In English, the relationship between knowledge and familiarity is entirely semantic, but in German it is phonological and morphological as well, suggesting a stronger and deeper affiliation. The verb *erkennen*, from which is formed the term German philosophers use for "knowledge" (*Erkenntnis*), has in its everyday usage the sense of "recognize." The sentence Kaufmann translates as "he knew me right away" can also be rendered as "he recognized me," with the attendant connotation of perceived familiarity (*recognize* is *re-cognize*, that is, *know again*). Nietzsche analyzes the sentence "er hat mich erkannt" as meaning the equivalent of something like "er hat das Bekannte an mir gesehen," an analysis that is perfectly reasonable for such a sentence spoken on the street. From there Nietzsche reasons that the people of the "Volk" understand knowledge to be the rediscovery of something already known rather than the discovery of "new" facts or relationships.

In his commentary on this passage, Kaufmann suggests that Nietzsche may have been thinking primarily of Hegel in suggesting that philosophers have often considered knowledge in this same way. It is just as likely, though, that he was thinking of Plato and the very ancient tradition that all knowledge is in fact nothing more than a re-cognition or remembering (as in the famous geometry lesson in the *Meno*).[31] The truth (Greek *aletheia*) is that which is "un-forgotten." Nietzsche goes on to level a critique at such philosophers for thinking that the discovery of the familiar is the acquisition of knowledge ("was bekannt ist, ist erkannt"). The critique goes in a peculiarly Neitzschean direction, however, because Nietzsche is not entirely sure that "knowledge," in the sense of a fundamental grasping of something, really exists. The error of philosophers might not lie so much in taking up the common people's notion of knowledge-as-familiarity as in reformulating it in the high-sounding terms of epistemology.

Nietzsche understands "knowing" (*erkennen*) in a rather different way: for him it means "to see as a problem" ("als Problem zu sehen"), an approach that is hardest to take with something that is familiar.[32] *Erkennen* would thus be most difficult in the case of "das Bekannte," the familiar. Nietzsche implies, though he does not explicitly say, that the philosopher's task must in part be to take what is familiar and to see it as a problem. How does one do that? How does one "defamiliarize" the familiar? I borrow the language of Russian Formalism here, not to imply any kinship between that movement and Nietzsche's work, but to suggest the fundamentally literary and rhetorical dimensions of the issue. The process of making the familiar problematic is precisely the process we have seen again and again in Nietzsche's practice of rhetorical rereading. What could be more familiar to us than the language of daily life, expressions like "er hat mich erkannt" or "Siebensachen" or "das A und das O"? It takes a special sort of imagination to see these commonplaces as problematic, an imagination that Nietzsche understands as belonging to both the poet and the philosopher. The mainstream of the Western intellectual tradition has tended to view this verbal mode of imagination as exclusively literary, however, and to regard as unorthodox those philosophers like Heidegger (particularly of the post-*Kehre* years), Derrida, and Nietzsche himself who embrace it openly. But philosophy, like literature, may not be in a position to free itself from the verbal imagination without suffering a crippling impoverishment. Nietzsche indicates exactly what form that impoverishment can take: the limitation of philosophical knowledge to a set of transformations of the unfamiliar into the familiar. Such a limitation, were it successful, would leave entirely to literature the most difficult and perhaps the most important intellectual task, that of seeing the familiar as a problem.

9

Nietzsche's Physiology of Ideological Criticism

Claudia Crawford

I would like to interpret the *act* of ideological criticism from the standpoint of a specific model of unconscious physiological perception which Nietzsche offers in his notes for a "Course on Rhetoric" (1872-74) in combination with notes from 1872.[1] Nietzsche's model, which finds only imitation in the conscious forms of language, also operates as a paradigm informing the work of cultural and ideological criticism. As a ground for developing Nietzsche's physiological model of unconscious perception, I will use the opening pages of John Berger's *Ways of Seeing*, in which he differentiates his reading of Franz Hals's two paintings *Regents of the Old Men's Alms House* and *Regentesses of the Old Men's Alms House* from that of a traditional art historian. By appropriating Berger's critical act I enter into a necessary agonistics[2] of both physiological and ideological activity with the aim of demonstrating how ideological criticism, in general, inevitably participates in an unconscious physiology of power relations.

Each critical act forms, as one of the definitions of "critical" reminds us, a crisis, a decisive moment of risk and anxiety. One enters a struggle or contest in which an attempt is made, through strategic maneuvers, to transform anxiety into power. From a postmodern perspective, it is not exactly a deconstruction of Berger's text which I offer; rather, the text serves as a paradigmatic example of ideological criticism useful for my argument. Of course, all criticism is ideological, as any evaluation, judgment, or critique inevitably arises within a specific historical moment. Therefore, ideology should be analysed as a separate yet inseparable element of criticism. Before I proceed to Nietzsche's model and my analysis of Berger's text, a few theoretical considerations may be helpful.

PHYSIOLOGY

A prerequisite to my discussion is a general understanding of Nietzsche's use of the term "physiology." Physiology is a complex element of Nietzsche's philosophy consisting of at least three differing perspectives. First, Nietzsche uses the term "physiology" in accordance with its general understanding as dealing with the primarily biological functions and vital processes of living organisms. In his reading of the natural and physical sciences, Nietzsche's interest in human physiology centered primarily upon discussions of human sensory perception, instinctual needs, and matters of preservation and enhancement of physiological functions.

Second, Nietzsche takes the point of view that the physiology which conditions the bodily existence of human beings provides the foundation or unconscious forms of their respective factual or conscious understanding of themselves. For example, in *Beyond Good and Evil*, Nietzsche writes: "By far the greater part of conscious thinking must still be included among instinctive activities, and that goes even for philosophical thinking... Behind all logic and its seeming sovereignty of movement, too, there stand valuations or, more clearly, physiological demands for the preservation of a certain type of life" (*BGE* 11).

Third, Nietzsche understands the physiological process as the struggle for domination among a number of interpreting power centers in the human being. "Every single drive would like only too well to present just *itself* as the ultimate purpose of existence and the legitimate *master* of all the other drives. For every drive wants to be master—and it attempts to philosophize in *that spirit*" (*BGE* 13-14).[3] Furthermore, on a social level, Nietzsche understands this physiological struggle of forces of preservation and enhancement of power as the determining factor in the ascent or decline of whole cultures, moralities, races, and so forth. Nietzsche suggests that an understanding of the "hegemony of physiology over theology, moralism, economics, and politics" might function as one of the most favorable remedies to the problems of modernity (*WP* no. 126).

The variability of the significations for the concept "physiology" which we find here, as biology, as the prerequisite for consciousness and as a process of struggle for power in connection with individuals, societies, and the human species, should warn us against assuming that it operates as any kind of fundamental "truth" for Nietzsche. Nietzsche's model of physiological perception details the unconscious operations by which the "human organization" masters the vast field of undifferentiated sensory stimuli. Perception is the expression of forces which appropriate nature. In the unconscious stages of the physiological production of images,[4] dominations operate, power determinations are applied, territories are marked out. "Our most sacred convictions, the changing elements in our supreme values, are judgments of our muscles" (*WP* no. 314). The unconscious figuration which leads to our cognition is ultimately a sign language for the body. "The unconscious disguise of physiological needs under the cloaks of the objective, ideal, purely spiritual goes to frightening lengths—and often I have asked myself whether taking a large view philosophy has not been merely an interpretation of the body and a *misunderstanding of the body*" (*GS* 34-35).

Nietzsche's application of physiology and the various definitions of its operations function within the thematics of the will to power, which I think Foucault has characterized rather well in *The History of Sexuality*:

Power must be understood in the first instance as the multiplicity of force relations immanent in the sphere in which they operate and which constitute their own organization; as the process which, through ceaseless struggles and confrontations, transforms, strengthens, or reverses them; as the support which these force relations find in one another, thus forming a chain or system, or on the contrary, the disjunctions and contradictions which isolate them from one another; and lastly, as the strategies in which they take effect, whose general design or institutional crystallization is embodied in the state apparatus, in the formulation of the law, in the various social hegemonies. [*HS* 92-93]

For Nietzsche, however, the power relationships which form social hegemonies are dependent upon or function in relationship with the hegemonies of bodily power relationships.[5] "The will to power 'appropriates' in the organism, before the 'name of man' may be broached." It is in terms of the body and power that language, its unconscious physiological operations and its conscious ideological creations, can be understood.

RHETORIC

Nietzsche's model is a rhetorical model.[6] In "Course on Rhetoric," Nietzsche writes: "The force [*Kraft*] which Aristotle called rhetoric, the power of unravelling, disentangling and of evaluating each thing, the effective force which makes its impression is the essence of language" (R 298). Rhetoric, by nature persuasion, at its most basic level seeks to wield power; it is the form of force which seeks to make its impression.

Nietzsche's rhetorical model emphasizes and expands upon the idea that conscious language is constituted as an *imitation* of the completely unconscious operations of tropology. "It is not difficult to demonstrate that what is called 'rhetorical,' as the devices of a conscious art, has been present as a device of unconscious art in language and its development" (R 297-98). In addition, I want to emphasize two collateral elements of its operation. First, as I have already noted, the model is grounded in physiological or organic impulses: "The man who forms language knows nothing of things or events, but of *excitations*" (R 298). A sensation takes the place of the thing itself. "In place of the thing, the sensation is nothing but a *mark*" (R 298). Second, Nietzsche's model of unconscious perception and its rhetorical strategies rely upon our conscious ideological positioning at any given time. The "sensation is then figured in an exterior sense by an image" (R 298). The character of the image which figures the excitation is determined only by the relationship that the perceiver has with the excitation, that is, it is determined by the "proper persuasion" of the perceiver at the moment of awareness of excitation. The basic rule of rhetoric for Nietzsche is that "rhetoric is only able to transmit a belief [*doxa*], and not a knowledge [*episteme*]" (R 298). "Believing is the primal beginning even in every sense impression: a kind of affirmation the first intellectual activity! A 'holding true' in the beginning!" (*WP* no. 506). The "proper persuasion," the "belief," the "holding true," arise out of ideological evaluations.

PHYSIOLOGY AND IDEOLOGY

Individuals and Societies

With regard to the individual, Nietzsche emphasizes that one is first a physiological being. The physiological or material condition is first; the ideological interpretation is added.[7] The subtitle of *Ecce Homo*, "How one becomes what one is," presents the essential question of the subject for Nietzsche and of postmodern definitions of the subject in general. Nietzsche does not write "How one becomes *who* one is" but rather "How one becomes *what* one is." The emphasis is not only on the *how* of the constitution of subjectivity but on the transformation of subjectivity into a "what."

First, one is a physiological economy of forces, an "instinct of self-defense" and prudence where energy is not wasted, where saying no as rarely as possible, having open hands, reacting as rarely as possible become the "issuing commandment" of self-preservation (*EH* 252). Nietzsche's economy of forces which make up the "what" of the subject reveals physiological strategies of power: protection, concentration of energies, and emergence of power.

Second, one is a variable field of power relationships rooted in specific historical and ideologically constituted discursive and nondiscursive moments. Foucault: "Discourse is not the majestically unfolding manifestation of a thinking, knowing, speaking subject, but, on the contrary, a totality, in which the dispersion of the subject and his discontinuity with himself may be determined" (*A* 55). Nietzsche: "To become what one is one must not have the faintest notion of *what* one is." For Nietzsche, the interchanges of the physiological and ideological economies of the individual do not arise as the result of the conscious willing of self-possessed subjects; rather, they are the result of unconscious instinctual operations.

> *Theory and Practice.*—Fateful distinction, as if there were an actual *drive for knowledge* that, without regard to questions of usefulness and harm, went blindly for the truth; and then, separate from this, the whole world of *practical* interests—I tried to show, on the other hand, what instincts have been active behind all these *pure* theoreticians—how they have all, under the spell of their instincts, gone fatalistically for something that was 'truth' *for them*—for them and only for them. The conflict between different systems, including that between epistemological scruples, is a conflict between quite definite instincts (forms of vitality, decline, classes, races, etc.). [*WP* no. 423)

Nietzsche questions the binarity and opposition of theory/practice, true/false, conscious/instinctual. For Nietzsche, ideologies, "truths," arise out of the physiological conflict of instincts of vitality and decline. However, in a circular movement, he also indicates that our initial physiological perceptions are conditioned by our ideological thinking, our particular "beliefs" and "proper persuasions."

In a parallel sense, the plurality and relativity of ideologies, according to Nietzsche, are necessary in the service of the utility, preservation, and growth of societies: "The continuum: marriage, property, language, tradition, tribe, family, people, state, are continuums of lower and higher orders. Their economy resides in the preponderance of the advantages of uninterrupted work.... The advantage resides in the fact that interruptions are avoided and losses that would arise from them are saved. Nothing is more costly than a beginning" (*WP* no. 731). What is in the interests of a society at a given moment of history will determine history's continuums of ideology. During the creative moments of a state, certain types of ideology are necessary to reinforce the dangerous drives, the enterprising spirit, foolhardiness, vengefulness, rapacity, and lust to rule. But once a community is fixed and is secure from external danger, many of the opposite ideologies become advantageous for its preservation and growth. Everything that elevates an individual above the herd is negated or eliminated, and new ideologies turn to values of fairness, modesty, submissiveness, and conformity (*BGE* 113-14). "We 'know' (or believe or imagine) just as much as may be *useful* in the interests of the human herd, the species; and even what is here called 'utility' is ultimately also a mere belief, something imaginary."

For Nietzsche ideologies do not operate *only* as a disguised form of oppression in the maintenance of a certain ruling class, although he does recognize their usefulness especially "between those who command and those who obey," but as signs or symptoms of physiological states of survival and growth in general (*GS* 298). The idea that ideology operates as a sort of veil covering over a "true" state of affairs to which the subject needs access in order to act effectively would constitute a new form of idealism for Nietzsche.[8]

Relationship between Language and Ideology

In *The Gay Science* Nietzsche writes: "The development of language and the development of consciousness go hand in hand," and *"consciousness has developed only under the pressure of the need for communication"* (*GS* 298). Thus consciousness is always positional, always historical, always bound up with relations of power of the social or herd. Ultimately, language and consciousness are ideological. "My idea is that consciousness does not really belong to man's individual existence but rather to his social or herd nature... consequently, given the best will in the world to... 'know ourselves' each of us will always succeed in becoming conscious only of what is not individual but 'average'" (*GS* 299). But Nietzsche also points to unconscious work as being an order of its own: "We could think, feel, will, and remember, and we could also 'act' in every sense of that word, and yet none of all this would have to 'enter our consciousness' (as one says metaphorically)" (*GS* 297).

Thus our unconscious could be a set of relations independent of language, but Nietzsche emphasizes that this is not the case: "Our thoughts themselves are continually governed by the character of consciousness—by the 'genius of the species' that commands it—and translated back into the perspective of the herd.... This is the essence of phenomenalism and perspectivism as I understand them: Owing to the nature of animal consciousness, the world of which we can become conscious is only a surface and sign-world" (*GS 299*). The realm of the physiological and unconscious perception of stimuli is not free of ideological influence. "The emergence of our sense impressions into our own consciousness, the ability to fix them, and, as it were, exhibit them externally, increased proportionately with the need to communicate them to others by means of signs" (*GS* 299). Thus ideologies, formulated in social language, offer the conscious form of unconscious physiological instincts and drives. In *Daybreak* Nietzsche points to an alternative sign system and suggests that one ought to look for the signs of physiological phenomena in an attempt to understand a particular ideological position. "It is always necessary to draw forth the *signs* ... that is to say, the *physiological* phenomenon behind the moral predispositions and prejudices—so as not to become the fools of reverence and injurers of knowledge" (*D* 214).

Postmodern readings assume the perspective that unconscious operations are unavoidably involved in the production of the subject and his language. In this regard Nietzsche and Lacan can be profitably paired for their readings, which conceive of the unconscious no longer as an exclusively private region inside us but as an effect of our relations with one another within specific cultural contexts. Nietzsche and Lacan understand language as the locus in which these relations are figured. Furthermore, the individual is not in control of language, with the result that subjects are constituted in an ongoing process of conflicting symbolic or ideological identifications which correspond to repressed desires and the struggle for power to satisfy and enhance such desires.[9] Nietzsche: "The assumption of one single subject is perhaps unnecessary, perhaps it is just as permissible to assume a multiplicity of subjects, whose interaction and struggle is the basis of our thought and our consciousness in general?" (*WP* no. 490).

THE TEXTS OF IDEOLOGICAL CRITICISM

Nietzsche asserts that unconscious language operates only upon the basis of sensations or "marks" in the place of things, and conscious language upon "signs" based upon those marks, with the result that ideological interpretation never concerns the object interpreted. The object or text only exists as a question of language, as a sign or symptom of contending physiological and ideological forces. Nietzsche: "No, [objective] facts are precisely what there is not, only interpretations. We cannot establish any fact 'in itself'"(*WP* no. 481). This critique of the object, whether it be a work of art or the center of a philosophical concern is by now a common theme in postmodernism. The tendency to think of language in terms of referents and words pointing to referents is resisted. After Foucault, discourses are treated no longer as groups of signs (signifying elements referring to contents or representations) but as practices that form the objects of which they speak. An appeal to the text as evidence or proof no longer functions in postmodern perspectives because it is the play of forces and ideological positions worked in language that are at stake in the critical act. As Stanley Fish writes: "Disagreements are not settled by the facts, but are the means by which the facts are settled" (WMIA 338). From this perspective, Berger is not interpreting Hals's paintings anew but is waging a battle against the language of the art historian. The paintings are only the occasion for a momentary linguistic play of forces in which meaning arises from the physiological force which appropriates and takes possession. Nietzsche: "Interpretation is itself a means of becoming master of something. (The organic process constantly presupposes interpretations)" (*WP* no. 643). Thus ideological critique of an object always recreates the object in language and cannot refer to an essence or thing in itself.

ACCOUNTABILITY VERSUS SEDUCTION

Berger's Marxist reading of Hals's paintings appears to conform in several respects to the postmodern perspectives just discussed. Berger writes: "The way we see things is affected by what we know or believe" (*WS* 8). "We are always looking at the relation between things and ourselves" (*WS* 9). And Berger also appears to adopt the subject as process: "The relation between what we see and what we know is never settled" (*WS* 7). Berger's is a phenomenological reading, however, rather than one conducted from a postmodern or

Nietzschean perspectivist point of view. Phenomenological interpretation privileges the activity of a self-possessed consciousness in its relationship with objects. Berger conducts his analysis under the auspices of "scientific language." He dons the mask of "objectivity," using the "evidence" of the paintings themselves: "study this evidence and judge for yourselves" (*WS* 13). Berger defines the "seduction" of Hals's paintings as their ability to work on us because of our shared ideological "knowledge"; he stresses historically specific meaning and the fact that the painting has been constituted through particular signifying practices meaningful to us because we share comparable social relations. Berger's ideological criticism is framed to enable his readers to "see" through the mystification of the bourgeois art historian. "If we 'saw' the art of the past, we would situate ourselves in history... in order to choose and to act" (*WS* 33).

Thus Berger's analysis betrays its investment in the ability of consciousness to describe, be objective, and have knowledge about things, in order to make judgments of value. In fact Berger reinforces this interpretation himself: "The world-as-it-is is more than pure objective fact, it includes consciousness" (*WS* 11). Berger's ideological reading of the history of the Western oil painting tradition is not aimed at "truth" in some absolute sense but at changing the perception of that tradition in order to create a new basis for activity. The art of the past has lost its "authority." "What matters now is who uses that language for what purpose.... A people or a class which is cut off from its own past is far less free to choose and to act as a people or class than one that has been able to situate itself in history. This is why— and this is the only reason why—the entire art of the past has now become a political issue" (*WS* 33).

The discourse of Berger's critical act, however, aims at a "truth" of another kind because it demands that such a critical discourse operate through fundamental processes of valuation and accountability. The discourse of ideological criticism, even when it is freed from some absolute truth, still implies a thetic position—explicit or not—in the form of a "thou shalt"/"thou shalt not." No matter what the theoretical objective, the critical act constructs a source, an audience, and a space of discourse which builds a representation of "the strong" and "the weak," those able to act with power (and thus, covertly, "with truth") and those who are unable to act with power. Nietzsche: "Every table of values, every 'thou shalt' known to history or ethnology, requires first a *physiological* investigation and interpretation, rather than a psychological one" (*GM* 55).

The point at which a relevant critique of Berger's ideological reading becomes possible, from Nietzsche's perspective, might find its metaphorical axis between the two words: accountability and seduction. For Berger, language functions as a vehicle of conscious explanation and judgment leading to the possibility of responsible action, whereas, for Nietzsche, language operates under the rubric of seduction. Language leads astray, it persuades not to responsibilty but rather to "wrongdoing." Nietzsche writes: "A quantum of force is equivalent to a quantum of drive, will, effect—more, it is nothing other than precisely this very driving, willing, effecting, and *only owing to the seduction of language*... which conceives and misconceives all effects and conditioned by something that causes effects, by a 'subject' can it appear otherwise" (*GM* 45).

For Nietzsche language is action, it is power, and it is, in the first instance, a physiological force. But language deceives and covers over the actuality of its birth in force and power relationships of force. Ideological discourse, like Berger's, talks about power and the effects of power as if they were something separate from the very instance of language used, as if language were a metadiscourse on power. Every instance of language is involved in a dynamics of physiological and ideological power relationships and persuasive techniques. "What the belief in a 'subject' allows is that the weak may be allowed to ask of the strong that they be accountable" (*GM* 45). Because ideological criticism usually participates in an attempt to unmask the "false" representation and liberate the "true" representation, it participates very fundamentally in the values of accountability and forgets itself as an instance of the seduction of language. Ideology is physiology translated through forgetfulness by the seduction of language.

AGONISTICS: TWO TYPES OF CRITICAL CONTEST

If one adopts Nietzsche's perspectives concerning the ongoing physiological and ideological constitution of the subject, the relationship of language both to the unconscious and to the object of critical analysis, then, it appears that ideological criticism no longer operates to reveal the "truth of the text," rather, it aims to intervene in the dynamics of power relations in and around the text so as to alter them.[10]

To back one interpretation is to declare war on another, if only for a given period of time in a specific social and historical context. Here, reference to Sam Weber's discussion of Nietzsche's *agonistics* reminds us, once again, that Nietzsche, and many postmodern interpretations, revolve around the aporia. In "Homer's Contest" ("Homer's Wettkampf"), a posthumouly published fragment written in 1872 as Nietzsche was developing his rhetorical model of language, he defines two types of contest integral to Homeric and pre-Homeric Greece which arose from the discord of envy (Eris). Nietzsche writes: "Hesiod calls one Eris evil—namely, the one that leads men into hostile fights of annihilation against one another—while praising another Eris as good—the one that, as jealously, hatred, and envy, spurs men to activity: not to the activity of fights of annihilation but to the activity of fights which are *contests*" (HC 35).

Weber transfers these distinctions into the thematics of game. The type of struggle connected with annihilation (*Vernichtungskampf*) is understood as a means to a "finality determined outside the game" (*JG* 105). The contest proper (*Wettkampf*), on the other hand, is struggle as an end in itself. While the first annihilates the opponent, the second operates through a mechanism of *ostracism* the spirit of which is contained in these lines from the Ephesians when they banish Hermodorus: "Among us, no one shall be the best; but if someone is, then let him be elsewhere and among others" (*HC* 36). If someone is the best, the game or contest can never begin. It is this exclusion, Weber writes; "which makes it possible for the agonistic field to define itself and especially, to maintain itself—to stay in the game...And if ostracism thus becomes the indispensable condition for the continuation of the contest, it is because the latter is understood from the start as a movement not of identity, but of otherness" (*JG* 106).

If the game holds itself as autonomous, it becomes self-destructive, for then its aim is the elimination of the other upon whom it nevertheless depends. Nietzsche writes that, if the contest proper is removed from Greek life, "we immediately look into that pre-Homeric abyss of a terrifying savagery of hatred and lust to annihilate" (*HC* 38). On the basis of this statement, Weber maintains that the fight of annihilation cannot be regarded as simply external to the contest or agon, properly speaking, because the fight of annihilation by its presence also makes the contest possible creating "two sides of a single—ambivalent—dynamic." Weber writes:

Agonistics, according to Nietzsche, always contains an element of domination, a desire to lay hold of the other, to curtail the otherness upon which the agonistics nevertheless depends. Agonistics is necessarily ambivalent, and the only question—the question animating Nietzsche's text—concerns the manner in which it tries to assume that ambivalence. The answer given in Nietzsche's text is to show how the Greeks succeeded in recognizing their identity as players as the effect of an irreducible otherness. [*JG* 107]

The fight of annihilation represents a form of criticism which Weber calls "prescription." It is a critical discourse which "attempts to hide its local determination behind an obligation claiming to come out of nowhere"; it makes the impossible attempt to "dissociate itself from its other" (*JG* 107-08). Its judgments call for accountability leading to an effect outside of the game. Thus, because the fight of annihilation takes its departure from outside itself and also has an end in view outside of itself, it operates only as a means. The contest proper, on the other hand, falls into the realm of seduction. It is criticism for its own sake, an agonistics of the will to power, which recognizes the ostracized other as integral to its activity and the annihilation of the other as its own downfall. For the contest proper the space of a game is created, but it is a space which recognizes its debt to and connection with that which is temporarily ostracized.

NIETZSCHE'S MODEL

Above I have described an agonistics of the cultural critical act. Nietzsche's physiological model of unconscious perception represents an agonistics and game of another sort.[11] In "On Truth and Lies in a Nonmoral Sense," Nietzsche writes his by now well-known formula of language: "To being with, a nerve stimulus is transferred into an image: first metaphor. The image, in turn, is imitated in sound: second metaphor" (*TL* 82). Nietzsche's model is his attempt to map out the mechanisms of the *first* metaphor, of the unconscious physiological processes leading from stimulus to image. Out of the chaos of stimuli, the space of a contest must be created in which a certain species is able to live. The rhetorical strategies of this contest depend upon the thematics of unconscious seduction in the sense of deception, of language's ability to lead astray. The strategies of this seduction include, at the beginning, and as precondition for all the others, ostracism/exclusion (*weglassen, übersehen, überhören*), then the activities of displacement (*umdeuten*), transposition (*Übertragung*), marking (*Bezeichnung*), and commutation (*Vertauschung*) follow. It is a "tricky" agonistics we conduct with ourselves to gain the power of the victor.[12] The five specific steps of Nietzsche's model place Berger's critical act in the context of the rhetorical seductions of unconscious perception.

Synecdoche/Ostracism

Nietzsche's first unconscious perceptual operation is synecdoche. We look, and synecdoche begins its work. Synecdoche in the unconscious reception of stimuli functions in a manner which indicates that "a partial perception introduces itself in place of the full and entire vision" (R 299). Synecdoche allows the "inexactitude of sight" (*PT* no. 54). It is the power within us "which permits the *major* features of the mirror image to be perceived with greater intensity. Its chief means are omitting, overlooking, and ignoring (*weglassen, übersehen, überhören*)." "Then we artistically add something to this by reinforcing the main features and forgetting the secondary ones," according to our persuasion, our particular relationship with things (*PT* nos. 54, 55). This process yields what Nietzsche calls "the most primal images." The operation of synecdoche selects and reinforces "its own persuasion," its particular "relationship with things," its unconscious, conscious, and ideological positions, in order to gain control over other forces. What does not have relevance in the perceptual moment is overlooked, omitted, repressed. Synecdoche as ostracism bars numerous stimuli so as to create a space for certain stimuli, those that do not annihilate the perceiver but are circumscribed to allow him to begin a contest of power and domination.

Berger opens his dicussion of the nature of seeing by writing: "Seeing is not mechanical reaction to stimuli. We see only what we look at. To look is an act of choice" (*WS* 8). In this phenomenological sense, Berger is aware that in looking at Hals's paintings, he synecdochizes a partial perception, that he chooses to see specific elements of the paintings according to his Marxist assumptions, according to his persuasion. What does Berger select and reinforce? What does he overlook, omit, repress? Both Berger and the art historian see the human figures which constitute the primary subject of the paintings, but of what do these human forms consist for each, according to Berger? For Berger, "the people, gestures, faces, and the institutions" they represent can be recognized and reinforced by us because they "correspond to our own observation . . . because we still live in a society of comparable social relations and moral values" (*WS* 14). He sees "the new characters and expressions of captialism," and "the administrators of public charity" in the human forms Hals represents. He represses among many other possibilities those elements which the art historian synecdochizes: "each woman," the "pattern of heads and hands," "vivid flesh tones," "deep glowing blacks," all a more literal reading of the elements of the composition of the painting. The art historian's synecdochizing process, Berger claims, stems from his "way of seeing," which takes the composition of the paintings "as if they were the emotional charge of the painting," thus transferring the image "from the plane of lived experience," to that of disinterested "art appreciation" (*WS* 13).

In this first step of synecdochization, Berger is aware that he chooses and reinforces elements of Hals's painting different from those of the art historian because he is focused on social reality, but is he as aware that he has staged the arena for a critical conflict by exaggerating the poles of the struggle in language? Nietzsche: "Course of the struggle: the fighter tries to transform his opponent into his *antithesis...*, as if his opponent were attacking reason, taste, virtue. The struggle compels to such an exaggeration" (*WP* no. 348). Berger's eye is focused and synecdochizes much more on the art historian's language than upon the elements of the painting. According to Berger, what the art historian synecdochizes is "mystification," "disinterested," "unchanging," and is "no better and no worse than the average." But look at the words Berger applies to his own synecdochizing activity: it is concerned with "lived experience," "conflict," "drama," "psychological and social urgency." The effectiveness of Berger's analysis and what impresses it upon our memories is not that we have come away with a different image of the figures in Hals's painting but rather that we have been implicated in a forceful instance of persuasive technique.

In the first moment of synecdochization, however, Berger views more than Hals's paintings and the language of the art historian. His critical act is, in a much more comprehensive sense, embedded in complicated networks of power between socioeconomic and cultural relationships and unconscious physiological instincts. Berger's critical act not only involves a synecdochization of a whole array of strategic procedures which serve to preserve his economic position, his relationship to peers, to his audience, and to his own unconscious needs but also operates as a nexus from which he seeks to enhance these. From this complex relationship of forces, Berger synecdochizes elements most advantageous to furthering this multiplicity of physiological aims within the specific critical context toward increasing his power. My own "inexactitude of sight" and operations of synecdochization, and Nietzsche's, are implicated in the same process.

Metaphor 1, Displacement: Forgetting

After the profusion of possible stimuli are reduced and reinforced into specific images, the second unconscious rhetorical operation begins: metaphor. Nietzsche distinguishes and defines three functions of unconscious metaphor. The first function is displacement (*umdeuten*) of signification (R 299). Here the individual in perception is forgotten in favor of tried images (see *TL* 83). This forgetting takes place through an unconscious process which Nietzsche calls "primal thinking" or "unconscious inference," which is imitation or comparison through analogical inference, identifying like with like. "Imitation presupposes first the reception of an image and then a continuous translation of the received image into a thousand metaphors all of which are efficacious" (*PT* no. 147). "The so called unconscious inferences can be traced back to the all-preserving memory, which presents us with experiences of a parallel sort and thus is acquainted in advance with the consequences of an action. It is not an anticipation of the effects (as in cause); it is rather the feeling 'similar causes, similar effects,' which is generated by a remembered image" (*PT* no. 115). This process extends to memory and the repetition of similar stimuli and metaphors "in the course of which related images from a variety of categories flock together." "Unconscious thinking must take place apart from concepts: it must therefore occur in perceptions" (*PT* no. 116).

> It is a matter of memory and sensation that when one substance comes into contact with another it decides in just *the way that it does*. At one time or another it *learned* to do so. Only like receives like: a physiological process...The same nervous activity produces the same image again. [*PT* no. 97]

> Thus there is sought not only some kind of explanation as cause, but a *selected and preferred* kind of explanation, the kind by means of which the feeling of the strange, new, unexperienced is most speedily and most frequently abolished—the *most common* explanations. Consequence: a particular kind of cause ascription comes to preponderate more and more, becomes concentrated into a system and finally comes to *dominate* over the rest, that is to say simply to exclude *other* causes and explanations.— The banker thinks at once of 'business,' the Christian of 'sin,' the girl of her love. [*TI* 497-98]

In this operation Nietzsche again emphasizes that the physiology of unconscious perception, in its connection with memory, operates according to ideological persuasion; it displaces, or arranges images "in just the way that it does" because it has "learned" to do so. In the space of the contest trusted "weapons" are brought forward.

Berger draws specific analogies according to "learned" or memorized metaphors arising from his persuasion. Berger has synecdochized or perceived elements of the painting and the language of the art historian which can be analyzed with his set of cause-effect memories. His Marxist presuppositions locate his perceptions in the economic and political setting in which the paintings find themselves. The paintings were "officially commissioned"; Hals was an old man of over eighty. He was destitute; most of his life he had been in debt, and he would have frozen to death if he had not been given three loads of peat by the administrators of charity whom he paints. Berger writes that the art historian records these facts and then "explicitly says that it would be incorrect to read into the paintings any criticism of the sitters. There is no evidence, he says, that Hals painted them in a spirit of bitterness" (*WS* 13). Berger sets up the art historian as naive and uncaring.

By focusing on Hals's economic position and his exploitation at the hands of the bourgeois administrators of an economic system with which we share "comparable social relations and moral values," Berger unconsciously makes rhetorical use of his reader's feelings of guilt, anger, and pity. He is implicated in the thematics of *ressentiment* and the fight of annihilation. Berger then aligns his readers with himself as having a certain righteous knowledge: "We do not accept Hals's sitters innocently." In his metaphorical displacements, Berger leaves the painting altogether and attempts rhetorically to persuade his audience, to intensify the poles of the struggle. The types of ideological analogies which Berger uses concern not only Marxist beliefs but also ideologies of moral responsibility, guilt, and pity. These learned inferences both helped produce Berger's original perceptions and continually reinforce them.

The traditional art historian, Berger tells us, is affected "by a whole series of learnt assumptions about art. Assumptions concerning: Beauty, Truth, Genius, Civilization, Form, Status, Taste, etc." (*WS* 11). "Many of these assumptions," writes Berger, "no longer accord with the world as it is"; they are "out of true with the present" (*WS* 11). Berger's staging of the perceptions of the art historian allows him to suggest that the art historian reinforces his synecdochization of Hals's painting with such unconscious analogical inferences as "life's vital forces," "the human condition," and "harmonious fusion," all elements of what Berger labels "disinterested art appreciation" stemming from a traditional humanistic viewpoint, disinterestedness which reflects an imaginary ideological stance under which the very real interestedness of the bourgeois art historian is hidden.

Berger presents himself as astute at unmasking the actual power plays and "learnt assumptions" inherent in the analysis and language of the art historian while remaining uncritical of his own. Berger writes: "In this confrontation the Regents and Regentesses stare at Hals, a destitute old painter who has lost his reputation and lives off public charity; he examines them through the eyes of a pauper who must nevertheless try to be objective, i.e., must try to surmount the way he sees as a pauper. This is the drama of these paintings" (*WS* 15). But this is also the drama of Berger's critical act. In the confrontation which Berger sets up between himself and the bourgeois art historian, Berger feels that he, too, must try to be objective, must try to surmount his "subjectivity."

When the metaphorical analogies of this second step of unconscious perception are made, certain analogies are to be masked under the guise of objective, scientific language. The physiological reactions of anger and bitterness, the will to dominate and to alter power relations, which constitute the basis of Berger's language, are to be repressed and formulated in an acceptable moral dialogue which calls forth our feelings of guilt and pity not only for Hals but for ourselves as well. In this sense, Berger's rhetoric betrays the actual physiological stakes in any critical act which seeks to appropriate, transform, and become master of the various discourses and power relations surrounding it.

Metaphor 2, Transposition: Positioning of the Subject

Nietzsche's rhetorical model of unconscious perception then continues with the very crucial second type of metaphorical operation, which consists of two steps of transposition (*Übertragung*): "space into time and time into causality" (R 299). The operation of transposition designates the process of moving something from one sphere into an entirely different one. "The combination of a felt stimulus and a glance at a movement produces causality" (*PT* no. 139). This process of metaphorization allows the step which "transfers personal psychological impulses into an impersonal world" (*PT* nos. 116, 144). *This is the set of operations by which the "subject" is constituted.* "The transposition which takes place and begins to allow the positing of an external world occurs when the sensation is identified with the sense" (*PT* no. 140).

In itself all that is given is a stimulus; it is a causal inference to feel this stimulus as an activity of the eye and to call it "seeing."

The first causal sensation occurs when a "stimulus is felt as an activity," when something passive is sensed as something active... The inner connection of stimulus and activity is transferred to all things. *The eye acts upon a stimulus,* i.e., it sees. We explain the world to ourselves in terms of our sensory functions, i.e., we presuppose causality everywhere, because we ourselves *continually experience* alterations of this sort. [*PT* no. 139]

Again, all perception of time and space pertains to the perceiver. The perceiver who is unconsciously appropriating and dominating the excitations and images puts herself in the active role, believes that her eye, and by implication, that she herself, is the cause of what is experienced. "Psychological history of the concepts 'subject.' The body, thing, the 'whole' construed by the eye, awaken the distinction between a deed and a doer; the doer, the cause of the deed, conceived ever more subtly, finally left behind the 'subject'" (*WP* no. 547).[13] Why, according to Nietzsche, is the subject a necessary construct? It is constituted out of fear and the desire to overpower that fear. It is the agonistic moment when anxiety must be turned to power. "The supposed instinct for causality is only fear of the unfamiliar and the attempt to discover something familiar in it—a search, not for causes, but for the familiar" (*WP* no. 551). Nietzsche compares this process to that of the amoeba: "The process of making equal is the same as the incorporation of appropriated material in the amoeba," which continually makes what it appropriates equal to itself and arranges it into its own forms and ranks (*WP* no. 501).[14]

Berger takes a position of power as subject through the transpositioning of space into time and time into causality. He orients himself historically in time and space, the space of bourgeois culture with time being "a sort of corridor from Hals to us." Both place him in a privileged position, at the center of the critical act as subject, as cause of what he "sees." Berger describes the art historian as positioning himself as a sort of omniscient and omnipresent subject, one who can speak with knowledge of "the unchanging human condition" (*WS* 13), who can "see" inside Hals, into his "personal vision," which "heightens our awe for the ever-increasing power of the mighty impulses that enabled him to give us a close view of life's vital forces" (*WS* 16). Again, Berger sets up the poles of a conflict between the art historian, as an omniscient "god figure," and himself as a historical human being. On the level of conscious cultural criticism this positioning appears natural and necessary.

This positioning of the "subject Berger," however, must again be seen in terms of physiological necessity not only with regard to Hals's paintings and the art historian but as a positioning in his world as a whole. Berger speaks from many locations and from many instances of causality. In each moment the "subject Berger" is similarly constituted, according to Nietzsche, from fear of the unfamiliar and the need to situate himself continually. He must continually create motivations arising from physiological and ideological positions which allow him to remain at the center where the diversity becomes manageable because of its causal reference to him. In order to become master over the multitude of undifferentiated stimuli, in order to find a position in time, space, and causal perspectives from which to enter the realm of communication and the counteractions of cultural evaluation, Berger must continually perform these metaphorical operations of transposition and domination. The positioning of the subject as able to dominate and control first, undifferentiated stimuli, then language, and ultimately cultural evaluations is a continual unconscious process.

Metaphor 3, Marking: Grammatical Categories

The third function of metaphor in Nietzsche's rhetorical model of perception is the marking or designation of grammatical genres. "Metaphor is also shown in the designation of genus; the *genus* in the grammatical sense, is a luxury of language and pure metaphor" (R 299). "All grammar is the product of that which one calls figural discourse *figurae sermonis*" (R 300). The genus of grammar indicated as subject is what Nietzsche calls a "semiotic" for an operation of human relations to stimuli. "Subject, object, a doer added to the doing, the doing separate from that which it does: let us not forget that this is mere semiotics and nothing real" (*WP* no. 634). Once the positioning activity of a "subject" has been established, all other grammatical relationships become possible. First, given the verb in its active sense, the action to which an actor is added becomes possible. "Two things, a particular sensation and a particular visual image, always appear together. That the one is the cause of the other is a *metaphor borrowed from will and act*: an analogical inference. The intention or willing yields the *nomina*; the acting, the *verba*" (*PT* no. 139).

The predicate and object follow. "From *quality and act*: One of our properties leads us to act, whereas it is in reality the case that we infer from acting to properties. Since we see actions of a particular

kind we assume the existence of properties. Thus, action comes first;
we connect it with a property. The word for the action originates first;
then the word for the quality is derived from it" (*PT no.* 139). The
continual process of "marking" out this unconscious grammar functions to situate the perceiving subject in time and space and with
reference to causality. "'Subject,' 'object,' 'attribute'—these distinctions are fabricated and are now imposed as a schematism upon all
the apparent facts. The fundamental false observation is that I believe
it is *I* who do something, suffer something, 'have' something, 'have a
quality'" (*WP* no. 549). Nietzsche takes the position that grammatical
forms govern speculation precisely because they lie unconsciously
preformed in the human mind.[15] In *Beyond Good and Evil* Nietzsche
emphasizes the unconscious physiological bases of the grammatical
functions: "Where there is affinity of languages, it cannot fail, owing to
the common philosophy of grammar—I mean, owing to the unconscious domination and guidance by similar grammatical functions—
that everything is prepared at the outset for a similar development
and sequence of philosophical systems . . . the spell of certain grammatical functions is ultimately also the spell of *physiological* valuations
and racial conditions" (*BGE* 27-28).

The implication of Nietzsche's model of unconscious grammar is
not only that these forms come to dominate conscious language
because they figure the unconscious operations of perception in
human beings but furthermore, that the very forms of our grammar
arise out of a relationship of forces in which the perceiver believes he
has become master. By categorizing the transmutation of power
relationships into fixed grammatical genera, legitimation of them and
the mastering activity of the subject arises and is continually
confirmed. "The so-called drive for knowledge can be traced back to a
drive to appropriate and conquer: the senses, the memory, the
instincts, etc., have developed as a consequence of this drive. The
quickest possible reduction of the phenomena, economy, the accumulation of the spoils of knowledge (i.e., of the world appropriated and
made manageable)" (*WP* no. 423).

The fixing of the subject with relationship to the rules of the
contest, the rules of grammar, allows its very significant corollary to
become possible: that the subject can be mastered, become accountable. The fixing of grammatical relationships and categories allows
the (grammatical) staging of power relationships in the critical act.
Once Berger experiences himself as a subject, at the center, as cause
and master of his actions, he is in a position to "act," to set up a world
of grammatical figures with relationship to himself. He identifies other

subjects: Hals, the art historian, the figures in the painting, his audience, and his peers; and objects: the paintings, that book he hopes to publish, the corpus of criticism which he hopes to influence. It is the strategic application of predicates, however, to Hals, to the bourgeois art historian, and to himself (and to his audience: you are exploited, ignorant, passive; you should be informed, engaged, active, alleviate the need for guilt) as well as to other subjects and objects in his world, which allows Berger to stage the real struggle or conflict for his reader. Hals is old, destitute, at the mercy of his sitters. The art historian is a mystifier, uses outmoded assumptions, offers an ideology which masks an actual state of affairs. Berger characterizes himself with predicates of clear sight, as possessing assumptions which accord with the world as it is, as being able to give back history. This grammatization of the critical situation, and the physiological and ideological socioeconomic setting in which it operates, allows demarcation of boundaries, fixing of power relations among a plurality of perceptual forces.

Metonymy/Commutation of Cause and Effect: The Pathos of Truth

To the rhetorical processes of unconscious synecdoche and the three instances of metaphorization, Nietzsche adds the third major rhetorical function of metonymy. Metonymy consists in the "commutation [*Vertauschung*] of the cause and the effect" (R 299). Commutation involves the activity of substitution, of making an exchange. "We say "the beverage is bitter" in place of "it excites in us a sensation of that kind," or "the stone is hard" as if "hard" is something other than a judgment on our part" (R 299). A belief, that is, a physiological sensation, is transposed into a statement of truth. "Such concepts, which owe their existence only to our feelings, are posited as if they were the inner essence of things: we attribute to events a cause which in truth is only an effect. The abstractions create the illusion as if *they* were the entity that causes the properties, whereas they receive their objective, iconic existence only from us as a consequence of these very properties" (R 319). "A particular body is the equivalent of so many relations." And a definition of something is arrived at by selecting properties which support relations. However, "relations can never be the essence (of the thing), but only consequences of this essence. A synthetic judgment describes a thing according to its consequences; i.e., *essence* and *consequences* become *identified*, i.e., metonymy" (*PT* nos. 141, 142, 152). The operation of metonymy first allows the "pathos of truth" to enter the game: "everything which distinguishes man from the animals depends upon this ability to volatilize perceptual metaphors in a schema, and thus to dissolve an image into a concept" (*TL* 84).

According to Berger, the art historian emphasizes the "wrong" properties, ones which "no longer accord with the world as it is," while he emphasizes the "right" properties, ones that do accord with the present, giving his judgment more value, more "truth." As a result his judgment should dominate and be the source of action. But as we saw in step four of Nietzsche's model, it was Berger who assigned the properties in the first place, properties which support his own activities of unconscious synecdochization and analogical inferencing or reinforcement. Nietzsche: "When someone hides something behind a bush and looks for it again in the same place and finds it there as well, there is not much to praise in such seeking and finding. Yet this is how matters stand regarding seeking and finding 'truth' within the realm of reason. If I make up the definition of a mammal, and then, after inspecting a camel, declare 'look, a mammal,' I have indeed brought a truth to light in this way, but it is a truth of limited value" (*TL* 85). What Nietzsche writes of the subject applies equally well to the ascription of properties: "The 'subject' is the fiction that many similar states in us are the effect of one substratum: but it is we who first created the 'similarity' of these states; our adjusting them and making them similar is the fact, not their similarity (—which ought rather to be denied—)" (*WP* no. 485). Substitution of cause and effect: an ideological belief is represented in a *certain* grammar as truth, as having arisen from the "facts," as a moral imperative calling for accountability. True, Berger attempts to escape this role by asking his listeners to be skeptical and by referring to the possibility that there could equally as well be a "pseudo-Marxist mystification" (*WS* 16) of Hals's paintings. Such rhetorical gambits, however, remain subsidiary disarming strategies amid the general physiological and ideological striving for power over an audience which the critical act embodies.

Nietzsche's description of the unconscious operations of synecdoche, the three types of metaphor, and metonymy constitute a thematics of repression. We are already familiar with Nietzsche's operation of forgetting, which in "On Truth and Lies in a Nonmoral Sense" allows the institution of a community language based upon agreement and a moral sense. Here at the level of unconscious operations, however, forgetting is not a moral obligation but a physiologically advantageous operation toward enhancement of the human organization. "There is in us a power to order, simplify, falsify, artifically distinguish. 'Truth' is the will to be master over the multiplicity of sensations" (*WP* no. 517).

The unconscious operations which Nietzsche describes also describe the operation of our conscious work with language. Whereas the unconscious operations have to do with a personal psychology of stimuli and images, conscious language, the transposition from images to sounds *with which to communicate* inevitably uses the same rhetorical operations, and still with the same end in view, the struggle for preservation and the enhancement of a certain physiological state of affairs. The act of cultural criticism adds to these dynamics the dimension of assessing what is "believed" to be an impersonal value which intensifies the desire for "knowledge" and "truth":

> Knowledge works as a tool of power. Hence it is plain that it increases with every increase of power—The meaning of 'knowledge': here, as in the case of 'good' or 'beautiful,' the concept is to be regarded in a strict and narrow anthropocentric and biological sense. In order for a particular species to maintain itself and increase its power, its conception of reality must comprehend enough of the calculable and constant [grammar, ideology, etc.] for it to base a scheme of behavior on it. The utility of preservation—not some abstract-theoretical need not to be deceived—stands as the motive behind the development of the organs of knowledge—they develop in such a way that their observations suffice for our preservation. In other words: the measure of the desire for knowledge depends upon the measure to which the will to power grows in a species: a species grasps a certain amount of reality in order to become master of it, in order to press it into service. [*WP* no. 480]

Criticism, which, on an ideological level, valorizes assumptions of subject, object, and logical argument, is only the surface of this drive for mastery. At the physiological level of unconscious perception, the action of purely bodily interpretation, ideological and cultural traces dominate. In the agonistics of power there are no polite boundaries between levels of human communication, whether unconscious, conscious, or cultural. Nietzsche: "The standpoint of 'value' is the standpoint of conditions of preservation and enhancement for complex forms of relative life duration within the flux of becoming" (*WP* no. 715).

It is essential to emphasize that this explication of Nietzsche's model does not constitute an ideological unmasking of the seductions of language, because this very deception is necessary to the human organism (see *TL* 86). Nietzsche's own standpoint of value, his physiological interpretations, and mine, are implicated in the same agonistics which I have attempted to demonstrate in the dynamics of Berger's critical act. The force of cultural or ideological assumptions operates in the first moment of unconscious and physiological perception. And the physiological necessities of preservation and growth of power operate in our most conscious cultural productions.

In closing, I would like to mention two points of view which I think characterize current thinking with regard to the implications of Nietzsche's model and its "deconstruction" of the critical act. In his book *Modern French Philosophy*, Vincent Descombes suggests that, after the recognition that "interpretation can never be brought to an end, that every sign is, in itself, not the thing susceptible to interpretation but the interpretation of other signs," that with Nietzsche "nothing is true, everything is permissible," what is left is nihilism, a stance which suggests that meaning is impossible (*MFP* 116-17). In his book *Deconstruction: Theory and Practice*, Christopher Norris writes that the "deconstructive text does not distribute opposition within a system of finite elements," rather, "it participates in irruptions of uncontrolled meaning in which the textuality asserts itself against any form of absolute methodical constraint." He continues, using Nietzsche and Foucault as instances: "This is not to condemn critical theory to an endless play of self-occupied textual abstraction. Rather it is to recognize, with Foucault, that texts and interpretive strategies compete for domination in a field staked out by no single order of validating method. Foucault follows Nietzsche in deconstructing those systems of thought which mask their incessant will to power behind a semblance of objective knowledge." Norris adds, significantly, that Foucault's "analysis of various 'discursive practices' constantly points to their being involved in a politics none the less real for its inextricably textual character" (*DTP* 87-88). One must find nihilism in the effluence of meanings, if by "meaning" one intends a fixed meaning. The subject as process, and now we must add, as physiological process, signifies a series of meanings and contests. Agonistics represents a complex of unconscious, conscious and cultural contests in which a subject is created and holds itself perilously poised in temporary arenas defined through exclusions and ostracisms upon which its very life depends, "as if hanging in dreams on the back of a tiger" (*TL* 80). I wish to second what Norris writes of Foucault by emphasizing that the Nietzschean perspective, which can "appear" nihilistic, *is* relevant for real political engagement. It is in the work of Nietzsche, Foucault, and other postmodernist thinkers that an effective discourse of politics becomes more possible precisely through a recognition of the complex agonistics in which all of us participate.[16]

ABBREVIATIONS

A   Foucault, Michel. *The Archaeology of Knowledge.* Trans. A. M. Sheridan Smith. New York: Harper and Row, 1972.

BGE   Nietzsche. *Beyond Good and Evil.* Trans. Walter Kaufmann. New York: Vintage Books, 1966.

BNL   Crawford, Claudia. *The Beginnings of Nietzsche's Theory of Language.* Berlin: Walter de Gruyter, 1988.

D   Nietzsche. *Daybreak.* Trans. R. J. Hollingdale. London: Cambridge University Press, 1982.

DTP   Norris, Christopher. *Deconstruction: Theory and Practice.* London: Methuen, 1982.

EH   *Ecce Homo.* In *"On the Genealogy of Morals" and "Ecce Homo."* Trans. Walter Kaufmann. New York: Vintage Books, 1967.

GM   Nietzsche. *On the Genealogy of Moral.* In *"On the Genealogy of Morals" and "Ecce Homo."* Trans. Walter Kaufmann. New York: Vintage Books, 1967.

GS   Nietzsche. *The Gay Science.* Trans. Walter Kaufmann. New York: Vintage Books, 1974.

HC   Nietzsche. "Homer's Contest." In *The Portable Nietzsche.* Trans. Walter Kaufmann. New York: Viking, 1968.

HS   Foucault, Michel. *History of Sexuality,* Vol. 1. Trans. Robert Hurley. New York: Vintage Books, 1980.

JG   Weber, Sam. "Afterword" to *Just Gaming,* by Jean-Francois Lyotard and Jean-Loup Thebaud. Trans. Wlad Godzich. Minneapolis: University of Minnesota Press, 1985.

MFP   Descombes, Vincent. *Modern French Philosophy.* Trans. L.
          Scott-Fox and J.M. Harding. Cambridge: Cambridge Uni-
          versity Press, 1980.

OL   Nietzsche. "On the Origins of Language." Trans. Claudia
          Crawford in BNL.

PT   Nietzsche. "The Philosopher: Reflections on the Struggle
          between Art and Knowledge." In *Philosophy and Truth:
          Selections from Nietzsche's Notebooks of the Early 1870's.*
          Trans. and ed. Daniel Breazeale. New Jersey: Humanities
          Press, 1979.

R   "Nietzsche's Lecture Notes on Rhetoric: a Translation."
          Trans. Carole Blair, *Philosophy and Rhetoric* (16:2)
          (1983), 94-129.

TI   Nietzsche. *Twilight of the Idols.* In *The Portable Nietzsche.*
          Trans. Walter Kaufmann. New York: Viking, 1968.

TL   Nietzsche. "On Truth and Lies in a Nonmoral Sense." In PT.

WMIA   Fish, Stanley. "What Makes an Interpretation Accept-
          able?" In *Is There a Text in This Class?* Cambridge, Mass.:
          Harvard University Press, 1980.

WP   Nietzsche. *Will to Power.* Trans. Walter Kaufmann. New
          York: Vintage Books, 1968.

WS   Berger, John *Ways of Seeing.* London: British Broad-
          casting Corporation, Penguin, 1972.

Part 4

Versions of the Self

10

Nietzsche and Postmodern Subjectivity

Kathleen Higgins

—And I saw a great sadness descend upon mankind. The best
grew weary of their works. A doctrine appeared, accompanied by
a faith: "All is empty, all is the same, all has been!"
—Nietzsche, *Thus Spoke Zarathustra*

THE POSTMODERNIST DEFINED

The term "postmodernism" has an oxymoronic sound. How, if
the word "modern" refers to the present, can currently living people be
"postmodern"? This question arises almost as a gut reaction. The word
seems a little uncanny. A "postmodernist" sounds like one of the living
dead or perhaps one of the living unborn—or maybe our sense of
temporality is simply offended. We can recall Kurt Vonnegut and
conceive of postmodernists as "unstuck in time."

Those who call themselves "postmodernists," however, are not
commenting on their own peculiar subjective condition. Their point is
a much more detached one, in keeping with the impersonal quality of
the term "postmodern." Postmodernists address themselves to the
condition, not of themselves personally, but of the whole modern age.
And for the most part, postmodernists describe this condition in
terms that are grim. Baudrillard straightforwardly characterizes
himself as a nihilist in a culture for which meaning of any sort is dead.[1]
Lyotard, although acknowledging a positive function of science and
intellectual inquiry in our era, nonethless despairs of any genuine

consensus among the diverse discourses through which we approach knowledge. For Lyotard, too, traditional "meaning" has come to an end.[2]

De Man, in his deconstructive reading of Nietzsche, draws similarly negative conclusions for the entire discipline of philosophy. "Philosophy," he maintains, "turns out to be an endless reflection on its own destruction at the hands of literature."[3] Along with Derrida, de Man endeavors to repudiate the cherished notion, fundamental to Western philosophy, that "truth can be made present to man.[4] There is no "beyond irony," de Man insists.[5] Philosphers, artists, and politicians alike are trapped in the position of "the child near the end of *The Birth of Tragedy* that is seen to be building and destroying the same sandcastle over and over again. This ever-recurring scheme of error repeats itself in all activities, in the political sphere as well as in the act of reading."[6]

The pervasiveness of negativity in the rhetoric of postmodernism leads critic Todd Gitlin to comment, "For the most part, postmodernist writing confesses (or celebrates!) helplessness. Make the most of stagnation, it says; give up gracefully. This is perhaps its defining break from modernism, which was, whatever its subversions, a series of declarations of faith."[7] Who are these postmodernists, these self-styled diagnosticians of our contemporary state? They do not comprise an easily characterizable group. For all of the characteristics one might isolate from the passages just cited, one could cite other postmodernists who would contradict them. Derrida, although as vehement as Lyotard in his denial of a fundamental "metanarrative" that can unify our fragmented discourses of knowledge, considers this an implicitly liberating realization. And Jameson denies that we are condemned to the fragmentary by our current cultural condition; he proposes that we develop new narrative structures in which to integrate the diverse elements of our experience.[8]

Why are the postmodernists such a difficult lot to assemble under one description? The reason is no doubt partly that their theories themselves commonly deny coherent, stable description in favor of a radically fragmented outlook on our experience. Thus, postmodernists tend not to describe themselves positively but instead assert themselves indirectly and polemically in their attacks on central concepts of our intellectual tradition. Typical foci of attack include truth, selfhood, substance, "presence," "metanarrative," totality, meaning, and "logos." Consistent with these attacks, postmodernists typically do not assert themselves as stable presences who engage us.

Another reason why it is hard to delineate the postmodernist position is that the term "postmodernism" depends for its meaning an often unspecified sense of "modernism." Kellner observes that part of the confusion about the term stems from the fact that different disciplines, with distinct respective views of modernism, start with very different assumptions when they assert that something is "postmodern."[9] Certainly, self-styled "postmodernists" are postulating a radical rupture between our cultural circumstances (or at least the theories they propose for interpreting these circumstances) and the whole tradition that flowered in "modernism." But in order to understand the rupture, we need to be clear about the modernism being rejected. And often in postmodernist writings, the significance of "modernism" is more assumed than clarified.

A further problem in specifying who the postmodernists are is the perspectivist orientation favored by many who are labeled by the term. Polemicizing in favor of perspectivism and (for the most part) against the need for or possibility of a "grand narrative" that would incorporate all points of view, postmodernists tend to radicalize their own perspective without attempting to integrate it into a socially agreed upon metanarrative or even into the discourse of other postmodernists.

Despite these difficulties with any attempt to pinpoint the core proponents and values of postmodernism, I think that certain contentions advanced by many so-called postmodernists can and should be evaluated. I propose to criticize some common themes assocaited with postmodernism by means of a consideration of Nietzsche's relationship to the movement (if, indeed, "movement" is an appropriate term). Postmodernists frequently claim Nietzsche as an intellectual ancestor. And certainly, some of Nietzsche's most provocative themes resemble features of contemporary postmodernism. He is asystematic, and he advocates perspectivism and a transvaluation of all values. Nevertheless, I will be arguing that certain apparent similarities between Nietzsche and the postmodernists are not, in fact, similarities at all and that Nietzsche can be seen as an implicit critic of postmodernism.

Central to what I see as Nietzsche's implicit critique of postmodernism is his radically different perspective on human subjectivity. Although both Nietzsche and the postmodernists advocate a fragmented, perspectivist orientation toward our experience, Nietzsche's purpose distinguishes him from his alleged intellectual heirs. Nietzsche's primary concern is the possibility of rich and meaningful subjective experience. His "postmodernist" critique of the dangers of "modern" pretentions serves this aim. And this same concern also leads Nietzsche to advocate certain decidely nonpostmodernist intellectual ploys: metanarratives and totalizing myths.

Postmodernists, in contrast, do not seem particularly concerned with personal subjectivity. Many explicitly despair of personal and societal meaning alike. And in general, the full human subject is absent from postmodern discourse. One of the reasons why it becomes difficult to say who postmodernists are, as we have observed, is that they typically reject as illusory any unified subjective being or experience. A postmodernist stance in writing is thus typically the stance of one who claims to be "elsewhere" (as contemporary debate about the "author" in relation to the text reveals). Perhaps one can, in a sense, "define" the postmodernist as someone who is somewhere else, someone who was someone else the last time, someone who will be someone else the next time. In this sense, Nietzsche is far from a postmodernist. His writing aims at direct and personally invested encounter far more than at a demonstration of the impossibility of "being there." "Of all that is written, I love only what a man has written with his blood."[10]

I will pursue my assessment of Nietzsche's implicit critique of postmodernism by focusing on three of his theoretical overviews on the nature of time and history: (1) his critique, in *On the Advantages and Disadvantages of History for Life*, of excessive historical consciousness; (2) his advocacy of "the gay science"; and (3) his doctrine of eternal recurrence. I will argue that in each of these overviews, Nietzsche rejects the historical orientation of postmodernists in favor of (1) personal, immediate engagement in termporality (as opposed to the development of theoretically distanced critiques of one's historical tradition), and (2) playful but serious appropriation of metanarratives as instruments for attaining subjective meaning (as opposed to postmodernist repudiation of all totalizing sagas and of "meaning" itself).

Before proceeding, however, I should explain why "history" is a reasonable focus for assessing Nietzsche's relation to postmodernism. The reason is that "postmodernism," despire the antihistorical overtones of the term, is not detached from history. Instead, postmodernism is a position *about* history. Postmodernists, like modernists, live in a historical world. Both presuppose that history is the context within which human activity occurs. The disagreement centers on the shape of that context and on the significance of that context with respect to our activity.

The modernist argues that our era has achieved a kind of progress over previous eras, judging in terms that have themselves developed as outgrowths of a historical tradition. The significance of our activity in the present age, therefore, is optimistically interpreted against the background of historical developments. The postmodernists, in contrast, argues that modernist "progress" is an illusion and that traditional terms for evaluating the achievements of our age either ought to be abandoned or must be. In positing a rupture with previous traditions, therefore, postmodernists continue to interpret contemporary developments in terms of history, albeit a history whose bequests should be scrapped. Postmodernists dissociate themselves from traditional criteria for assessing the significance of our "achievements" in the present, with the consequence that many deny that "meaning" itself has any meaning for our era.

Both modernists and postmodernists, therefore, presuppose "history" in the elaboration of their theories. The notion that historical context is the background against which human activity occurs, a modern idea, came to dominate Western thought only in the nineteenth century. Thus a "modern" perspective continues to express itself in "postmodern" discourse, if only as a presupposition that ought to be deconstructed. Postmodernists and their critics debate about whether or not postmodernism is so completely embedded in history that postmodernism inherently asserts the arrival of a "postmodern age" as a new historical period.[11] But in either case, postmodernists are historicists to the extent that they define their positions in reaction to a long-evolving historical tradition beyond which they believe we, in our era, should or must move.

In this respect, postmodernists frequently turn to Nietzsche as an ally; for Nietzsche is similary critical of a lengthy historical tradition, which he similarly urges us to reject. But Nietzsche is also critical of the historicist turn itself as a radical modern move that should be subjected to critical scrutiny. I will be arguing below that Nietzsche, if a postmodernist of sorts, is at the same time implicitly a critic of postmodernism in his analysis of modern historicism. According to Nietzsche's critical analysis of the historicist move, certain perspectives linked with postmoderism appear as pathological symptoms of the modern enthrallment with history, not as cures for its dangers.

If one lacked aesthetic scruples, one might call Nietzsche a "post-postmodernist." For if postmodernism takes a critical step backward from modern faith in historical progress, Nietzsche advocates taking one more step away from the entire historical mode. But "post-postmodernism" would be a misleading label for further step that Nietzsche advocates. For the next step he proposes is not backward into a more distanced theoretical vantage but forward—not toward a stance of further detachment but toward a state of immediate involvement.

Nietzsche's skeptical analysis of the modern quest for historical knowledge is itself directed toward immediate experience. The danger he observes in his contemporaries' obsessive concern with history is a danger to their subjective condition. Excessive preoccupation with history, he argues, can damage a person's sense of self and of immediate connection with a larger world. And this damage has, for many, already occurred. I will argue in what follows that many postmodernists, for whom "self" as "present" is theoretically anathema, would be among those Nietzsche sees as already damaged.

NIETZSCHE'S CRITIQUE OF HISTORICAL KNOWLEDGE

In his early work *On the Advantage and Disadvantage of History for Life*, one of his "Untimely Meditations," Nietzsche argues that the value of historical knowledge must be assessed in terms of its influence on the human being's sense of life. The work is best known for Nietzsche's analysis of the ways in which history can and does make important contributions to the life of both cultures and individuals. His famous account of the three kinds of history—monumental, antiquarian, and critical history—corresponds to the positive functions that Nietzsche sees history as performing. Monumental history inspires by reminding us of what is humanly possible; antiquarian history stirs feelings of reverence and gratitude that enhance satisfaction with one's life and culture; and critical history provides a basis for judgment, so that such satisfaction does not become blind.[12] These modes of history and their corresponding positive contributions constitute the advantages with which a sense of history provides life.

When the quest for historical knowledge becomes an end in itself, no longer associated with one of these positive projects, however, it can rob the person seeking it of his or her basic sense of life. Unfortunately, Nietzsche sees this as the situation of many in his own day. Nietzsche's explanation of the reasons have often been rehearsed, but his emphasis on the extent to which personal, subjective experience has been devastated by the influx of modern historical know-ledge has perhaps been underemphasized. I will therefore review his list of the five harmful effects of modern historical awareness. Each of these, we shall see, is a harm to the individual's sense of being a living self in vital connection with a living world.

First, historical consciousness nullifies the individual's sense of joy in the present. The ocean of historical facts of which the modern human being is made aware contextualizes his or her understanding of the present. Whatever one encounters in the present appears as just another episode, whose genuine significance is determined by this larger span of events. The result is that the individual is rendered increasingly incapable of appreciating the present as an occasion of self-sufficient happiness. "The least happiness," claims Nietzsche, "if only it keeps one happy without interruption, is incomparably more than the greatest happiness which comes to one as a mere episode." But this is to say that the presssure of modern historical conscious-ness undermines the human being's potential for happiness. In order to experience happiness, one must be able "to live unhistorically while it endures."[13]

Second, modern historical consciousness inhibits the individual's creative activity. By diminishing the prominence of the present in the oceanic sweep of history, the modern historical perspective impairs the individual's conviction that action in the present can effectively transform the inheritance of the past. Healthy life, for both individuals and their culture, depends on what Nietzsche calls "the plastic power" of the person or society, namely "the power distinctively to grow out of itself, transforming and assimilating everything past and alien, to heal wounds, replace what is lost and reshape broken forms out of itself."[14] Modern human beings, however, tend to be so overpowered by the diverse collection of things past and alien that the conviction that one (or one's age) can master and reshape them is extinguished.

Third, modern historical awareness creates chaos in the inner human being and generally weakens one's sense that this inner being is connected to the larger world. Too much information about anything prevents digestion. In the case of excessive historical information, moreover, the facts about which one is knowledgeable are alien and disconnected, "at war with each other."[15] In order not to disintegrate, the individual resigns him or herself to the war within. But a consequence of this war is the individual's loss of confidence in the inner person's ability to guide action. External behavior becomes more and more a matter of conforming to convention. Thus the inner being and external behavior become increasingly out of touch with one another, and the inner person comes to take the actual (external) world less and less seriously.

Fourth, the modern historical consciousness increasingly renders the individual a jaded nonsubject. A being, according to Nietzsche, is a subject only insofar as it is affected by objects. But modern people, too attentive to knowledge of history, have become too distant from the actual, present world to be affected or moved by anything. And by attending excessively to theoretical knowledge about all manner of past things, the modern person becomes incapable of surprise at anything the present could offer. Thus the modern individual easily becomes indifferent to virtually everything that is present. In addition, historical knowledge teaches that "things were different in all ages, it does not matter how you are." And this relativism further encourages the attitude that the actual situation in the present need not deeply concern one. The jading influence of historical knowledge uproots the future as well as the present. For in order to act with the hope of creating a future, one needs "the unconditional faith in something perfect and righteous" and illusions that foster unconditional love.[16] But the modern approach to historical knowledge kills illusion; it demythologizes and dissects.

Fifth, modern historical knowledge renders individuals ironic, even cynical, about their own roles in the world. Made aware of how many possibilities have been actualized, they see themselves as latecomers. Their own lives appear to them almost as historical afterthoughts, "episodes" in which nothing radically new or significant can be accomplished. The modern individual suffers from an "inborn grayheadedness" whose chief symptoms are paralysis and a sense of personal impotence.[17] Everything that the individual attempts is attempted with the self-ironic sense that nothing much will come of it.

Nietzsche's complaints about the effects of excessive historical awareness on the individual subject can be criticized for their sketchiness and their generality,[18] but they show that Nietzsche links the modern approach to history to psychological damage in the human subject. And for our purposes, it is significant that his criticisms suggest a case against modernism that resembles that made by certain contemporary postmodernists, such as Jameson, who are interested in social theory.[19] The vision that we are captives of history, incapable of surmounting its determining flood of influences, is a vision that Nietzsche, like Jameson, rejects.

It is signficant, however, that Jameson, unlike many others who are called "postmodernists," sets out to analyze and critique contemporary culture, which he designates as "postmodern" as distinguished from a previous "modern" era of capitalism. His own critical stance toward what he understands to be our contemporary cultural situation differentiates Jameson from those "postmodernists" who view "postmodernism" as an aesthetic, epistemological, or philsophical ideal as well as from those (like Baudrillard) who accept the current cultural situation (which they analyze as "postmodern") as something they are powerless to change. In my suggestion below that Nietzsche implicitly criticizes postmodernism, I have in mind primarily these latter forms of postmodernism rather than Jameson's. Indeed, if Nietzsche can appropriately be compared to any of the contemporary postmodernists, I think he is most akin to Jameson in his overall orientation (although obviously not in his practical politics). Both analyze culture from a critical standpoint that calls for change, and both consider the aesthetic to be the arena in which cultural change must be instigated. Even so, there are signficant dissimilarities between Jameson and Nietzsche, the most striking being that Jameson bases his critique on Marxist dialectic, while Nietzsche proposes radically individual transformation as the originating basis for any cultural change that he recommends.

No doubt, other prominent postmodernists beside Jameson might be described as cultural critics. Derrida, for instance, in his efforts to deconstruct some of the privileged concepts of the Western philosophical tradition, is often described as cultural liberator, who aims to free our worldview from the dominant, often oppressive values that our tradition has taught us.[20] The liberation that Derrida heralds, however, is not directly linked to any practical proposals for either political, social, or existential change. Indeed, Derrida's deconstruction (not to mention de Man's) has often been criticized for its politically noncommittal character. And the theoretical negativism involved in strategy of "deconstructing" the systems of others does seem satisfied with itself, not implicitly directed toward specific positive alternatives. For that matter, if one of deconstruction's theoretical underpinnings is the view that any philosophical system is in principle deconstructible, it is hard to see how the movement *could* consistently defend a particular practical strategy for change.[21]

Unlike even those contemporary enthusiasts of postmodernism who might seek independence from tradition through theoretical critique, however, Nietzsche has a radically individualistic focus in his rejection of our tradition's inheritance. The transformation he urges more and more stridently in his later works is a change in the *individual's* subjective sense of self in the context of the world. Fundamental to this transformation is a change in the individual's temporal orientation. Nietzsche's list of ill effects that stem from excessive historical awareness, in fact, pertains primarily to the individual's sense of self in time. His critique of the modern obsession with history is thus directed at the personal instead of the societal.

This call to existential, subjective self-transformation differentiates Nietzsche from the large number of postmodernist theorists
who deny the meaningfulness of the idea of a coherent self.[22] In fact, if
we survey Nietzsche's list of ill effects of excessive historical awareness, we discover that many postmodernists are more critiqued than
vindicated. As a checklist of problems one might have in formulating a
healthy sense of self, it represents an *ad hominem* argument that fits a
number of postmodernism's proponents.

Reviewing Nietzsche's list with the postmodernists in mind, we
make five discoveries.

1. The inability to see the present as a moment of self-sufficient
happiness is thematic in the writings of postmodernists Baudrillard.
Baudrillard considers our era as one in which all distinctions have
"imploded,"[23] as one in which the masses have become a "black hole"
that "engulfs the social" and renders all meaning meaningless.[24]

2. De Man despairs of the possibility of progress in our interpretation of the world[25] and even of the possibility of political progress.[26]
De Man is hardly convinced that action in the present can effectively
transform the inheritance of the past. We are condemned, he claims,
to repeat the same errors over and over again.[29] The postmodernist
predilection for pastiche of eclectic elements, moreover, suggests a
deterioration of what Nietzsche calls "the plastic power" of persons
and societies. As critic Gitlin observes, "Pastiche lives off borrowed
energies. The post-modern mode is compilation, recombination...
When writing is imprisoned within previous writing, it can't attend to
what hasn't been written, what hasn't yet been imagined."[28]

Pastiche is viewed by many postmodernists as appropriate not
only to art, but to our general orientation toward our world.
Baudrillard considers "playing with the pieces" of past culture to be
the singular postmodern possibility[29] Lyotard characterizes the
current condition of knowledge in a similar vein: "All we can do is gaze
in wonderment at the diversity of discursive species."[30] A new
integration of the diversity strikes him as neither possible nor
desirable in our era. "Let us wage war on totality," he argues in *The
Postmodern Condition.*[31]

3. Lyotard thus asserts that our irreversible epistemic condition
is a war of "facts" from different spheres of knowledge—the very "war"
that Nietzsche associates with spiritual chaos. Lyotard even makes
this war of incommensurable "facts" a principle of contemporary
epistemology. He thus describes and celebrates our era as one in
which information must remain nonintegrated.

The spiritual calamity that Nietzsche links with this situation may well seem applicable to such postmodernists as Lyotard who insist that we must resign ourselves to our cultural condition. Nietzsche considers conformity to convention as the ironic result of our "modern" cacaphony of information. And postmodernism, for all its jargon of a rupture with the past, does not generally oppose convention. Instead, it tends to embrace the cultural climate, however described, a fact that has led critics such as Habermas to link the entire postmodernist movement to a neoconservative spirit.[32]

4. The jaded nonsubject that, according to Nietzsche, replaces the individual in an era of excessive historical consciousness would seem to be the postmodern human being *par excellence*. At least this is the kind of human being that is described in the literature of and about postmodernism. Gitlin generically characterizes the stance of postmodernism as one of "self-regarding irony and blankness."[33] The demystifying tenor of many postmodernist writings seems to invite subdued affect instead of enthusiasm. "Disenchantment," in Baudrillard's view, is fundamental to postmodernity.[34] Jameson associates postmodernist culture with a "waning of affect."

Significantly, Jameson explicitly links this phenomenon with the postmodernist theory of such poststructuralists as Derrida, de Man, and Baudrillard: "The very concept of expression presupposes indeed some separation within the subject, and along with that a whole metaphysics of the inside and the outside, of the wordless pain the moment in which, often cathartically, that 'emotion' is then projected out and externalized, as gesture or cry, as desperate communication and the outward dramatization of inward feeling."... In light of the fact that much of postmodernist theory undermines the very distinction (between "inside" and "outside") on which the concept of expression depends, Jameson concludes that such theory is itself "a very significant symptom of the very postmodernitst culture which is our subject here."[35] Surprise (Nietzsche's affect of preference) is not only a cultural anachronism, as Jameson sees it;[36] it is theoretically objectionable to most postmodernists as well.

5. Irony, to many postmodernists, is the only legitimate stance of discourse. De Man embraces irony as inescapable.[37] Lightheartedness is difficult to find in the tone of most of the theorists we have been discussing. And to the extent that postmodernism denies the possibility of a metanarrative or a totalizing discourse, irony would appear to be its natural medium (despite Lyotard's insistence that we should learn to be content with discrete "little narratives."[38] Baudrillard

manifests what Nietzsche terms "inborn grayheadedness," moreover, insisting that we are condemned to fragments of past traditions which we are powerless to reintegrate. This is precisely the viewpoint described in the epigraph to this chapter, a viewpoint that Nietzsche lampoons and ultimately has Zarathustra reject in *Thus Spoke Zarathustra*.[39]

NIETZSCHE'S ANTIDOTES TO ABUSED HISTORY

The harms that Nietzsche associates with excessive historical consciousness seem to afflict the worldviews of many of his alleged postmodernist descendents. This fact suggests that his theoretical perspective on history is not fully in keeping with theirs, for he criticizes as dangerous the views that postmodernist theorists assert. Nietzsche's antidotes to excessive historical consciousness, proposed later in "On the Advantage and Disadvantage of History for Life," further suggest a disparity between Nietzsche's views and certain favored postmodernist themes.

The two basic antidotes Nietzsche terms "the unhistorical" and "the superhistorical." The unhistorical involves the ability "to *forget* and enclose oneself in a limited *horizon*."[40] This perspective is precisely the opposite of what Lyotard aims to remind us: that no horizon can encompass the entire range of discourses by which we comprehend our world and that we should actively attempt to develop "our ability to tolerate the incommensurable."[41] The superhistorical involves a shift of gaze from the becoming of ongoing history to "that which gives existence an eternal and stable character, toward *art* and *religion*."[42] Nietzsche advocates here precisely what many postmodernests reject or abandon: a metanarrative, a totalizing story that locates the fragmentary in a context. Hope is necessary, Nietzsche tells us, to cure ourselves from the modern malaise that history has bequeathed us. But we can take hope from the model of the Greeks, who organized the chaos of materials they absorbed from foreign cultures by "reflecting on their genuine needs."[43] This strategy, Nietzsche suggests, is the one that we should employ to become vital human subjects once again.

With respect to history, Nietzsche's vitalism not only dominates those tendencies that ally him with postmodernism; it also leads him to propose decidely nonpostmodernist remedies for some of the problems he observes in contemporary culture. The antidotes that he recommends involve immediate engagement in the present and the use of grand metanarratives as means of orienting oneself within time. In addition, the focus of Nietzsche's concern for vital experience is the subjective person, a focus quite different from that of contemporary postmodernists. Speaking of those who join him in hoping for a return to the Greek strategy of imposing order on chaos, Nietzsche asserts, "I know that these hopeful ones intimately understand all these generalities and that with their very own experience they will translate them for themselves into a doctrine meant personally."[44]

Nietzsche's own translations of these generalities into doctrines meant personally are articulated only in works of a later period. I will now turn to the later doctrines of the gay science and eternal recurrence and show how Nietzsche uses them to provide the kind of antidotes demanded by his earlier essay. The fact that Nietzsche continues to pursue antidotes for the harms he links to excessive concern with history suggests that his implicit critique of many postmodernists remains one of his concerns into his mature period. These later recommendations, moreover, aim at something entirely different from the goals of most contemporary postmodernists: a fuller, more personally understood temporality that would replace an entirely historicist perspective on one's age.

THE GAY SCIENCE AS A TEMPORAL PERSPECTIVE

Nietzsche's notion of "the gay science" is developed in his book of the same name. The intimately personal character of what Nietzsche means by this expression is evident in his preface to the book's second edition. Nietzsche notes that the gay science was his own spiritual condition of hope that occurred in the wake of a malaise. "'Gay Science': that signifies the saturnalia of a spirit who has patiently resisted a terrible, long pressure—patiently, severely, coldly, without submitting, but also without hope—and who is now all at once attacked by hope, the hope for health, and the *intoxication* of convalescence."[45] Nietzsche portrays the malaise that preceded his saturnalian mood in terms reminiscent of his earlier account of the malaise of the historically educated. "And what did not lie behind me then! This stretch of desert, exhaustion, disbelief, icing up in the midst of youth, this interlude of old age at the wrong time,...this radical retreat into solitude as a self-defense against a contempt for men that had become pathologically clairvoyant—this determined self-limitation to what was bitter, harsh, and hurtful to know."...[46] Nietzsche's description here of the premature old age, excessive knowledge, and self-protective isolation that preceded the mood of the gay science recalls even the terminology of this earlier discussion. I shall argue below that it describes the tone of certain postmodernists as well.

The preface to the second edition of *The Gay Science* concludes, moreover, with a characterization of "gay science" that coincides in spirit with the recommendation that Nietzsche made in his untimely meditation on history. The practitioners of the gay science, Nietzsche tells us, have turned their sights away from the project of trying to know everything, of "truth at any price." "For that we are too experienced, too serious, too merry, too burned, too *profound*." Again Nietzsche points to the Greeks, whose perspective on these matters was more healthy than that of the majority of moderns. The Greeks, instead of aiming to know all that they could, were "superficial—*out of profundity*."[47]

And this, contends Nietzsche, is what we should become again— and what those who pursue knowledge (or science) gaily are, by definition. Nietzsche's implied maxim "Become superficial out of profundity" is not only definitive of the gay science, however. It also condenses the major points of his recommendations to those suffering from history. Those who are superficial out of profundity have the ability "to stop courageously at the surface . . . to adore appearance."[48] They limit their horizon and in this way resemble the unhistorical person. At the same time, they artistically impose order on chaos, finding in the forms they invent a kind of stable ground for their existence in the fashion of the superhistorical person. Significantly, this superficiality that Nietzsche recommends postdates commitment to the scientific quest for knowledge. In this respect, Nietzsche's concern with appearances differs markedly from that of Baudrillard, who proposes that we play with appearance only because we have nothing left. Nietzsche's superficiality is "superficiality out of profundity" precisely because a certain depth of awareness has already been penetrated.

One might read Nietzsche here as adopting a "postmodernist" perspective in that the gay science presupposes a Lyotardian awareness of the fragmentary chaos that comprises the field of modern knowledge. The chaotic juxtaposition of materials that one encounters in *The Gay Science* might seem a kind of Lyotardian gaming with a disconnected assortment of things. But on closer inspection, we find not a mere pastiche à la Lyotard but a diversity of points of view meant to support each other as elements of a coherent vision.

Two currents dominate the presentation in *The Gay Science*, both of which concern the individual's temporal orientation. On the one hand, the work contains discursive treatments of wide-ranging theoretical topics, many of which are focused on history and temporality. (Examples include discussions of the shifting human perspectives on the purpose of life (section 1), of the amazing durability of scientific laws (section 46), and of the retroactive reinterpretation of history on the basis of one's present experience (section 34). But these abstract discussions are accompanied by reveries, accounts of personal moods and attitudes, and veritable advice columns that offer rather intimate personal suggestions. These two currents of the book's contents converge in their focus on the transient and on the wealth of creative options we have, both theoretically and personally, for imposing order on the chaos of temporal flux. Thus, contrary to most contemporary postmodernists, for example, Baudrillard, Lyotard, Derrida, and de Man—but not Jameson), Nietzsche positively advocates metanarratives and takes this advocacy as one of his major themes.

The book's opening section sets the tone for the theoretical discussions by linking "the gay science" to a sense of the rhythm of ebb and flow in history. Distinguishing tragic and comic perspectives on life, Nietzsche notes that the tragic view that has inspired our religions and moralities, although it urges us to beware of what lies beneath life, nonetheless promotes life. It gives people a sense that there is some purpose in what happens, even though the truth is that what happens occurs "necessarily and always, spontaneously and without any purpose." The comic view of life is the more profound view, for it recognizes that the movement of the world is spontaneous and ultimately purposeless. Because it is the more penetrating view, the comic view always triumphs over the tragic. "The waves of uncountable laughter'—to cite Aeschylus—must in the end overwhelm even the greatest of these tragedians."[49] One might, using Nietzsche's analysis, describe postmodernism as comic, for it stresses the chaotic and resists idealization.

The human race, Nietzsche contends, has a periodic need for belief that life has a purpose. And so, although the comic view will always triumph, the tragic view will recurrently arise and satisfy this human need. The conclusion Nietzsche draws is more suggestive than definitive, but it decidedly defies the historical vision that enchants the modern age. "Consequently—. Consequently. Consequently. O, do you understand me, my brother? Do you understand this new law of ebb and flood? There is a time for us, too!"[50]

The orientation toward history that Nietzsche offers here contrasts markedly with that which he criticizes in "On the Advantages and Disadvantages of History for Life." He is far from seeing history as a causal chain of influences that molds the present— farthest of all from the Hegelian view of history as an inevitable, teleological unfolding. In contrast, he envisions the movement of history as akin to that of ocean waves. On this model, the amount of historical knowledge that modern scholars have acquired need not seem an oppressive burden on the present. Instead, it informs us about previous configurations of the chaotic texture of life, a texture which we ourselves transfigure artistically.

Our action in the present, on Nietzsche's view, is as much and as little efficacious in the scheme of history as is the movement of the present ocean wave. Although its shape and specific contents are influenced by those of its predecessors, the present wave is original, and like the Kantian object of beauty it exhibits "purposiveness without a purpose." It directs itself aggressively in accord with its own inner momentum. The wave, moreover, is beautiful, not because of its role with respect to some profound purpose, but because of its purposive superficial form.

Our present activity, when observed from the standpoint of the gay science, assumes a similar aspect. Although its shape is influenced by historical currents, our present activity is an original outburst, expressive of our inner beings. Without being tied to a relentless historical teleology, our activity is nonetheless purposive. And because its significance is not determined by the larger historical currents that lie behind it, activity in the present can be enjoyed with an aesthetic delight, which takes pleasure in the mere form of purposiveness.

Nietzsche compares human activity more directly to waves in section 310 of *The Gay Science.* "You and I," he addresses some ocean waves, "—are we not of one kind?—You and I—do we not have *one secret?*"[51] And Nietzsche also depicts this analogy more figuratively.

> How greedily this wave approaches, as if it were after something! How it crawls with terrifying haste into the inmost nooks of this labyrinthine cliff! It seems that it is trying to anticipate someone; it seems that something of value, high value, must be hidden there. —And now it comes back, a little more slowly but still white with excitement; is it disappointed? Has it found what it looked for? Does it pretend to be disappointed—but already another wave is approaching, still more greedily and savagely than the first, and its soul, too, seems to be full of secrets and the lust to dig up treasures. Thus live waves—thus live we who will—more I shall not say.[52]

The more personally addressed advice of *The Gay Science* converges with this depiction of human action in time. Section 295, to take just one example, is a paean to "brief habits," temporary personal modes for organizing an aspect of life. These brief habits seem all-satisfying while they endure but give way eventually to some new discovery that rearranges habits in its own image. "This is what happens to me with dishes, ideas, human beings, cities, poems, music, doctrines, ways of arranging the day, and life styles." Nietzsche contrasts brief habits both with enduring habits and "a life entirely devoid of habits, a life that would demand perpetual improvisation."[53] Again the theme of artistic imposition of form on the flux of experience is in evidence and again this imposition of form is tied to subjective satisfaction. At the same time, Nietzsche praises the assertion of subjective freedom in the present, however much experience has gone before.[54]

We are now in a position to see that the gay science functions as an antidote to the previously considered five harms that result from modern historical consciousness (1) The gay science counteracts the nullification of joy in the present by viewing the present with an aesthetic satisfaction. (2) The present can be enjoyed aesthetically because the gay science also counteracts inhibition of the individual's creative activity. The gay science promotes creative activity by emphasizing our present creative power to give form to the range of contents that the past has bequeathed us. (3) The gay science reverses damage to the individual's sense of self in vital contact with the world. It does so by emphasizing the self-assertive character of imposing order on the flux of temporality. Not only is the individual not withdrawn from the external world in which historical consequences occur; the individual, in the view of the gay science, has the active role of ordering and redefining the significance of those consequences. (4) The gay science counteracts the jading tendencies of modern historical consciousness by developing the individual's capacity for "superficiality out of profundity." By focusing on the present surface of experience, rather than on some teleological saga of which it may be a result, they gay science restores a kind of innocence to the individual's immediate experience. (5) The gay science also undercuts modern individuals' ironic view of their own historical role, which stems from their sense that they have been born too late to determine the purposes that guide the world. The gay science undercuts this ironic perspective by treating it, too, with a further ironical move. To the ironic view that modern people are belated, the gay science adds the ironic perspective that this sense of belatedness is a localized phenomenon in the ebb and flow of history and a phenomenon that will recurrently pass away and develop again. In general, the gay science offers a full, personally meaningful temporality as opposed to a historically obsessed vision of time that robs the present of subjective significance.

DO POSTMODERNISTS PRACTICE GAY SCIENCE?

We can observe some similarities between the gay science and the perspective of our present-day postmodernists. The gay science rejects the modern, exclusively historicist interpretation of the present, the interpretation that conceives the present as a product of historical currents that flow into it. This perspective, from the vantage of the gay science, appears as only one possible perspective and not even the most accurate account. In this respect it resembles the postmodernist view that the dominant modes of thought and value that inform our history are ultimately ungrounded and that we can (and implicitly should) distance ourselves from them. In its negative polemic, Nietzsche's account of the gay science resembles the polemic of current postmodernists.

On superficial examination, the positive suggestion involved in the conception of the gay science also appears postmodernist. For the perspective that Nietzsche advocates would involve awareness of the fragmentary and transient character of experience, as opposed to an absolutist interpretation of all experience within a totalizing scheme.

But on further inspection, the positive suggestion of the gay science looks less postmodernist. *The Gay Science* advocates appreciation of the transient by means of a turn toward aesthetic immediacy. At the same time, the gay science involves appropriation of the immediate through the imposition of metanarrative order on the flux of experience. In these respects, Nietzsche's account of the gay science parts company with present-day postmodernism.

One finds little evidence of appreciation for sheer immediacy in postmodernist writings. Derrida makes absence—the impossibility of immediacy—a principle of communication. Lyotard's emphasis on the war of incompatible language games leaves no room for "superficial," immediate embracing of one of them. Baudrillard does believe that present appearance is all we have, but the "fundamental tonality" of this situation is, in his view, "melancholy."[55]

The postmodernist inheritance from Nietzsche, if anything, is perspectivism, the view that every view is an interpretation. (Indeed, it seems that each postmodernist interprets this claim anew.) But unlike Nietzsche's perspectivism, that of the postmodernists is not conjoined with "gay science." There is typically no "gay" perspective from which to observe with amusement the limitations of their own methods (including the limitation of being unable to totalize). In fact, the common postmodernist polemic against metanarratives absolves the postmodernist position ittself from internal critique, for any totalizing overview from which it might be criticized is itself undermined by postmodernist theorizing. The postmodernist position does not view itself "lightly," for it undercuts all *terra firma* outside it. The postmodernist has nowhere else to go, theoretically, and thus tends to take the postmodernist stance as the single vantage that one can trust. As Kellner observes, the "war on totality" declared by Lyotard itself is premised on an unacknowledged totalizing view.[56].

And even if the postmodernist perspective can, in a sense, be classed with Nietzsche's "comic" perspectives, it is certainly not "comic" in the sense that Nietzsche associates the comic with immediate, nonpurposive delight. The postmodernist perspective is more akin to Schopenhauerian sourness than to Nietzsche's comic "gaiety." Focused on interpretation and on the diversity of interpretive possibilities, postmodernist discourse stresses not the aesthetic immediacy of our experience, but the ways—more aptly, the pitfalls of the ways—we use to mediate it.

But it may seem that postmodernism does advocate a kind of aestheticism. For "play" is endorsed in many postmodernist quarters. Baudrillard condemns us to "play," while Lyotard promotes the full range of language games. Indeed, "playful" has almost become a Homeric epithet for Derrida.

But postmodernist "playfulness" is not the aesthetic stance of the gay science. It is primarily a stance toward texts (broadly construed) and modes of discourse. And while this playfulness is attitudinal, it is not an existential attitude toward one's life in the world. Admittedly, some postmodernists do contend that their stance toward texts can be extended into a subjective stance toward the larger world. (Indeed, de Man suggests that if we are aware of the ultimate groundlessness of our interpretations, we cannot do otherwise.) But even if one takes this course, one does not thereby assume a lighthearted aesthetic attitude toward the living world. The postmodernist who makes this move renders the world seriously problematic—the world becomes a text that demands interpretation. We are condemned by this move to the lot of Sisyphus, for no interpretation can finish the project. We must interpret constantly, never to do so adequately.

Most fundamentally, the gay science differs from the stance of postmodernism in that the gay science is a deeply personal stance.

The postmodernist worry about who, what, and where an author might be—argued at length and in print by many authors—is an indication of the detached tenor of the discussion. The gay science, in contrast, is posed as a formula for the interpenetration of thinking and living—in a full, deeply personal sense—and for subordinating intellectual inquiry (*and* its totalizing schemes) to this existential purpose.

The gay science might be termed "postmodern" in light of its rejection of the historicist character of the spirit of modernism. But in its positive suggestions, it resembles the stance of current postmodernists very little. In particular, the gay science involves a personal stance of immediate engagement, and it stresses the value of metanarratives for psychic health and even aesthetic enjoyment. We shall next observe the same pattern of resemblance and dissimilarity between postmodernism and Nietzsche's most famous doctrine concerned with temporality, that of eternal recurrence.

NIETZSCHE'S AHISTORICAL PERPLEXITY

The doctrine of eternal recurrence, which asserts that the cycle of time repeats itself an infinite number of times—has long disturbed readers of Nietzsche. The basis of disturbance is that it is not clear either what kind of theory the doctrine is or what difference the doctrine would make if it were true. I will not consider the various interpretations that have been suggested. I will simply acknowledge my agreement with Bernd Magnus's view that the doctrine of eternal recurrence is an expression of a particular life-affirming attitude toward life.[57]

Elsewhere I have argued that this attitude toward life expressed by eternal recurrence resembles the attitude toward music that the appreciative listener assumes.[58] I will suggest the points of analyogy that I see between eternal recurrence and music in order to suggest an intuitive sense of the attitude that eternal recurrence expresses. With a sense of this attitude in mind, we will be in a position to see why eternal recurrence, like the gay science, functions to counteract the subjective harms that Nietzsche links to modern historical consciousness in a manner that is unpostmodernist. In order to sketch the analogy between eternal recurrence and music, however, I must begin by saying more about the model of time proposed by the doctrine of eternal recurrence.

Eternal recurrence appears to give each moment in time the same degree of importance. Each recurs the same number of times;

each is causally connected to past and future in the same way; each is as much a future event as a past event. But this apparent equality among moments is deceptive, for this view ignores the standpoint of the individual who might assume the attitude to which the doctrine refers. Any such individual is situated in a present moment, and from any such standpoint, the doctrine of eternal recurrence gives that present moment a unique importance among moments in the cycle.

Why? Basically, because the present moment is the *only* moment in the sweep of time in which human action can occur. The past and the future are, for the individual in the present, equally impotent. The present moment is the unique point at which all the elements causally conditioned by the past can be reinterpreted and reordered purposively toward future ends, and these ends themselves are subject to evaluation and reformulation in the present.

Further inspection of the model of eternal recurrence indicates another feature that has import for the signficance of the present moment. On the model of eternal recurrence, the past and the future collapse into one another. Because all moments of time recur eternally, all moments of the future have already occurred. But all past moments, because they will recur again, are also a part of the future.

One consequence of this collapse of past and future is that some future endpoint cannot be the teleological purpose that gives significance to the events that lead up to it. Any future endpoint is also a point that lies behind us, and no genuine endpoint at all. Another consequence of the collapse of past and future is that the present, as the active moment in which the materials of the past are reformulated, reformulates the materials of the future as well. The future is a part of the past. Metaphorically, the present moment is like an engine that pulls the train of all temporal moments, past and future, along with it and wherever it wants to go.

The doctrine of eternal recurrence thus focuses on the present as the moment that bestows significance on the entire span of history, both social and individual. But what does this amount to in the subjective state of mind of the doctrine's adherent? How does this model translate into an attitude?

Here, I believe, we can enlist musical experience as our key. For in experiencing music, our approach to temporality in many ways coincides with that described by the doctrine of eternal recurrence. As this musical approach to temporality conditions our subjective musical experience, so does the approach to temporality implicit in the doctrine of eternal recurrence condition our subjective experience generally.

MUSICAL TEMPORALITY AS A MODEL
FOR ETERNAL RECURRENCE

Victor Zuckerkandl analyzes the temporality of musical experience in his book *Sound and Symbol: Music and the External World.* When we experience a musical tone, he contends, we experience in immediacy. But the significance of the tone lies not merely in its present statement but in its "promise of the whole of the work."[59] This is to say not that future tones determine the meaning of the present tone but that a tone's meaning lies in its "pointing" forward toward other tones, tones which the structure of the music suggests to us. We experience musical tones as aimed at resolution.

At the same time, a sense of past is also inherent in the musical present. For music involves the ebb and flow of rhythm. We sense the waves of rhythm as a process "'away from—back to,' not a flux but a constantly repeated cycle."[60] Besides experiencing futurity in the present tone's pointing, we experience its position in an already established wave cycle.[61] The present tone thus combines immediate impressions of past and future within itself.

And yet does this mean that the present musical tone is the product of past determination or is only significant as a means to a future end? Not at all. Zuckerkandl notes that any effort to return to past musical moments not only does not provide a key; it *destroys* understanding of the musical present. "Let anyone who is capable of it call to mind the immediately preceding tone of a melody that he is hearing. *The instant he does so, he will have lost the thread of the melody*....Any turning back of consciousness for the purpose of making past tones present immediately annuls the possibility of musical hearing."[62] Nor does the eventually attained future retrospectively determine the meaning of a musical tone. "The expectation that I feel upon hearing a tone is not toward any *event*...; it is directed toward futurity, toward what can never become present....Without leaving the present behind me, I experience futurity as that toward which the present is directed and always remains directed."[62] The meaning of the musical present is not established by some other moment or moments in musical time. Instead, the temporal whole of past and future are contained experientially in the present musical tone.

How does this situation resemble eternal recurrence? This model of musical temporality privileges the present moment as the living moment of music that reflects the whole of musical time. The model of eternal recurrence, similarly, privileges the present moment as the active moment that ties together the causal streams of past and future. Both theories, through this emphasis on the present, indicate that the present is the part of time to which one's attention should properly be directed. And in both cases, the attitudinal consequence of this focus is an aesthetic perspective on events. In the case of the model of musical temporality, this perspective is that of musical appreciation. In the case of the model of eternal recurrence, this perspective is that of the active innovator who "artistically" assembles materials derived from the past into forms that accord with his or her aspirations toward the future.

Significantly, both models imply that the present can be viewed as meaningful only with some reference to future ends. The meaning of the present depends on its assuming a role in a nonchaotic temporal matrix. Striving toward either a musical goal or a humanly invented one is essential to vital life in time, and Nietzsche's eternal recurrence provides a model for reconciling this fact with a sense of aesthetic delight in the present.

The model of eternal recurrence suggests that striving and purposive activity make sense even in the absence of belief that progress is being made or that we can determine its significance only within a full account of history. The musical model that we have considered gives us an intuitive sense of this attitude toward purposive activity. In music we experience as meaningful the present, purposive tone which, although connected to the past, is underdetermined by it, and which, although pointing toward future resolution, leaves us uncertain as to where it will move.

The musical meaning we experience in listening is not a comprehensive knowledge of the work's structure but a continuing and growing delight in what is present. Musical listening, in this way, involves a stance of "superficiality out of profundity." With the doctrine of eternal recurrence, Nietzsche describes an ideal attitude of present-centered purposiveness without a purpose. In subjective experience, such an attitude is rightly described as aesthetic.

Understood in this way, the doctrine of eternal recurrence counteracts the same harmful tendencies of modern historical consciousness that the gay science counteracts. (1) As a model of time that focuses on the primacy of the present, eternal recurrence is designed to *foster* aesthetic joy in the present, unadulterated by teleological concerns. (2) With its emphasis on creative activity as the means by which the past is given meaning, eternal recurrence promotes rather than inhibits such activity. (3) This same emphasis also instills a sense of subjective connectedness with and efficacy in the larger world. (4) By emphasizing the possibility of continually revising the significance of the past by means of present action and evaluation, eternal recurrence counteracts tendencies toward jadedness in outlook. (5) Like the gay science, the employment of the model of eternal recurrence casts a further ironic perspective on the self-undercutting ironic sense that we are belated in history. The model of eternal recurrence renders the idea that we are historic "latecomers" laughable, for by means of it the present moment and all other moments can each be viewed as either the latest or the earliest point in history or as any point between earliest and latest.

ETERNAL RECURRENCE AND POSTMODERNISM

Having used a musical analogy, perhaps we are especially prepared to notice a dissonance in tone between the present-centeredness of Nietzsche's doctrine of eternal recurrence and the term "postmodernist." Postmodernism is a doctrine of self-styled belatedness, while Nietzsche's doctrine makes this notion a joke. The doctrine of the gay science may treat history lightheartedly, but the doctrine of eternal recurrence undercuts the very idea of "history." Offering a model of time in which the terms "past" and "future" are more or less arbitrary, the doctrine of eternal recurrence undercuts the linear account of time on which history is written.

The doctrine of eternal recurrence has a certain affinity for postmodernism's strategy of undercutting traditional assumptions firmly lodged in our thinking—for the linear view of time is such an assumption. But even to locate such an assumption on the map of history is a postmodernist move that Nietzsche's ahistorical doctrine does not make.

More important, the positive vision of the doctrine of eternal recurrence is decidedly unpostmodernist. One reason is that the doctrine offers a vision of time that is totalizing, albeit in an unconventional way. Moreover, the doctrine's attitudinal perspective on time involves a stance of personally felt aesthetic immediacy. The very purpose of its totalizing vision is to assist a sense of subjective meaning in one's present activity. Again, and in the same respects we have observed above, the orientation of one of Nietzsche's most fundamental doctrines is at odds with the detached theoretical stance of postmodernism.

FRAGMENTS AND FRAGMENTS

My argument so far has been that although Nietzsche resembles contemporary postmodernists in criticizing the modernist view of history, his antidotes are decidedly unpostmodernist. I will close with some reflections on the fragmentary. For I suspect that Nietzsche appears to many to be more postmodernist than he is precisely because of his predilection for the aphoristic and the fragmentary.

My point on the fragmentary is a simple one. Fragments can be used for a wide variety of purposes. A fragment, if carefully selected, can represent the whole. This is the idea behind the 'representative passage" in considerations of literature. Or even if it is not so carefully selected, a fragment can serve as a reminder of the whole, as in the case of a nostalgic artifact that is to remind us of an earlier decade in this century. Or a fragment might be aesthetically appreciated in itself. A part of a seashell or a piece of driftwood can be enjoyed in this manner. Or a fragment might serve as an aesthetic suggestion, as in many haiku poems.

The simply fact that Nietzsche employs fragments does not imply that he employs them to the same ends as postmodernists who glory in the fragment. Fragments can emblemize both positive and negative entireties. Fragments can serve the positive, sometimes delightful functions just listed. Or as Arthur Danto observes, they can be constructed into aphorisms that are so striking as to assure that we will remember them.[64] Danto considers this to be Nietzsche's purpose in using aphorisms, whose "pointed terseness is a means of ensouling the message it carries, and to counteract the predictable deteriorations of memory."[65]

Fragments can also be employed in a negative mode, however, serving to symbolize negative, even morbid ideas. A fragment can symbolize dismemberment and disintegration if it is interpreted as "disjoined from the whole." A fragment can represent meaninglessness if the interpreter focuses on the fact of its being dissociated from a meaning-giving context.

As I understand the writings of most postmodernists, I am convinced that their fragments tend toward these more negative roles. Even when a fragment is employed as representative, as is often the case in deconstruction, the representation involved is typically enlisted to indicate a deeply self-sabotaging character of the text under discussion. The representation involved is thus representative lack of integrity.

No doubt there are postmodernists and deconstructionists who employ fragments to reveal the mysterious. This pursuit underlies the effort to link deconstruction to religious understanding, and certainly this is a different pursuit from any that I have so far mentioned. Even in such cases, however, the mission of the fragment is a destructive mission, in the wake of which spiritual insight is to follow. And emphasis on a positive spiritual orientation in the wake of postmodernist devastation is not the dominant tone in postmodernist writings, at least not the writings of those postmodernists I have primarily considered here. The destructive moment as an end in itself is valorized in most of these writings—and in this respect, these writings aim at something quite different from even the most fragmented writings of Nietzsche.

An objection might be raised, however. Have I not conceded a lot to the postmodernists who claim Nietzsche as ancestor when I acknowledge that Nietzsche often depicts totalizing narratives as ultimately unfounded? After all, what else can he be doing when he describes comic ages as those in which their unfounded character is recognized as true? And if this is one of Nietzsche's major points, has not Nietzsche, like the postmodernists, insisted that we are condemned to the fragmentary?

Indeed, Nietzsche does agree with the postmodernists in denying that there is any absolute, ultimate story that serves as an epistemological foundation for all truths. Ultimately, our metanarratives are our creations, and no particular one is immortal. The death of God represents a death of faith in the absolute correctness of any one story.

But unlike the postmodernists who oppose metanarratives and wage war on totality, Nietzsche insists that totalizing schemes are existentially necessary whether or not they constitute a valid epistemological grounding for world interpretation. Nietzsche, admitting the epistemological questionability of all totalizing schemes, nevertheless finds them indispensable for us as human beings. The Apollonian illusion remains, throughout Nietzsche's work, a necessary condition of human life. And if epistemology cannot grant us a totalizing story that we can claim with certainty to "know," we must turn elsewhere for the metanarratives that ground subjective meaning. Nietzsche does not primarily concern himself with epistemology but turns to other arenas for metanarratives, particularly to those of the aesthetic and the religious.

Focusing on the status of "knowledge," "interpretation," and "the real," contemporary postmodernists give considerably more play to epistemology and the dreams of epistemology than does Nietzsche. As a result, their denial of the soundness of any epistemological ground provokes them to radical reactions—to insistence that we can speak only ironically and that we can never again accept a "big picture" on the world.

Nietzsche, however, sees the ultimate groundlessness of meta-narratives to be no reason to reject them. Not abandoning metanar-ratives, Nietzsche enjoys the plethora of possibilities. Feeling no need to wage war on totality, "meaning," or "the real," Nietzsche responds to his metaviews as an artist. Meaning is not absolute, not a function of a firm metanarrative. But Nietzsche concludes from this that we should see meaning itself as a temporal, creative activity. Far from battling against the metanarrative, Nietzsche sees metanarrative as an existen-tial, subjective task for each of us. Using the fragments of history and experience as materials, we should invent big stories as a means of making jubilant, subjective peace with the fact of flux.

One hears little of Nietzsche's ecstatic tone in the writings of contemporary postmodernists. If anything, one hears overtones of *Zarathustra's* Soothsayer. To the somber postmodernist doctrine, "All is empty, all is the same, all has been!" Nietzsche poses *Zarathusra's* lighthearted, laughing outlook on "big pictures": "Was *that* life? ... Well then! Once more!"[66]

11

The Mask of Nietzsche's Self-Overcoming

Charles E. Scott

'Mask' does not suggest in Nietzsche's writing a deceptive countenance placed on a self-revealing identity. It is not an ontological opposite to 'ground' or to transcendental reality. It does not mean something that covers something else that is more basic but indicates rather the enigma and dissemblance of phenomena. Phenomena, on Nietzsche's account, do not veil something else. They show the enigma of all things, that is, of all phenomena, by virtue of their own dissemblance. Nietzsche calls the force of dissemblance the will to power: the moving force of all things that is not subject to logical or reflective comprehension and that is the continuing force of appearing, that is, the continuing force of masking. 'Mask' paradoxically means in the context of Nietzsche's thought that our traditional concepts and experiences of reality cover over the nonreally real, the nonsubstance of the world. Chaotic appearing is masked by systems of knowledge, meaning, and signfication. Consequently Nietzsche's own concept of will to power is itself a deception to the extent that it functions as an organizing principle that explains things or that refers to something that is real in itself. Will to power in Nietzsche's work is a phenomenon primarily in its deceptive temptation to organize a discourse by its *meaning*. As a mask will to power reveals itself. As a nondeceptive idea, it withdraws into meaning.

In contrast to Greek art, which, according to Nietzsche, provides a beautiful veil to cover the terrors of chaos, his own thought is an attempt to let chaos be shown through the mask of his thought. In this sense we can say that one of Nietzsche's projects is to let the mask show itself as mask. Before this can happen, his interpretations must do more than call attention to themselves as interpretations. They need to move in such a way that their force is not one of systematic self-maintenance or insistence upon their own truth. Their force is rather one that withdraws their truth and meaning by the power that establishes their claims to truth and meaning. It must be a force of self-overcoming that makes evident the masking process in the manner in which that process goes on. When self-overcoming takes place, the veil of truth is persistently drawn away to show masking without truth and thus to show chaos without being or existence. If he succeeds and is also able to experience affirmation of the process in it, his thought of self-overcoming will constitute an art by which Greek terror and its lineage in Western thought will have been modified and perhaps, in his discourse, overcome.

The first step in understanding the mask of self-overcoming is to follow not the concept of self-overcoming but the self-overcoming process in Nietzsche's writing. I shall work on self-overcoming in relation first to the recoiling movements in Nietzsche's thought and then in Nietzsche's third section of *The Genealogy of Morals* on the ascetic ideal in order to begin an account of his own self-overcoming. Recoiling is one of the primary movements of self-overcoming and is a movement of masking in Nietzsche's writing that reveals no meaning at all. By noting the different types of recoil in his writing, we are showing the dynamics of self-overcoming in his thought. Our attention is focused on the roles of recoil and self-overcoming in his account of them.

THE FUNCTIONS OF RECOIL

Types of Recoil

Recoiling movements in Nietzsche's thought constitute a way of thinking that does not authoritatively reestablish itself or look to a completion of itself by the manner in which it moves and develops. There are four senses of *recoil* that may be taken to elaborate self-overcoming: rebound, falling back under the impact of a force, quail or wince, and coil again.

Recoil in the sense of "rebound." This is a movement of springing back in consequence of a release of pressure. This movement is evident, for example, in the rebounding effect of values that are released from traditional and opposing pressures in such contexts as Judaeo-Christian morality, nationalism, and Platonic and Aristotelian metaphysics. When suppressed valences rebound in the absence of traditional opposition, they form multiple foci of organizing powers for thought and action. The power of the ascetic ideal is dispersed in its genealogical account, for example, by the powers of what Nietzsche calls "affirmative" uncovering and making public and by the powers of sensuality, self-interest, appearance, and mortality. Such rebounding recoil, by its movement of dispersion in traditional, philosophical ways of thinking, has a destructive effect on the central organizing force of such ideas as linear time, the choosing subject, and essential unity. It has a similar effect on the affiliation of 'unity' with 'reality', the positive value of the idea of wholeness, and the explanatory value of the Kantian conception of subjectivity. The positive effect of rebounding recoil is found in the release whereby multiple forces of making, freeing, and affirming have priority over the traditional ways of establishing truth by the exclusion and suppression exercised by the power of the idea of unity. By attending to this recoiling movement, we put in question the tendency to think of Nietzsche as either a metaphysician or an antimetaphysican, that is, the content of his claims and critiques is found to be secondary to the self-overcoming movement of his thought. Rebounding recoil is a significant aspect of the self-overcoming movement of Nietzsche's discourse and is a movement to which all aspects of his thought are subject.

Recoil as falling back under the impact of a force. Many of the ideas and values that have positive functions in Nietzsche's thought fall back under the impact of his genealogical approach to those very ideas and values. In the *The Genealogy of Morals*, for example, his own attempt to remember by his genealogical work and his conscience regarding weakness and fear are clearly a part of the ensemble of values that this genealogical study negatively impacts. Both his memory and his conscience invoke the traumatic suffering that he accounts as part of their formation. Nietzsche's intention of finding the energy common to all forms of life recoils under the impact of his idea that *all* descriptive claims are interpretations within a specific descent as well as under the impact of his claim that the force of all formations—including the formation of the idea of common force—is beyond meaning and sense. The authority of Nietzsche's constructive ideas falls back—recoils—in the impact of their descent and the discursive contingency of those ideas. In this recoiling movement they lose their claims to authority except within their own discursive organization. This is a nonauthorizing movement—in this context, a movement without an author—that pervades Nietzsche's writing. His discursive organization as a whole, as a limited organic unity, is characterized by the movement of self-overcoming: there is the falling back from the authority of Nietzsche's organizing ideas and values, and there is the self-overcoming of the discourse as a whole in the impact of the force of dispersion which degenerates the authority of the given discursive unity. His genealogies are thus forces in the impact of which his own leading ideas fall back from the authoritative position that Nietzsche at times gave them.

Recoil in the sense of "quail" and "wince." Nietzsche's writing recoils before the foolishness of the values that have extremely serious impact in his tradition of thought. Redemption, self-giving love that has been idolized under the name of *agape*, seriousness of mind, honest truth, scholarly objectivity, passionate commitment to God, philanthropic concerns: Nietzsche's discourse repeatedly winces before such value as their internal motivational structure and historical formations come to light. Knowing himself to be under their effects, Nietzsche is driven like Zarathustra by the force of his wincing recoil to paradocize and ironize them and himself, not in the hope of eliminating them entirely—he too is all too human—but with the intention of putting into effet a disgust, a quailing, before their refusal of their own secret interests and before their pious blindness. Zarathustra's nausea and self-sickening are not incidental parts of Nietzsche's writing and are in part physical appropriations of wincing recoil. This movement has moment particularly for us who might read Nietzsche without paradocizing and ironizing him and ourselves too in the reading process. To take him with a heavy spirit of seriousness is no less a violation of the discourse's wincing recoil than to follow someone like Thomas Aquinas or Mother Theresa without comedy, parody, and irony. If we are unable to mock our own mocking of him, we are unable to follow one of the recoiling strands of his writing and thought.

Recoil as coiling again. We can think of this movement in relation to the ideas of eternal return and will to power. On the one hand the idea of eternal return involves a series of claims about the meaninglessness of time and the trajectory of will to power. On the other, this notion, which Nietzsche calls "the great cultivating idea," involves *in its conception* a coiling again of traditional ideas, a recollecting and gathering of inherited forces, a type of torsion among them that can release a bevy of nontraditional effects by way of directions of action, collections of newly formed or reformed presuppositions, different organizations of values and thoughts, and possibly beings different from our traditional humanity and from us who are constrained to think of terms in beings and the complicated metaphors and grammar that collect around 'being', 'thought', and 'time'. A literal or proper sense of eternal return is that all things repeat themselves in an endless circular movement. But we must ask ourselves how this claim *functions* in Nietzsche's writing. We find a double recoiling action: there is the claimed eternal recoiling again of each event before it springs forward again, expending itself, burning out, and slowly coiling again in an unthinkable return of life force to the event's constellation; then there is the coiling again in the claims of the ideas of eternal and return, of the early Greek image of time, the conflict of meaning and meaninglessness, the peculiar Western anxiety over death and loss, the twin anxieties of keeping and releasing, and all the other bits of thought and sense that compose the idea of eternal return—these composing elements are coiled again in Nietzsche's metaphor, but this recoiling movement changes the patterns of force in which all the elements have combined, in their inherited associations, and the idea of eternal return releases these elements with meanings and senses they did not have in their other metaphysical formations. In the second sense of coiling again, the ideas that have led to and made possible the idea of eternal return are themselves released from the ideologies and passions that have held them and now lead to thoughts and passions that depart from and contradict the earlier, authoritative structures. In this movement eternal return also puts in question its own authority as a definitive concept or meaning and sets in motion a self-overcoming movement within Nietzsche's thought. This recoiling movement is away from a static maintenance of the thoughts that compose it.

The movement of coiling again in the idea of eternal return, if it is itself a movement of recoils, is not a familiar one. These recoiling movements, as we find them in Nietzsche's writing, are not governed by the ideas of same, identity, or self, and the *again* of coiling again does not suggest in this context the repetition of some fundamental sameness, such as being, oneness, spirit, subjectivity, divinity, or energy with a self-realizing telos. This recoil, rather, promises a 'beyond' that verges on the horizon of our thought, on an *über*. This horizon verges not on our dominant traditions but on the movements by which those traditions decompose. This recoiling suggested by eternal return is part of the self-overcoming in Nietzsche's discourse. We find in *The Genealogy of Morals*, for example, a coiling again of the ascetic ideal. On the one hand it is the object of severe genealogical critique. On the other, it plays a major role in the genealogicial critique, and the essay coils again in the power of the ascetic ideal, now that the ascetic ideal in Nietzsche's discourse knows its lineage and amoral power. In this movement there is both coiling again and a springing rebound that pushes the discourse to the edge of its ability to speak and propels it beyond itself in a self-overcoming movement that cannot know its future or its effects. I find this the most forceful recoil in *The Genealogy of Morals*: it propels itself beyond itself in its genealogical knowledge of its own ascetic ideal.

Genealogy and the Ascetic Ideal

"Ascetic" means self-denial by means of severe abstinence. Its antithesis is, in our tradition, sensuality and the body's life. Yet *antithesis* is hardly appropriate for *body*: already an asceticism is at work in my use of *antithesis*, as though body were a thesis that could be anti. Already too much meaning is bestowed on body, already the body's density is denied in its affirmation as the antithesis of *ascetic*. From what does the meaning of ascetic ideal derive? In part, Nietzsche says, it derives from the unstable equilibrium between the animal and the angel in humans and from the human desire to survive, that is, from the human will to will (*GM*, III, 1-2). A stability is imposed on this instability that pervades human mentation and animality, but this stability has fear and the will to will as its progenitors, and fear combined with the will to will is not the hallmark of stability. The ascetic ideal is generated by lack of stability, and it pervades stability *in* this instability: it promotes the very instability that it means to overcome. We may say that it recoils in its own instability. When we hold in mind that the ascetic priest generated the space for philosophical thought, according to Nietzsche, we are prepared to see that this stabilized instability is definitive of our traditional work, that to think genuinely and seriously as a philosopher is to be marked by the ascetic ideal. We find our thinking called into question by virtue of the heritage of our endeavor.

The signature of the ascetic ideal is guilt: the felt and affirmed indebtedness of being an animal with the presence of the "angelic," an individual's being an unjustifiable, meaningless breach, an individual's lacking one central essence, an individual's being under the authority of an image of centered unity in one nature that gives and takes life. To be this breach is to be a self in need of fundamental correction within a hierarchy of greater or lesser reality. To be this breach is to be guilty.

The discipline of the ascetic ideal is self-denial in the form of continuous correction and submission of the animal, the chaotic, the meaningless: it is a discipline that subtly humiliates the meaninglessness of life by imposing a meaning for life under the transcending authority of pure life/pure being. This is a discipline that calls for the spectator's distance from the animal, the dense, the confused, the superficial, the vacuum.

The pervasiveness of this ideal cannot be overstated on Nietzsche's terns. Aside from its obvious relation to religious morality and practices, it structures both philosophical and artistic endeavor. It is found in the multiple goals of realizing a higher nature or spirituality by means of superior systems of morality, thought, and enjoyment, by the insights of privileged souls. We are naturally inclined by our discourses to find the highest forms of worship, the best forms of criticism, the most subtle wines, the loftiest music, the purest foods, the most whole-engendering methods of health care, the best causes for social action, the best morality, the formulas for realizing our true and best nature, and the best and truest thoughts: we are driven by our discourses to find the truth of ourselves by disciplines of self-realization and self-denial, like the athlete who trains for movement and endurance by austere denial of most satisfactions and by elevating a few severe activities over all others. When such endeavors are attached to the idea of virtue, we have at work the ascetic ideal and the shade of the ascetic priest.

The pervasiveness of the ascetic ideal suggests to Nietzsche the appropriateness of suspicion of our most passionate life-affirmations. He finds, for example, even in Wagner's enthusiastic affirmation of sensuality an unconscious desire for redemption, conversion, and salvation. Wagner's very seriousness betrays his chaste desire for truth in his revolt against the morality of his age: Wagner's pious, driven seriousness is the carrier of the will to truth and the ascetic ideal of that will. We find the same kind of seriousness in the phiilosophical drive for exactly accurate thought, transcendental grounding for phenomenological description, and loftiness of spirit beyond the fallen world of everyday desire and occupation. "Every spirit has its own sound and loves it's own sound," Nietzsche says, and that sound in willing itself attempts to drive out other voices and to elevate itself in the form of hierarchies of value (*GM*, III, 8). Whenever we find exclusively self-authorizing systems of values—even if those values make sensuality primary—we find the ascetic ideal at work. Such structures of value will be poor in things of nonspiritual living; they will be pure and chaste in their discipline of forming hierarchies and humble before the authority of their truth, whatever their truth might be. Our values of careful objectivity, rational explanation, suspended belief in disciplined investigation, and serenity in the face of confusion and uncertainty, we find in this genealogy, are formed by and express the ascetic ideal.

We are already familiar with Nietzsche's descriptive claim that the disciplines of knowledge and morality are themselves unconscious expressions of will to power, and we note now that these disciplines are expressions of will to power *in* their ascetic ideal. The ascetic ideal is both an articulation of the unovercomable breech in human existence, a breach that is bordered by what our tradition names spirit and animal, and an expression of will to power. As unconscious will to power, the ascetic ideal is a forceful affirmation of human meaning that enables the human organism to affirm itself in the face of no meaning at all. As unconscious expression of the void of existence, it is an affirmation that radically denies its own occurrence and that sickens itself by willing its own denial in the illusion of self-affirmation. Nietzsche's way of stating this paradox is that all willing which takes its direction from the ascetic ideal longs to escape from appearance, change, becoming, and death, and in denying the very elements of human life it denies its own happening and wills nothingness in the illusion of spirituality: the ideal wills the void—death—in spite of itself (*GM* III, 28). But it remains will. In spite of sickening itself in its self-denying will to truth and meaning, it *wills*, and the issue for us is how we are to think in this will that weakens its own organism by the nonselfconscious strategy of the ascetic ideal.

This self-consciousness is at once a process whereby the ideal continually perishes. We note first that in Nietzsche's genealogy we are involved not in an antithesis of the ideal but in the ideal's own development. The genealogy is characterized by recoil before the ugly self-contradictions that constitute the ideal, its lack of ideal in its ideal self-assertions, its dumbness, its impurity, its hubris, and its accumulation of power and authority. The genealogy's wincing recoil expresses the ascetic ideal and is structured by it. The genealogy seeks—wills—the truth of the ascetic ideal and in this endeavor finds itself submitted to the law of self-overcoming that is found in traditional morality and thought.

But this recoil is compounded by another recoil. The genealogical knowledge coils again in the energy of ascetic self-awareness, now affirmed without repression, and in this compounding torsion it interprets itself by its own paradox and meaninglessness. The genealogy finds that its own meanings are breached by no meaning at all, that its order is always in the horizon of mere lack of order, and that it does not represent an antithetical position to the objects of its critique.

What is this nontheoretical, nonantitheoretical movement? In III, 27, Nietzsche names it the "law of the necessity of self-overcoming." In the context of guilt, self-overcoming releases and reinscribes its participants in guilt, "letting those incapable of discharging their debt go free" (II, 10). Justice is overcome by a mercy closely associated with the Judaeo-Christian experience of forgiveness. But that rendering names a quasi-mercy that is itself traditionally spiritualized in the cruel and stringent terms of the ascetic ideal. It is a movement of self-overcoming in the history of resentment but a movement that traditionally reinscribes resentment and asceticism in a more stringent, yet more self-deceived spirituality of justice and mercy.

The law of the necessity of self-overcoming means in part that no spirituality—religious or philosophical or aesthetic—has authority outside its own configuration, and it means that its own unappropriated chaos will catch up with its own substantial self-deception and explode it away from itself like the recoil of a supernova. The will to power never rests in its expressions, and it never stabilizes the authorities by which it comes to stand in a given environment. It too is subject to self-overcoming.

For our purposes, the question has to do with the recoil of this law as it rebounds from itself in its authoritative status in Nietzsche's discourse. Metaphysical readers of Nietzsche take this law, as well as his ideas of will to power and eternal return, to be claims about what is really real, and many interpret his position as nihilistic because *metaphysically read* he appears to mean that what is really real lacks ultimate meaning or sense: Nietzsche's position then has the kind of negative purity that radicalizes the tradition of metaphysical skepticism. But such readings neither recognize the function of self-overcoming in the texts of this law and these ideals nor themselves engage in self-overcoming thought.

This law, the discourse of its authority, is part of the process of self-overcoming in the tradition of the ascetic ideal and the will to truth. Or we may say that it has authority on its own terms only in the organism of its own discourse. In *The Genealogy of Morals*, Nietzsche has shown that self-overcoming functions within Western morality as a law of life. This law assumes the suppression of mere void by the meanings of the ascetic ideal as well as assumes the paradoxical, decomposing void of its own meanings. Without the suppression characteritic of Western morality and its accompanying sickening and decomposition, the law does not occur. It is a law within the movement of the meanings of the ascetic ideal by virtue of those meanings' combined refusal and unconscious expression of what Nietzsche variously calls void, nothingness, and breach. The function of Nietzsche's interpretation of the law of the necessity of self-overcoming is thus to undercut its own authority outside its heritage by showing its genealogy and by maintaining the awareness generated by the genealogy.

We can see now that self-overcoming defines the movement of the ascetic ideal as well as the movement of Nietzsche's genealogical account of that ideal. Self-overcoming is primarily not a theory but a discursive movement that he identifies in Western thought and practice as well as in his own writing. When self-overcoming is treated primarily as a theory or as a paradoxical kind of intentional activity, void and breach appear to be lost in the activity and passivity of the interpretive structure: it becomes another meaning which might perplex us but which we could not be said to think as we undergo it. We are not, however, the subjects or the objects of self-overcoming. As humans, as instances of Judaeo-Christian humanitas, we are of it, and it is our submerged movement as we live out its denial. It is a movement that by reverting to itself decomposes its own theoretical standing and rebounds beyond its possible meanings into nothing that is self-overcoming itself. In this recoiling, self-overcoming movement Nietzsche's mask takes place not as a concept or a description of realty but as the enigma of meaning and no reality at all in the art of his discourse. In this sense the movement of his writing composes a mask of appearance without reality, a movement that we undergo as we follow his discourse.

Our account of Nietzsche's genealogy of the ascetic ideal has as one of its own genealogical aspects something that Nietzsche's did not have: Nietzsche's genealogy. We have verged on thinking beyond Nietzsche as we have organized his writing in a voice that was not his to control—the voice of self-overcoming—and as we have followed the effects of that movement. We have not undergone his pain over the loss of infinite meaning, for example. We have not felt Zarathustra's nausea. We could say the reason is that we have not felt deeply enough or spiritually enough. But we know that Nietzsche has put in question the meanings of both 'depth' and 'spirituality', and we pause before capitulating to their attraction. The ambivalence that Nietzsche experienced between laughter and terror over the loss of founded, teleological time need not be as poignant for us as it was for him when we have undergone the movement of his discourse. Whereas he struggled to find courage to endure the self-overcoming of both religious and moral beliefs, the passage of the monopolizing power of those beliefs has passed on to a much less troubled discursive organization. No matter how fervently we participate in religious and moral faiths, we may know that their meanings are optional and feel, perhaps with alertness, both the vacuum of human meaning and no inclination to worship, pray, praise, or confess in that vacuum, or to look for transcendent justification of our values and continuity of meanings among our transactions. We know that both religion and morality may well not only carry their own means of destruction but also be destructive for us when we live by them. These emotions and knowledges indicate part of the effects of Nietzsche's self-overcoming. We can be no more than tempted by aspects of our tradition whose passing threatened catastrophe for Nietzsche.

On the other hand, we do not need to look beyond ourselves to register the continuing effects of the ascetic ideal. I have said that one of this ideal's phenomena is found in our own reading of Nietzsche. But we can also trace the effects of self-overcoming in the weakening of those emotions that collect around the loss of foundations, the nineteenth-century idea of subjectivity, God, and the power of the idea of unity. The traces of Nietzsche's self-overcoming are found as well in the growing attraction of the ideas of breach, division, fragment, scission, void, torsion, recoil, verge, and horizon. For us probably a strong temptation is to feel satisfaction in intellectual types of humility, poverty, and chastity regarding texts, and one way beyond the ideal is concentration on self-overcoming which recoils and repeatedly occurs without reestablishing a center of focus that escapes the voice of its own overcomings. In this case, self-overcoming does not suggest dominance and exclusion in the name of the traditional notions of right. Options to the traditional ethics of suppression and outcasting, of the insistence on founded meanings, might emerge from this movement. Even that hope, however, may legitimately raise our suspicions. The nonethics of self-overcoming doubtless threatens a loss of those satisfactions we feel when we struggle for right and justice as we have inherited those concepts. But in the recoil of self-overcoming that overthrows morality from within its own genealogy, and in the rebound to options that we cannot posit from the riches or the poverty of our tradition, we might expect less of that asceticism that is able to affirm life only by distorting it in the names of meaning and goodness, that remembers only by outcasting its mere vacuum, and that fears its own margins more than it fears its closure to its own voice of self-overcoming.

Has a springing out from Nietzsche's genealogy occurred during this discussion? Has there been a recoil in our reading of Nietzsche, a recoil that moves in and to and beyond the horizon of Nietzsche's thought? In *The Genealogy of Morals* the ascetic ideal comes to horizonal awareness in which the genealogical discourse on the ascetic ideal recoils in the discovery that it has given its own lineage and found in itself the ascetic ideal. This discourse is not beyond the ideal but is aware in it, and this awareness appears to give a different horizon from that of the ascetic ideal. This genealogy discovers itself as a spectator of the ascetic ideal and as a recoiling part of the ascetic ideal. In willing its own truth the genealogy wills the self-overcoming recoils that move without awareness in the ascetic ideal. Genealogical discourse is beyond the ascetic ideal only in the sense that it affirms the recoils that pollute the ascetic ideal and infect it with self-overcoming and the emptiness to which self-overcoming bears witness. I have emphasized this discursive movement, not the experience of a genealogist, not the self-consciousness of an individual, but the discourse that puts the genealogy beyond the reach of any instance of consciousness or experience. Is this reading in the springing movement of Nietzsche's genealogy one of its products that is different from what he would or could have done? In recoiling back to Nietzsche's genealogy, are we a step removed from the ascetic ideal that his genealogy found within its own discourse? Or are we within the shade of the ascetic priest, entranced by his/her play of shadows, less aware of his/her shadow than Nietzsche? My dilemma has involved a posture of thinking and reading that distances, disciplines, and purifies Nietzsche's texts. My question is whether there is a recoil in this distance that is springing from the part played in our lineage by Nietzsche's genealogy, whether in coiling again this discourse is under the force of Nietzsche's spring which pushed his own language to a place in which the individual's experience could be undone by discourses that move in coils that are of the language's own making. My cue has been the vacuum of self-overcoming which no longer seems terrible, Nietzsche's pathos which is now less intense in the lineage that has sprung from his work, the space of spectating which might be able to will more freely its own pollution of meaninglessness and differences without identity. I am ending with the question of the mask and the question of ethics, with questions that demand not answers but rather their own continuation as questions by recoiling on themselves, with the thought that the priority of question recoils in Nietzsche's affirmation of self-overcoming, affirmation that moves thought through the nihilism of self-overcoming to self-overcoming as the spring for thought without the necessity of asceticism's denial of its own self-overcoming movement. In Nietzsche's mask of self-overcoming, question dominates solution and sets in motion a distinctive way of thinking that forms in the self-overcoming movements.

The distance of our stance is thus the question. If this masking distance moves in the springing recoil of Nietzsche's genealogy, if it is a distance of recoiling in vain, it is not a purified space for meaning, but is the movement of question without answer, a movement that in recoiling produces neither solutions nor moralities but a Dionysian quality which approaches us as a shade without a will to certainty, a Dionysian quality that is the mask of self-overcoming. The discipline of the distance of our stance regarding Nietzsche is found in maintaining the priority of question. Does *this* discipline recoil on the ascetic ideal of the academic disciplines? By maintaining the priority of question are we engaged in a self-overcoming of the ascetic ideal in our work as philosophers? Do you, like me, find it disconcerting that we, by this discipline of distance regarding Nietzsche's texts, have less of the ascetic ideal to live by? Less meaning? Do you find more to will—more will—in this loss of meaning? Can we be philosophers who do not mortar and fill in the cracks among the fragments of values and meanings? Can we as philosophers suffer and paradocize the 'why'? Know without wanting to be wise? Read with laughter the great thoughts and live without heroes? Can we maintain the distance of the questioning discourse in Nietzsche's recoils? Or must we once again return to the comforts of the ascetic priest, will meaning among all things, and answer the question, why man at all, in order to have the energy to think and to be?

12

Zarathustra's Three Metamorphoses

Robert Gooding-Williams

"On the Three Metamorphoses," the opening speech of part 1 of Nietzsche's *Thus Spoke Zarathustra*, has inspired numerous commentaries, ranging from the traditional biographical gloss to a more recent alchemical analysis of Zarathustra's language.[1] In this essay, I will argue for still another approach to this very difficult speech, by interpreting it in light of the assumption that *Zarathustra* is Nietzsche's philosophical explanation of the possibility of creating *new* (that is, non-Christian-Platonic) cultural values. In other words, my reading of "On the Three Metamorphoses" will be based on the premise that the central theme of *Zarathustra* is the *avant-garde* pursuit of novelty and originality which typifies modernist literary and artistic practices. Thus, despite the spate of recent commentators who stress Nietzsche's "postmodernism," I shall be presupposing that one of Nietzsche's preeminent philosophical concerns is the *modernist* project of cultural renewal. If Nietzsche is in fact a postmodernist, then his postmodernism is a distinctively (and paradoxically) modernist postmodernism.[2]

I

In what follows, I will be discussing each of the three metamorphoses in some detail. I want first, however, to describe briefly my understanding of the relationship between "On the Three Metamorphoses" and

Zarathustra's significance as a mode of philosophical explanation. I shall do no more than adumbrate my view of this relationship, since I cannot, within the space of a single essay, provide this view the kind of elaboration and justification it demands.

"On the Three Metamorphoses" describes the overall dramatic structure of *Zarathustra*. Indeed, the three metamorphoses of which Zarathustra speaks specify modes of action, the repeated enactment of which enables Zarathustra to become a creator of new values. The plot of *Zarathustra*, by dramatizing Zarathustra's performance of the three metamorphoses, is precisely that aspect of Nietzsche's fiction which explains the possibility of creating new values.

In order to clarify further the relationship of the three metamorphoses to the structure of *Zarathustra*, we may well recall that the figure of the child, with which the three metamorphoses ends, is the figure that the old saint applies to Zarathustra in the second section of the prologue. The saint's assertion that "Zarathustra has become a child" suggests that Nietzsche's protagonist possesses the child's capacity for new beginnings, even at the outset of the book's novel-like plot.[3] Zarathustra, from the moment of his first appearance, seems ready to participate in the sort of value-creating activity that Nietzsche, in *Beyond Good and Evil*, attributes to new philosophers. Yet I would claim that, as Zarathustra opens, Zarathustra is only potentially a new beginner, only potentially a child and value creator.

When Zarathustra initially appears, he has yet to observe his own counsel; that is, he has yet to become who he is. The story narrated in *Zarathustra* is the story of how Zarathustra fulfills his destiny, or, more exactly, the story of how he *becomes* the child and the value creator *he is potentially*.[4] That there is a story here to be told at all presupposes that Zarathustra's destiny has been deferred, or, in other words, that he has not immediately achieved his potential. A recurrent pattern of action, marked and delineated by the three metamorphoses, structures Zarathustra's effort to become actually the child he is potentially when he departs from his mountain and meets the old saint.

In general, the plot of *Zarathustra* is shaped by an opposition between Zarathustra's intention to fulfill his destiny and the obstacles which block his pursuit of his intention. These obstacles take the form of figures of repetition that speak against the possibility of creating new values. For example, Zarathustra (in part 2) hears the prophecy of a Soothsayer, which prophecy implies that the creation of new values is impossible. In the Soothsayer's vision, Zarathustra confronts the nightmare of an unending repetition that would make his

intention to fulfill his destiny ineluctably a velleity. Similarly, Zarathustra encounters distortions of his teach (in part 2) that construe it to
be a disguised reiteration of the Christian-Platonic view of human
existence. Because Zarathustra's ability to create new values requires
that he convince his audience that his views do not repeat the ideals of
Christianity and Platonism, the distortion of these views constitutes
an obstacle to his undertaking. Though less menacing than the
Soothsayer's prophecy, which envisions the fulfillment of Zarathustra's destiny as metaphysically impossible, the misinterpretation of
Zarathustra's teaching likewise opposes a form of repetition to the
consummation of his purpose.[5]

Zarathustra enacts the first metamorphosis of the spirit, symbolized
by the figure of a camel, whenever he encounters representations of
repetition (for example, the Soothsayer's prophecy and the distortion
of Zarathustra's teaching) that discourage his desire to create new
values. He performs the second metamorphosis, symbolized by the
figure of a lion, by placing himself in defiant opposition to these
representations of repetition. Finally, Zarathustra brings about the
third metamorphosis, signified by the figure of a child, when he
forsakes the defiant posture of the lion and attempts to be a value
creator. The claim at the beginning of the book, that Zarathustra has
become a child, suggests that he has already been a camel and a lion.
As the plot of the book unfolds, we find Zarathustra having to become
a camel and a lion *again*, twice in the prologue and twice in the main
text, before finally, at the end of the book, he can complete his destiny
as a child. Zarathustra completes this destiny when he finally frees
himself of the representations of repetition he has known as a burden
(as a camel) and as an object of defiance (as a lion), and thus finds the
inspiration and the power to become who he is. The repeated
enactment of different metamorphoses shows how and that it is
possible to atualize the child's potential, by depicting the conditions
which enable Zarathustra to keep faith in his destiny and transcend
its deferment.

II

I want now to consider each of the three metamorphoses individual-
ly, beginning with the figure of the camel. Christian-Platonic asceticism defines the cast of mind which Nietzsche identifies with this
figure. To use the language that Nietzsche employs in *On the
Genealogy of Morals*, the camel signifies an attitude toward human

existence according to which nothingness, or the ascetic ideal, is the purpose of that existence. For Nietzsche, the ascetic ideal expresses "a hatred of the human, and even more of the animal, and more still of the material, this horror of the senses, of reason itself, this fear of happiness and beauty, this longing to get away from all appearance, change, becoming, death, wishing, from longing itself—all this means —let us dare to grasp it—a will to nothingness."[6] Zarathustra can describe the camel's life as a desert (*Wüste*), because the camel denies and represses everything vital in human existence, to the point of transforming human existence into something barren and lifeless. In its Christian-Platonic form, the asceticism of the camel is tied inextricably to certain values, an adherence to which promotes the will to nothingness. In "On the Three Metamorphoses," Zarathustra characterizes these values in terms of the "thou shalt" ("du sollst") morality of the Old Testament. Here, as elsewhere in the text, he insists that Christian-Platonic values, which the camel reveres, burden the camel in the manner of a heavy (*schwer*) weight that is difficult to bear. In Zarathustra's view, the camel is an image of life turned against itself, of a will that stands in awe of values that threaten to crush the human will and destroy it.[7]

Nietzsche offers at least two reasons for the belief that Christian-Platonic values express a will to negate life. First, he maintains that these values, by virtue of their *content*, slander the passions, sensuality, beauty, and so forth. They identify as wrong or sinful particular aspects of human life that seem essential to human beings' existence as embodied beings in time. Second, and perhaps more important, Christian-Platonic values express an unconditional morality, and "confronted with morality (especially Christian, or unconditional, morality), life *must* continually and inevitably be in the wrong, because life is something essentially amoral—and eventually crushed by the weight of contempt and the eternal no, life *must* then be felt to be unworthy of desire and altogether worthless."[8] What Nietzsche has in mind, when he alludes to unconditional morality, are values the justification of which purports to be independent of the preferences and situations which distinguish and divide human beings. Such values are unconditional because they claim to be binding on all individuals, regardless of the circumstances and interests which separate them. Nietzsche believes that unconditional morality is hostile to life, since it expresses a desire to eliminate conflict among alternative schemes of interests and values—a form of conflict that Nietzsche thinks is *essential* to life—in favor of the universal rule of one and only one value scheme. Christian or Christian-Platonic values characterize an unconditional morality, because they present themselves as the only values which human beings should ever observe. These values are symptomatic of a will to negate life, because they demand the eradication of a mode of conflict that, in Nietzsche's mind, is one of life's necessary conditions.[9]

Zarathustra introduces the second metamorphosis of the spirit with reference to the unconditional morality of the camel:

> In the loneliest desert, however, the second metamorphosis occurs: here the spirit becomes a lion who would conquer his freedom and be master in his own desert. Here he seeks out his last master: he wants to fight him and his last god; for ultimate victory he wants to fight with the great dragon.
>
> Who is the great dragon whom the spirit will no longer call lord and god? "Thou shalt" is the name of the great dragon. But the spirit of the lion says, "I will." "Thou shalt" lies in his way, sparkling like gold, an animal covered with scales; and on every scale a golden "thou shalt."
>
> Values, thousands of years old, shine on these scales; and thus speaks the mightiest of all dragons: "All value of all things shines on me. All value has long been created, and I am all created value. Verily there shall be no more 'I will'." Thus speaks the dragon.[10]

Erich Heller is right, I think, to find in the conflict between the lion and the great dragon an important allusion to Wagner's *The Ring of the Nibelung*, in particular to Siegfried's clash with Fafner.[11] It would be premature and perhaps futile, however, to attempt an analysis of this allusion without a more detailed discussion of *Zarathustra* as a whole, especially of parts 1-3. Let me turn, then, to what Zarathustra actually says about the lion and the great dragon. What characterizes the lion essentially is his defiance of the dragon's unconditional and Christian morality, the morality of the "thou shalt." Zarathustra identifies the dragon with this morality ('Thou shalt,' besides being emblazoned on each of the dragon's scales, is also his name), and thus suggests that the spirit's last god (*"letzter Gott"*) is indeed the Christian God. The great dragon, then, is a figure for the absolute power and authority which the camel invests in the values that govern his existence. "All value of all things shines on me..., and I am all created value," thus speaks the great dragon. The lion's defiance of the great dragon and his repudiation of the camel's asceticism are actions with a complex significance. In what follows, I shall attempt to elucidate the meaning of these actions, by focusing on three distinct but related themes: supersession, priority, and freedom.

III

The theme of supersession becomes evident for the first time in Zarathustra's claim that the lion "would...be master [*Herr*] in his own desert...," where "he seeks out his last master [*letzten Herrn*]." These words imply that the lion means to be master just where the dragon has been master. The lion wants to supplant the dragon as the lord of a desert in which the dragon previously prevailed. From the lion's perspective, the dragon is a usurper, because he is master in a domain—the lion's own (*eignen*) desert—in which the lion alone has the right to hold sway. The desert, once again, is Zarathustra's figure for the impoverishing impact of ascetic self-denial on human exist-ence. Life is a desert for the lion because he is an heir to the asceticism of the camel. To be precise, the life that the lion finds given to him *has become* a desert, because the ascetic ideal has dominated that life. Though the lion rejects this ideal, the life he claims for himself is its creation. The second metamorphosis does not undo the effects of repression and the will to nothingness on human life but subjects this life, without qualification, to a new master, namely, the lion's will. This will wants there to be neither no masters nor many masters but aims to be by itself the only master. In essence, the lion's will is a will to rule human existence with an unrestricted power and authority. The lion seeks out his *last* master, that is, his last master other than himself, in order to destroy a last restriction on his will. This will, or, as Zarathustra puts it, the lion's "I will," now claims for itself the same exclusive and absolute power and authority to command human existence that the Christian camel worships in the great dragon and his "thou shalt" morality.

What conceptual presuppositions motivate Nietzsche to interpret the defiant spirit of the lion as a will to supersede the great dragon? Why, in other words, does the lion's naysaying to Christian asceticism take the form of a desire to *supplant* the Christian God, or, more exactly, to represent the "I will" as the camel represents the 'thou shalt," namely, as an expression of absolute power and authority? One plausible and illuminating answer to this question is that Nietzsche conceives the conflict between the lion's will and the Christian God essentially in Reformation terms. According to Luther, it is in the nature of man's "natural" will not only to want to be a god but to want to be a god in place of the one God who actually exists. From this monotheistic perspective, which grants the possible existence of none but one God, the will to be a god cannot be a will to be but one god among many. Rather this will must be a will to annihilate the one God, in order to possess in his place his power and authority. In Luther's view, the will to annihilate God can be undone only by an act of grace.[12]

Now Nietzsche's lion, I want to suggest, is modeled on Luther's conception of a natural will that has been unaffected by God's grace. The lion, like this natural will, refuses to share the divinity he seeks. He simply will not countenance a polytheistic world in which many gods (or masters) effectively limit each other's power and authority. No less than the Christian God himself, the lion and the graceless natural will are monotheistic in their theological commitments. Each admits the existence of only one God and master, which God and master *each* strives to be. If the lion is to be the absolute power and authority he wants to be, then the great dragon must be slain. Like Luther's natural will, the lion's "I will" must will God's (the dragon's) annihilation. In fact, the lion's "I will" and the dragon's "thou shalt" cannot but exclude each other. Each can prevail only on the condition that the other fails to triumph. That even the dragon knows this is only too clear from his insistence that "Verily, there shall be no more 'I will.'"

The act of supersession is in essence an act of negation. It is, in other words, the sort of act that Nietzsche identifies elsewhere as reactive. As is typical of reactive agents, Zarathustra's lion defines himself in and through the denial of his difference from a force that dominates him. By willing to supersede the Christian God, he wills to obliterate his own difference from the power and authority that this God represents.[13] In this way, the lion denies that God's power and authority transcend him, or, what is the same thing, asserts that there is nothing to distinguish this power and authority from the "I" (his "I") which wills. But this is just another way of saying (or implying) that the lion's will wills God's annihilation or that the "I will" excludes the "thou shalt." For from the perspective of the lion's will, modeled as it is on Luther's natural will, to identify oneself with God's power and authority (to take God's place) is at once or already to have annihilated God, along with all his unconditional moral commands.

The theme of priority is related essentially to Nietzsche's notion that the lion's will is a will to supersede the Christian God. I will approach this theme by carefully considering the only words that Zarathustra attributes to the great dragon: "All value of all things shines on me. All value has long been created, and I am all created value. Verily there shall be no more 'I will.'" Part of what the dragon asserts here is the unconditional nature of the morality he represents. He implies that the values which constitute this morality are all and thus the only values that apply to human existence. The dragon, in essence, proclaims the unqualified and universal validity of a single scheme of values. But this is not the end of what he insinuates. In addition to depicting Christian values as unconditional, the dragon invests them with historicity. Speaking retrospectively, he avers that the "thou shalt" morality is a created morality that has been handed down from the past as an inescapable facticity. Speaking prospectively, he alleges that all values have long been created (" Aller Werth ward schon geschaffen"), or, in other words, that all values that could ever exist have already been created. He holds that there will be no more creation of values—no more "I will"—which is to say that the future will provide nothing in the way of new values. From the dragon's point of view, or from that of Christianity as Nietzsche conceives it, Christian values are and must be the only values, now and forever. Besides demanding an unqualified and universal obedience to its values, Christianity insists that there are not and simply cannot be any others. It is in this insistence that Christianity expresses its most virulent hostility to life.

I can now explain the claim that Zarathustra enacts the first metamorphosis of the spirit when he encounters representations of repetition that discourage his desire to create new values. As we have seen, the figure of the camel signifies an absolute submission to the Christian view of human existence. This submission in part involves acceptance of the proposition that the future will yield no new values, a proposition that follows from the great dragon's belief that already existing Christian values are and must be the only values. In the view of the camel, the future offers human beings no escape from the values that burden them, namely, no release from a facticity that is part of the legacy of the Christian God.[14] From this perspective, the future must repeat the past, to the extent that human beings must continue to live their lives in accordance with Christian values. It is not surprising, then, that Zarathustra undergoes the first metamorphosis precisely on occasions that move him to see things as a camel sees them. To be precise, Zarathustra becomes a camel only when he confronts representations of repetition (for example, the Soothsayer's prophecy or the distortion of his teaching) that amount to a reiteration of the claim that the future will or has to be a repetition of the Christian past.

To be a camel is to internalize the outlook of the great dragon, that is, to suppose that the "thou shalts" commanded by God exhaust all possibilities of value creation. The camel assumes, in effect, that God's will has expressed itself prior to every other will and thus preempted for itself all possible values. For the great dragon, there shall be no more "I will" because the divine "I will," which is the source of the divine "thou shalt," has left nothing for any will, including the human will, to accomplish in the way of value creation. Now, though the camel accepts this dogma, the lion does not. On the contrary, says Zarathustra, the lion assumes "the right to new values."[15] How does the lion do this?

The answer is that the lion denies the priority of the divine will. In fact, this denial is implicit in the lion's will to have for himself the power and authority that the camel cedes to God. As we have seen, it is in the nature of the lion's will to will God's annihilation, that is, to will that God not exist, in order to possess God's power and authority. To will that God not exist is, for the lion, to will that there not exist a will that has exhausted all possibilities of value creation, *prior* to the lion's assertion of his will. When the lion claims for himself God's power and authority, when he puts himself in God's place, he preempts for himself all possibilities of value creation. This is not to say that the lion actually creates values—indeed, Zarathustra explicitly denies that he does so—but only that the lion, in ascribing to himself God's power and authority, claims an exclusive power and *right* to create values. In other words, the lion denies that there can be any creation of value that does not express the power and the authority of his will. Whereas the great dragon purports to represent the accomplished creation of all possible values, the lion asserts that there can be no value creation that does not have and rightfully have its origin in his will. The lion implies, then, that *if* there are created values, his will, and his will alone, is the source of those values.

The theme of freedom is implicit in the lion's reaction to the representations of repetition according to which the future has to be a repetition of the Christian past. The lion defies these representations of repetition by denying that Christian values are necessarily the values of the future. This act of denial is at once an assertion of independence and a preparation for the creation of new values. "To create new values—that even the lion cannot do; but the creation of freedom for oneself for new creation—that is within the power of the lion."[16] The lion, since he is the second of the three metamorphoses, is an intermediary figure who achieves a freedom *from* Christian values and a freedom *for* the creation of new ones.[17] The lion says "no" to duty and thus wills the annihilation of the "thou shalt" he has loved "as most sacred," by finding "illusion and caprice even in the most sacred."[18] In other words, he frees himself from the Christian God, and from this god's claim to have prempted the lion's "I will,'" by declaring this god to be a nonexistent fiction. The independence from Christianity that the lion thus attains lets him believe that his future need not repeat the Christian past. The lion is free for new creation, that is, he can acknowledge the possibility of creating new values, because he liberates himself from the perspective of the camel, which perspective regards all future willing as the inevitable reassertion of past value creations.[19]

IV

I shall now turn to the third metamorphosis. Nietzsche's conception of this final transition was probably influenced by Goethe's *Novelle*.[20] Whatever its origin, the movement from the lion to the child has a special significance. This change marks the beginning of *Zarathustra* yet only reaches its climax at the end of the book. To show and explain how Zarathustra becomes who he is, and thus fulfills his destiny, is to show and explain how he completes the third metamorphosis of the spirit.

Nietzsche describes the third metamorphosis with the following words: "The child is innocence and forgetting, a new beginning, a game, a self-propelled wheel, a first movement, a sacred 'Yes.' For the game of creation, my brothers, a sacred 'Yes' is needed: the spirit now wills his own will and he who had been lost to the world now conquers his own world."[21] Nietzsche's portrait of the child occupies about a fourth as much space as his individual depictions of the camel and the lion. This portrait also seems vague and insubstantial.[22] Yet this should come as no surprise. In a sense, the central purpose of *Zarathustra* is to fill out the figure of the child, that is, to develop a philosophical vocabulary that characterizes and helps to explain the possibility of a being who creates new values. So while the description of the child in "On the Three Metamorphoses" is a thin one, much of what we find in the rest of the book compensates for it. Nonetheless, in this essay, I will limit myself to a discussion of Nietzsche's description of the third metamorphosis. In particular, I shall focus on two features of this description, namely, the child's innocence and his forgetting.

Because the figure of the child is so burdened with romantic connotations, it is not easy to do justice to the significance which Nietzsche attributes to this figure. The problem is rendered even more complex by Nietzsche's own ongoing obsession with romanticism. This obsession involves Nietzsche's repeated but often unsuccessful attempts to distance himself from romantic writers as well as his occasional palinodes, expressing the self-critical insight that sometimes these attempts have failed miserably.[23] One is not surprised, then, to discover an overriding disposition among Nietzsche's commentators to interpret the figure of the child in essentially romantic terms. Among recent critics, Erich Heller's attempt to assimilate Nietzsche's conception of this figure to the idiom of romanticisim is particularly explicit. In Heller's view, Nietzsche's child is the symbol of a paradise regained (or attained). He is a figure for a naïveté, innocence, and unity with nature that signify a dissolution of self-consciousness. In all of these respects, claims Heller, Nietzsche's child symbolizes a vision of "pure and unselfconscious being" that Nietzsche shares with Rousseau, Schiller, Kleist, Wordsworth, and Hegel.[24] Like Heller, J. P. Stern sees in Nietzsche's child a metaphor for Woodsworthian innocence. Similarly, Karl Löwith, and again recently Joan Stambaugh and Roger Hollinrake, suggest that this figure betokens an immediate oneness with being.[25]

Löwith, Stambaugh, and Hollinrake all base their views on the assumption that Nietzsche identifies the figure of the child with the motto 'I am'. This assumption finds some support in one of Nietzsche's posthumously published notes: "Higher than 'thou shalt' ranks 'I will' (the heroes); higher than 'I will' ranks 'I am' (the gods of the Greeks.)"[26] The affinity of this remark to what Zarathustra says in his first speech is obvious. What is less obvious is that the motto 'I am' should be identified with the conception of the child that emerges in "On the Three Metamorphoses." Though the phrases 'thou shalt' and 'I will' do appear in Zarathustra's accounts of the lion and the camel respectively, the phrase 'I am' nowhere occurs in Zarathustra's discussion of the child. Indeed the only 'I am' in the "On the Three Metamorphoses" is the 'I am' attributed to the great dragon, who says that "I am all created value." Moreover, what is essential to the third metamorphosis is not a transition from willing to being (for example, from "*I* will" to "*I* am") but the disappearance of the idea of a substantial subject (a so-called doer behind the deed) to whom various acts of willing can be ascribed. The child, far from saying, "*I* am," or "*I* will," does not say "I" at all. Rather he "wills his own will," which is to suggest that he acknowledges no substantial subject but only willing willing itself.

None of this shows, of course, that the motto 'I am' is irrelevant to our attempt to make sense of the figure of the child. Yet I do want to insist on a reading of "On the Three Metamorphoses" that precludes the soundness of both Hollinrake's suggestion that the child is simply being and Stambaugh's romantic belief that the child is "wholly immersed in its being."[27] If the figure of the child signifies "being," then the being it signifies has a genuine complexity, a complexity characterizing a form of willing that bears a *reflexive* relation to itself (the will of the child wills itself). The child cannot be simply being, nor wholly immersed in its being, nor, as Heller suggests, pure unselfconscius being, if only because the child exists *for-itself* as will. This is not to say, on the other hand, that the child represents an organized innocence that encompasses divided self-consciousness within a mediated or "higher" unity. If the idea of the substantial subject as such disappears with the advent of the child, then one cannot identify this figure with the substantial supersubject which idealism and romanticism en-vision as surmounting all divisions and differences.[28] I emphasize my belief that Nietzsche's child exists for-itself only in order to justify the contention that the innocence of the child cannot be the innocence of unmediated being. This contention is true, not only because the child's will wills itself, but also because the child's will is a new beginning, that is, an example of intentional activity that transcends what is ("being," as Heller understands it) toward what is yet to be. Above all else, the child is defined by his beginning intention, namely his intention to create new values.

Zarathustra identifies neither the camel nor the lion as innocent. He thus suggests that the camel and the lion have an affinity that distinguishes them from the child. As we have seen, the lion, no less than the Christian camel, believes that all created values have their origin in a cause that is the first and only cause of all created values. And despite his naysaying to those values that seem to derive from the Christian God's power and authority, the lion does embrace one Christian value, namely, that of possessing the sole and unrestricted power and authority to create values. The lion's will, like Luther's natural will, because it wants to supersede God, never questions the value of *being God*.[29] In fact, the lion's act of accrediting divine power and authority to himself is precisely the act by which he seems to redeem (make good or valuable) the impoverished existence he inherits from the camel. But what is it to be God? What is the nature of the being which the lion claims for himself, when he attributes to himself God's power and authority?

The answers to these questions can be found in the language which mediates the lion's struggle against the great dragon. This language interprets willing as a deed performed by a doer or an ego substance that underlies, unifies, and is independent of its thoughts, desires, and actions. The doer-deed dichotomy, and what Nietzsche understands to be the *fiction* of the substantial subject, are implicated in the lion's "I will," in the dragon's "thou shalt," and even in the "I am" which the dragon applies to himself.[30] When the lion supersedes the great dragon, he purports to put his ego substance, his "I," in the place of the

"I" of his nemesis. To supplant God, in the view of the lion, is to identify one's own ego substance as the only possible origin of created value. To *be* God, from this perspective, as well as from the perspective of the Christian camel, is to be the ego substance or substantial subject in which all created values originate and inhere.

As I noted above, the child does not interpret willing as the activity of a substantial subject. An important passage in *Twilight of the Idols* suggests that this rejection of substance ontology extends to the child's vision of the world as a whole. The same passage also explains Zarathustra's claim that "the child is innocence."

> There is nothing besides the whole. That nobody is held responsible any longer, that the mode of being may not be traced back to a *causa prima*, that the world does not form a unity either as a sensorium or as "spirit"—that alone is the great liberation; with this alone is the innocence of becoming restored. The concept of "God" was until now the greatest objection to existence. We deny God, we deny responsibility in God: only thereby do we redeem the world.[31]

With this statement, Nietzsche questions the principle that there is always a reason that things are thus and not otherwise (the principle of sufficient reason). He criticizes as well a particular application of this principle, according to which God, his sensorium, or his spirit, is the sufficient reason for the world's mode of being. In Nietzsche's view, one can experience becoming innocently only if one denies that the unity of the world ("the whole") is the product of a causa prima. More generally, he implies that the essence of innocence consists in relinquishing the belief that the character of the world derives ultimately from a deed done by a first doer or ego substance. On this account, the innocence of Nietzsche's child has nothing to do with achieving an immediate oneness with being but expresses the notion that there exists no causa prima, that is, no God or godlike substantial subject who is the origin and ground of all else. In "On the Three Metamorphoses," this same notion finds expression in the child's freedom from the struggle to be the one and only God who is the first and singular cause of all created values. The child is thus distinguished from the camel and the lion, as well as from the great dragon, by his liberation from the monotheistic theological thinking which these other figures have in common.

Nietzsche's claim that "the child is...forgetting" is intrinsically related to his conception of the child's innocence. Nietzsche's child forgets not himself but a theologically informed self-interpretation. Unlike the camel and the lion, for example, the child does not define himself with reference to the assumption that it is good to be the one and only God. The child's forgetting might seem, then, simply to sustain and reinforce the lion's defiance of Christianity, by extending that defiance to the very value of being God. According to this view, the child's rejection of substance ontology expresses a naysaying to the will to possess God's power and authority and thus a final naysaying to Christianity. Yet Zarathustra never describes the child as a defiant naysayer but attributes to him a sacred "Yes" that contrasts with the sacred "no" of the lion. In other words, he does not conceive the child to be a reactive spirit who constitutes his identity through acts of resistance to already established values. Whereas the lion says "no" to the dragon's "thou shalt," the child says nothing of the sort to the assumption that it is good to be God. Forgetting, unlike naysaying, is not an act that negates or contradicts previously posited theses. To contradict a thesis is to oppose that thesis to an antithesis. To forget a thesis, on the other hand, is to render conscious opposition to it impossible. The yea-saying of the child is not responsive to the claim that it is good to be God or to the dragon's "thou shalt" but presupposes that each of these theses has been consigned to oblivion. The power of forgetting is not the power of reaction but the power to release oneself from those claims that otherwise engender reaction.[32]

My account of the child's innocence and forgetting leaves a number of critical questions unanswered. How, for example, are innocence and forgetting related to the creation of new values? Does the child's innocence help facilitate such creation, or is this innocence a product of the child's discovery that he has the capacity for new creation? To what, furthermore, is the child's yea-saying responsive if not to the dragon's "thou shalts" or to the value of being the one and only God? As we have seen, the portrait of the child provided in "On the Three Metamorphoses" is just too limited to provide clear answers to these questions. This is not to say, however, that no answers are available. As the plot of *Zarathustra* unfolds, Nietzsche elaborates his conception of the child. The depiction of Zarathustra in "Zarathustra's Prologue," the discussion of creation in part 1, and Zarathustra's response to the Soothsayer in part 3 all illuminate this conception, though most illuminating is the ending of *Zarathustra*, part 4. The importance of this ending cannot be overestimated, since it is only here that Zarathustra fulfills his destiny and truly becomes the child he is potentially.

V

As I suggested at the beginning of this essay, my reading of "On the Three Metamorphoses" presupposes that *Zarathustra* is a future-oriented text whose principal theme is the modernist pursuit of cultural rupture and discontinuity. I assume, in other words, that *Zarathustra* is Nietzsche's philosophical explanation of the possibility of creating new values and that *Zarathustra* accounts for this possibility by describing the actions which enable its protagonist to become who he is. Thus, my suggestion that at the end of *Zarathustra* Zarathustra finally realizes his potential as a child is essentially related to my interpretation of *Zarathustra* as a whole.

Zarathustra can become a creator of new values because he can endure, defy, and free himself from the Christian-Platonic cultural inheritance which repeatedly besets him: this is the lesson of "On the Three Metamorphoses." The crux of this lesson is that action forms and is formed by character. As Zarathustra pursues his destiny, he enacts and reenacts the different metamorphoses of the spirit. The changes in character which produce and accompany these dramatic performances constitute the process by which he becomes a creator of new values. The three metamorphoses, because they shape and structure this process, contribute essentially to its intelligibility as an explanation of the possibility of modernism.

Part 5
Postmodernism Pro and Contra

13

Nietzsche and the Condition of Postmodern Thought:
Post-Nietzschean Postmodernism

Babette E. Babich

THE POSTMODERN CONNECTION

Whatever the tessellated schema of the postmodern may comprise, it is not principally or even in significant part illuminated by the name of Friedrich Nietzsche. Thus, beyond spontaneous and tacit invocation, neither his philosophy nor his style are much featured in discussion or debate on the postmodern. Even as Fredric Jameson broadly emphasizes the influence of Nietzschean strategies in Jean-Francois Lyotard's "differentiation between story telling and 'scientific' abstraction,"[1] Lyotard himself actually cites Nietzsche only in a restricted, background context.

Cataloguing the postmodern condition of knowledge, Lyotard criticizes the instability of modern scientific master narratives, rejecting the ostensibly absolute provenance of totalizing formulaic or theoretic idealism as well as positivistic realism. In the course of his study, Lyotard valorizes and details the inherently pluralistic (and typologically talmudistic) model of partial narratives or stories. For

Lyotard, "narration is the quintessential form of customary knowledge, in more ways than one."[2]

But in his account, Lyotard relies upon "ethnological description,"[3]
via the epic hero of myth and the Cashinahua Indian storyteller. Thus
in the modernistically recidivist French tradition of anthropology
after Lucien Lévy-Bruhl and Claude Lévi-Strauss, Lyotard prefers to
make reference to third world culture. Yet the talmudic tradition
interior to modern European culture offers an alternative and
inherently more illuminating reference. As the forgotten "other" of
Judaeo-Christian culture, this explicitly narrative tradition under-
girds the "grand" narratives of modernity. Even in the slim reference
that can be spared for this introduction, a hermeneutic of the
talmudic tradition sheds at least as much light on the pragmatics of
narrative knowledge as Lyotard's own ethno-distant reflection on "the
savage mind."[4]

The talmudic account is not only the contextual story of a story but
as the word at least of a teacher, if not of an exceptionally good and
wise man, the story told is also always 'true'. Hence, in its talmudistic
significance, Lyotard's narrative pluralism is never a relativism. The
connection between Nietzsche and the talmudistic expression
Lyotard has brought to bear on the question of the postmodern is
propadeutic; the latter pluralism works by way of Nietzsche's antece-
dent perspectivalism.

Articulating the postmodern condition of knowledge, Nietzsche
recognized that "'European nihilism' resulted from the truth requirement of science being turned back against itself."[5] On the level of
culture-criticism, the Nietzschean philosophical perspective questions the bourgeois humanist tradition on the terms of the centrality
and authority of the subject. On its most controversial and to date
inarticulable epistemic level, Nietzsche's perspective challenges the
possibility of any univocal truth and the illusion of seamless technico-
scientific mastery.

Even so, it must be conceded that Lyotard himself does not endorse
the explosive significance of Nietzsche's diagnosis for his own depiction of the postmodern. Likewise, beyond Jameson's technical acknow-
ledgment of Nietzsche's importance for Lyotard, Nietzsche's name
does not figure in his own carefully Marxian treatment of political and
cultural postmodernity. Similarly, but much further afield, Canadian
writers on the postmodern, most notably Kroker and Cook, mention
Nietzsche's name with stuttering but ultimately merely talismanic
frequency.[6] Hassan more or less omits Nietzsche from his schematism,[7] and Huyssen aligns Nietzsche with the misogynistic moderns

against the French critics' (read as Kristeva) recent description of "modernist and avant-garde writing as predominantly feminine."[8] Only Spanos seems to mention Nietzsche with philosophic sensitivity, but even this concession remains titular.[9] I discuss Jencks's classification of Nietzsche and Hutcheon's oblique review of Nietzschean influence in detail below.

It is symptomatic of the problem in question that Nietzsche's image appears on the cover of a recent German paperback on the topic of postmodernity. Typically, or because of the irony of the text's cover, the collection mentions Nietzsche only in a few places and then in connection with another topic or author/ity. In Wolfgang Welsch's leading essay, he notes that of the three putative first appearances of the term 'postmodern', the earliest is apparently to be found in Rudolf Pannwitz, *Die Krisis der Europäischen Kultur* (1917), in a context Welsch declaims as "Nietzsche-Aufguss um nicht zu sagen Nietzsche-Kitsch"—which is to say, Kitsch-Nietzsche rehashed![10] For Welsch, Nietzsche's diagnosis of the pathology of modern culture and its correction by way of the generation of the overman is the dyadic stimulus for Pannwitz's hysteric denunciation of the decline (nihilism) of modern Europe and ecstatic proclamation of a postmodern *Lösungsperspektive* via a proto-Nazi "post-modern human" ideal. Beyond Pannwitz, one imagines, one could add the names of Spengler, Jünger, and, of course, Heidegger. Thus a glimpse into its deepest waters unsettles a review of the postmodern reception of Nietzsche.

It seems to me that the ordinary vector connecting Nietzsche and the postmodern works along the axis of contiguity. This association is the prime working of an indeliberate reticence, which psychoanalytically inspired readers are proud to call repression. But the more obvious problem is the deliberate ambiguity of the allusion/elision characterizing Nietzsche's style. One literally does not know whereof one speaks when one names Nietzsche. The writer who asked "Have I been understood?" began his life reflection on his writings with the Schopenhauerian inclination his interpreters have always hastened to absolve, "non legor, non legar"[11]—"I am not read. I will not be read." Nietzsche is only uneasily installed in the pantheon of tacit and automatic reference: Freud, Marx, Nietzsche. This is not to affirm that of this holy trinity, or any other, only Nietzsche's name would be out of place. The author is always forced out of the text as interlocutor to become the name god of incantatory significance when the challenge of a reading requires so much power at one's thoughtful disposal that one would be compelled to think *up* to what one is reading. Nietzsche demands a melancholically resigned postmodern reader *already* "drunk with riddles, glad of the twilight, whose soul flutes lure astray to every whirlpool."[12] Searching for the "perfect reader," Nietzsche imagines "a monster of courage and curiosity," a reader "capable and worthy of the same pathos," because, he anguishes, until such a reader is found, "Nobody will understand the art that has been squandered here."[13] At the end, in the section "Why I Am a Destiny," he repeats, "Have I been understood?"[14] "Have I been understood?"[15] "Have I been understood?"![16]

NIETZSCHEAN STYLE:
THE CONCINNOUS POSTMODERN

In the following discussion I shall propose Nietzsche's stylistics as an exemplification of the communicational situation and strategy named postmodern. What I regard as the *concinnity* of Nietzsche's style can be understood, then, as a precociously postmodern compositional technique. Concinnity is derived from the Latin *concinnus*. In its colloquial adjectival significance, the word suggests a consummate performance, a 'smooth' accomplishment. The verb *concino*, means "to sing in chorus." In the sense in which I employ the term, concinnity corresponds to its technical, musical function, describing syn-phony, that is, the smooth harmony of disparate or dissonant themes. In writing, a concinnous style has two significant registers, in the first place, what is expressed by the writing as a consequence of the stylistic play and interplay of written texts, and beyond that, given the importance of Nietzsche's reader-specific, evocative style, in the second place, the appropriate(d), creative response of the reader to the text, that is to say, what the reader can work up out of the text.

Nietzsche's concinnity is a playing of and between his own texts, evoking an echoing reception or choral response by playing between and among the reader's own background of anticipation, textual affinities, and reflective/projective recollections. Thus Nietzsche's stylistic concinnity or auto-text-deconstructive style has a varying resonance for the general, atonal as well as for the sensitive or attuned reader.[17] Nietzsche's concinnity recalls Linda Hutcheon's parodic heterogeneity or double voicing, exemplifying in an evocative/provocative textual construction the Jenckian architect's double coding.[18]

Coordinate with Umberto Eco's characterization of the postmodern cultural condition via the impossible fairy tale of innocence, Nietzsche's stylistic concinnity effects the inscription/subversion of the enduring dream of innocence as a cultural ethos, simultaneously undermining its illusory totality. When Eco notes the absence of the authentic innocent or the genuine, his most important implication is neither the philosopher's homelessness nor the novelistic dictum "you can't go home anymore." For Eco has elected to acknowledge the living consequences of the conflicting but still fusing horizons of modern cultural experience and limited worldly resources. These living consequences include, for example, saying "I love you" in an age of advertisement, television, movie, and music video love affairs. Such a conflict is manifest in the American dream conviction that financial success can be won by anyone at all, Irish, Jewish, or even a Korean greengrocer, even while its attainment is predicated upon the surpassing of all competitors and the vulgar contrast between bruised third-world poverty for so many millions and the safe security of an investment bond, representing so many millions. The standard for poverty is arbitrary, but the standard for success is not: the preterite disproportion is required. As Bataille reminds us, in a truculent exaggeration of Heideggerian inauthenticity, we most of us, proximally and for the most part, see not ourselves but others as inauthentic, substandard, and so undeserving.[19] Hence the key to the longevity of late capitalism is not its technologized industry, crystallizing investment value and magnifying labor, but what this same intensification of scale heightens at the very value of the extreme.

Eco's recognition of the loss of originality and meaning in the age of image and repetition is more descriptive than prescriptive, more phenomenological than cavalier. The only way to approach the sober innocence and ideological idealism of the past is by the gently dehiscent way of irony, which invocation both sustains poetic reference and underscores our tacit recognition of its shimmering illusion. For Eco, what we know, now, is that rather than the modern occlusion of the past in the anticipatory service of an eschaton, "the past ... must be revisited." This revisitation opposes the monotony of Habermas's protests, and never aspires to the delusions and the nostalgic vision of romantic neoclassicism, for the past is to "be revisited with irony, not with innocence."[20] The ironic retrieve does not champion a lost ideal. Stylistically parodic, with sage and melancholy sympathy, the ironic retrieval confirms the illusion of the past as such, recollecting it for old time's sake. The past revisited with jaded parody or dry irony is never its reprise.[21] The ironic trope is nothing less than what Nietzsche named the artistic truth of illusion in its subsistent unsaying of what it says. But Nietzsche is a master not only of irony but also of consummate parody, as Zarathustra offers the superb proof, as he goes down and over. Thus it is important to attempt to map Nietzsche's role in the figuring of the relation between the master tropings of modernity and the postmodern concession that the truths of modernity are unavoidably chained in the circles of their communication.

An explicit critic of modern man, modern culture, modern politics, and so forth, Nietzsche may nevertheless be named "modern" by a writer such as Habermas, among others, just because reflexive critique is a defining characteristic of the Enlightenment project of the modern. If the postmodern also involves critique, postmodern critique does not advance understanding beyond prejudice but only acknowledges its inevitable constriction. This is not identical to the projection of the hermeneutic circle of understanding, because one does not actually believe one's prejudices as well as because one knows oneself to be confirmed within their value scheme. Yet, in and after all, Nietzsche's name typically has been linked to the project of modernity, whether as antipode or as its prime exemplification.[22] Is it to be claimed that Nietzsche is modern *as well as* postmodern? This claim would be more informative if there were a difference between the postmodern simple and the postmodern modern. But there is no such difference, and in its ineluctable conjunction with the modern, the postmodern may be articulated as the spoiled project or strained confidence of modernity. Like someone who no longer believes in a friend without however being able to break off the friendship, the postmodern depends upon the modern, *without* sharing the illusion of its promise as truth.

As Nietzsche suggests, the ethos of modernity as the projection of progress has long failed to live up to its own promise.[23] This failure is appropriate to and consistent with the effective functioning of a promise as such. Hence from the perspective of the modern as from that of the postmodern, there is no way to escape the failure of the modern project: the difference is simply the tenor of the (weak) optimistic modern or (strong) pessimistic postmodern response.[24] Nietzsche's importance for an understanding of the postmodern situation is his reflection on the rule of error and the illusion of truth that is not a (weak) skepticism but an affirmative experimentation with illusion (in art) and thus a (strong) confirmational incorporation of error in life (that is, in the grand style).

NIETZSCHE AND POSTMODERNISM

It is by now redundant even to acknowledged that the postmodern is perniciously chimerical.[25] For each different author, and each generic appropriation, the postmodern subject acquires a different definition. To offer an (arbitrarily) brief statement of the postmodern, it can be said that it means about what it seems to mean, that is, "approximately after modernity." The word "after" is not meant to suggest that the postmodern designates the sudden irruption of the future, as a particular period closing modernity. Likewise, what I name modernity or the modern is not interposed as a diachronic period. Indeed, the modern has been more suggestively defined as a project of antitraditional innovation.

After Baudelaire, the emphatically novel modern is the anxious exhilaration of being on the brink of every important, life-advancing answer for every intellectual, practical-social, politico-aesthetic, or even spiritual need. The claim of this answer and its scope are consequent upon the modern and still contemporary scientific ideal. In his antagonism toward the ultimacy of modern answers, Nietzsche derides less the nihilism of the modern world as such than the convicted project of incipient happiness which characterizes the modern temper. This devotion to the contentment/consumption ideal of happiness attends what Nietzsche calls the 'prosaic' (anti-artistic) style of the modern. The progress ethos of the modern with its unblinking confidence in the power of reason was the crowning project of classical philosophy. As Nietzsche remarks at the bold beginning of his career, "Socrates is the prototype of the theoretical optimist who, with his faith that the nature of things can be fathomed, ascribes to knowledge and insight the power of a panacea...To fathom the depths and to separate true knowledge from appearance and error, seemed to Socratic man the noblest, even the only truly human vocation."[26] The optimistic temper of modernity is a necessity. Driven by its consequential interest in totalizing knowledge, "science, spurred by its powerful illusion, speeds irresistibly toward its limits where its optimism concealed in the essence of logic, suffers ship-wreck."[27] Thus, the self-destruction of the modern project of rationality found its abstract but irreversible epistemological denouement in Kant and Schopenhauer. Today, in the natural field, the efforts and discoveries of science tend toward the same end of devalued cognitive transparency.[28] But for its part, science is necessarily ambivalent regarding the limits of knowledge/progress. If science embodies the modern project of rational knowledge, it self-destructively affirms its own limitations in the service of its own knowing activity. Yet that same knowing activity counts as progress, that is, as totalizable knowledge, for all practical purposes.[29]

If the postmodern condition of scientific knowing continues the knowing ethos of the modern, it is enmeshed in the contradiction it names anathema. Following Lyotard's account, the master narrative is doomed to a nontotalistic subservience because the narrative, however grand, can never be the last word on a matter. It is preeminently for this reason that the postmodern cannot be a register or period term.[30] Instead, the postmodern characterizes the reverberatory effect (or wake) of a nonrealized (better: *un*realizable) rational ideal in the recognition of the factical misappointment of the ideal of economic and spiritual progress through scientific technology and democratic enfranchisement.

In its core, as has been repeatedly observed, the postmodern perspective is fundamentally parasitic, which is also to say that it necessarily recognizes the appeal of modernity's ultimacy as a value. Hence it inscribes the discourse of the ultimate value of modernity while challenging the actual value of these values in the world of real inadequacies and endless complexity. The subversive resistance to the modern emerges as postmodernism renounces the life-leveling goals of modernity while acknowledging the essentially illusory allure of modernity as inevitably, inherently unrenounceable for mass culture.

In the (Lyotardian) literature of the postmodern, further elaborations describe the postmodern condition as a proliferation of part narratives after the dereliction of the gargantua: the ultimate answer, the one truth. For my purposes, I can only summarize/conflate the various accounts offered by Jameson, Jencks, Huyssen, Kroker, and others by defining postmodernity as an antitotalizing, affirmative, melancholic perspective challenging the totatlizing, excelsior-ultimacy of modernity.

In the remainder of this chapter I will seek to extrapolate the reasons why Nietzsche is only obliquely acknowledged in the otherwise almost obsessionally promiscuous literary, aesthetic, and philosophic debate on the postmodern. This clarification is needed not because such a revelation would serve as an improving rectification, altering the character of the postmodern but rather because such an account may indirectly illuminate that very character. For this reason, the following proposes not a reading of Nietzsche as postmodern but rather a reading of the postmodern *after*, in the light of, or post-Nietzsche.

In recent meditations on the meaning of the modern subject after the Enlightenment or, in a broader articulation, the postmodern formulation of the question of humanism, Nietzsche's importance is clear enough. But that context is not yet the context of postmodernism. No less a canonized-canonizing author than Charles Jencks, in his book folio *What Is Post-Modernism?* finds Nietzsche to be paradigmatically modern. As Jencks defines the postmodern incorporation of the modernist change in worldview, he typifies the modernist worldview as "brought on by Nietzsche, Einstein, Freud."[31] Now, the modern is variously reviewed by many authors as a critically ironic view of the past in ways that conduce to an equivocation on the modern and the postmodern. As I have noted above, the convergence of the terms as such is not problematic. What is more, in architectural styles, the modern is hardly likely to suffer a collapse into a distinctly opposing style. The usual building materials and guidebook designations assure that security. But in historiography, in philosophy, in fiction, even in graphic, plastic art, such a transmutation is not only an easy possibility but occasionally impossible to foreclose. Thus, as we have seen, in its literary, philosophic, cultural expression, the postmodern is the modern in its fullest extension. Otherwise said: the postmodern is the failure of the modern. It is the rupture of the project of rationality—but it retains, like the pieces of a shattered mirror, or the reticulation of a cracked surface of acrylic or autoglass, the surface function or the marginal contours of its original integrity.

Thus it is only of interest to reflect that what Jencks does by associating Nietzsche and the saints of modernity is symptomatic of the conceptual condition of the postmodern. As Jencks reviews the characteristic excesses of the incorporative ethos of postmodernism vis-à-vis the modern, while simultaneously refusing that same incorporation, Jencks evokes a substantive style of reflection and repetition. This style is a quintessentially Nietzschean trope which Jencks, of course, cannot identify as such but merely—felicitously—names "double coding," which at this juncture must pass as a ruptured code. Nietzsche's concinnous texts exemplify this "double coding," self-rupturing style.

Both Nietzschean concinnity and what Jencks has called double coding name the same thing. Both testify to the *doomed* reflective attempt to both do/say something and not to do/say that thing.[32] This coded coding, this having it both ways or, better, this knowing better but going along anyway, embodies the only style of life-election remaining for the postmodern times Eco names the "age of lost innocence."[33] The ironic tactic of affirming/subverting one's circumstantial sophistication by exposing its inadequacy while yet trading on its inevitable necessity operates in both Nietzsche's style and what Lyotard, Eco, Jameson, Jencks, and others name the (commerically Las Vegan) postmodern.

With a protentional reference to the postmodern question of interpretation and humanism, Hans-Georg Gadamer attributes to Nietzsche's legacy "that it is interpretation, with its legitimate cognitive interpretive aim, that first grasps the real which extends beyond every subjective meaning...interpretation is expected to go behind the subjectivity of the act of meaning."[34] And it seems to me that David Carroll is right to observe, as Gadamer himself had done in another context, that "Foucault, Lyotard, and Derrida have many important predecessors in the critical project (Blanchot, Merleau-Ponty, Adorno, Benjamin, Heidegger, the German Romantics, and Kant, to name only these), but of all their predecessors, Nietzsche is undoubtedly the one who most explicitly laid the groundwork."[35] But notwithstanding, Carroll's bid for Nietzsche's foundational preeminence, Linda Hutcheon's exposition of the literary, cultural, critical strategy of the postmodern in *A Poetics of Postmodernism* exemplifies the oblivious appropriation of Nietzschean themes. Like Jencks, again, Hutcheon's tacit, unheeding importation of Nietzsche's perspectives to articulate her own poetics is effected without intent and surely without malice. Furthermore, my identificational analysis of this importation is deliberately proposed as an ad hoc, patently unfair interpretation. It is not proposed as an analysis of the origin of Hutcheon's thought. I can do no more than note that Hutcheon has doubtless read Nietzsche, and her sense for precedents and exemplificational instances in cultural practice and artifact is brilliant. Yet she disregards the intellectual historical sense in which her own poetics is indebted to Nietzsche's originalizing writing and thinking, *and* she does so in fine faith. It is because this structural debt is unconscious that this positional insensitivity crystallizes the interpretive nexus I detail in reviewing the value of the post-Nietzschean (Nietzschean) for the conceptual condition of the postmodern (modern) condition.

To underline, then, as Hutcheon does, that what the postmodern redounds to "is that there all kinds of orders and systems in our world—*and* that we create them all," repeats Nietzsche's most basic perspective. To continue by emphasizing that "that is their justification and limitation,"[36] is further to recapitulate Nietzschean perspectivalism, employing the same value terms and emphases (plurality of orders, creation of values/systems, justification, limitation) while eschewing direct reference. This reticence with regard to referencing quotation is odd, given the fearless paradoxicality or express parodicality—to employ Hutcheon's useful expression of the typology of the parodic—of academic discourse on the postmodern as such. The blind foreclosure of Nietzsche in the nomenclature of postmodern stylists is not a consequence of Hutcheon's parody, and if it does recall the spirit behind what Jameson calls pastiche, the negation of the Nietzschean prefiguration of postmodernism is an almost invisible, or else illiterate, ultimately unconscious pastiche. The significance of this negation must be traced further just because there are so many authors who do the same thing.

That this interpretive insensivity to Nietzsche is not in fact a culpable failure in Hutcheon's or any other writing on the postmodern needs repeated emphasizing. But I do wish to maintain that the thought of the postmodern is best apprehended *after* Nietzsche, that is, in his fashion and with the reflective benefit of his philosophic stylistic or poetics of the modern and the postmodern.[37] As a project for another day, this elusive aspect can be traced, and finding it, we can begin to experiment with style, that is, after Nietzsche, we can better see the significant value and functional employment of post-modern double coding.

Nietzsche's perspectivalism affirms a multiplicity of perspectives, none of which, including the operating perspective of the philosopher of perspectivalism, has any absolute claim. The emphasis upon the *Übermensch* or "posthuman" in Nietzsche succeeds a critical under-standing of the human as such, shifting its position to the sliding or precessionally decentered subject of interpretive style. But for a postmodern position, the anti- or posthumanism of Nietzsche's perspectivalism reveals its unimpeachable ambivalence. As even Ihab Hassan, who has catalogued the antihumanism of postmodernity, would affirm, postmodern political reflections are not written against humanity but in the name of the possibility of its very egalitarian, liberal plurivocity. This plurivocity is Nietzsche's own antipode and still modern socius, that is, Democracy. Nietzsche's thought on the use and abuse of history, on the subject of discourse and the discourse of the subject, and, above all, on truth and lie, and so forth, involves a textual inscription/subversion of heterogeneity that can continue to count as postmodern, but its ambivalent regard for that same heterogeneity, manifest in the name of egalitarian Democracy, con-founds classification.

Here it is imperative to recall that the watchword and touchstone of Nietzsche's antitotalizing perspectivalism is its resolute provisionality. Accordingly, Nietzsche's multivalently heterogeneous perspectivalism anticipates the inherent ambivalence of the postmodern challenge to hierarchized discourse, specifically to the question of its authorial or traditional authority and the presumption of a final word.

Nietzsche's self-deconstructing, culture-deconstructive, "double-coded" textual style works as proof against the straight inevitability of the 'grand' narrative. The return of the question from reader to author, speaker to speaker, undercutting authority and thereby undercutting the modern tradition, is a Nietzschean stylistic chiasmus. This double-coded, Nietzchean style works as a multiregister movement interior to the discourse which not only subverts the reader's self-presumption but is its own overt, self-subverting reflection.

POST-NIETZSCHE: POSTMODERN

Postmodernism retains the critical, scientific vision of modernity but, together with this sophisticated self-reflexive awareness, it avows or more precisely *admits* the impossibility of scientific totalizing or absolutist knowledge. It acknowledges its implication in the modernist project through a glancing, subverting, or teasing surface affirmation which thus manifests the transparency of its eschatological movement toward the absolute. The postmodern recoil of incredulous credulity is more than the modernist hyperbolic interrogation because it also challenges the credibility of its doubt (and, accordingly, does not hesitate to undercut the doubting subject).

This return of the question is supervalently Nietzschean. And it is to Nietzsche that we turn to find the style of critical reflection articulated via a multiregister movement interior to the discourse which is not only self-reflexive but self-subverting. When Nietzsche, writing on 'The Prejudices of the Philosophers' in his (topologically and indeed topically postmodern) book *Beyond Good and Evil*, declares that the physical scientist's understanding of the law of nature is nothing but a (bad) interpretation, he cannot help concluding with a malicious concession: "Granted this too is only interpretation—and you will be eager enough to raise this objection?—well, so much the better.—"[38] Prepostmodern and with no talk of double coding, Nietzsche's style nevertheless illustrates the way it is done in the given context of explicit challenge (to the physicists) and complicit subscription (to the scientific standard). Thus we have an object textual illustration of the double turn or ambivalence of a discourse characterized by parody and the sustained question of factitious and so inherently plurivocal truth. It is imperative to note that such a text must be one that autonomically undercuts its *own* authority. While thus articulating itself in the style of totalizing discourse, the Nietzschean or postmodern text refuses itself as totalizing or absolute.

Hence it is possible to view the entire body of Nietzschean writings, or at least the individual texts themselves, as effectively self-subverting efforts working through a constant play on the reader's expectations and the philosopher's resistances.[39] In *Beyond Good and Evil*,

Nietzsche writes, "Supposing truth to be a woman—what?"[40] and so coins his own metaphor for the metaphorical goal of a classical search. But Nietzsche then moves to his own "truths," replacing a question mark with an exclamation point and writes, "But she does not *want* truth: what is truth to a woman!"[41] With this emphatic turn, Nietzsche reclaims the metaphor for the kitchen, the parlor, the world of culture, games, and nineteenth-century sex. In this way he can abuse "the scholar, the average man of science," by descrying "something of the old maid about him."[42] And at his breathless, intoxicated conclusion, Nietzsche invokes Dionysus, naming him a philosopher, to declare that gods philosophize and that the god "once said 'Under certain circumstances, I love mankind'—alluding to Ariadne, who was present—"[43] How is this statement to be read? Nietzsche scholars are themselves recalcitrantly, clumsily importunate dogmatists—what then!—and accordingly, they desex Ariadne. Dionysus, who, like Phoebus, touches Nietzsche's trembling ears, alludes to Ariadne. But who is to play Ariadne? Is it Lou—who loved only Nietzsche's ears and his hands? But is Lou then Dionysus? Or is Nietzsche Dionysus, as he declared, almost as he declared himself to be Ariadne? To be both things to himself, since he could not manage things any other way? Such a foray into the domain of Nietzschean stylistics goes too far afield. I mention it here only by way of showing that throughout the text in question, as throughout all of Nietzsche's texts, women, truth, and even philosophers are concinnously double played, or, at the very least, double voiced.

To leave off the reading I promised not to commence, it can be concluded that the postmodern, Nietzschean style of philosophy declaims the impossibility of the (master) narrative while already recognizing that language, the illusory rule of grammar and the phantasy consequences of syntax, provides its own inscription of a univocal, hypostatizing, and so 'master' narration. Denying (or underscoring) the totalizing character of one's own discourse does not redound to a logical regress but much rather to the inadequacy of the logical. In a language that qualifies domains and universes such that it is possible to say "There is no truth" or "There is at least one truth" and so on, there is no way of pronoucing the end of totalizing discourse except by means of self-totalizing discourse: hyperbole, parody, the aphorism, the sustained or catachrestic contradiction. That Nietzsche's notoriously protean text employs all of these forms to extraordinary effect suggests the intelligibility or viability of paradoxicality.

A deliberate or stylized self-opposition throws the whole project-possibility of totalizing discourse into disrepute. As Nietzsche's reflection suggests for our most comprehensive understanding, the implication(s) of an author's position, of the speaker's discourse for what is traditionally represented or spoken, may not but at the same time always must include the speaker, who, since Plato's thetic and illustrative exposition, has been meant to assume a neutral, objective, and only thus absolute stance. And what if the speaker's authority is questioned? Even in Plato's original context, this absolute stance is surreptitiously confirmed as ultimately vulnerable. Without a receptive reader/interlocutor, the author/speaker's bid for objectivity is doomed.

The dilemma of the speaker's self-evidence illustrates communicative perdition. This condemnation is engendered by the structure of passivity, of desire after Nietzsche, "a thought comes when 'it' wishes, and not when 'I' wish."[44] It is both possible and impossible for the speaker to betray himself to his interlocutor because as, Heidegger says, *Die Sprache spricht*, "Language speaks,"[45] which is then to say with Lacan, "that the subject is spoken rather than speaking."[46] Even at this provisionary juncture, the structuring of language demands much more elucidation. In the concluding space of this essay, I can offer no more than a sliding reflection on the task to be begun.

POSTMODERN TRUTH: DUPLICITY AND THE SIMULACRA

"All Cretans are liars!" said (or lied?) the Cretan. The question is the truth of the truth, which is also to say, the truth of untruth. If the Cretan is to tell the truth, he thereby takes a holiday from his heritage for our sake. He sides with his interlocutor's prejudices for the space of a wink or a word, and arch irony or a relaxed sophistication are the only means to put the "truth" about Cretans across. This truce at the source, like the soft vulnerability of the possum "dead" on the road, open to antagonistic inspection, only works if, amused by the innocence of its attempted disingenuousness, we see his ruse and are moved to leave him to it rather than deliberately killing or only blindly missing him. The low-ranking wolf employs the same semiotic to the same effect, exposing his throat in combat with a wolf of a higher rank. And a deliberate affectation of innocence can gain an employer's indulgence where an attempt to offer the convolutions of personal justification will not do. Thus while the actual event may have transpired in fact, and once upon a time, a friendly, drunken, or sagely melancholic (postmodern!) Cretan may have shared a secret confidence with an Athenian or, more credibly, a Boeotian companion, this banal event only undermines itself at the same time that it threatens the inevitability of the mole's efficacy. The Cretan can tell the truth about his lying, but we will believe him only if his revelation accords with our previously measured calculations in his regard. The logical contradiction is not what kills the truth of the Cretan self-revelation. What kills truth at the start is the psychological suspicion of the motive within and above both Trojan contradiction and Cretan consistency.

Accordingly, even the best-intentioned, ingenuously self-expressive Cretan could not help but damage the totalizing implications of the secret information shared, both then and now. The revelation, like all universal designations, has its ordinary progression in which the value of the individual is effaced. All Cretans lie. One knows that all Cretans lie. All one knows is that Cretans lie. Enough of that *all* and at the end of the day, one cannot be far from the suspicion "why isn't this guy—isn't this guy still—lying to me?"

As if prefigured, the same words and reduplicative hermeneutic sound in the chagrin of disappointed calculations manifest in Freud's expression of expository suspicion: "Two Jews met in a railway carriage at a station in Galicia. 'Where are you going?' asked one. 'To Cracow,' was the answer. 'What a liar you are!' broke out the other. 'If you say you're going to Cracow, you want me to believe you're going to Lemberg. But I know that in fact you're going to Cracow. So why are you lying to me'"[47] For Lacan, parodying this problematizing dynamic of the interlocutor's expectation and the speaker's concomitant authorial frustration for his own thetic purposes: "I can lure my adversary by means of a movement contrary to my actual plan of battle, and this movement will have its decisive effect only in so far as I produce it in reality and for my adversary." Lacan is rehearsing the theoretical dialectic of communicative prediction and control, suspicion, and covert operation from the side of the subject to the object as it is played on the battlefield, the modern market, or in the schoolyard. "But," as Lacan continues to explain, the dialectic is indeed two-sided on both sides: my own side and that of my adversary, hence "in the propositions with which I open peace negotiations with him, what my negotiations propose to him is situated in a third locus which is neither my speech nor my interlocutor."[48] The problem is the problem of the signifying structure of language. That problem is not an issue for semiotic analysis as much as it remains a problem for philosophers just because, as Freud himself keenly saw, the issue is nothing less than the (Nietzschean) truth of truth. Freud writes, "the more serious substance of the joke is the problem of what determines the truth. The joke, once again, is pointing to a problem and is making use of the uncertainty of one of our commonest concepts."[49] For Freud, what distinguishes the pointing aggression of these jokes is that they attack "not a person or an institution but the certainty of our knowledge itself, one of our speculative possessions."[50]

Still innocent of the hermeneutics of postmodern suspicion, Freud's modestly modern claim is that the challenge to our knowledge of the truth does not challenge an institution. But it is as telling as anything else to note that, for a postmodern scientific culture, the speculative conviction of truth *does* have the epistemic status of an institution as a kind of fetish or phantastic ideal that Freud could hardly have conceived and that postmodern Marxist thinkers have only now begun to articulate vis-à-vis the question of Otherness, particularly in feminist and third-world contexts. It is a postFreudian, postMarxist, that is, *postmodern* and *Nietzschean*, strategy to declaim the impossibility of truth and simultaneously to recognize that, in its inscription, theorizing writing itself lays claim to the same institution. Beyond the truth of the subject, there is the subject of truth. But that too is a subject that has lost its original innocence. Nietzsche teases that he keeps "in readiness at least a couple of jabs in the ribs for the blind rage with which philosophers resist being deceived. Why *not?*"[51]

The vision of totality is tantalizing, and it would remain so if there were any yet untarnished contenders in the heaven of distant values. But we look hard to find any still inspiring possibilities as time passes and as our memories grow historiographically, scientifically sharper. Once tried, once ab-used, the name of absolute truth loses its appeal for the conviction of the phallogocentric perspective.

As Nietzsche has taunted us, taught us, there is, ultimately, no one truth but this truth that there is no one truth. And even this truth of nonsingular truth may not designate truth after all because it is one perspective and nothing more. All truths are *particularized* viewpoints, useful within particular contexts but utterly unnecessary and possibly even useless outside them.

The question to be answered is not, of course, the question of the real or authentic *meaning* of the postmodern, of postmodern*ity*, or of postmodern*ism*. The postmodern is a quintessentially topical construct, ranging over the contextual surfaces of its applications in as multifarious a variety as those applications themselves. If anything conjoins this variety, and so entitles it to the homogeneity of a single rubric, it is the negativity imposed by postmodern/ity/ism. In the field of philosophy, the epistemic posture of knowledge, the status of truth, the standing of being—in the discipline of the love of wisdom, the discourse of the master knower, the knower of mastery, of discourse, of truth and lie—the postmodern condition is the condition of the end and the end of the end. It is the end at all events and turns, the end of the answer, the end of the understanding of the question as propadeutic to an unknown answer because the question that leads to an answer only leads to an answer in a duplicity or imitation of a seeking. And an authentic search need never be attempted, because what is sought has already been found, as Pascal, already arch, already posed in the vault of modernity, has reminded the belated, blinking readers of the question of the question. But to ask the question one needs more than a faith in answers; one needs more than belief. In place of the faith of our fathers, the faith of religion and the faith of science—in the place, that is to say, of the *answer*—one needs the rare ability to think, and the daring that is the exact prerequisite for its very exercise which is its only consummation.

For the philosopher, the seeker of wisdom, the devoted friend of truth, truth should never have been conceived as an ultimate answer. But as Nietzsche muses, the danger of this conception is unabated and "the innocence of thinkers has something touching and inspiring of reverence in it which permits them even today to go up to consciousness and ask it to give them *honest* answers."[52] After Freud, and after Lacan's retrieve of what Freud discovered as the insistent horror of the unnamed (*es/ça*) that speaks in our place, we begin to recognize that the cognitive ideal of truth has been installed in the place of the (unconscious) object of desire. For again as Heidegger has it, "Language speaks."[53] But this again, is to say what Lacan says on the matter, "the subject is spoken, rather than speaking."[54] Lacan introduces this Heideggerian expression of human Dasein as 'spoken rather than speaking' by affirming that "there is no speech without a reply."[55] Human beings are the locus of the discourse of the other, of what Freud called a memory and Lacan names the unconscious. This unconscious functions by inscribing its similes in the body, in its symptoms, in the words that the subject speaks when it speaks where it does not think to think.[56] When truth comes to stand in the empty place of a lacking, the insurrection of a failure to be on the plane of the simulacrum, the register of the imaginary impinges with perfect resonance upon the domain of the symbolic.

After the mechanic of the Marxian, Freudian, Nietzschean power genealogy has unhinged the innocent convictions of knowledge, the postmodern in philosophy is the condition of knowledge. The names Marx, Freud, and even Nietzsche are only a ruminative species of Lacan's suggestive "points de capiton": they are useful for their suggestive power, because of the metaphorical connections that can substitute for them, and because as names for talmudists, they conduce beyond themselves, and are metonyms for the question concerning human being and truth. The postmodern condition of knowledge can then be thought throughout its manifestations in the consecrating legitimations regarded variously as common sense (the lesser Cartesian conviction, I know this, that I am), philosophic wisdom (the Kantian vision of restraint, whatever I know is only by way of what I can know), political liberalism (just one more effort, one more negotiation, one more rehabilitative definition of mutuality, and the end of communicative discourse will be in sight), and scientific truth (the approximation of the closure between facts to be known and the productive manipulation that proves knowledge in the offerings of consumable technologies). Thus a reflection on the relevance of Nietzsche to the postmodern condition of thought is a reflection on the relevance of the question of the question, the ability to question, and to think. This reflection can begin in a time after the prize of thought, the illusion of the accession to the ultimate object, has been dismantled. The broken shards of the illusion, the shattered mirror of representation, offer a metonymic conduction which lines the thinker up, but not as before, either on the right, on the side of primacy, fulfillment, or truth, or on the left, on the side of failure, incompletion, or illusion, and leads, as a tentative question that asks where it does not know what it will find, to the inevitable shifting of the signifier, and the ambiguity of the Real that impossibly circumscribes the human condition.

---------14---------

Nietzsche, Postmodernism, and Resentment:
A Genealogical Hypothesis

Robert C. Solomon

Postmodernism is the current intellectual commodity for sale and it's being flogged shamelessly by cultural critics and university professors ... Postmodern culture also privileges those representations which can operate as exchange values ... the chief values of a consumer society. Yet underlying these values one can also detect the resonance of the catastrope, destruction and nihilism.

—*Border/Lines*

The idea is to create a mediatory concept, to construct a model which can be articulated in, and descriptive of, a whole series of different cultural phenomena. This unity or system is then placed in a relation to the infrastructural reality of late capitalism. The aim, in other words, is to provide something which can face in two directions.

—Fredric Jameson

Fundamentalism is "our fascism"—a class-, region-,. and race-based response to modernism.

—*The Nation*

What is postmodernism? Is it in fact a new twist or turn of the Zeitgeist, a new phase in that temporal slaughterbench called history (*whose* history?), or is it only an ill-defined rumble in literature and the arts, perhaps just one more intellectual fad, filled with its own pretensions, emanating from Paris with adolescent anarchism and expressing itself in the American academy as "theory"? When did this postmodern epoch begin—if it began—and what characterizes its spirit (or lack of spirit)? Is postmodernism in fact a rejection of modernism, or is it rather, as several authors have suggested, a revised version of modernism, perhaps modernism with a loss of nerve, or that omnivorous modernism which swallows and digests all things and finally even itself? Is postmodernism something new and exciting, or is it, perhaps, just an exhausted version of something all too familiar? Is it, worse, an expression of just that self-indulgent and self-righteous intellectual imperialism that it so bitterly criticizes, the attempt to cram all of the complexities of (post)modern life into a single "Unity or system"? Why would one (still) want to do that?

If there is a beginning to postmodernism (let us ignore all of those writers dating back to Heraclitus who have also been cited as "postmodern" authors), it is probably to be found in the work of the German philosopher Friedrich Nietzsche. His death in 1900 provides a convenient mark for historians, numerologists, and other scholars who find some special significance in the turn of centuries or in double-zeros, and the fragmentary, passionate, and prophesying nature of his work has special appeal to those who are on the lookout for apocalyptic trends, systematic breakdowns, historical ruptures, and 'discontinuities.' It also appeals to those with a predilection for decadence but some residual resistance to debilitating pessimism. This catalogue certainly describes Nietzsche himself, who called himself "untimely" and declared his own philosophy an "attack on modernity." He predicted a new century fraught with irrationality and danger, and he billed his own philosophy (in *Beyond Good and Evil*) as "a prelude to a philosophy of the future." If there is a general phenomenon of postmodernism, an apocalyptic break with the past, and if philosophy is an expression of it, then Nietzsche might well be heralded as its prophet and he himself as the first true postmodernist.

In this essay, I am going to try to throw some light on the common casting of Freidrich Nietzsche as the primordial postmodern philosopher and, at the same time, cast a bit of a dark shadow on the bright idea of a postmodern culture. I want to use Nietzsche—and in particular his diagnosis of *ressentiment*—to pursue my own misgivings about the hot topic of postmodernism. My ultimate suspicion is that not only does "postmodernism" fail to refer to anything interesting but (like the word "liberal" in recent national politics) it distracts from and distorts whatever substantial issues we might otherwise be discussing. And (as again in recent national politics) the language of postmodernism displays an uncomfortable if covert sympathy with some of the most reactionary voices of our times. I would not want to push this comparison too far, but it should be enough to give us pause and send us back to Nietzsche, not as the spokesman for what we unimaginatively call "postmodernism" but for his warnings against it.

Let me begin by distinguishing between postmodernism in philosophy and a broader postmodern movement which may, perhaps, include a number of other academic and artistic disciplines. (It would be surprising indeed if they all were to fit the same model.) Let us further distinguish between postmodern theory in general and what has been called the "postmodern condition" and "postmodern culture," in part because it is quite unclear whether the reference is to a culture that subscribes to postmodern theory or whether it rather fits certain contentious theories about the prognosis of contemporary American society in particular. I would of course be the last person to insist that these are entirely separate considerations. Every culture is aimed and driven by its own pet theories, whether or not these are fully articulated by some philosopher or other, and every theory reflects its parent culture, whether self-consciously or not, even if it sees itself as attacking or undermining that same parent culture. We should not be surprised, therefore, if the postmodernist attack on modernity is itself born of modernistic assumptions or if the very idea of a postmodern culture turns out to be the most visible symptom of its own diagnosis.

FRIEDRICH NIETZSCHE AND POSTMODERN PHILOSOPHY

The question is whether an alternative conception of philosophy emerges at some point in the nineteenth century, perhaps at the precise moment on January 3, 1889, when Nietzsche collapses into insanity. By leaving us a fragmentary, aphoristic collection of philosophical writings, Nietzsche provides a model for philosophy that is so different from the model of Kant and other moderns that we are forced to call it "postmodern."[1]

—David Hoy

Is Nietzsche a postmodern—or a postmodernist—however "untimely"? Should we look at his work or his life, for the one might be postmodern and the other of no interest at all? Or are we any longer able to tell them apart, in the case of this man who (according to Alexander Nehamas)[3] created himself through his work as Plato created Socrates (that is, the only Socrates whom we know)? If there is a postmodern interpretation of Nietzsche, how seriously are we to take that? Should we treat it as "just" another interpretation? As the "true Nietzsche"? (What could be less postmodern?) And yet, we have been overwhelmed lately with such interpretations. Is the postmodern Nietzsche a postmodern construction, not even an interpretation nor an invention either but a pastiche, a collage, of little pieces of Nietzsche, many of them merely marginal? Indeed, is "Nietzsche" himself not merely a text—in fact not even a text—from which anyone can make anything one wants of him? After all, Martin Heidegger (himself a sometimes postmodern hero) bases much of his own interpretation of Nietzsche on Nietzsche's unpublished notes, and some current French and Yale critics feel quite free to interpret Nietzsche (the 'true' Nietzsche) on the basis of an essay he only sketched out and never published.[4] But even if we feel properly constrained by the texts, there is room for a multiplicity of interpretations, especially considering the fragmentary and inconsistent style and the fact that Nietzsche often wrote without paying much attention to what he had said a decade, a book, or even a page earlier. Nietzsche clearly did not always mean to be taken literally, given his sense of irony and hyperbole, not to mention the Nietzschean/ Straussian/postmodernist strategies of "reading between the lines" and in the margins (where other readers usually perceive nothing but empty page). There are different styles, there is refracting rhetoric, there are alternative perspectives, contrasting interpretative frameworks, indeed several different Nietzsches, depending on the book, the period, and the mood.

Of particular importance to the postmodernist interpretation(s) of Nietzsche is the experimental perspectivism of his "middle" period. (The classification is Walter Kaufmann's.)[5] In those works, ranging from *Daybreak* to *Gay Science* in particular, Nietzsche promoted his aphoristic style, conscientiously shifted from idea to idea and from perspective to perspective, "looking now out of this window, now out of that one." It can be argued, of course, that his list of possible perspectives was more than somewhat truncated, and his perspectivism was itself a sustained philosophical polemic in defense of a substantial number of philosophical theses. But more troubling is the fact that it is not at all clear that Nietzsche's middle period should be taken as definitive or even as formative. To be sure, some of Nietzsche's most important themes emerge there, particularly his attack on Christian psychology and his critical thoughts on the nature of morality.[6] But this is just to say that perspectivism was never itself the key to Nietzsche's outlook or method and his rhetoric was always aimed at some profound philosophical (which is not to say metaphysical) prejudices. To read Nietzsche in this way, however, is to interpret him less as a postmodern than as a modern enlightenment polemicist battling against pretense and superstition, against premodern provincialism and philosophical dogmatism. Indeed, one recent author has even argued that the whole idea of interpreting Nietzsche in "fragments" is ridiculous and that Nietzsche's work should be read as nothing less than the pursuit of a single set of attitudes defined by the ancient Greeks. It is, consequently, an attack on much of what not only is "modern" but is today called "postmodernism."[7]

Even within the now traditional reading of Nietzsche, the interpretations proliferate, and the reading of the texts belies both the "single idea' and the "fragmentary" readings. How should we read Zarathustra—as Nietzsche's spokesman, as alter ego, as a parody of Christ, as a merely literary buffoon? Is Zarathustra a modernist tract, "elaborating the conditions under which the creation of new values would be possible"[8] or rather a postmodernist fragmentation, an explosion of that very ambition (with an emphasis on the problematic fourth book of that work).[9] And how should we regard that last mad or in any case maddening work, *Ecce Homo*—as the capstone and summation of Nietzsche's life work (as Nehamas has recently argued with flair and brilliance) or as one more dubious set of "interpretations" of Nietzsche which is no more "privileged" than any other? On either reading, has the modern notion of the "author" ever been called more into question and the writer's ego thrust further front and center? In short, where should we locate this "postmodern" Nietzsche that we've heard so much about, and what must we presume (or ignore) about his texts to find him—or to find the Nietzsche who is proclaimed as postmodernist prophet? Or is the postmodern appropriation of Nietzsche a misappropriation, a misinterpretation, another expression of that same cocky modernism that he so often attacked and most despised—a defensive misreading to satisfy the desperate need to find kinship when one's own intellectual confidence is without adequate foundation? But in any case, it is clear that Nietzsche gives us lots of room for multiple interpretations, and this alone makes him attractive for postmodern interpretation and interpretation as a postmodernist.

PLURALISM AND POSTMODERN PHILOSOPHY

Henceforth, my dear philosophers, let us be on guard against the dangerous old conceptual fiction that posited a 'pure, will-less, painless, timeless knowing subject'... an eye that is completely unthinkable, an

eye turned in no particular direction.... There is only a perspective
seeing, only a perspective knowing."[13]

—Nietzsche, *Genealogy*

However else Nietzsche might be considered, he was and is
primarily a philosopher, and it is his philosophy that is (or is not)
postmodern in its temperament. But what is postmodern philosophy?
How is it that modern philosophy has "ended"? My colleague Bernd
Magnus has listed six possible characterizations of what has recently
been celebrated (by postmodernists) as the "end of philosophy" or
(more in house) "the postmodern turn in philosophy."[11] This statement could mean, he suggests, (1) the completion of philosophy,
surpassing all previous achievements and setting them aside, or (2)
"the Politburo solution," in which all books attempting or advocating
open inquiry were banned or burned in favor of some established
philosophical dogma or (3) skepticism, as the conclusion that no
knowledge is possible (and not just a philosophical position itself), or
(4) the cultural loss, perhaps forgetting of philosophy, and (5) the end
of intelligent life on earth and, therefore, the end of philosophy (at
least on earth). Magnus pursues only the sixth notion, which he calls
"therapeutic" (also "Hermeneutical and pragmatic") and is directed
primarily against the first sense. It is (6) that what has been called
philosophy, at least for the past few centuries and perhaps since
Plato, has been an illusion. and (6a) there is no subject matter
properly called "philosophy," (6b) there is no method peculiar to
philosophy, (6c) there are no solutions to so-called philosophical
problems, and (6d) the history of philosophy is nothing but the failed
attempt to define philosophical problems, apply those
supposedly philosophical methods, and find those evasive solutions.
Magnus distinguishes this thesis sharply from nihilism (as I will here)
and insists instead on a sense of liberation from a constricting and
ultimately inappropriate sense of philosophy. What does not become
clear (indeed even the question is dubious) is what postmodern
philosophy—philosophy after the "end" of philosophy—is supposed to
look like. What can we talk about? But it is not just the profession—
with its entrenched and established interests—that will not close up
shop and go away. It is also those ancient, if constantly revised,
questions that ordinary nonpostmodern folk still ask, about how to
live and what to value. What does postmodern philosophy—philosophy—have to say to them?

Nietzsche's famous answer, as nondogmatic and as nontraditional
as one can imagine, is "find your own way." But is postmodernism
really so pluralist? Indeed it would seem that one dominant strain of

postmodern thinking is precisely that "one's own way" no longer exists, that our fragmentation and domination by the media has robbed us not only of "the way" but of our own way as well. But it is not as if Nietzsche actually believes Zarathustra's advice here either. Much of his philosophy is disparaging and a critique of other "ways." How can he both attack dogmatism in ethics and assert without damaging qualification his own values? The problem here is an old one, which I have elsewhere called (in a different context) "the existentialist paradox." It is: how can one reject philosophical dogmatism and then hold some more than merely subjective opinion about how it is that one (not just I) ought to live? Nietzsche is immensely sensitive to this question, and his cautious retreats to perspectivism are part of his answer. But the larger part of his response to this dilemma is outright moralizing, couched in relativistic, historical, and psychological terminology, perhaps, but it is moralizing all the same. "Become who you are" is no mere tautology; it becomes a harsh indictment of much moral and modern thinking. It is also an indictment of much postmodern thinking, with its emphasis on mass market and media thinking and its unceasing attacks on individualism and moral thinking as such.

I have seen catalogues of no fewer than a dozen such characterizations of postmodernism in general, which not only include numerous contradictions but lead us to the absurd conclusion that postmodernism began as far back as the preSocratic Greeks. Some of these lists are no more than ill-organized collections of some dominant features of late twentieth-century cultural life; others strain to develop a systematic theory. Some display an appallilng disregard for their own consistency, while others display considerable philosophical sophistication.[11] But of the many available definitions and characterizations of postmodernism, let me focus on that one admirable trait that is particularly central to philosophy, letting the semantic chips in other disciplines fall where they may. That central ingredient in philosophical postmodernism is the (in fact modernist) sensibility called "pluralism." This has a spectrum of interpretations and defenses, from Richard Rorty's declarations belligerent and therefore much in vogue, that there is no Truth and traditional Philosophy is dead as a doornail to William James's more truly pragmatic sense of tolerance for competing but equally justifiable worldviews. But on any interpretation there is no privileged intellectual or cultural position or discipline, whether philosophy, science, or Yale literary criticism, no excuse for extending the hegemonic Western moral and political position to the rest of the world in the name of "reason" and ignoring other voices, other traditions, other truths, no justification for insisting in philosophy on airtight necessary and sufficient conditions without regard to context or the vagueness and vicissitudes of ordinary thought and language. This is, I believe, the positive, even "joyful" way of presenting the usually merely negative attack on "Truth," classical metaphysics and epistemology, a way of stressing diversity rather than skepticism. Much more follows from this, and there is much to say about what distinguishes postmodernism from the dominant enlightment tradition that might well be equated with "modernism" and the complex connections between postmodernism (so conceived) and romanticism. But at any rate, the chronology should be kept within bounds. Greek and medieval pluralists may abound, but let us restrict our sense of postmodernism to those movements and figures which oppose the enlightenment tradition, especially romanticism but also certain forms of pragmatism, existentialism, and poststructuralism.

But even here, ambiguities abound. Hegel attacked the enlightenment and was instrumental in its undoing but also brought some of its most cherished ambitions to full fruition. The movement generally called romanticism declared itself the foe of enlightenment cosmopolitanism but in many ways mirrored its pretensions and is as such part of modernism as well as of postmodernism.[12] Some influential figures in contemporary philosophy are unabashedly antipluralist even while inspiring postmodernist pluralism; consider, for example, Edmund Husserl, who set the stage for much of the modern revolt but himself carried out a relentless attack on Wilhelm Dilthey and all forms of "relvativism, psychologism and anthropologism."[13] Existentialists such as Kierkegaard and Sartre often bend both ways, endorsing some of the key claims of postmodern pluralism but, in the latter case, retreating to a distinctively modernist conception of self and, in the former, a premodern conception of faith. Indeed, one prominent characterization of postmodern philosophy (and postmodernism in general) is precisely that fragmentation of self and the desperate return to earlier forms of faith. Yet another, more academic version of this retreat is the (not unwelcome) rediscovery of the history of philosophy in even the most steadfastly analytic philosophy departments. The problem with the present, postmodern or otherwise, is that it inevitably finds itself specious, and every "movement" seems to need some other against which to prove and define itself.

IS NIETZSCHE A POSTMODERN PHILOSOPHER?

Recent literature suggests agreement that Nietzsche is properly understood as a postmodern philosopher. But why? On the one hand, there are the arguments that emphasize Nietzsche's anti-realism and his attack on the myth of the given. Read with reference to these motifs, Nietzsche has been presented as a postmodern precursor of post-modern American philosphers, e.g. Goodman, Quine, Sellars and Rorty. On the other hand, Nietzsche's postmodernism can be equally well identified with his belief that the modern of classical episteme is one of domination.[14]

—Robert Gooding-Williams

If postmodern philosophy is the philosophy of pluralism, then the one philosopher who seems to stand out as the unimpeachable prophet of postmodernity is Nietzsche. He announced his distaste for modernity precisely because of its dogmatic universalism and declared himself a pluralist par excellence, especially in the guise of what he called his "perspectivism," the idea that, in his words, "there are only interpreta-tions." At the extreme, Nietzsche (and virtually Nietzsche alone, before this century) boldly declared that "there is no truth" and, more paradoxically, that "truth is error," and by no means did he exclude himself when he pointed out, at the beginning of *Beyond Good and Evil*, that philosophical systems were to be understood as the "moral prejudices" of their creators. Such declarations have too often sidetracked discussion of Nietzsche into protracted debates about his "self-referential paradox." ("When he claims that there is no truth, doesn't he mean such a declaration to be true?")[15] But the more urgent question seems to me to be the nature of those "moral prejudices." Is morality indeed a facade for prejudice? What, then, is the argument against prejudice? Is it that prejudice is a betrayal of weakness, of ressentiment? And is so, what is wrong with that? Can one possibly understand Nietzsche's charges without presuming some moral high ground—whether "morality" or not? There is also the more general problem, whether pluralism inevitably leads to relativism or subjectiv-ism, and then to conceptual chaos, such that any view is just as valid—or as invalid—as any other. This would lead to the awkward conclusion that "slave" and "herd" moralities, despite their obviously derogatory names and analyses, are just as acceptable as "master" moralities and/or no morality at all. Nietzsche's perspectivism, coupled with his comments elsewhere, has given rise to the common but wholly mistaken idea that Nietzsche is ultimately a "nihilist," but Nietzsche attacks nihilism and rejects subjectivism as nonsense and relativism as "childish." He would have little truck with that newer form of postmodern nihilism which harps on the perspectival nature of truth and interpretation as a means of avoiding any stance or commitment of one's own, even denying the significance or responsibil-ity for one's own past. Today, this is often defended in Nietzsche's name, but despite his perspectivism, there is no question about the fact that Nietzsche clearly had an affirmative ethics in mind (and on paper) and stood for something. He was no mere rhetorician or protodeconstructionist.

His perspectivism and his pluralism mark Nietzsche as the exemplary postmodernist philosopher, and of course his timing (no matter how "untimely" he considered himself) was exactly right. He wrote the main body of his work in the 1880s, vegetated in the 1890s, died precisely in 1900, and began to have a significant impact in Europe just as the chaotic new century was starting. The violence of Nietzsche's writing was perfectly appropriate to an epoch that would be wholly lacking in gentility, and it is not insignificant (though easily misinterpreted) that *Thus Spoke Zarathustra* was the most popular and most hated book of World War I (among the Germans and their enemies, respectively). Unlike the other great thinkers of Germany who preceded him, Nietzsche had no system, condemned systematization ("a lack of integrity"), and could not reach any grand synthesis (though he tried periodically) concerning the ultimate nature or significance of his own philosophy. His philosophy remained in fragments, his notes in fragments, his ideas and opinions in fragments, his life in fragments. If there is a postmodern philosophy, Nietzsche is clearly its exemplar, if not its prophet or father, but rather as a kind of failing rather than by intent.

But can postmodernism have a prophet, with its suspicions of temporality and barely suppressed fear of the future? Nietzsche's own anxious enthusiasm about the future, coupled with his fascination with the past, makes him a poor postmodern and at best a hapless postmodernist critic. And his harsh attacks on fellow philosophers are not merely deconstructive; they always come with an alternative thesis waiting in the wings. Indeed, from some of his own comments (for example, on his discovery of Spinoza), one forms the clear impression of a traditional philosopher in search of his own system and a set of "new values" (in fact the very old values of nobility and the very modern value of creativity). The mature Nietzsche (from *Zarathustra* on, at any rate) was no perspectivist, not much of a pluralist, and consequently not much of a postmodernist either.

Only in his middle, "experimental" period did Nietzsche pursue perspectivism with a vengeance. And even then, the scientistic backdrop of this experimentalism, a prejudice hardly compatible with the sympathies of most postmodernists, is not sufficiently appreciated.[16] But the critical possibilities of Nietzsche's middle period were limited, in contrast to the more celebratory enthusiasm of his first and more philological period and the more muscularly assertive polemics of his third and last "Zarathustrian" period, culminating in *The Antichrist* and *Ecce Homo*. He had easily enough pointed out and deflated the "prejudices of morality" in *Daybreak* and *Human-All-Too-Human*, but the development of a more "scientific" moral theory required something more rigorous and sustained. To this end, Nietzsche developed his view of himself (quite inaccurately) as "the first philosopher who was also a psychologist" and as a "genealogist," a concept still much in dispute and much misunderstood. The two best products of this new methodology (which together form one of the seminal works in ethical theory) are *Beyond Good and Evil* and *On the Genealogy of Morals*. The core of this theory is the idea that morality—or more accurately, Judeao-Christian morality—is the product of resentment. The question is what this theory means and amounts to and what Nietzsche wants to do with it. I think that part of the answer is unambiguous. Nietzsche seeks not only understanding but a reevaluation and even a revolution in morals.[17] He plays off one perspective against another, perhaps, but there is no question that he takes sides. In *Beyond Good and Evil* and in *On the Genealogy of Morals*, Nietzsche's view is not perspectival or pluralistic except in a degenerate sense, that some people are undeniably *better* than others and the lambs have their outlook just as the eagles do. He bragged (in *The Will to Power*) that he was interested in rank order, not egalitarian pluralism, and if postmodernism is perspectivism without privilege, or the doing away with elitism in favor of the vernacular, then Nietzsche should not be counted among the postmoderns. Or perhaps the category of postmodernism in philosophy just is not very revealing or helpful.

Resentment and Postmodern Philosophy

Out of the ressentiment of the masses it has forged its chief weapon against US, against all that is noble, gay, high-minded on earth, against our happiness on earth. "immortality" concede to every Peter and Paul has so far been the greatest, the most malignant, attempt to assassinate noble humanity.[18]

—Nietzsche, *The Antichrist*

Resentment is treated by Nietzsche and by most of his commentators as a despicable emotion that poisons anyone it enters. I want to argue that the case is more complicated than that description would suggest. The genealogical account traces "slave morality" back to literal slaves, the most downtrodden and deprived peoples of ancient times. But according to Nietzsche (and Scheler after him),[19] the modern age is virtually defined by bourgeois resentment—the resentment of a class that is no longer "slave" in any ordinary sociological or political sense but is still wholly servile in a profound psychological sense. Resentment elaborates an ideology of combative complacency, a "leveling" effect that declares society to be "classless" even while maintaining powerful class structures and differences. It is also the pretense of a self-imposed helplessness (unlike the real hopelessness of an actual slave) and a consequent passivity—except for a very active moralism and spirit of condemnation—toward the world. Nietzsche's (and Scheler's) view, in contrast, is that resentment is disastrous, incapacitating to the strong (as "bad conscience") and injurious to the weak as well. It would not be misleading (but the perspective would be odd) to say that the emotional thrust of Nietzsche's philosophy, from *Birth of Tragedy* to *Ecce Homo*, is to diagnose and extinguish resentment from our basic repertoire of emotions.

If resentment defines and so debilitates modernism, then post-modernism must overcome the spirit of resentment. Not surprisingly, the attack on resentment also turns to the political expressions of resentment, democracy, and socialism in particular. On one standard account, the modernist avidly defends egalitarianism and pluralism as weapons of social stability and progress. The postmodernist would like to take these values seriously, but the question is whether any such values are possible without resentment as their originating motive, whether egalitarianism is, as Nietzsche charged, just an extension of mediocrity, complacency and hypocrisy under the guise of self-righteousness. Accordingly, more than a few postmoderns have avoided politics altogether, or they have found themselves drawn to a very different kind of politics, and Jürgen Habermas is not alone in suspecting that the politically reactionary aspects of postmodern thinking are not merely coincidental but essential and have as much to do with their emotional structure (that is, resentment) as their notorious forgetfulness of the past.[20] (Habermas casts the net too broadly, attacking postmodern thinking as a species of romanticism. But a great many passions are both romantic and democratic and quite different from resentment.)

Resentment—I will continue to dispense with the more general meaning and the more specialized tone of the French in favor of the more familiar and accurate English word—is an emotion distinguished, first of all, by its concern and involvement with *power*. It is not the same as self-pity, with which it often shares the subjective stage; it is not merely awareness of one's misfortune but involves a kind of personal outrage and an outward projection or overwhelming sense of injustice. But neither is it just a version of hatred or anger—with which it is sometimes conflated, for both of these presume an emotional power base which resentment essentially lacks. Resentment is typically obsessive; "nothing on earth consumes a man more quickly," Nietzsche tells us, and its description often embodies such metaphors of duration and consumption as "smoldering," "simmering," "seething," and "fuming" (rather than "raging," which would indicate more activity and direction). Resentment is notable among the emotions for its lack of any specific desire. In this, it is not the same as envy—a kindred emotion—which has the advantage of being quite specific and based on desire. Envy wants, even if it cannot obtain and has no right to do so. If resentment has a desire, it is, typically, the total annihilation, prefaced by utter humiliation, of its target—though the vindictive imagination of resentment is such that even that would probably not be enough, if it were possible, which it is not. So too, resentment is quite different from spite, into which it occasionally degenerates, for resentment is nothing if not prudential, even ruthlessly clever. It has no taste at all for self-destruction; on the contrary, it is the ultimate emotion of self-preservation and distinction (we are not speaking of survival) at any cost.

Nietzsche has mixed feelings about resentment. If creativity is one of the highest virtues—and it certainly seems to be for him—then resentment would seem to be one of the most virtuous emotions, for it is certainly among the most creative, perhaps even more so than inspirational love (the schemes of Iago and Richard the Third, compared with the witlessness of Othello and Orlando, for example). Insofar as language and insight, ruthless criticism, and genealogy are skills worth praising—Nietzsche is willing to build an entire self from them—then resentment would seem to be one of the most accomplished emotions as well, more articulate than even the most righteous anger, more clever than the most covetous envy, more critical than the indifferent spirit of reason would ever care to be. Not surprisingly, our greatest critics and commentators are men and women of resentment. (Good historical examples are both Rousseau and Voltaire; contemporary examples are Andrea Dworkin and Alexander Cockburn.) Nietzsche is surely right, that our most vocal and influential moralists are men and women of deep resentment—whether or not this is true of morality as such. Our revolutionaries are men and women of resentment. In an age deprived of passion—if Kierkegaard is to be believed—they alone have the one dependable emotional motive, constant and obsessive, slow-burning but totally dependable and durable. Through resentment, they get things done. Whatever else it may be, resentment is not ineffectual. To note that resentment lies at the source of postmodernism is not to deny its potential power.

Resentment as Power, Resentment as Impotence

> Aggrieved conceit, repressed envy—perhaps the conceit and envy of your fathers—erupt from you as a flame and as the frenzy of revenge.[22]
> —Nietzsche, *Thus Spake Zarathustra*

Resentment may be an emotion that begins with an awareness of its powerlessness but by way of compensation—or what we call "expression," resentment has forged the perfect weapon—an acid tongue and a strategic awareness of the world, which in most social contexts—especially in the so-called liberal arts—guarantees parity, if not victory, in most social conflicts. The neo-Nietzschean stereotype is too often the cultivated master and the illiterate slave—perhaps because we cultivated ones, imagining a choice, cannot conceive of choosing slavery. But the tyopology that counts in the genealogy of resentment and morals is the articulate slave and the tongue-tied, even witless master. The slave is sufficiently ingenious to do what even Nietzsche despairs of doing, namely invent new values. And the master, not the slave, becomes so decadent and unsure of himself that he allows himself to be taken in by this "revaluation of values." Hegel had it right in the *Phenomenology*; so did Joseph Losey in his 1963 movie *The Servant*. Speech is the swordplay of the impotent, but in the absence of real swords it is often overpowering. Language may be the political invention of the "herd" (as Nietzsche suggests in *Gay Science*), but it is also the medium in which real power is expressed and exchanged. Irony is the ultimate weapon of resentment, and as Socrates so ably demonstrated, it turns ignorance into power, personal weakness into philosophical strength. It is no wonder that Nietzsche had such mixed feelings about his predecessor. In the weaponry of resentment, he created the "tyranny of reason" as the successful expression of his own will to power.

Resentment presupposes a sense of impotence, and Nietzsche's claim is often thought to be that only the weak feel resentment. But the text of *Genealogy* makes it quite clear that this is not so. The strong feel resentment too, for they too find themselves facing a world that is not always in their control or to their liking. The most illuminating cases of resentment are to be found not in the pathetic digs of the underclass but in the highest rings of power. In the Washington White House, for example, we are now used to the spectacle of the most powerful person on earth seething with resentment, every act expressing a sense of frustration and impotence. Nietzsche says that the difference between the weak and the strong is not the occurrence of resentment but its disposition and vicissitudes. A strong character may experience resentment but immediately discharges it in action; it does not "poison" him. But it then becomes clear that strength cannot be a public measure of power, for it is easy to see the wisdom of the Zen master and the Talmudic scholar who are never poisoned by resentment because they never allow themselves those desires and expectations which can be frustrated and can lead to resentment. Here, of course, we remember Nietzsche's bitter criticism—"only the emasculated man the good man"—but now we need a far more subtle ethics of emotion than some crude scale of intensity of passion. The man of resentment is hardly devoid of passion—even intense passion; his is the ultimate passion, which burns furiously without burning itself out. I have come to suspect, however, that this description fits all too well the low-keyed fury that manifests itself in so many postmodern and postmodernist tracts and theses, the attack on masterpieces and the concept of "the author" by those who (have tried but) will never write masterpieces, the attack on the future by those who fear that they see where it is going, the attack on enlightenment thinking by those who have given up on civil rights and social action. Postmodernism may be a useless category for understanding or even describing the world, and the postmodernist movement may not last past the next conference (in any case it will have a hard time surviving MTV), but the underlying passion that provokes it will probably be with us for a good long time.

Nietzsche envisioned a postmodern culture, in *Thus Spoke Zarathustra* and elsewhere, but ours is certainly not it, and Zarathustra himself certainly did not know where to find it. Nietzsche looked forward to an epoch free of resentment, or at least an epoch that would include a number of Übermenschen and "new philosophers" who would be free of resentment. Their time has surely not yet come. What we find instead is a resurgence of a resentment most profound, replacing the optimism of enlightenment modernism with not romantic pessimism nor even cynicism but bitter disappointment. Postmodernism is today's "futurism" but without the optimism—and without a sense of the future.

THE PASSIONS OF POSTMODERNISM

No style, no subject is intrinsically superior to any other. Vulgarized pluralism is the cultural logic of laissez-faire—'anything goes'...Postmodernism is above all post—60s; its key note is cultural helplessness.[22]
—Todd Gitlin, "Hip Deep in Postmodernism"

Postmodern is sometimes presented as a welcome rejuvenation of the new, as an avant garde that rejects the very notion of an avant garde, in any case as a breakthough, an exciting new "discontinuity" in Western history, a transcendence of a certain kind of falsehood called "modernism."[23] Definitions of modernism and postmodernism vary considerably, but I think that it is justifiable to identify the core of modernism with the idea of progress and the ideas of teleology, in the sense that there is indeed, at the end of our efforts, a goal, a kind of achievement, the Truth. Postmodernism rejects the idea of progress, rejects teleology, rejects the ideal as well as the reality of "Truth." All the rest—the fragmentation of self, the discontinuity of history, the loss of faith in institutions, the rejection of "masterpieces" in literature, the rejection of the enlightenment in ethics and epistemology in philosophy—is detail. Postmodern pluralism is first and foremost an expression of disappointment, a retreat, a purely negative thesis.

In this obvious sense, "postmodernism" is defined by its negativity, by its posture as a naysaying, however delightful some of its best known positive practices—Derrida's infamous puns and wordplay or Philip Johnson's and Michael Graves's striking squiggles, colors, and playfullness. Postmodernism, as its name shows so clearly, is a reaction, a negation, a turn against the easy confidence and optimism that were the basis of modernism. Thus the enthusiasm of postmodernism is often at odds with the theses defended in its name which tend to emphasize decadence, loss of confidence, fragmentation, disintegretion, devolution, and an obsession with excretion (at least according to *The Postmodern Scene*, by Arthur Kroker and David Cook). And despite the agreed-upon rejection of progress, it is by no means clear how postmodernism as a historical phenomenon is to be understood (in part because the periodization of history is itself a distinctively modernist strategy). The confusion and inconvenience arising from the lack of agreement on postmodernism's crucial characteristics often make it seem as if "postmodernism" is nothing but another academic coinage looking for a phenomenon. It is disconcerting, at least, to see so much ink spilled and so many trees felled just in the attempt to ascertain whether there is any such phenomenon and if so how it is to be defined.

There are almost as many definitions of postmodernism as there are postmodern authors, but although most of them refer to the state of the culture at large, the truth seems to be that they apply precisely only to a small coterie of intellectual specialists. It has often been argued, for example, that postmodernism has no place in the *Zeitgeist* but dangles as an academic epiphenomenon from multidimensional modernism. (Ironically, the insistence that postmodernism is vernacular—rather than elite—has itself been put forward as a criterion for postmodernism by Charles Jencks.) It has also been argued that the diagnosis of "decadence," and perhaps even the more noncommittal claims of "discontinuity," are themselves historical and teleological concepts. Indeed, by the end of any postmodernism seminar or conference, it is all too easy to fall into appropriate skepticism, suspicious that there is no phenomenon to which "postmodern" applies. But such an attitude may be a mistake. In certain well-defined and very protected arenas, postmodernism has been quite well defined.

There are particular postmodernisms that are (more or less) well defined and may evade the Nietzschean diagnosis anticipated above. In architecture, for instance, a rather distinctive postmodernist movement can readily be characterized in terms of the stylistic preference for eclecticism and, perhaps, a somewhat contemporary, if not exactly novel, philosophy of spatiality. The interpretation of architectural postmodernism in the light of more academic theories, however, displays that familiar postmodern arrogance and projection when, for instance, Fredric Jameson waxes eloquent about the spatial fragmentation and self-involution of the especially hideous and notoriously inconvenient Bonaventure Hotel in downtown Los Angeles (to which Russell Jacoby smartly replies that the structure of the building reflects the aim of excluding the local black and Hispanic residents.) In literature, postmodernism is sometimes defined (for example, by Louis Mackey) in terms of its tendency to self-undermining self-reflection, with Stern's *Tristram Shandy* and Pynchon's *Gravity's Rainbow* as examples, but it is far from clear that such novels signal the change in "human fate in contemporary society" that some postmodernist spokespeople announce. The threat of post-modern criticism and such tactics as deconstruction and "reader response theory," however, is that they undermine the traditional academic way of doing literary business. To English professors, at least, postmodernist criticism is very real and a danger to their authority in the classroom. In philosophy, postmodernism is almost always mentioned in conjunction with the collapse and ruination of the entire philosophical enterprise, as it dates back to Descartes, if not to Plato. The names of Derrida and Rorty, for example, can be guaranteed to send shivers of indignation through many a professional audience, for if they are right (right?), they signify the end, if not the death, of Philosophy.

But even in these academic disciplines, there is considerable confusion about the nature of the postmodern turn, and this confusion suggests that the need to insist on the existence of such a turn is more urgent than the observations that constitute its evidence. Many of the same authors and artists are mentioned (by different

theorists) on both the modernist and the postmodernist side—
Friedrich Nietzsche for one—and such diverse and opposed phenomena as Soviet social realism and Yankee hedonism are thrown
together as essential postmodern tendencies. Postmodernism is
identified with postindustrialism, with post-structuralism, with post-
Marxism, with contemporary narcissism, with the return of fantasy
and flightiness. Indeed, even the name is remarkably unimaginative
and noncommittal, indicating a mere *reaction*, a falling apart, or
falling short, a disappointment, a diagnosis, perhaps a "catastrophe"
(Kroker and Baudrillard). Despite the exuberance of some of its
defenders, with their excremental imagery (no modernist Freudian
interpretations, please!) postmodernism, beginning with the word
itself, is a cry of desperation, a philosophy of victimization, an
expression of deep ressentiment, which, as Nietzsche often argued,
can be frighteningly self-satisfied and even joyful in its impotent
attacks and its desire to see all things opposed to itself (as itself) in a
state of irremediable degeneracy.

Postmodernism and The Evangelical Right

> Fundamentalism is our fascism—a class—, region—, and race based
> response to modernism.[24]
>
> —The Nation

From the point of view of history, of course, all of this academic fuss
about "postmodernism" is a tornado in a teapot and, outside the
cloistered walls, a matter of utter indifference. "Postmodern" is just
the latest mindless journalistic euphemism for the New, the strange,
the conscientiously out-to-lunch. Academic postmodernism presents
itself in bold perspective, as a revolution, a breakthrough, but its
critics quite rightly see it as a breakdown in university life, a loss of
scholarly nerve, a reaction to academic life based on resentment. This
is not, of course, a specific ad hominem claim, as if its support were to
be found in the seething resentment of its most successful practitioners. Fred Jameson, from what I've seen of him, seems quite
content, if cantankerous and jolly enough, but what he represents and
talks about, the source of his great appeal, cannot be explained in
terms of intellectual curiosity alone. He is the latest Piper for a legion
of disgruntled academics, with or without his political preferences

and professional success, who see in the accusations of postmodernism an expression of their own frustration and disappointment with university life. (Jameson's own identity as a postmodernist, as opposed to his role as its foremost expositor, has often been questioned. It is not at all clear how Marxism—the epitome of modernism—and postmodernism could ever be compatible.) The vacuity of "postmodernism" and the empty battles fought in its name point unmistakably to a form of frustration that would rather not admit its own nature, its own limits, or its own causes.

Postmodernism, I want to suggest, is an expression of frustration, desperation, and resentment. Whether or not Nietzsche is himself a postmodernist (and it is easy to see how he might well fit into this portrait), he clearly diagnoses the phenomenon in the culture at large. But if so, then it is not hard to find a cultural reaction against modernity which is not at all academic and no doubt very dangerous. If we want to see the real power of postmodernism at work, I suggest we turn not to these academic conferences nor to the already trite use of "postmodern" in popular culture to refer to anything a bit unusual, new, or kinky but to an enormous group that, for the most part, never even heard the word. If postmodernism is an outright attack on modernity and in particular on the modern ideals of progress and the secular successes of the Enlightment, it does not follow that the ultimate postmodernists are those who explicitly and articulately recognize the historical nature of their targets but rather those who are, through Hegelian historical cunning, its mindless instruments.

This thoroughgoing attack on modernism, along with its quite literal announcement of the apocalypse and the resultant fragmentation of the world, I find in the New Right, the "Moral Majority" and its adherents. Not that the evangelical Right could solicit even a dollar with the claim, but in the name of attacking the particulars of modernism—collectively identified now as "secular humanism" but in fact better characterized as pluralism—right-wing evangelism has won over millions of people, hundreds of millions of dollars, and a dominant position in American politics. Karl Marx called religion "the opiate of the people," but I think he vastly underestimated the role of religion as critique, the attractiveness of religious utopias and heavens of all sorts, the power of religion in opposing (as well as promoting) secular progress and acting as a voice of the powerless, the disenfranchised, and the damned.[25] Religious fundamentalism in America, as in Iran, has become the popular amphetamine, the source of an enormous bust of passion that would gladly change the world.

Academia may be running out of gas, but there is plenty of emotional fuel left in the culture at large. There is indeed a postmodernist reaction afoot in the world, but it is not to be found just in a few fanciful buildings, a handful of self-referential novels, and the professional despair of those residual post-positivists who have given up on their search for an adequate theory of Truth.

Postmodernism and Emotion

> The history of philosophy is a secret raging against the preconditions of life, against the value feelings of life.... Philosophers have never hesitated to affirm a world provided it contradicted this world and furnished them with a pretext for speaking ill of this world. It has been hitherto the grand school of slander.[26]
>
> —Nietzsche, *Will to Power*

Postmodernism is typically presented in terms of theory, or as a theory, which again tends to make it a more or less exclusive academic phenomenon. It is a certain worldview—or set of worldviews, a "way of seeing, a view of the human spirit."[27] But I believe that postmodernism might better be understood, both in and out of academy, in terms of emotion or, to be a bit more phenomenologically global and Heideggerian, in terms of a mood. Postmodernism, I want to argue, represents a mood far more than it signifies any particular vision or theory, which is why there are so many mutually antagonistic characterizations of the phenomenon. That mood is one of resentment, an affect structured by the sense of failure, whether personal or collective. Of course, one could also write insightfully and entertainingly about fame, fraud, and fortune on two not entirely dissimilar evangelical circuits, but here I want to talk only about Nietzsche's diagnosis of resentment and the role of that emotion in history and morality.

Emotions, like art, literature, philosophy, truth, and morals are historically determined and culturally bound. If there is anything like a decisive cultural break between high modernism and postmodernism, we would expect one of its prominent symptoms to be some dramatic discontinuity in our emotional life—perhaps, as Fredric Jameson has suggested, "a waning of affect," but probably some more remarkable change such as the appearance of a new emotional phenomenon or the dramatic expansion or disappearance of an old one. Indeed, if postmoderism is a violent reaction, we should expect an emotion that is suitably violent and enduring and anything but "waning." I want to argue that Jameson is just plain wrong on this one, that the current cultural climate—even (especially?) within most

English departments—is explosively charged with affect, and this emotion is resentment, fueled by impotent self-righteousness and aimed at nothing less—in various revolutionary formulations ranging from deconstruction to Marxism and evangelicalism—from the odd phenomenon of professors attacking their own bread and butter and declaring it worthless to the broad theoretical denial of the major institutions of this society.

Every emotion has its "quantum of reason," Nietzsche once argued, but resentment has much more than a quantum; it also has quality. It is an articulate, tactical, even brilliant emotion. Emotions are typically teleological and serve purposes, whether noble or degenerate. The goal of resentment is a combination of nobility and degeneracy— though Nietzsche stresses the latter—and that goal is to regain self-esteem, to balance the injustice perceived in the world, to "get even"— and then some. "The heart has its reasons," wrote Pascal, but so does the spleen. It also has strategies and weaves intricate conspiracies, in which reason may be an unwitting accomplice. Despite the traditional celebration of "apatheia" in philosophy, the most violent emotions drive even our seemingly most dispassionate beliefs and values. Thus it was that Nietzsche diagnosed the whole of Judaeo-Christian morality as the expression of resentment and dubbed Kant a master of deceit. The new religious Right, whatever its claims of love and righteousness, is clearly based on just that same insidious passion. So is academic postmodernism but without the pretensions of love.

The Genealogy of Postmodernism: A Polemic

> If Naziism is a caricature of Nietzsche's social and political philosophy that loses touch with the unified culture based on Dionysian flux that underlies Nietzsche's view, some form of postmodernism is a similar caricature in terms of contemporary psychology and culture. We can't stand over and against the world, observing it as though it were a spectable, simply taking it in from moment to moment.[28]
> —Robert Ackerman, *Nietzsche: A Frenzied Look*

My hypothesis then, not meant to be unpolemical, is that academic postmodernism is an expression of just that discomfiture, that bitterness, that resentment that drives the New Right. It does not matter that the one manifestation is well articulated by some of the cleverest minds in Paris and New York, while the other is expressed mainly in biblical twattle by hams and hypocrites in Tennessee and southern California, it is not very important that the one flirts with nihilism, while the other insists on absolute truth; it matters little that one defends a sophisticated theory of textural inaccessibility, while the other takes a single text as literal authority and immediate presence. As Nietzsche so often observed (one of many Hegelian aspects about him), polar opposites are more often similar than different. What matters is the source of these two postmodern manifestations, and that source is the shared resentment of a sizable group of 'outsiders,' shut out of the mainstream(s) of contemporary society—the sixties eclipsed by Reaganomics and AIDS, "traditional family values" gone to pot—with a strong voice and a powerful vehicle of expression—through academic channels or via television, "transvaluing" the established values of the dominant culture, rejecting such central notions as the importance of progress, and adopting instead the mutually fashionable notion of a catastrophe and apocalypse. Again, it matters little that this for one group is an undefined chaos in which Hedonistic consumerism reigns and media images rule, while the other believes in Judgment Day as described in the *Book of Revelation*. But hedonism, crass symbolism, and apocalypse are less opposed than they may seem. Some of Bob Dylan's early songs capture all three conceptions at once, and Nietzsche often talks in much the same way, for example, in his celebration of that suprastoic form of resignation called amor fati. Nor does it matter that the postmoderns lampoon the vapidities of contemporary society, while the New Right attacks its obscenities. After all, are they not often the same? The most opposed reactions—depending on education, cultural background, and the immediate source of one's frustration—may be the result of the same virulent passion and that passion is self-righteous resentment.

This "naysaying," whether or not in the guise of a celebration, characterizes much of postmodern literature and criticism, and resentment, if anything, summarizes the so-called postmodern culture and its attitudes toward itself, its modernist past, and its own future. I think that Habermas is wrong to characterize this anti-Enlightenment stance as "romantic" but right to accuse it of an incipient even if unacknowledged and unwilling sympathy for fascism. one doesn't have to accept the Manichean slogans of the sixties to accept the common wisdom that for the bastards to get control those individuals who have the knowledge and skill to protest and change things need only do nothing. And one does not have to accept as typical the genuinely awful political pronouncements of some of the leading French postmodernists to acknowledge that the politics of postmodernism tend at best to be laissez-faire and merely contemptuous, a grumpy resignation to a life of suburbs, shopping malls, television, academic conferences, and (mainly) money mixed with an apocalyptic fatalism.

CONCLUSIONS: AGAINST POSTMODERNISM

Nietzsche moves toward a form of control and consistency that is inconsistent with a laissez-faire post-modernism. That there is no unified self is part of Nietzsche's diagnosis; the Übermensch moves from this in the direction of being the only truly unified individual.[29]

—Robert Ackerman

I suggest, that postmodernism is an expression of academic ressentiment, though an adequate demonstration that this is so would require much more documentation than I have mentioned here. It is, for now, a charge born of suspicion, of a (crypto-)modernists' distrust of too much uneducated enthusiasm among literary critics for the most difficult philosophy, a disgust with the proliferating numbers of philosophers who have turned against philosophy (without leaving it), and professors who have lost their enthusiasm for the masterpieces they teach, a controlled sympathy but also suspicion of those intellectuals who resent their marginal role in society. In short, postmodernism is the resentful projection of too many self-important smart people feeling slighted by the Zeitgeist. Again, I do not mean to say that everyone who calls him or herself a postmodernist or writes on postmodernist culture is expressing personal resentment. Intellectual life, like morality, can be explained in terms of geneaology, but not every individual case can or should be so explained (though of course the possibility of doing so always raises the question.) Postmodernism is an academic's unimaginative work looking for a subject matter and a definition. But it is not as if there are not enough interesting and substantial problems to work on in the world, not enough masterpieces still worth reading and rereading, not enough unsolved questions that do not collapse under the pluralist's insistence that there may be no single universal answer.

I have been challenged by some of my best (postmodern) friends, who want to know why I am so harshly critical and inflammatory on the subject of postmodernism. Indeed, have I myself not been pushing postmodern themes for two decades, attacking mechanical Cartesianism and mainstream formalism in philosophy, celebrating pluralism and passion as opposed to professional dogmatism, hyperrationality, and pretentiousness? Is not my fondness of Nietzsche itself a mark of my admiration for the diagnostic experimentalism and intellectual rebellion that is the best part of postmodernism? If so, why the vitriol, even the "bitterness"? Why try to remove Nietzsche from postmodernism and turn him against it, when it seems that he and I both embrace this new way of thinking.

Part of the reason is the utter waste of time and energy spent fighting over the definition and delineation of a period (if it is a period) that as yet has no shape or contours, much less a definition. It is no surprise that, even in the absence of any substantial "progress" in postmodern thinking, the term has already degenerated into an item of media kitsch. To be sure, the advocates of postmodernism are not entirely to blame for this degeneracy—even if they certainly ought to be more embarrassed (and the media hype does seem to follow from some of their own theories). But if nothing else, this would seem to indicate something about the term's utter vacuousnous and promiscuity.

Moreover, I find myself angered by discussions of postmodernism because so much about it—its style as well as its theories, not to mention the incredibly crass, porcine comments of some its French and Francophile advocates—promotes and even celebrates political irresponsibility and utter callousness. This is not a new charge, of course. Fredric Jameson has expressed similar reservations, and Jürgen Habermas has launched an all-out attack on postmodern thinking as nothing less than "fascist" because "romantic." My argument, in contrast, is that what is wrong with postmodernism is (to attack one crude attempt at periodization with another) that it is not romantic enough! It lacks passion (as opposed to the usual academic heat, which is not the same thing). It exercises and expresses the *wrong* passions. It lacks (and attacks) a sense of purpose. One need not read much new postmodern criticism to detect the self-congratulation and disdain for those who still believe in progress, who hold holy a cause, who want to do something about the vile state of the world rather than to generalize and moralize amorally about it. Nietzsche himself was no activist, but the one thing that cannot be said of him is that he believed in nothing. He may have lampooned "the improvers of mankind" (in *Twilight of the Idols*, not one of his better moments), but his whole philosophy was driven by a sense of purpose and guided by a keen sense of health and decay. This sense I miss in much of postmodernism, that very quality of health (as opposed to the celebration of decadence and decay), that notion that we can make a difference and are not mere passive spectators condemned to impotence by fragmentation and a leveling pluralism.[30]

I have no objection to a "new way of seeing" and of doing philosophy that is pluralistic and fragmented, whose target is academic dogmatism and the hegemony of an "enlightened" way of thinking whose main purpose seems to keep the same incompetents in power. But here as elsewhere, postmodernism seems to be more akin than opposed to what it attacks. It rejects those visions of society that make real change possible, just as it rejects or ignores those aspects of Nietzsche that make his new readers so enthralled and inspired. It fails to see (as so much of professional philosophy has failed to show) that philosophy is not just for philosophers, that philosophy is not just intellectual masturbation (as my sophomores would put it), that it is not just "spirit disporting with itself" (as Hegel more elegantly put it). The alternative to postmodern philosophy is not a return to current "mainstream" philosophy, with its residual Cartesianism and positivism and its tedious obsession with epistemology and formalism. It is not a return to the grand metaphysical speculations of yesteryear either. It is just *doing* philosophy, asking those questions that people (not just philosophers) have always asked, about living life to the fullest, about one's place in society, if not in the cosmos, about the nature of our natures (if not of human nature), self-examination and criticism which is all too absent from the pomp and Germanic playfullness that describes so much of postmodern criticism. I hear very little in postmodern chitchat about the homeless, about the racism that is still so rampant in our society. For that matter, I hear very little about friendship or ethics or death or life. From postmodernists I hear only about postmodernism. Of course, Nietzsche at the end of his mental life was talking only about himself as well, but we care about Nietzsche, for other reasons, and we rightly take that late egomania as a sign of his own hopeless decline.

So Is There a Postmodern Nietzsche?

If we read Nietzsche with the rhetorical awareness provided by his own theory of rhetoric we find that the general structure of his work resembles the endlessly repeated gesture of the artist 'who does not learn from experience and always again falls in the same trap.'[31]

—Paul de Man "Nietzsche's Theory of Rhetoric"

It has too long been fashionable to dismiss Nietzsche for his hyperbole and crypto-fascists remarks, but now Nietzsche seems to be subjected to an equally devastating mode of dismissal which turns him into a mere metaphilosopher and ignores the very "dangerous" substantial issues he raises for (against) us. Indeed, the jargon of postmodernism is even used to deny the existence of "substantial issues"—easy enough in the ethereal comfort of the seminar room but not even plausible while reading the newspaper. It ignores Nietzsche's insistence on the need for ideals and the need to take a stand. Indeed, it defends the importance of not taking a stand. What troubled Europe for so much of this century and awakened so many bright undergraduates was not Nietzsche's metaphilosophy but his uninhibited accusations and invitations to a boldness in thinking about our lives that had all but disappeared from philosophy. I would like to think that this is what postmodern philosophy is all about—moving beyond the formulaic and overly technical academic dogmatism of the recent past to personal involvement and a pluralism that is concerned with how a particular philosophy contributes to a particular life rather than how a jargonized essay fits into the latest professional fashion. There is currently a widespread suspicion that much of postmodernism is an excuse not to believe in anything, to avoid both personal and political involvement and take refuge in apathy, despair, or mere ambition. But it seems to me that Nietzsche stood for a postmodernism that involved far more. I am reminded of a statement that Peter Schjeldahl made some years ago, commenting on the artist Mark Rothko as a precursor of postmodernism: "He was too early to know that believing in something is always risky; we have the edge on him." So, too, one forms the impression, reading so many postmodern authors and commentators, that anything can be said, without responsibility, without any risk at all. But the Nietzschean conclusion to be drawn from that postmodern observation should not be retreat; it invites engagement. Postmodernism is nothing but an unusually hysterical reaction to the quickening historical process of evolution and change. It is, in that sense, the very opposite of that attitude of amor fati, which Nietzsche opposed to ressentiment and tried so hard to make his own. In this bold sense, amor fati is not resignation but the willingness to throw ourselves into our projects and into history. But this willingness seems to me to be the dominant urge of modernism, not postmodernism, and if Nietzsche is a postmodernist in this sense, he resembles Marx far more than he does Derrida (though the aims of the revolution are obviously quite opposed). There are many Nietzsches, and only one of them is the Nietzsche who anticipated the worst features of modern European history. I find it disturbing that this Nietzsche is today being resurrected and celebrated as "postmodern."

What is postmodernism? My conclusion is that postmodernism does not deserve recognition as a historical, cultural, or philosophical category and that what is today called postmodern deserves diagnosis rather than continued analysis. Is there a postmodern Nietzsche? I think our answer should be that this question is neither important nor interesting. But what Nietzsche has to say against such pessimistic and passive pretentions as postmodernism is very important and quite interesting, and perhaps the time has come to end this discussion and turn back to the texts. What Nietzsche wanted to say is not just "post-" anything.

NOTES

Introduction

1. "Interview with Stanley Fish," in *The Current in Criticism: Essays on the Present and Future of Literary Theory*, ed. Clayton Koelb and Virgil Lokke (West Lafayette, Ind.: Purdue University Press, 1987), 96.

2. But this is, when examined at all carefully, a very postmodern answer.

3. One observer who evidently thinks so is Stephen H. Watson. See, for example, his "The Adventures of the Narrative: Lyotard and the Passage of the Phantasm," in *Philosophy and Non-Philosophy since Merleau-Ponty*, ed. Hugh J. Silverman (New York: Routledge, 1988), 174-190. In giving his account of Lyotard's philosophy, he scarcely mentions *The Postmodern Condition*.

4. Harry Levin, "What Was Modernism?" in *Refractions: Essays in Comparative Literature* (New York: Oxford University Press, 1966), 277.

5. *The Postmodern Condition: A Report on Knowledge* (Minneapolis: University of Minnesota Press, 1984), 79 (cited in the text henceforth as *PC*).

6. From the close of the preface to the second edition of *The Gay Science*.

7. See, for example, Clayton Koelb, "'Tragedy' as an Evaluative Term," *Comparative Literature Studies* 11 (1974), 69-84; and Koelb, "The Problem of Tragedy as a Genre," *Genre* 8 (1975), 248-66. As noted below, I do not wish to imply by this comparison that "postmodernism" has the same cultural importance as "tragedy."

8. Gayatri Chakravorty Spivak, "Imperialism and Sexual Difference," in *The Current in Criticism*, 320.

9. Barbara Herrnstein Smith, *Contingencies of Value: Alternative Perspectives for Critical Theory* (Cambridge, Mass.: Harvard University Press, 1988), 151. By quoting Smith's book, which is itself arguably a version of the postmodernist position, I doubtless stack the deck on behalf of one side of the question.

Chapter 1: Redeeming Revenge

Earlier versions or portions of this paper were presented at the Collegium Phaenomenologicum in Perugia, Italy, at the Program in Comparative

Literature of SUNY-Buffalo, and at the Philosophy Department of Memphis State University. I am extremely grateful to Tomoko Masuzawa and Dennis Schmidt for their helpful comments.

1. See Irving Wohlfarth, "Resentment begins at Home: Nietzsche, Benjamin, and the University," in Gary Smith, ed., *On Walter Benjamin* (Cambridge: MIT Press, 1988), 227.

2. Walter Benjamin, *Ursprung des deutschen Trauerspiels* [1916/1925], in *Gesammelte Schriften* (Frankfurt am Main: Suhrkamp Verlag, 1980), Bd. I.1, esp. 279ff. *Gesammelte Schriften* is henceforth cited as GS. Unless otherwise indicated, where a German text is cited in English I will use the currently available English translations, as noted.

3. "Karl Kraus," *GS* II.1, pp. 366f.

4. Ibid., 361.

5. Karl Löwith, *Nietzsches Philosophie der ewigen Widerkunft des Gleichen* (Berlin, Verlag Die Runde, 1935), cited repeatedly by Benjamin in "Konvolut D: Die Langeweile, ewige Wiederkehre," *Passagenwerk*, *GS* V.1, 174-77.

6. "Zentral Park," *GS* I.2, p. 660.

7. Ibid., 262f.

8. See, for example, Benjamin's letters to Scholem of Jan 20, 1930 (on the disparity between Benjamin's and Heidegger's conceptions of history) and April 4, 1930 (on Benjamin's plan—never realized—to "demolish" [*zertrümmern*] Heidegger in a reading group with Brecht); his letter to Rychner of March 8, 1931 (declaring his distance from the "Heidegger school"); his letter to Gretel Adorno of July 20, 1938 (expressing his outrage at being identified, by *Internationalen Literatur*—a Moscow-based publication— as a follower of Heidegger). See Walter Benjamin, *Briefe*, hrsg. Gershom Scholem and Theodor Adorno (Frankfurt am Main: Suhrkamp Verlag, 1978). See also Benjamin's attempt to differentiate the critical intensity of the "dialectical image" from Heidegger's allegedly essentializing conception of "historicity" (*Passagenwerk*, *GS* V.1, p. 577).

9. T. W. Adorno, Ästhetische Theorie (Frankfurt: Suhrkamp, 1973), 78; *Aesthetic Theory*, trans. C. Lenhardt (London: Routledge and Kegan Paul, 1984), 72.

10. See "On Redemption," *Thus Spoke Zarathustra*, trans. Walter Kaufmann in *The Portable Nietzsche* (New York: Viking, 1968), 250-53 (henceforth cited as *TSZ*).

11. Heidegger, "Who is Nietzsche's Zarathustra?," in *Nietzsche* vol. II, trans. David Farrell Krell (New York: Harper, 1984), 211-33.

12. See the *Nachlass* fragment—quoted by Heidegger at "Who is Nietzsche's Zarathustra?," 229—in which Nietzsche affirms "a kind of sublime malice and extreme exuberance of revenge."

13. Ibid., 229.

14. *TSZ* 254.

15. *TSZ* 211. At *TSZ* 329, Nietzsche identifies rainbows with "illusive bridges" [*Schein-Brücken*].

16. *TSZ* 269-272.

17. *Werke* II, 1190-1195; *The Antichrist* (herafter cited as *AC*) in *The Portable Nietzsche*, 599-606. See below.

18. "To stamp [*aufprägen*] Becoming with the character of Being—that is the supreme *will to power*." *The Will to Power* §617, translated by Walter Kaufmann and R. J. Hollingdale (New York: Random House, 1967), 330 (slightly modified). I will cite *The Will to Power* hereafter as *WTP*. Heidegger quotes and comments on this fragment repeatedly throughout the *Nietzsche* volumes and elsewhere, citing it as evidence of Nietzsche's intrametaphysical propensities to eternalizing, to fixing, and to a general privileging of the present. On Heidegger's own use and abuse of this passage—his eagerness to cite as a "definitive recapitulation" what is in fact only an isolated fragment, his omission of the sentences immediately following in the *Will to Power* which show Nietzsche to be in fact *exposing* what Heidegger would have him *propose*, and so on—see David Krell's remarks in his translator's notes in *Nietzsche* vol. II, 201n and 257n.

19. Heidegger, *What is Called Thinking?*, trans. J. Glenn Gray (New York: Harper and Row, 1968), 100.

20. "Von Nutzen und Nachteil der Historie für das Leben," *Werke*, hrsg. Karl Schlechta, Bd. 1 (Munich: Hanser Verlag, 1969), 209; "On the uses and disadvantages of history for life" in *Untimely Meditations*, trans. R. J. Hollingdale (Cambridge: Cambridge University Press, 1983), 59. I will hereafter cite these works as *Werke* and *UM*, respectively.

21. *Werke* I, p. 259; *UM* 94

22. *TSZ* 281.

23. *Genealogy of Morals* II. §26, trans. Walter Kaufmann (New York: Random House, 1967), 158 (hereafter cited as *GM*).

24. *Werke* I, p. 262; *UM* 104.

25. *Werke* I, p. 263; *UM* 105.

26. *Werke* I, pp. 242f; *UM* 87.

27. *Werke* I, p. 239; *UM* 84.

28. *Werke* I, p. 240; *UM* 85.

29. *Werke* I, p. 240; *UM* 85.

30. *Werke* I, p. 242; *UM* 87.

31. *Werke* I, p. 257; *UM* 99.

32. *Werke* I, p. 238 *UM* 83. Hegel's picture gallery of Spirit cannot be too far from Nietzsche's mind.

33. "Schopenhauer als Erzieher," *Werke* I, p. 293; *UM* 132.

34. *Werke* I, p. 228; *UM* 75.

35. *Werke* I, p. 232; *UM* 78.

36. *Werke* I, p. 228; *UM* 75.

37. *Werke* I, p. 268; *UM* 110.

38. *Werke* I, p. 263; *UM* 105.

39. *Werke* I, p. 265; *UM* 106.

40. *Werke* I, p. 263; *UM* 105.

41. *Werke* I, p. 274; *UM* 114.

42. *Werke* I, p. 269; *UM* 110.

43. "Über den Begriff der Geschichte," GS I.2, p. 695; "Theses on the Philosophy of History," in *Illuminations* (henceforth cited as *Ill.*), trans. Harry Zohn (New York: Schocken, 1969), 255.

44. *GS* I.2, p. 696; *Ill.*, 256.

45. *GS* I.2, p. 702; *Ill.*, 262.

46. *GS* I.2, p. 702; *Ill.*, 262.

47. *GS* I.2, p. 704; *Ill.*, 263.

48. *GS* I.2, p. 693; *Ill.*, 254 (modified).

49. *GS* I.2, p. 700; *Ill.*, 260.

50. G. W. F. Hegel, *Vorlesungen über die Philosophie der Geschichte, Werke in zwanzig Bänden*, Bd. 12 (Frankfurt am Main: Suhrkamp Verlag, 1970), 12.

51. See Hegel, *Wissenschaft der Logik, Werke in zwanzig Bänden*, Bd. 6, p. 13.

52. "Zum Bilde Prousts," *GS* Ill, pp. 320f; *Ill.*, 211 (slightly modified).

53. See *GS* II.1, p. 311; *Ill.*, 202.

54. "Der Surrealismus," *GS* II.1, pp. 299f; "Surrealism," in *Reflections,* trans. Edmond Jephcott (New York: Harcourt, Brace, Jovanovich), 181f.

55. Compare Philippe Ivornel, "Paris, Capital of the Popular Front; or the Posthumous life of the Nineteenth Century," *New German Critique* 39 (Fall 1986), 61-84.

56. T. W. Adorno, *Negative Dialektik* (Frankfurt: Suhrkamp, 1966), 15; trans. E. B. Ashton (New York: Continuum, 1983), 3.

57. *Werke* II, p. 333; *TSZ* 183.

58. T. W. Adorno, *Minima Moralia: Reflexionen aus dem beschädigten Leben* (Frankfurt: Suhrkamp, 1980), 20.; trans. E.F.N. Jephcott (London: NLB, 1974), 19.

59. *Werke* II, p. 395; *TSZ* 253.

60. T. W. Adorno, "Erpresste Versöhnung," in *Noten zur Literatur*, Bd. II (Frankfurt: Suhrkamp Verlag, 1961).

61. Franz Kafka, *Parables and Paradoxes*, bilingual ed., ed. Nahum Glatzer (New York: Schocken, 1946), 80f.

62. *Werke* II, p. 873ff; *GM* 132ff.

63. *Werke* II, p. 881; *GM* 141 Cf *Werke* III, p. 711; *WTP* 133.

64. *Werke* II, p. 789; *GM* 45.

65. *Werke* III, p. 711; *WTP* 133. Cf *Werke* III, pp. 456, 480, 485, 489, 501, 540ff, 767f; *WTP* 293-300.

66. *Werke* II, pp. 1190-92; *AC* 600-2.

67. *Werke* I, p. 1191, *AC* 602.

68. *Werke* II, p. 394; *TSZ* 252.

69. R. J. Hollingdale, trans., *Thus Spoke Zarathustra* (Harmondsworth: Penguin, 1961), 162.

70. See n. 72 below.

71. *Minima Moralia*, 14.

72. *Werke* I, p. 275; *UM* 115.

73. *Werke* II, p. 751; *Beyond Good and Evil*, trans. R. J. Hollingdale (Harmondsworth: Penguin, 1973), 196f.

Chapter 2: Translating, Repeating, Naming

1. Friedrich Nietzsche, "*On the Genealogy of Morals*" and "*Ecce Homo*," trans. Walter Kaufmann (New York: Random House, 1967), 313. This translation will be cited hereafter as *GM*.

2. Jürgen Habermas, *The Discourse of Modernity*, trans. Frederick Lawrence (Cambridge, Mass.: MIT Press, 1987), 125-26.

3. Michel Foucault, "Nietzsche, Genealogy, History," in *Language, Counter-Memory, Practice*, trans. Donald F. Bouchard and Sherry Simon (Ithaca: Cornell University Press, 1977), 140-42. This essay will be cited hereafter as NGH.

4. Nietzsche's name is almost completely absent from the genealogy *à l'américaine* that Stephen Toulmin and Alan Janick have sketched in *Wittgenstein's Vienna* (New York: Simon and Schuster, 1973). Yet Nietzsche's name and writings were inescapable in the Vienna in which Wittgenstein lived.

5. NGH 145.

6. NGH 141.

7. *GM* 15.

8. NGH 161.

9. See Mikhail Bakhtin, *Problems of Dostoyevsky's Poetics*, ed. and trans. Caryl Emerson (Minneapolis: University of Minnesota Press, 1984).

10. NGH 146.

11. NGH 148.

12. See Foucault, *The Use of Pleasure*, trans. Robert Hurley (New York: Pantheon Books, 1985), 236, 238, 239.

13. *The Birth of Tragedy*, trans. Walter Kaufmann (New York: Random House, 1967), 91.

14. Roland Barthes, *Fragments of a Lover's Discourse*, trans. Richard Howard (New York: Farrar, Straus and Giroux, 1978). Jacques Derrida "Plato's Pharmacy" in *Dissemination*, trans. Barbara Johnson (Chicago: University of Chicago Press, 1981), 61-171.

15. See Mark Poster, "Foucault and the Tyranny of Greece," in *Foucault: A Critical Reader*, ed. David Hoy (New York: Blackwell, 1986), 205-20, esp 216.

16. See Michel Foucault, *Folie et déraison: Histoire de la folie* (Paris: Plon, 1961). Jacques Derrida, "Cognito and the History of Madness," in *Writing and Difference*, trans. Alan Bass (Chicago: University of Chicago Press, 1978),

31-63; Michel Foucault, "My Body, This Paper, This Fire," trans. Geoff Bennington, *Oxford Literary Review* 4: 1 (1979), 9-28.

17. See *Descartes: Philosophical Writings*, trans. and ed. Elizabeth Anscombe and Peter Thomas Geach (London: Thomas Nelson and Sons, 1954), esp. 61-65. Perhaps Anscombe and Geach were aided in translating as they did by the example of the play of voices and question-and-answer style in Wittgenstein's *Philosophical Investigations*.

18. Derrida, *Of Grammatology*, trans. Gayatri Spivak (Baltimore: Johns Hopkins University Press, 1976), 141 (cited hereafter as *OG*).

19. *OG* 114.

20. Cited in *OG* 124.

21. See *GM* essay 3.

22. *OG* 123.

23. *OG* 124.

24. *GM* 153.

25. Claude Levi Strauss, *The Savage Mind* (Chicago: University of Chicago Press, 1966), 269.

26. *GM* 55.

27. *GM* 161.

28. *OG* 101.

Chapter 3: Nietzsche's Madman

1. For a provocative discussion of the role of parable in Nietzsche's writing, see J. Hillis Miller, "Gleichnis in Nietzsche's *Also Sprach Zarathustra*," *International Studies in Philosophy* 17:2 (1985), 3-15.

2. Jacques Lacan, "Desire and the Interpretation of Desire in *Hamlet*," *Literature and Psychoanalysis*, ed. Shoshana Felman (Baltimore, MD.: Johns Hopkins University Press, 1982), 28.

3. Ibid., 29.

4. Friedrich Nietzsche, *Joyful Wisdom*, trans. Thomas Common (New York: Frederick Ungar, 1971), 167-68.

5. Jacques Lacan, "The Gaze," in *The Four Fundamental Concepts of Psycho-Analysis* (New York: W. W. Norton, 1981), 88, 89.

6. John Berger, *Ways of Seeing*, (New York: Penguin, 1972), 16.

7. Lacan, "The Gaze," 86.

8. Berger, *Ways of Seeing*, 13.

9. For an alternative analysis of the relationship between the camera and perspective which nevertheless reaches the conclusion that the camera does not negate the notion of the center, see Fredric Jameson, *The Political Unconsciousness* (Ithaca, N.Y.: Cornell University Press, 1981), 160.

10. For a complete statement of this position, see Wilfrid Desan, *The Planetary Man* (New York: Macmillan, 1972).

11. See, for example, J. P. Sartre's *Being and Nothingness*, trans. Hazel E. Barnes (New York: Washington Square Press, 1969).

12. Nietzsche, *Joyful Wisdom*, 168.

13. For a detailed discussion of Nietzsche's nihilism, see Martin Heidegger, *Nietzsche*, vol. 4, *Nihilism*, trans. Frank A. Capuzzi (New York: Harper and Row, 1982).

14. Nietzsche, *Joyful Wisdom*, 168.

15. Ibid.

16. Ibid., 169.

17. Ibid., 167.

18. Simone de Beauvoir, "Conversations with Jean-Paul Sartre," in *Adieux* (New York: Pantheon Books, 1984), 438.

19. See Nietzsche's *The Use and Abuse of History*, trans. Adrian Collins, (New York: Library of Liberal Arts, 1957), and Debra Bergoffen, "Seducing Historicism," *International Studies in Philosophy*, Vol. 19/2, 1987, 85-98.

20. Nietzsche, *Joyful Wisdom*, 168.

21. The idea that the same words may express different desires and may hence mean differently is explicitly found in the section "On Passing By," in *Thus Spoke Zarathustra*, trans. Walter Kaufmann (New York: Penguin, 1954), 175-78.

22. Lacan, "The Gaze," 87.

23. I am indebted to Fredric Jameson *The Political Unconsciousness*, 163, for the concept of the interpretive center, though the use he makes of it is different from that developed below.

24. Gilles Deleuze and Felix Guattari, *Anti-Oedipus Capitalism and Schizophrenia*, trans. Robert Hurely, Mark Seem, and Helen R. Lane (Minneapolis: University of Minnesota Press, 1983), 76.

25. Nietzsche, *Joyful Wisdom*, 169.

26. Nietzsche, *Thus Spoke Zarathustra*, trans. Walter Kaufmann (New York: Penguin, 1978) 182 ("On Apostates," book 3).

Chapter 4: Language and Deconstruction

The first three sections of this essay have been published previously as "Deconstructing *The Birth of Tragedy*," *International Studies in Philosophy* 19 (1987), 67-75. The final section will be included in my forthcoming book on Nietzsche in the Modern European Philosophy Series of Cambridge University Press. I am grateful to Susan Fox and other members of the English Department of Columbia University for the inspiration to put my thoughts on *The Birth of Tragedy* into writing and to Sue Larson for many helpful discussions on Davidson, truth, and metaphor.

1. John Wilcox, *Truth and Value in Nietzsche* (Ann Arbor: University of Michigan Press, 1974), 109.

2. For a detailed discussion of redemptive strategies in *The Birth of Tragedy*, see Robert E. McGinn, "Culture as Prophylactic: Nietzsche's *Birth of Tragedy* as Cultural Criticism," *Nietzsche-Studien* 4 (1975), 75-138.

3. Translations are from Walter Kaufmann's edition of *The Birth of Tragedy* (New York: Vintage, 1967) (*GT*), with minor changes based on volume III/1 of the *Kritische Gesamtausgabe* edited by Giorgio Colli and Mazzino Montinari (Berlin: DeGruyter, 1972). Numbers in the text following *GT* indicate the section of the work; "V" denotes Nietzsche's later preface to *GT*, "Versuch einer Selbstkritik."

4. Nietzsche seems to treat "the thread of causality" as equivalent to "the thread of logic," something much easier to associate with Socrates.

5. This understanding of Schopenhauer's view of the ultimate significance of the a priori forms time, space, and causality is suggested by section 34 of the first volume of *The World as Will and Representation*, in which he claims that the final goal of knowledge structured by these forms is to relate things to one's own will.

6. Nietzsche transforms Schopenhauer's will into an "artist-god" who frees himself from the contradictions in his soul by creating the empirical world: "The world—at every moment the attained salvation of God, as the eternally changing, eternally new vision of the most deeply afflicted, discordant, and contradictory being who can find salvation only through *illusion* [*im Scheine*]" (*GT* V, 5). The empirical world thus appeases the creator's desire for Apollinian art and must itself be illusory.

7. If art is not more truthful than theory, Nietzsche has no basis for considering it more life affirming either. The Socratic also compels us to go on

living and, according to Nietzsche in section 15, is apparently more important for the preservation of life than is art. Within the confines of the argument of *GT*, only insofar as art is considered more truthful than theory can it be said to affirm life more fully. See my argument in "An Alternative Account of the Contradictions" and note 11 below.

8. John Searle, "The Word Turned Upside Down," review of Jonathan Culler, *On Deconstruction: Theory and Criticism after Structuralism*, New York Review of Books, October 27, 1983, p. 74.

9. Numbers in the text correspond to pages in Paul de Man, *Allegories of Reading* (New Haven: Yale University Press, 1979).

10. See Stanley Corngold, "Error in Paul de Man," in *The Yale Critics: Deconstruction in America* (Minneapolis: University of Minnesota Press, 1983), for a discussion of de Man's own errors in the translation of the passage from which he draw this argument.

11. Here I follow the argument in Wilcox, *Truth and Value in Nietzsche*, 190.

12. My treatment of metaphor is greatly influenced by Donald Davidson's account in "What Metaphors Mean," *Inquiries into Truth and Interpretation* (New York: Oxford University Press, 1984), 245-64.

13. Jacques Derrida, *Speech and Phenomenon*, trans. David Allison (Evanston, Ill.: Northwestern University Press, 1973), 139.

14. See especially "Reality without Reference" and "The Inscrutability of Reference," in Davidson, *Inquiries into Truth and Interpretation*.

15. John Wallace, "Only in the Context of a Sentence Do Words Have Any Meaning," *Midwest Studies in Philosophy 2: Studies in the Philosophy of Language* (Minneapolis: University of Minnesota Press, 1977), 152.

16. Ibid., 163.

17. Ibid., 151.

Chapter 5: Nietzsche contra Nietzsche

I thank the National Endowment for the Humanities and the Andrew W. Mellon Faculty Fellowships at Harvard University for their generous support. My thanks also to Sara Blair, Laurence Lampert, Graham Parkes, and Robert Pippin for their helpful criticisms of earlier drafts of this essay.

1. In the spirit of deconstruction, many commentators have in turn questioned the authority of deconstruction itself. See David Wood: "Decon-

struction is intimately concerned with power ... but does not the deployer of such strategies of reading actually acquire, for him/herself or their own texts, enormous power? ... while [deconstruction] can always, in a certain way, handle straightforward philosophical objections, the question of its own power, vulnerability, desire, might prove to be its Achilles' heel" ("Following Derrida," in *Deconstruction and Philosophy*, ed. John Sallis [Chicago: University of Chicago Press, 1987], 157-58.

2. Rudolf Kuenzli also maintains that Nietzsche welcomes the deconstruction of *Zarathustra*, in "Nietzsche's Zerography: *Thus Spoke Zarathustra*," *Boundary 2* (1981) 99-117. According to Kuenzli, *Zarathustra* exemplifies Nietzsche's "zerography," which Kuenzli defines as "the writing process, the strategy by which the whole is deconstructed and rendered as a cipher, the signifier is liberated from the 'primary signified'" (104). As I argue below, we need now view the deconstruction of *Zarathustra* as an exercise in zerography.

3. In *Nietzsche as Philosopher* (New York: Macmillan, 1965), Arthur Danto maintains that the text "may be entered at any point" (20), for it is unified only to the extent that it "acquires a certain external structure by having each segment pose as a homiletic uttered by Zarathustra" (19). Echoing these sentiments in *The Portable Nietzsche* (New York: Viking, 1977), Walter Kaufmann avers that, "after all has been said, *Zarathustra* still cries out to be blue-penciled" (106) and warns the reader that Nietzsche essentially begins anew at the close of part 3: "Part Four forms a whole, and as such represents a new stylistic experiment" (344). In his own translation of *Zarathustra* (Harmondsworth, Middlesex: Penguin, 1969), R. J. Hollingdale submits that "the book is very loosely constructed, but it does possess direction and a plot of sorts" (31). See also Eugen Fink, *Nietzsches Philosophie* (Stuttgart: Kohlhammer Verlag, 1960), 64.

4. Several commentators have recently celebrated the textual discontinuities of *Zarathustra*, by means of which Nietzsche challenges the established conventions of traditional philosophy and literature. Alan Megill, for example, maintains that *"Zarathustra* simply will not fit into a critical or analytical framework ... *Zarathustra* is a work of literature, an imaginative aesthetic creation in which Nietzsche's vision of crisis and 'return' finds its highest expression. This is not to say that *Zarathustra* can somehow be taken as a paradigm of what literature is, but only that the category of literature seems to be the only one within which *Zarathustra* fits at all" (*Prophets of Extremity* [Berkeley: University of California Press, 1985], 61-62). Gary Shapiro suggests that *"Zarathustra* is a rhetorical *Spiel*. It plays with serious affairs of the understanding but does not aim at persuasion. It speaks without authority" ("The Rhetoric of Nietzsche's *Zarathustra,*" in *Philosophical Style*, ed. Berel Lang [Chicago: Nelson Hall, 1980], 355). Stanley Rosen similarly maintains that since *Zarathustra* "is a revelation rather than a treatise ... we may expect a certain oddity of language with concomitant problems of interpretation" (*The Limits of Analysis* [New York: Basic Books, 1980], 201). Although

Jacques Derrida is not concerned in *Eperons* specifically with *Zarathustra*, he attributes to Nietzsche a style designed to render "undecidable" the traditional constituent values of philosophy and literature. See *Spurs/Eperons*, trans. B. Harlow (Chicago: University Chicago Press, 1978).

5. I refer throughout this essay by number to the pages of Walter Kaufmann's translation of *Zarathustra* in *The Portable Nietzsche*.

6. See Thomas Pangle, "The 'Warrior Spirit' as an Inlet to the Political Philosophy of Nietzsche's *Zarathustra*," *Nietzsche-Studien* 15 (1986), 153.

7. "With these words Zarathustra leaped up, not like a frightened man seeking air but rather as a seer and singer who is moved by the spirit...a coming happiness lay reflected in his face" (195).

8. Nietzsche himself often notes that the respective bursts of creative energy that spawned parts 1 and 2 were separated by the space of an entire year. In a letter to Köselitz on July 13, 1883, Nietzsche claimed that the deviations of part 2 "would be almost indecent to a musician: a different harmony and modulation than in the first part" (*Nietzsches Briefwechsel* [hereafter cited as *NBW*] III 1, ed. G. Colli and M. Montinari (Berlin: Walter deGruyter, 1981), no. 433, p. 397. In a letter to Köselitz written in August 1883, Nietzsche remarked that "in detail, there is an incredible wealth of personal experience and suffering [in part 2] that is intelligible only to me—some pages strike me as almost *drenched with blood*" (*NBW* III1, no. 460, p. 443).

9. Pangle suggests that Zarathustra's enemies are former disciples who have grown powerful, rebelled against Zarathustra, and ridiculed his teaching, (151).

10. One often encounters commentators who indiscriminately attribute Zarathustra's teachings to Nietzsche. According to Werner Dannhauser, "The simplest answer to the question [Who is Nietzsche's Zarathustra?] is that Zarathustra is Nietzsche himself" (*Nietzsche's View of Socrates* [Ithaca: Cornell University Press, 1974], 241). See also Walter Kaufmann, *Nietzsche: Philosopher, Psychologist, Antichrist*, 4th ed. (Princeton: Princeton University Press, 1974), 198-204; Ofelia Schutte, *Beyond Nihilism: Nietzsche without Masks* (Chicago: University of Chicago Press, 1984), chap. 6; J. P. Stern, *A Study of Nietzsche* (Cambridge: Cambridge University Press, 1979), chap. 9.

11. See Laurence Lampert's developmental reading of *Zarathustra*, in *Nietzsche's Teaching* (New Haven: Yale University Press, 1986). Anke Bennholdt-Thomsen agrees that "the construction of the work is constituted by Zarathustra's realization of his communication-problem" (*Nietzsches "Also Sprach Zarathustra" als literarisches Phänomen* [Frankfurt am Main: Athenäum Verlag, 1974], 24).

12. Kathleen Higgins also notes the Bildungsroman structure of *Zarathustra*, in *Nietzsche's Zarathustra* (Philadelphia: Temple University Press, 1987), 104.

13. Nietzsche's choice of words for Zarathustra's descent is important: for although *untergehen* is literally rendered by "to go under," it more generally means "to perish" or "to die." Nietzsche enables us to take seriously both senses of *untergehen*; as Zarathustra will soon discover, to go under *is* to perish.

14. The fragility of Zarathustra's teaching is manifest in his very first social encounter. While talking to the old saint who lives in the forest, Zarathustra offers contradictory explanations of his decision to go under. After initially professing his love for humankind, Zarathustra suddenly reverses himself: "Did I speak of love? I bring men a gift" (123). Zarathustra's vacillation suggests the ambiguity of his relation to those to whom he descends: is Zarathustra a lover of man or the bearer of an ambiguous Promethean gift?

15. In his unpublished notes, Nietzsche occasionally refers to this condition as *incomplete nihilism*: although the death of God is acknowledged, another entity is recruited to fill the place of the deceased, thus reinforcing the appraisal of human nature as inherently deficient. See *Nietzsche Werke: Kritische Gesamtausgabe*, ed. G. Colli and M. Montinari (Berlin: deGruyter, 1972), Vol. 8/2, entry 10 [42], p. 142.

16. The later speech "On Great Events" makes it clear that most of part 2 transpires on Zarathustra's "Blessed Isles" (241).

17. Pangle sees nothing suspicious about Zarathustra's emigration to the Blessed Isles. He conjectures that Zarathustra's disciples emigrated there following the close of part 1, having "spent years in withdrawn meditation upon, and discussion of, [Zarathustra's] earlier appearance among them" (151).

18. Although the book presents the Blessed Isles as an actual, specific place to which Zarathustra has emigrated, we should perhaps understand "the Blessed Isles" as a geographical metaphor for a communication situation that promises the success of Zarathustra's pedagogical project. These Isles are "Blessed" primarily because they are (allegedly) inhabited by auditors who are prepared to accept Zarathustra's teaching.

19. Lampert suggests that the emergence of this subtext is attributable to Zarathustra's "reticence" in light of his own teaching; Zarathustra therefore "practices ways of speaking that are much less direct than the persuasive speeches of Part I" (84).

20. Lampert helpfully refers to these songs as contributing to "an interlude of inwardness" (84).

21. Friedrich Nietzsche, *Ecce Homo*, trans. Walter Kaufmann, in *"On the Genealogy of Morals"* and *"Ecce Homo"* (New York: Random House, 1969), 306.

22. Nietzsche's manipulation of the light/darkness imagery contributes to the anti-Platonic undercurrent of *Zarathustra*. Whereas Socrates in the

Republic identifies himself and his philosophers with the "sunlight" of the True world—as opposed to the "darkness" of the cave—Nietzsche represents this sunlight as insufficient, as requiring the mediation of darkness. Hence for Nietzsche, the *genuine* cave is the philosopher's solitude. I further explicate the anti-Platonic imagery of *Zarathustra* in "Solving the Problem of Socrates: Nietzsche's *Zarathustra* as Political Irony," *Political Theory* 16:2 (1988), 257-80.

23. Pangle maintains that "the situation that brings forth the lament... is the situation Zarathustra finds himself in, as the 'Sun' who can see around himself only darkness and needy offspring illuminated by light which is ultimately all traceable to him, the Sun" (164). But by concentrating on Zarathustra's auditors' lack of light, rather than on Zarathustra's own lack of darkness, Pangle misses the point of Zarathustra's lament: that he is *only* light.

24. Following Zarathustra's initial failures in the prologue, where his sole auditor was a corpse, he precipitately vowed: "No shepherd shall I be, nor gravedigger. Never again shall I speak to the people: for the last time have I spoken to the dead" (136).

25. Lampert refers to *The Tomb Song* as "a song of hope" (109), but it strikes me as a song of despair. To be sure, the chapter itself ends on a hopeful, "resolute" note, as Zarathustra invokes the terrible strength of his will, but this hopeful conclusion is perhaps better understood as a self-deceived reaction to the despair evinced in the song itself.

26. The next speech is "On Self-Overcoming," which is followed in turn by an examination of several types who ostensibly overcome themselves.

27. Lampert agrees that these speeches address those who, though admirable, still fall short of Zarathustra's ideal (123).

28. Zarathustra's "shadow" departs the Blessed Isles for the island with the smoking mountain (241-42), thus reprising Zarathustra's subtextual departure in *The Tomb Song* (222).

29. In part 3, while reflecting on his travels, Zarathustra realizes that "the wanderer's shadow and the longest boredom and the stillest hour—they all urged me: 'It is high time'" (274).

30. The soothsayer's vulgarization, "All is empty, all is the same, all has been" (245) probably refers specifically to the doctrine of eternal recurrence, which Zarathustra has not yet promulgated. I view the eternal recurrence of the "small man" as a corollary to the Übermensch ideal that Zarathustra cannot yet endure.

31. Here Nietzsche introduces a phrasal motif for the dissipation of Zarathustra's self-deception: "Like one coming home from a long sojourn in strange lands ["aus langer Fremde heimkehrt"] he looked at his disciples and

examined their faces; and as yet he did not recognize them" (248). Compare pp. 264, 295. In *Beyond Good and Evil* (295), Nietzsche speaks of his own philosophical development in terms of this motif. As Lampert notes, Zarathustra also responds to his disciple's interpretation by shaking his head "a third and final time, having seen the limitation of all his disciples" (139).

32. Here the appropriateness of the staff as a gift for Zarathustra becomes more evident, for he has cultivated a relation of redeemer/redeemed with his auditors.

33. In the chapter "On Great Event," for example, Zarathustra's auditors were much more interested in his apparitional descent to Hell—a mere "rumor" (242)—than in his teaching (245). See Lampert, pp. 132-33.

34. I have thus assumed that the child's mirror accurately reflects Zarathustra's image, that the reflection is not the (distorted) product of the child's own interpretation. Lampert identifies the child as "a disciple whose...immature creativity reflects a Zarathustra who, to Zarathustra's eyes, has become a devil" (86), thus attributing the diabolic reflection to the inadequacy (that is, immaturity) of Zarathustra's auditors.

35. The title of this passage is indeed portentous, for we have already been told that "the greatest events—they are not our loudest but our stillest hours" (243). In fact, this chapter not only explains what "stillest hours" are and why they are important but also *becomes* Zarathustra's own "stillest hour" (39). Bennholdt-Thomsen maintains that "The Stillest Hour" contains "the decisive break which changes Zarathustra's task" from that of teaching (17).

36. According to Lampert, we should not interpret Nietzsche's speech on "The Stillest Hour" as a truthful, literal account of his predicament. Lampert maintains that Zarathustra "mask[s] himself before his disciples by presenting himself as weak and divided in will, as still only a herald, though he has seen and accepted for himself with a single will the task that the superman must undertake" (152).

37. In light of Paul de Man's commitment to the irreducible figurality of all language (a commitment he also attributes to the young Nietzsche), I take it that he would contend that no such "author-less" reconstruction is possible. As I understand de Man's theory, Nietzsche's accommodation of the deconstruction of his authority would itself be subject to deconstructive criticism. De Man maintains that "the wisdom of the text is self-destructive (art is true but truth kills itself), but this self-destruction is infinitely displaced in a series of successive rhetorical reversals which, by the endless repetition of the same figure, keep it suspended between truth and the death of this truth. A threat of immediate destruction, stating itself as a figure of speech, thus becomes the permanent repetition of this threat" (*Allegories of Reading* [New Haven: Yale University Press, 1979], 115). I believe that Nietzsche would accept this qualification of his strategy.

38. I regret that a more detailed interpretation of part 3 of *Zarathustra* lies beyond the scope of this essay.

39. See Kuenzli, 109-110.

40. In order to explicate Nietzsche's reconstruction of *Zarathustra* on the authority of his readers, I draw upon the interpretation of part 4 that I presented in "A Moral Ideal for Everyone and No One," *International Studies in Philosophy* 21:2 (1990).

41. Whereas *Zarathustra* is quite obviously a parody of the Passion of Christ, Nietzsche elsewhere expresses a genuine admiration for Christ's public practices: "In truth, there was only *one* Christian, and he died on the cross" *(The Antichrist(ian)*, trans. Walter Kaufmann, in *The Portable Nietzsche*, 612).

42. See Alexander Nehamas, *Nietzsche: Life as Literature* (Cambridge, Mass.: Harvard University Press, 1985), 232-34.

43. Many interpretations of the text insist upon Zarathustra's inability, reluctance, or failure to become the Übermensch (See Tracy Strong, *Friedrich Nietzsche and the Politics of Transfiguration* [Berkeley: University of California Press, 1975], in 331, n. 2; Martin Heidegger, "Who Is Nietzsche's Zarathustra?" trans. B. Magnus, *The New Nietzsche*, ed. D. Allison (New York: Dell, 1977), 68; Gilles Deleuze, *Nietzsche and Philosophy*, trans. Hugh Tomlinson (New York: Columbia University Press, 1983), 192; Rosen 214; Pangle, 75-76). These interpretations correctly observe that Zarathustra does not become what he heralds. Yet these interpretations also fail to appreciate that Zarathustra *abandons* his original ideal of Übermenschlichkeit in parts 3-4. Zarathustra consequently does not accede to the station of world-historical Übermensch but only because he abandons this ideal in favor of another. As an example of a "higher type," Zarathustra therefore *does* become "in relation to mankind as a whole, a kind of Übermensch" (*The Portable Nietzsche*, 571). Nietzsche himself says of Zarathustra: "the concept of '*Übermensch*' has here become the greatest reality" (*Ecce Homo*, p. 305). I thus understand *Übermensch* to designate the ideal of human greatness promoted by Nietzsche; see Lampert, 253.

44. For an alternative interpretation, see Megill, who claims that "the Zarathustrian mind *demands* that we accept its view of the universe; it does not attempt to argue for such an acceptance...it stands as an absolute to itself, natively self-confident, delighting in its free play, which it seeks, without further justification, to impose upon the world" (63).

45. Pangle restricts Zarathustra's status to that of "herald": "Zarathustra does not create and therefore does not demonstrate the possibility of values in the full sense of the term as he understands it. We have yet to be shown here human beings, ways of life, that are ends in themselves and not merely 'bridges' to something else", (177).

46. Now it may have been so or otherwise...in short, as the proverb of Zarathustra says, 'What does it matter?'" (430). See Shapiro, "Festival, Parody,

and Carnival in *Zarathustra IV*," in *The Great Year of Zarathustra (1881-1981)*, ed. David Goicoechea (Lanham, Md.: University Press of America, 1983), 61.

Chapter 6: De Man Missing Nietzsche

1. Rotry incorporates Nietzsche into his pantheon of pragmatists—those philosophers who have abandoned philosophy, or at least the epistemological end of it. Putting him in bed with Williams James, Rorty says of Nietzsche that he was "content to take the halo off words like 'truth' and 'knowledge' and 'reality', rather than offering a view about the nature of the things named by these words" (Rorty, "Idealism and Textualism," in *Consequences of Pragmatism* [Minneapolis: Univerity of Minnesota Press, 1982], 150). I will have occasion here to challenge this statement almost point for point, without answering all of Rorty's often compelling pragmatic assertions. It seems clear to me, however, that Nietzsche would roll over in his grave at the conjuration of any text linking his name to the adjective "pragmatic."

2. Paul de Man, "Action and Identity in Nietzsche," *Yale French Studies* 52 (1975), 16; reprinted in *Allegories of Reading* (New Haven: Yale University Press, 1979), 119.

3. Paul de Man, *Allegories of Reading*, 116, 126-28.

4. Nietzsche, *Morgenröte* (Dawn of Day), aphorism 84.

5. Nietzsche, *Zur Genealogie der Moral (On the Genealogy of Morals)*, preface, aphorism 8.

6. Alexander Nehamas, *Nietzsche: Life as Literature* (Cambridge, Mass.: Harvard University Press, 1985), 2.

7. Toward the end of *Epérons (Spurs)*, Derrida makes much of a single aphorism in which Nietzsche speaks of "meine Wahrheiten" ("my truths"). Pervading Nietzsche's late texts, however, the unmodified word "truth" appears, and its rhetorical impact on the reader cannot be avoided by selective readings. See Derrida, *Eperons: Les styles de Nietzsche (Spurs: Nietzsche's Styles* [Chicago: University of Chicago Press, 1978], 105), and see notes 14 and 25.

8. "For such truths do exists," *Genealogy*, essay I aphorism 1.

9. Jean Granier, *Le problème de la vérité dans la philosophie de Nietzsche* (Paris: Editions du Seuil, 1966).

10. Sarah Kofman, *Nietzsche et la métaphore* (Paris: Payot, 1972), 193 (my translation).

11. Gillian Rose, *Dialectic of Nihilism: Post-Structuralism and Law* (New York: Blackwell, 1984), 87-91. Rose provides a superb discussion of the centrality of justice ("die Gerechtigkeit") to Nietzsche's thought, a far more

thorough and accurate discussion of the concept than that provided by Kofman (who has an axe to grind). See Kofman, *Métaphore*, 67-71. Rose effectively indicates that Heidegger (partly because he was, unlike Nietzsche, a hermeneutical innovator), could not—or would not—grasp the importance of the Nietzschean approach to justice. The relationship of justice to textuality is explored further in this paper.

12. *Jenseits von Gut und Böse (Beyond Good and Evil)*, aphorism 35. (I have generally followed the excellent translation of Marianne Cowan in all references to *Beyond Good and Evil* (Chicago: Gateway, 1966).

13. Hendrik Birus, "Nietzsche's Concept of Interpretation," in *Texte: Revue de critique et de théorie littéraire* 3 (1984), 78-102.

14. Kofman, *Métaphore*, 197.

15. Derrida, *Spurs*, 107.

16. Birus, "Nietzsche's Concept," 90.

17. Stanley Fish, *Is There a Text in This Class?* (Cambridge, Mass.: Harvard University Press, 1980).

18. Cited in Birus, "Nietzsche's Concept," 90.

19. *Genealogy*, essay 2, aphorism 12.

20. See on this point my "Text into Theory: A Literary Approach to the Constitution," *Georgia Law Review* 20 (1986), 939.

21. Kofman discusses justice at length in her book (see note. 10 above), 67-74, but remarkably omits *Genealogy*, II 11, the largest and clearest passage on justice in all of Nietzsche. The omission is deliberate, for that aphorism negates her entire argument.

22. Paul de Man, "Heidegger's Exegesis of Hölderlin," in *Blindness and Insight* (Minneapolis: University of Minnesota Press, 1983), 249-50.

23. Paul de Man, "The Rhetoric of Blindness: Jacques Derrida's Reading of Rousseau," in *Blindness*, 102.

24. Ibid.

25. Derrida, *Spurs*, 50. (The translation of this passage into English is incorrect in the cited edition. It should be "I mean that the world abounds in beautiful things but is nonetheless poor in beautiful moments or in beautiful descriptions of such things.")

26. Hence Kofman's insistence on the metaphoric aspect of all things in Nietzsche, whereas in fact Nietzsche makes distinctions among kinds of matter and therefore kinds of approaches to such matter by healthy wills to

power. The approach to text, for example and as we have seen, is character-ized more in terms of *identity* (the text as text) than in terms of metaphor (the text as interpretation). Because of her insistence on metaphor, and despite her (correct) assertion that "la philosophie de Nietzsche n'est pas un humanisme" (p. 206), Kofman often sounds like the kind of pluralist and relativist that Nietzsche of course abhorred. See especially pp. 149 and 202.

27. Even historical events are sometimes characterized as texts by Nietzsche and are therefore privileged as texts above interpretation. Hence the famous aphorism 38 (wrongly cited as 28 by Kofman on p. 194) of *Beyond Good and Evil*, where Nietzsche equates the French Revolution with a text and observes that "the noble and enthusiastic spectators of all Europe so passionately read their own outrage and enthusiasms into it that the text disappeared behind the interpretation ["bis der Text unter der Interpretation verschwant"]!".

28. I use throughout for *Ecce Homo* the R. J. Hollingdale translation. (Penguin, 1985). Nietzsche, *Werke* (Berlin: DeGruyter, 1969), vol. VI/3, 231, my translation.

29. Birus translates *ephexis* as "restraint"—evoking again the centrally discussed aphorism of this paper. See Birus, "Nietzsche's Concept," 91.

30. Kofman demonstrates what Nietzsche would have called interpretive "dishonesty" in treating this word and this passage on her p. 166. She mistranslates *Auslegung* as "interpretation," thus furthering her own exegesis but missing the philological distinction offered by the choice of word. More gravely, she chooses to cite only half the passage, leaving out the central notion of "rumination" that privileges the text as a kind of nourishing matter impervious to, but necessary for, the reader's growth. Only thus can she conclude, totally falsely where the passage is concerned, that "la forme aphoristique est l'écriture même d'une force artistique posant des formes nouvelles et aussi nombreuses qu'il y a de lecteurs qui conquièrent, qui s'approprient un texte." The conquering reader, vanquishing the text in a completely subjectivist manner, is as untrue to the image of the ruminating cow as Kofman's pluralistic interpretive community is to Nietzsche's strictly hierarchical world.

31. See especially the "Rhetoric of Tropes (Nietzsche)," in *Allegories*, 103-118.

32. See Weisberg, *The Failure of the Word: The Protagonist as Lawyer in Modern Fiction* (New Haven: Yale University Press, 1984), chap. 1.

33. De Man, *Allegories*, 125.

34. See note 7 above.

35. *Allegories*, 126.

36. Aside from the discussion of this point above, see especially *Beyond Good and Evil*, aphorisms 260 (on the total indifference of the noble act to subsequent verbal ratification) and 268 (on the weakness of language compared with experience).

37. *Allegories*, 126.

38. Ibid., 127-28.

39. See my discussion of Heidegger (and de Man) in this regard in Weisberg, "Text into Theory: A Literary Approach to the Constitution," *Georgia Law Review* 20 (1986), 939, 946-62.

40. *Allegories*, 128.

41. *Allegories*, 128.

42. "But the real philosophers are commanders and legislators. They say 'It shall be thus!'...This 'knowing' is creative. Their creating is legislative" (*Beyond Good and Evil*, aphorism 211; Cowan, 135).

43. Nietzsche, *Werke*, vol V/1, 76. Aphorism 84, translated by Birus, see n ote 13, p. 92.

Chapter 7: The Dance from Mouth to Hand

1. See the epigraph to the first chapter of Jacques Derrida, *Of Grammatology*, trans. Gayatri Chakravorty Spivak (Baltimore: The Johns Hopkins University Press, 1976), 6, which iterates Nietzsche's characterization of Socrates as "he who does not write." Later in the chapter Derrida writes that Nietzsche "has written that writing—and first of all his own—is not originally subordinate to the logos and to truth" (p. 19). Derrida does not develop the idea, and it is the antithesis between this pregnant but unelaborated utterance and the superficial favoring of speaking over writing in *Zarathustra* that is the motivation for the present essay. The richness of the ramifications of the relations between the speech/writing imagery in this text and Derrida's ideas of trace, type, *différance*, and so forth, however, can be only alluded to rather than thoroughly developed in what follows.

2. *Thus Spoke Zarathustra*, prologue sec. 5. Subsequent references will be to the numbers of the part (in Roman) and chapter (in Arabic) of the text, so that the quotations may be located in any edition. I used Friedrich Nietzsche, *Sämtliche Werke, Kritische Studienausgabe*, 1980. For the sake of faithful preservation of the imagery, I myself translated the passages from Nietzsche.

3. See the section entitled "Nietzsche *versus* Socrates" in Werner J. Dannhauser, *Nietzsche's View of Socrates* (Ithaca and London: Cornell

University Press, 1974), chap. 5, for an illuminating discussion. The similarities and differences between Plato's relations to the figure of Socrates and Nietzsche's to that of Zarathustra, as well as the relations of both pairs to each other, are rewarding to ponder. Lawrence Lampert's reading in his book *Nietzsche's Teaching: An Interpretation of "Thus Spoke Zarathustra"* (New Haven: Yale University Press, 1986) is also sensitive to the Plato/Nietzsche= Socrates/Zarathustra nexus. Lampert also delineates carefully the developing complexities of Zarathustra's relations with his external audience.

4. In addition to the fairly common form of vocalization that is whispering, we hear calling and crying, screaming and sighing, bellowing and roaring, wailing and moaning, humming and murmuring, puffing and blowing, chattering and stammering, cackling, neighing and whining, gurgling and grunting, yelping and howling, panting and wheezing—sounds like labor, many of them: hard work at the birth of the word.

5. *Phaedrus* 276b-277a. See Derrida's deft handling of this theme in "Plato's Pharmacy," in *Dissemination*, trans. Barbara Johnson (Chicago: University of Chicago Press, 1981), especially sec. 8. "The Heritage of the Pharmakon."

6. All the sections of part 1 bear titles beginning with "On.../Von..." (even though the second speech of the book is in fact delivered not by Zarathustra himself but by a parody figure of him). Apart from the refrain "Thus spoke Zarathustra," which closes every section, there are passages of third-person narrative in only six of the twenty-two sections. The number of sections named after titles of Zarathustra's speeches decreases as the book progresses, reflecting the speaker's increasing realization of the diminishing effectiveness of speech as a means of communiction. (The number of speeches in parts 1 through 4 is: 22, 15, 10, 2; and the number of songs: 0, 3, 3, 3.)

7. *Zarathustra* II.5. This image has, however, a significant counter-resonance: "ploughshare" is a common metaphor for "stylus," and so it is possible that Zarathustra's words may also reach his audience through the medium of the "furrowed" page. For a discussion of this field of imagery, see Ernst Robert Curtius, *European Literature and the Latin Middle Ages*, trans. Willard R. Trask (Princeton: Princeton University Press, 1973), chap. 16, "The Book as Symbol."

8. Among the occurrences not to be discussed here: over a gateway, and above a door and a path, there are words written, such as "moment" (III.2), "impossibility" (III.1), and "the path to the holy" (IV.13). It is interesting that no writers are mentioned in these contexts. In two places we read of written signs: "the contemporaries" are, ironically, "fully inscribed [*vollgeschrieben*] with the signs of the past" (II.14), and Zarathustra speaks earlier of the priests' writing "signs of blood on the path they followed" (II.8).

9. "Tinten-Fischen und Feder-Füchsen:" "ink-fish and pen-foxes" (III.11, sec. 1). *Feder* literally means "feather," and the association of writing with feather quills would lead naturally to the image of the bird, which is actually reached later in the text via the phenomenon of birdsong. The only other mentions of feathers occur in part 4: in the chapter "On Midday," sleep is said to *dance* "feather-lightly" (*federleicht*) on Zarathustra's eyes (IV.10), and he later speaks of his distaste for unfruitful scholars, before whom "all birds lie defeathered [*entfedert*]" (IV.13, sec. 9). One might suppose that such scholars, in their desire to get down to some serious writing, have plucked the feathers to use as quills—oblivious to the lesson of the *Phaedrus* that the soul must not lose its wings if the creator is to be inspired.

10. Curtius, p. 304. It is true, as Curtius remarks, that ancient Greece—whence Nietzsche drew his primary inspiration—is an exception in this respect. See also Derrida, "Plato's Pharmacy," sec. 3: "The Filial Inscription: Theuth, Hermes, Thoth, Nabu, Nebo." (It is also true that Nietzsche is fond of opposing his Zarathustra to the historical figure.)

11. See Gherhardo Gholi, "Zarathushtra," in *The Encyclopedia of Religion* ed. Mircea Eliade (New York: MacMillan, 1986), vol. 15. It is significant that these Gathas are *songs*—a mode of discourse Nietzsche's Zarathustra will come to prefer. While the last of the five Gathas "was probably written after the prophet's death," the historical Zarathustra apparently wrote at least four works more than Nietzsche's character.

12. *Zarathustra* III.2, secs. 1-11. In both cases the writing appears to be a laborious business: it takes Moses forty days and forty nights to transcribe the commandments, a rate of less than two a week, and whoever is inscribing Zarathustra's new tablets appears to be even slower: the three examples given of inscriptions are "Do not spare your neighbor," "noble," and "become hard" (III.12, secs. 4, 11, 29)—and yet the new tablets amid which Zarathustra sits are only "half inscribed."

13. The only occasion on which Zarathustra appears to come close to writing occurs just after his mention of ink fish and pen foxes: "My hand is a fool's hand," he says, "woe to all tables and walls and whatever else has room for foolish decoration and foolish scribbling" (III.11, sec. 1). He hardly sounds like much of a writer here—a demented graffiti artist at best. And within a few lines, his speech has turned to the topics of flying, birds, and song.

14. *Zarathustra* I.7, "On Reading and Writing." Nietzsche was surely familiar with the apothegm from Gottfried Keller which speaks of writing in blood:

> Es ist ein weisses Pergament
> Die Zeit, und jeder schreibt
> Mit seinem roten Blut darauf,
> Bis ihn der Strom vertreibt.

[Cited in Curtius, 347]

In holding blood as a writing medium to be spirit, Zarathustra is reversing the traditional Western view that the spoken word is the essential soul or spirit of language, while the supplement of writing corresponds to the contingent body: "Writing, the letter, the sensible inscription, have always been considered by the Western tradition as body and matter external to the spirit, to breath, to speech, and the logos" (Derrida, *Of Grammatology*, 52).

15. The relations between writing and death are articulated by Derrida in a number of texts: see, for example, *Of Grammatology*, 17, 25, 39, 68-69, 143, 183-85, 196; "Plato's Pharmacy," 91-3, 103-5; *Writing and Difference*, trans. Alan Bass (Chicago: University of Chicago Press, 1978), 71; *Margins of Philosophy*, trans. Alan Bass (Chicago: University of Chicago Press, 1982), 82-86.

16. The connection established in "On Reading and Writing" between laughter and lightness and elevation is reinforced later several times (see II.7; III.12, sec. 2; IV.1).

17. *Zarathustra* III.2. Zarathustra speaks of the thought's "biting" him in the following section, and identifies himself in "The Convalescent" (III.13) as the one who was rendered speechless by the heavy black snake's crawling into his mouth. One is reminded of the necessity expressed in "On Reading and Writing" of being able to "laugh over . . . what is black and heavy" ("schwarz und schwer": a richly alliterative pair of qualifiers). One might also think of the way in which Angst constricts the throat and renders speech impossible in Heidegger's *Sein und Zeit* (sec. 40).

18. *Zarathustra* III.13. The image of rainbows as shining bridges recalls a passage, a favorite of practitioners of deconstruction, from the early essay "Über Wahrheit und Lüge": "A nerve-stimulus first translated into an image! first metaphor. The image then re-formed into a sound! second metaphor! And each time a complete leaping out of one sphere into a totally different and new sphere." With respect to this passage from "The Convalescent," the talk of tones and hearing (some of it omitted in the quotation) in the context of the interplay between inside and outside may be amplified by reading it in conjunction with Derrida's "Tympan" (in *Margins of Philosophy*).

19. One thinks of Herakleitos, fragment 93: "The master of the Oracle at Delphi says nothing and conceals nothing, but gives a sign *[semainei]*"— silently, one may surmise.

20. *Zarathustra* IV.10. Many aspects of both the setting and action of this section—the midday heat, the concern with sleep, conversation on the grass with or about the soul, images of psyche and lightness and wings—are reminiscent of the *Phaedrus*.

21. Derrida alludes to the speaking of Nietzsche's hammer in "Tympan," in the context of making resonate fully the interconnections between the phenomena of hearing by way of the eardrum, the percussion of membranes,

and the pressures of manual printing presses (*Margins*, ix-xxix). It may be worth remarking in this context upon the fact that, during most of the period of his writing *Zarathustra*, Nietzsche was the proud owner of a typewriter—though one that was apparently as susceptible as its owner to physical breakdown. A photograph of the magnificent machine can be found on p. 99 of Ivo Frenzel's small biography, *Friedrich Nietzsche* (Hamburg: Reinbek, 1966).

22. *Zarathustra* IV.19, sec. 9. This kind of harvesting imagery—sickles, ripe vines, and their erotic overtones—appears to echo the following passage from the Book of Revelations, which concerns, significantly, an injunction to write: "And I heard a voice from heaven saying unto me, Write... And I looked, and behold..., another angel came out from the altar, which had power over fire; and cried with a loud cry to him that had the sharp sickle, saying, Thrust in thy sharp sickle, and gather the clusters of the vine of the earth; for her grapes are fully ripe" (14:14-18).

23. "What the Germans Lack," 7. See also "Aphorisms and Arrows," 34, where another connection between thinking and the feet is made, through Nietzsche's response to Flaubert's contention that one can think and write only when sitting: "Only thoughts arrived at through *walking* are worth anything." How much more worthwhile, then, would be thoughts that are reached by way of dance.

Chapter 8: Reading as a Philosophical Strategy

A portion of the material in this essay is reprinted from chapter 5 of *Inventions of Reading: Rhetoric and the Literary Imagination*, by Clayton Koelb, copyright © 1988 by Cornell University. It is used with the permission of the publisher, Cornell University Press.

1. Carole Blair, "Nietzsche's Lecture Notes on Rhetoric: A Translation," *Philosophy and Rhetoric* 16: 2 (1983), 106-7.

2. I cite "On Truth and Lie" in English from *The Philosophy of Nietzsche*, ed. Geoffrey Clive (New York: New American Library, 1965), 503-15; and in German from Nietzsche, *Werke in Drei Bänden*, vol. 3 (Munich: Hanser Verlag, 1966), 309-22. This passage is from *Philosophy*, 508; *Werke*, 314. "Was is also Wahrheit? Ein bewegliches Heer von Metaphern, Metonymien, Anthropomorphismen, kurz eine Summe von menschlichen Relationen, die, poetisch und rhetorisch gesteigert, übertragen, geschmückt wurden und die nach langem Gebrauch einem Volke fest, kanonisch und verbindlich dünken: die Wahrheiten sind Illusionen, von denen man vergessen hat, dass die welche sind, Metaphern, die abgenuzt und sinnlich kraftlos geworden sind, Münzen, die ihr Bild verloren haben und nun als Metal, nicht mehr als Münzen, in Betracht kommen."

3. *Philosophy*, 508; *Werke*, 314. "Nach einer festen Konvention zu lügen, herdenweise in einem für alle verbindlichen Stile zu lügen."

4. See Gregory Ulmer, *Applied Grammatology: Post(e)-Pedagogy from Jacques Derrida to Joseph Beuys* (Baltimore: Johns Hopkins University Press, 1985).

5. Ulmer, *Applied Grammatology*, 315.

6. *Philosophy*, 506; *Werke*, 311. "Ist die Sprache der adäquate Ausdruck aller Realitäten?"

7. *Philosophy*, 507; *Werke*, 312. "Das 'Ding an sich' (das würde eben die reine folgenlose Wahrheit sein) ist auch dem Sprachbildner ganz unfasslich und ganz und gar nicht erstrebenswert."

8. I cite *The Gay Science* in English from *The Gay Science*, trans. Walter Kaufmann (New York: Vintage Books, 1974); and in German from the *Kritische Gesamtausgabe* of Giorgio Colli and Mazzino Montinari, Vol. V, 2 (Berlin: de Gruyter, 1973). For everyone's convenience I will cite by aphorism (or poem) number rather than by page. (Note that the Colli/Montinari edition uses *ss* regularly instead of β.) "Zu Mindesten giebt es Wahrheiten von einer besonderen Scheu und Kitzlichkeit, deren man nicht anders habhaft wird, als plötzlich,—die man *überraschen* oder lassen muss.

9. See fragment 18 [5] from the *Nachlass (Kritische Gesamtausgabe* V, 2, p. 571).

10. *Nachlass* 12 [2] (p. 474).

11. "Take a chance and try my fare: / It will grow on you, I swear; / Soon it will taste good to you. / If by then you should want more, / All the things I've done before / Will inspire things quite new."

12. See Clayton Koelb, *The Incredulous Reader: Literature and the Function of Disbelief* (Ithaca: Cornell University Press, 1984), 192-215.

13. "Interpreting myself, I always read / Myself into my books. I clearly need / Some help. But all who climb on their own way / Carry my image, too, into the breaking day."

14. "So may a friend be my interpreteter. / And should he climb on his own way, / He'll carry his friend's image onward with him" (my trans.).

15. "Lured by my style and tendency, / you follow and come after me? / Follow your self faithfully— / take time—and thus you follow me."

16. "My youthful wisdom's A and O / I heard again. What did I hear? / Words not of wisdom but of woe: / Only the endless Ah and Oh / Of youth lies heavy in my ear."

17. "Wie weit der perspektivische Charakter des Daseins reicht oder gar ob es irgend einen anderen Charakter noch hat, ob nicht ein Dasein ohne Auslegung, ohne 'Sinn' eben zum 'Unsinn' wird, ob, andererseits, nicht alle Dasein essentiell ein *auslegendes* Dasein ist—das kann, wie billig, auch durch die fleissigste und peinlich-gewissenhafteste Analysis und Selbstprüfung des Intellekts nicht ausgemacht werden.... Die Welt ist vielmehr noch einmal 'unendlich' geworden: insofern wir die Möglichkeit nicht abweisen können, dass sie *unendliche Interpretationen in sich schliesst.*"

18. Aphorism 374. "Ach, es sind zu viele *ungöttliche* Möglichkeiten der Interpretation mit in dieses Unbekannte eingerechnet, zu viel Teufelei, Dummheit, Narrheit der Interpretation,—unsre eigne menschliche, allzumenschliche selbst, die wir kennen."

19. Poem 44. "A seeker, I? Oh, please be still! / I'm merely *heavy*—weigh many a pound. / I fall, and I keep falling till / At last I reach the ground."

20. "Wer singt uns ein Lied, ein Vormittagslied, so sonnig, so leicht, so flügge, dass es die Grillen nicht verscheucht,—dass es die Grillen vielmehr einlädt, mit zu singen, mit zu tanzen?"

21. Aphorism 383. "Die Tugenden des rechten Lesens—oh was für vergessene und unbekannte Tugenden!"

22. "Ein andres Ideal läuft vor uns her ...: das Ideal eines Geistes, der naiv, das heisst ungewollt und aus überströmender Fülle und Mächtigkeit mit Allem spielt, was bisher heilig, gut, unberührbar, göttlich hiess...; das Ideal eines menschlich-übermenschlichen Wohlseins und Wohlwollens, das oft genug *unmenschlich* erscheinen wird, zum Beispiel, wenn es sich neben dem ganzen bisherigen Erden-Ernst, neben alle Art Feierlichkeit in Gebärde, Wort, Klang, Blick, Moral, und Aufgabe wie deren leibhafteste unfreiwillige Parodie hinstellt—und mit dem, trotzalledem, vielleicht der *grosse Ernst* erst anhebt, das eigentliche Fragezeichen erst gesetzt wird."

23. I use the phrase "verbal imagination" to refer in general to the capacity to produce texts based upon rhetorical reading. This point is explained more fully in chapter 1 of *Inventions of Reading.*

24. "So leben die Wellen,—so leben wir, die Wollenden!—mehr sage ich nicht."

25. "Das macht, wir selbst wachsen, wir wechseln fortwährend, wir stossen alte Rinde ab, wir häuten uns mit jedem Frühjahre noch."

26. "Schein ist für mich das Wirkende und Lebende selber, das soweit in seiner Selbstverspottung geht, mich fühlen zu lassen, dass hier Schein und Irrlicht und Geistertanz und nichts mehr ist,—dass unter allen diesen Träumenden auch ich, der 'Erkennende,' mein Tanz tanze, dass der Erkennende ein Mittel ist, den irdischen Tanz in die Länge zu ziehen und

insofern zu den Festordnern des Daseins gehört, und dass die erhabene
Consequenz und Verbundenheit aller Erkenntnisse vielleicht das höchste
Mittel ist und sein wird, die Allgemeinheit der Träumerei und die Allverständ-
lichkeit aller dieser Träumenden unter einander und eben damit *die Dauer
des Traumes aufrecht zu erhalten.*"

27. From the close of the preface to the second edition (*Gay Science*, 38;
Kritische Gesamtausgabe, 20).

28. See *The Will to Power*, ed. Walter Kaufmann (New York: Random House,
1968), 342; and Stanley Corngold, *The Fate of the Self* (New York: Columbia
University Press, 1986), 126.

29. Corngold, *Fate of the Self*, 126.

30. "Ich nehme diese Erklärung von der Gasse; ich hörte Jemanden aus
dem Volke sagen 'er hat mich erkannt'—: dabei fragte ich mich: was versteht
eigentlich das Volk unter Erkenntniss? was will es, wenn es 'Erkenntniss' will?
Nichts weiter als dies: etwas Fremdes soll auf etwas *Bekanntes* zurückgeführt
werden. Und wir Philosophen—haben wir unter Erkenntniss eigentlich *mehr*
verstanden?"

31. *Meno* 81 e ff.

32. Aphorism 355. "Das Bekannte ist das Gewohnte; und das Gewohnte ist
am schwersten zu 'erkennen,' das heisst als Problem zu sehen, das heisst als
fremd, als fern, als 'ausser uns' zu sehn."

Chapter 9: Nietzsche's Physiology of Ideological Criticism

1. Although I call the unconscious pattern of activities I am about to
present a model, it should be understood not as a structure in the limited
structuralist sense but as a focus for use in questioning a dynamics. The 1872
notes to which I refer are designated *PT* in the abbreviations.

2. I will return to this term later in my discussion.

3. These three distinctions concerning Nietzsche's physiology are taken
from Wolfgang Müller-Lauter, "Artistische decadence als physiologische
decadence: Zu Friedrich Nietzsches später Kritik am späten Richard Wagner,"
in *Communicatio Fidei: Festschrift für Eugen Biser*, ed. Horst Bürkle and
Gerhold Becker (Regensburg: Verlag Friedrich Pustet, 1983). For a discussion
of specific readings in the natural and physical sciences which influenced
Nietzsche, see *BNL*. For further work relating Nietzsche to the physical and
natural sciences, see George Stack, *Lange and Nietzsche*, (Berlin: de Gruyter,
1983), and Alwin Mittasch, *Friedrich Nietzsche als Naturphilosoph*
(Stuttgart: Alfred Kröner, 1952). Müller-Lauter also mentions *Nietzsche
Studien* 7 (1978), 189-223, which discusses Wilhelm Roux's influence upon
Nietzsche concerning the organism as inner struggle.

4. When I speak of image in the context of this discussion, it is not in the sense of the idealist definition of perception as forming images or pictures in the mind. Today the term "mental structures" seems to be a more useful conception, because what is at issue is less the subjective experience of "having an image" than the ability to make whatever new observations are called for, to retrieve new comparisons from the remembered (but absent) object or scene.

5. See, for example, *WP* no. 492.

6. In two articles, Anthonie Meijers, "Gustav Gerber und Friedrich Nietzsche," and Martin Stingelin, "Nietzsches Wortspiel als Reflexion auf poet (olog)ische Verfahren," in *Nietzsche Studien* 17 (1988), Meijers and Stingelin offer evidence and a concordance of Gerber's *Sprache als Kunst* which demonstrates Gerber's influence upon Nietzsche's notes for a "Course on Rhetoric." See chapter 14 of *BNL*, which addresses these articles. The tropological or rhetorical framework which Nietzsche uses in the notes for a "Course on Rhetoric," in the notes from 1872, and in "On Truth and Lies in a Nonmoral Sense" is adopted from Gerber. The specific ideas concerning the physiology of perception and its relationship to language production, however, to which Nietzsche applies the rhetorical framework, had been developed independently and over a long period of time through the earlier influences of Schopenhauer, F. A. Lange, and Eduard von Hartmann. Nietzsche also read works in the natural and physical sciences by Helmholtz, Fechner, Wundt, and Zöllner, works in which processes of unconscious thinking, specifically unconscious inferences ("unbewussten Schlüsse"), were discussed. The idea of unconscious inferences was conceived by analogy with logical inferences of thought. The idea was that, at an unconscious level, perceptions in the form of images or impulses had to be worked on, circumscribed, classified, and determined before conscious thought could integrate them into its realm. Nietzsche's model of physiological perception is his attempt to describe the processes of unconscious inference as closely as possible. Nietzsche's turn to the rhetorical model offered by Gerber was a continuation of these researches.

7. See, for example, *WP* no. 334.

8. Nietzsche's criticisms directly approach the problem inherent in the Althusserian definition of ideology. Althusser limits his definition of the "subject" of ideology to Lacan's imaginary and thus the subject remains essentially unitary and noncontradictory. This subject, which is constituted through ideologies and which has the conscious ability to make history and change society, is hindered because the nature of ideology as an imaginary relation to the real conditions does not give the subject a full and sufficient knowledge or control over the actions it takes. And Berger adopts this understanding of ideology.

9. Lacan has stated, of course, that "the unconscious is structured like a language." Lacan differs from Nietzsche, however, in his understanding of this phrase. Lacan insists, in "Of Structure as an Inmixing of an Otherness Prerequisite to Any Subject Whatever," in *The Structuralist Controversy*, ed. R. Macksey and E. Donato, (Baltimore: The Johns Hopkins University Press, 1972), that "the unconscious has nothing to do with instinct or primitive knowledge or preparation of thought in some underground. It is a thinking with words, with thoughts that escape your vigilance" (189). Lacan shifts the locus of the unconscious from within the self (organism) to beyond it. For Nietzsche, however, language has everything to do with instinct. Following von Hartmann in his *Philosophy of the Unconscious*, Nietzsche writes in "On the Origins of Language," "it remains only to consider language as a product of instinct, and instinct is one with the innermost kernel of a being" (OL 222-23). As Nietzsche's model of unconscious perception demonstrates, there is a completely unconscious language with a specific structure which *is* a prerequisite for conscious thinking.

For Lacan the structure of language resides in Saussure's signifier/ signified, and he emphasizes the domination of the signifier over the signified. There is a *metonymic* chain of signifiers, with each signifier having meaning only in differential relations with the other signifiers of the chain. Therefore the sign is never constant. In "Agency of the Letter in the Unconscious," in *Ecrits*, trans. Alan Sheridan (New York: W. W. Norton, 1977), Lacan writes: "Only the correlations between signifier and signifier supply the standard for all research into meaning.... For the signifier, by its very nature, anticipates meaning by unfolding its dimension before it" (153). The signifier is never in direct relationship with the signified which slides beneath it [in a *metaphorical* operation] and therefore, meaning is caught in the relationships of signifiers to other signifiers.

I would like to propose, using Nietzsche's model of unconscious language, that what we have is a more complicated relationship of signifiers, signifieds, and signs as well as a much more complicated process of rhetorical operation. Let me explain, using Barthes's model of connotation, in which the signs of one system make a lateral shift and become the signifiers of the next staggered system, wherein the signifieds of the connotative system become ideologically diffused and global. Nietzsche's description of language in "On Truth and Lies in a Nonmoral Sense" consists of two metaphors: a first metaphor, stimuli into images which can be represented as:

signifier (unconscious image)
signified (stimulus).

This sign then becomes the signified of Nietzsche's second metaphor, images into sound, and Saussure's sign:

signifier (sound-image)
signified (Saussure's concept/Nietzsche's unconscious image).

Now, one goes to the cultural or ideological level, with Saussure's sign becoming the signifier:

signifier (sound, word, image, etc.)
signified (ideological meanings).

If one remains at the level of Saussure's signifier as Barthes and Lacan do, it is true, one seems to be implicated in a play of signifiers with no sure connection to specific signifieds. If one adds the language of unconscious signification, however, then Saussure's sign rests upon Nietzsche's unconscious sign which does arise from physiological (that is, instinctual) needs. (But lest we fall into the error of taking Nietzsche's unconscious sign as a basis for representational language, remember that stimuli are not things in themselves but only marks in their places.) Nietzsche's position is in contradistinction to that of Lacan, who repeatedly maintains that instincts are not instrumental in preparing for conscious language. Nietzsche's unconscious language of physiology and instinct already makes conscious language a connoted system, and therefore any cultural production becomes a connoted system of a third semiological order. Now, of course, what Nietzsche says, and what this discussion tries to make explicit, is that the third-level cultural significations operate in the purely instinctual and physiological operations of the first unconscious sign. Thus the model of language and ideology is less a chain than a circle, a sort of vicious circle implying that there is no privileged moment in the production of meaning, not unconscious instinct, not conscious thought, and not cultural ideologies. Whereas Lacan characterizes the unconscious in a rhetorical relationship with conscious and cultural levels of signification (through the ostracism of instinct), Nietzsche emphasizes that instincts can operate as signifiers to cultural signifieds. For example, Nietzsche coins the concepts of the "knowledge drive" (*Erkenntnistrieb*, which can also be translated as "instinct for knowledge") and the "drive for truth" (*Trieb zur Wahrheit*). These and similar terms are used repeatedly in Nietzsche's writings, especially during the period in which he writes "On Truth and Lies in a Nonmoral Sense," "Pathos of Truth," "Course on Rhetoric," and the notes translated in *PT*.

10. Of course, some Marxist and Neo-Marxist strains of postmodernism also operate with these perspectives.

11. In his article "On the Linguistic Approach to the Problem of Consciousness and the Unconscious," in *The Framework of Language*, Michigan Studies in the Humanities (Ann Arbor: University of Michigan Press, 1980), Roman Jakobson explores some of the history and ideas which surround the conception of unconscious language. I refer you to that article to demonstrate that what Nietzsche has to offer in the following pages reflects the historical development of language study at the time he wrote "Course of Rhetoric" and the 1872 notes and to observe that some of the specific unconscious operations which Nietzsche offers are also described by other linguists to one degree or another.

12. The three types of metaphor which Nietzsche's model of unconscious perception outlines can be compared to some extent with the three operations of Freud's dreamwork. Nietzsche's metaphor 1, displacement (*umdeuten*), can be compared with Freud's operation of displacement (*Verschiebung*). For both Freud and Nietzsche, displacement involves energy that is displaced or moved from one image to another. For example, Nietzsche writes: "Unconscious inferences are no doubt a process of passing from image to image. The image which is last attained then operates as a stimulus and motive" (*PT* 116). Nietzsche's metaphor 2, transposition (*Übertragung*), can be compared with Freud's condensation (*Verdichtung*). In Freud's condensation, one idea represents several associative chains of ideas and is at the center of them, receiving all their energy. This is an excellent description of Nietzsche's understanding of the constitution of the subject which takes place in the operation of transposition. Nietzsche's metaphor 3, marking (*Bezeichnung*) of grammatical categories, can be compared with Freud's concept of considerations of representability ("Rücksicht auf Darstellbarkeit"), but the process would be the reverse of regression. In regression, dream thoughts undergo selection and transformation in order to make them able to be represented in images. The process of unconscious grammar in Nietzsche's metaphor 3 allows the unconscious images to be able to be represented in sounds or words. Freud's distinction between thing presentations and word presentations preserves this distinction between an unconscious language of images and the preconscious system in which thing presentations are linked with word presentations, a process which then makes conscious use of language possible. Nietzsche does not distinguish a preconscious in Freud's sense. Although Freud does not develop the operations of dreamwork in rhetorical terms, Benveniste in an essay "Language in Freudian Theory" in *Problems in General Linguistics*, Miami Linguistics Series 8, trans. Mary Meek (Miami: University of Miami Press, 1971), suggests that the proper study of the unconscious could most beneficially lie in the "*stylistic* devices of discourse" (75). He writes:

> For it is style rather than language that we would take as term of comparison with the properties that Freud has disclosed as indicative of oneiric "language".... The unconscious uses a veritable "rhetoric" which, like style, has its "figures," and the old catalogue of tropes would supply an inventory appropriate to the two types of expression [that is, oneiric or unconscious language and conscious language].... The nature of the content makes all the varieties of metaphor appear, for symbols of the unconscious take both their meaning and their difficulty from metaphoric conversion.... They also emply what traditional rhetoric calls metonymy and synecdoche. [Ibid].

13. So far Nietzsche's model of unconscious perception, conceptualized through the tropes of synecdoche, metaphor 1, and metaphor 2, agrees almost step for step with current theories of perceptual "information processing" taken from Julian E. Hochberg, *Perception*, 2d ed. (Englewood

almost step for step with current theories of perceptual "information processing" taken from Julian E. Hochberg, *Perception*, 2d ed. (Englewood Cliffs, N.J.: Prentice-Hall, 1978), 162-63. First, there is the "momentary sample" that is vision or the single glance in which "what is sampled is a relatively small section of a larger object, scene or continuously changing event." Second, there is a process of "extraction, comparison, and encoding." The momentary glance provides a patterned flash of color, texture, a movement. It must be compared to some criterion. For example, did you see the letter T? Compare it to F, E, and so forth. Comparison yields the encoding of the shape perceived as a T—then other information in the momentary glance, color, brightness, precise shape, may be discarded. Third, storage of short-term or long-term memory takes place. The encoded information must be stored in short term memory until the perceiver can report it, combine it with the information from the next glance, or transfer it to long-term memory. The fourth step in information processing is the "combining of successive samples." "In normal perception, as when a viewer looks at the different parts of some object, the samples he receives are not independent glances. They are not independent because the physical world has consistencies, or structure, so that each glance provides for some anticipation of the next, and the schema whose features are to be tested on any glance is often already in immediate memory from the preceding glances." This tying together of glances and transposition of space into time and time into cause first creates the position of the subject. Some of the basis for similarity between Nietzsche's model and modern perception theory lies in the common element of the work of Hermann von Helmholtz with which Nietzsche was very well acquainted and which still informs a great deal of the basic assumptions of modern perception theory.

14. See also *BGE* 104-5 and 160 as well as *TI* 496-97.

15. This is an idea that Nietzsche adopts from von Hartmann. See *BNL* 33-35.

16. Nietzsche often considers the possibility that all our evaluations, our fictions, our politics, have only the character of a means to the development of the organism itself. See, for example, *WP* no. 676.

Chapter 10: Nietzsche and Postmodern Subjectivity

I thank Jenene J. Allison, Douglas Kellner, and Robert C. Solomon for their help in my revisions of this essay.

1. Jean Baudrillard, "On Nihilism," *On the Beach* 6 (Spring 1984), 39.

2. Jean-François Lyotard, *The Postmodern Condition* (Minneapolis: University of Minnesota Press, 1984), 26.

3. Paul de Man, "Nietzsche's Theory of Rhetoric," *Symposium* 28:1 (Spring 1974), 42-43.

4. Paul de Man, *Allegories of Reading* (New Haven: Yale University Press, 1979), 88.

5. de Man, "Nietzsche's Theory of Rhetoric," 48.

6. Ibid., 50.

7. Todd Gitlin, "Hip Deep in Post-modernism," *New York Times Book Review*, November 6, 1988, p. 35.

8. Fredric Jameson, "Postmodernism; or, The Cultural Logic of Late Capitalism," *New Left Review*, 146 (1984), 53-92.

9. Douglas Kellner, "Postmodernism as Social Theory: Some Challenges and Problems," *Theory, Culture and Society* 5 (1988), 239-41.

10. Friedrich Nietzsche, *Thus Spoke Zarathustra*, in *The Portable Nietzsche*, trans. and ed. Walter Kaufmann (New York: Viking, 1968), 152. This work is hereafter cited as *TSZ*.

11. See Michel Foucault. "What Is Enlightenment?" in *The Foucault Reader*, ed. Paul Rabinow (New York: Pantheon, 1984), 39.

12. See Friedrich Nietzsche, *On the Advantage and Disadvantage of History for Life*, trans. Peter Preuss (Indianapolis: Hackett, 1980), 14-22. This work is hereafter cited as *Advantage*.

13. Ibid., 9.

14. Ibid., 10

15. Ibid., 23

16. Ibid., 39.

17. Ibid., 44.

18. They might also be criticized as being applicable only to intellectuals, not to society in general. For a defense of regarding the intellectual as characteristic of the modern era, see Carl Jung, "The Spiritual Problem of Modern Man," in *The Portable Jung*, ed. Joseph Campbell (New York: Viking Press, 1971), 456-60. For my purposes, the possibility that Nietzsche's analysis applies more to intellectuals is not a problem, for the "postmodernists" to whom Nietzsche's critique implicitly applies are academics, intellectuals *par excellence*.

19. See Jameson, 198-217. See also Kellner, 259-60.

20. See Mark C. Taylor. "Ironies of Deconstruction," *Los Angeles Times Book Review*, July 31, 1989, p. 18. See also Jacques Derrida, "Racism's Last Word," *Critical Inquiry* 12:1 (1985), 85.

21. Cf. Jon Wiener, "Deconstructing de Man," *The Nation*, January 9, 1988, 22.

22. See, for example, de Man, "Nietzsche's Theory of Rhetoric," 39-40.

23. See Baudrillard, "On Nihilism," 39.

24. See Jean Baudrillard, *In the Shadow of the Silent Majorities* (New York: Semiotext(e), 1983), 1-4.

25. See de Man, "Nietzsche's Theory of Rhetoric," especially 38-43.

26. Ibid., 50.

27. Jameson associates contemporary disbelief in the possibility of practical action with a "schizophrenic" breakdown in our sense of temporality. "The breakdown of temporality suddenly releases this present of time from all the activities and the intentionalities that might focus it and make it a space of praxis..." Jameson does not conclude that the vividness of the present that results from this sense of its disconnection with time is necessarily negative. The "charge of affect" that results can be "described in the negative terms of anxiety and loss of reality," but it could also be described "in the positive terms of euphoria, the high, the intoxicatory or hallucinogenic intensity" (Jameson, 71).

28. Gitlin, 35. Jameson similarly describes preference for pastiche as a characteristically postmodern phenomenon. See Jameson, 64-65. Jameson associates the contemporary cultural tendency to see all cultural productions as "heaps of fragments" with a crisis in our temporal orientation along lines that interestingly parallel Nietzsche's complaints. See ibid., particularly 71ff. For a postmodernist attack on originality, and thus a defense of "living on borrowed energies," see Rosalind Krauss, *The Originality of the Avant-Garde and Other Modernist Myths* (Cambridge, Mass.: MIT Press, 1985).

29. Jean Baudrillard, "Games with Vestiges," *On the Beach* 5 (Winter 1984), 24.

30. Lyotard, 26.

31. Ibid., 82.

32. See Jürgen Habermas, "Modernity versus Postmodenrity," *New German Critique* 22 (1981) 10-14.

33. See Gitlin, 1.

34. Baudrillard, "On Nihilism", 38-39.

35. Jameson, 61.

36. Ibid., 56.

37. See de Man, "Nietzsche's Theory of Rhetoric," 44-45.

38. See Lyotard, 60.

39. See *TSZ* 245-46 and 353-56.

40. *Advantage*, 62.

41. Lyotard, xxv.

42. *Advantage*, 62.

43. Ibid., 64.

44. Ibid., 63.

45. Friedrich Nietzshce, *The Gay Science: With a Prelude in Rhymes and an Appendix of Songs*, trans. Walter Kaufmann (New York: Random House, 1974), 32.

46. Ibid., 32-33.

47. Ibid., 38.

48. Ibid., 38.

49. Ibid., no. 1, pp. 74-75.

50. Ibid., no. 1, p. 76.

51. Ibid., no. 310, p. 248.

52. Ibid., no. 310, p. 247.

53. Ibid., no. 295, p. 237.

54. Recurrenty in *The Gay Science*, Nietzsche gives similar hints as to how subjective experience can be viewed as an active, artistic enterprise that involves forming and reforming the chaos which is the true content of time. These hints include his admonition to give style to one's character (no. 290), his account of how differently we think when we are bold than when we are not (no. 311), and his reverie on the happiness he felt in thinking a thought that vanished when he tried to contain it in words (no. 298).

55. Baudrillard, "On Nihilism," 39.

56. See Kellner, 252-53.

57. See Bernd Magnus, *Nietzsche's Existential Imperative* (Bloomington: Indiana University Press, 1978).

58. See Kathleen Marie Higgins, *Nietzsche's Zarathustra* (Philadelphia: Temple University Press, 1956), 179-184.

59. Victor Zuckerkandl, *Sound and Symbol: Music and the External World*, trans. Willard R. Trask, Bollingen Series 44 (Princeton: Princeton University Press, 1956), 37.

60. Ibid., 168.

61. Ibid., 173.

62. Ibid., 231.

63. Ibid., 233.

64. See Arthur C. Danto, "Some Remarks on *The Genealogy of Morals*," in *Reading Nietzsche*, ed. Robert C. Solomon and Kathleen M. Higgins (New York: Oxford University Press, 1988), 13-28.

65. Ibid., 16.

66. *TSZ* 430.

Chapter 12: Zarathustra's Three Metamorphoses

This essay was completed with the help of a grant from the National Endowment for the Humanities. I thank Judith Ryan, the Simmons College English Department Colloquium, and two anonymous readers for comments on an earlier draft.

1. See, for example, Erich Heller, *The Disinherited Mind* (New York: Harcourt Brace Jovanovich, 1975), 304-26, and Richard Perkins, "Analogistic Strategies in *Zarathustra*," in *The Great Year of Zarathustra*, ed. David Goicoechea (Lanham, Md.: University Press of America, 1983), 316-38.

2. I argue that *Zarathustra* can be read as a philosophical explanation in my "Literary Fiction as Philosophy: The Case of Nietzsche's *Zarathustra*," *Journal of Philosophy* 83 (November 1986), 667-75. For a justification of my belief that Nietzsche's postmodernism can be characterized as a "modernist postmodernism," see my "Nietzsche's Pursuit of Modernism," *New German Critique* 41 (Spring-Summer 1987), 95-108.

3. Friedrich Nietzsche, *Thus Spoke Zarathustra*, trans. Walter Kaufmann, in *The Portable Nietzsche*, ed. Walter Kaufmann (1954; rpt. New York: Viking, 1977), 123 (hereafter I will cite this translation and edition as *TSZ*); Friedrich Nietzsche, *Nietzsche Werke. Kritische Gesamtausqabe*, ed. Giorgio Colli and Mazzino Montinari, 20 vols. (Berlin: Walter de Gruyter, 1967-82), Vol. 6, pp. 6 (this edition will henceforth be cited as *KGW*). For a discussion of the affinity of *Zarathustra* to the nineteenth-century novel, see my "The Drama of Nietzsche's *Zarathustra*: Intention, Repetition, Prelude," *International Studies in Philosophy* 20 (Summer 1987), 105-116.

4. See *TSZ*, 351; *KGW* VI:1, 293, "For *that* is what I am through and through: reeling, reeling in, raising up, raising, cultivator, and disciplinarian, who once counseled himself, not for nothing: Become who you are!" Also see, in this same section, Zarathustra's allusions to his destiny (*Schicksal*), which has yet to be fulfilled.

5. In "The Drama of Nietzsche's *Zarathustra*: Intention, Repetition, Prelude," I explain in greater detail my belief that the plot of *Zarathustra* is structured by an antithesis of intention and repetition.

6. Friedrich Nietzsche, *On the Genealogy of Morals*, trans. Walter Kaufmann and R. J. Hollingdale, in *"On the Geneology of Morals" and "Ecce Homo,"* ed. Walter Kaufmann (New York: Vintage Books, 1969), 162-63 (hereafter I will cite this translation and edition as *GM*); *KGW* VI:2, 430.

7. *TSZ* 138, 305; *KGW* VI:1, 26, 239.

8. Friedrich Nietzsche, *The Birth of Tragedy*, trans. Walter Kaufmann, in *"The Birth of Tragedy" and "The Case of Wagner,"* ed. Walter Kaufmann (New York: Vintage Books, 1967), 23; *KGW* III:1, 13. See also, in the same passage, Nietzsche's allusion to Christianity's particular antipathy to sensuality, the passions, and so forth. For Nietzsche's tendency to associate the phrase 'thou shalt' with "Christian, or unconditional, morality," see Friedrich Nietzsche, *Beyond Good and Evil*, ed. and trans. Walter Kaufmann (New York: Vintage Books, 1966), 110 (hereafter I will cite this translation and edition as *BGE*); *KGW* VI:2, 121-22, and *KGW* VII:2, 101.

9. For a similar but more elaborate account of Nietzsche's critique of unconditional morality, see Alexander Nehamas, *Nietzsche: Life as Literature* (Cambridge, Mass.: Harvard University Press, 1985), chaps. 4 and 7.

10. *TSZ* 138-39; *KGW* VI:1, 26.

11. See Heller, 316-18.

12. My Luther interpretation is based on Hans Blumenberg's discussion of proposition 17 of Luther's *Disputatio contra scholasticam theologiam*. See Hans Blumenberg, *Work on Myth*, trans. Robert Wallace (Cambridge, Mass.: MIT Press, 1985), 541, 545, 672.

13. As is well known, the text in which Nietzsche most persuasively develops his analysis of reactive force, its relation to the negation of difference and so forth is *On the Genealogy of Morals*, especially the first essay. The best available commentary on these aspects of Nietzsche's thought is Gilles Deleuze, *Nietzsche and Philosophy*, trans. Hugh Tomlinson (New York: Columbia University Press, 1983).

14. Cf. Harold Alderman, *Nietzsche's Gift* (1977; rpt. Athens: Ohio University Press, 1979), 33. Alderman is right, in his discussion of Zarathustra's camel, to stress the theme of facticity and tradition. What he misses, in

"On the Three Metamorphoses," is the claim of facticity and the past to exhaust creative possibility.

15. *TSZ* 139; *KGW* VI:1, 26.

16. Ibid.

17. Karl Löwith's claim that the lion enjoys a freedom to be nothing seems to me to slight Nietzsche's assertion that the lion achieves a freedom *for* new creation. See Karl Löwith, *From Hegel to Nietzsche*, trans. David Green (Garden City, N.Y.: Anchor Books, Doublday, 1967), 191-92.

18. *TSZ* 139; *KGW* VI:1, 26-27.

19. J. P. Clayton defends a more traditional account of the lion's freedom, by assimilating this freedom to Kant's conception of autonomy. He claims that Nietzsche is rehearsing "the classic conflict between moral laws imposed from without and moral laws generated from within, the conflict between what Kant would have called heteronomy and autonomy" (J. P. Clayton, "Zarathustra and the Stages of Life's Way: A Nietzschean Riposte to Kierkegaard," *Nietzsche Studien* 14 [1985]; 190). Clayton's discussion cannot do justice to Nietzsche's text, because Kant's "Der Wille" creates moral value, in the form of moral law, whereas Nietzsche's lion creates no value whatsoever. Clayton is mistaken, then, to ascribe to the lion a self-legislated morality. For a view similar to my own that stresses the lion's future-oriented freedom for the creation of new values, see David Goicoechea, "Love and Joy in Zarathustra," in *The Great Year of Zarathustra*, ed. David Goicoechea (Lanham, Md.: University Press of America, 1983), 41.

20. See Malcolm Pasley, "Nietzsche and Klinger," in *The Discontinuous Tradition*, ed. P. F. Ganz (Oxford: Clarendon Press, 1971), 147-48.

21. *TSZ* 139, *KGW* VI:1, 27.

22. Cf. J. P. Stern, *A Study of Nietzsche* (Cambridge: Cambridge University Press, 1979), 181.

23. For a brief but very illuminating discussion of Nietzsche's struggles with romanticism, see Heinrich von Staden, "Nietzsche and Marx on Greek Art and Literature: Case Studies in Reception," *Daedalus*, Winter 1976, 85-93.

24. See Heller, 321-26. Heller's account of the "paradise regained" motif in romantic writers involves some oversimplification. For example, he does not distinguish a primitivist "return to nature" from the pursuit of a "second-order" or "organized" innocence that subsumes and preserves difference, multiplicity, self-consciousness, and so forth. For two useful discussions of the importance of this distinction to our understanding of the writers that Heller mentions, see Geoffrey Hartmann, "Romanticism and 'Anti-Self Consciousness,'" in *Romanticism and Consciousness*, ed. Harold Bloom (New York: W. W. Norton 1970), 46-56, and M. H. Abrams, *Natural Supernaturalism* (New York: W. W. Norton, 1971), 141-324.

25. See Stern, 181, n. 1, Roger Hollinrake, *Nietzsche, Wagner, and the Philosophy of Pessimism* (London: George Allen and Unwin, 1982), 7; Joan Stambaugh, "Thoughts on the Innocence of Becoming," *Nietzsche Studien* 14 (1985), 164-78; and Löwith, 191-92 (Löwith also discusses "On the Three Metamorphoses" in chapter 3 of his *Nietzsches Philosophie der ewigen Wiederkehr des Gleichen*). Heidegger's and Fink's distinctive interpretations of Nietzsche's playing and innocent child are also interesting and worthy of attention. Cf. Martin Heidegger, *Nietzsche, Vol. 2: The Eternal Recurrence of the Same*, trans. David Farrell Krell (New York: Harper and Row, 1984), 77-78, Martin Heidegger, *Nietzsche, Vol. 4: Nihilism*, trans. Frank A. Capuzzi (New York: Harper and Row, 1982), 235-37, and Eugen Fink, *Nietzsches Philosophie* (Stuttgart: Kohlhammer, 1960), 187ff.

26. *KGW* VII:2, 101. The translation is my own.

27. Stambaugh, 174.

28. For a useful discussion of the role of the "supersubject" in idealist philosophy *and* romantic literature, see Abrams, 90-92, 197-324.

29. According to Deleuze's reading of Nietzsche, the will to ascribe established value to oneself (in the case of the lion, the established value of possessing God's power and authority) is typical of slavish or reactive dispositions. This reading is consistent with my earlier interpretation of the lion as reactive and finds textual support in *BGE*, no., 261; *KGW*, VI:2, 222-24. See Deleuze, 9-10, 81-82.

30. See *BGE*, no. 17; *KGW*, VI:2, 24-25. For a further sampling of Nietzsche's criticisms both of the doer-deed dichotomy and the assumption that the self is an ego-substance, see *GM*, 44-46; *KGW*, VI:2, 292-95, and Friedrich Nietzsche, *Twilight of the Idols*, trans. Walter Kaufmann, in *The Portable Nietzsche*, ed. Walter Kaufmann (1954; rpt. New York: Viking, 1977), 482-83 (I will henceforth cite this translation and edition as *TI*); *KGW* VI:3, 71-72.

31. *TI* 501; *KGW* VI:3, 90-91.

32. See *GM*, 36-39, 57-58; *KGW* VI:2, 284-88, 307-8. Also see Deleuze, 113-14, and Alphonso Lingus, "The Will to Power," in *The New Nietzsche*, ed. David Allison (New York: Delta, 1977), 54, 58.

Chapter 13: Nietzsche and the Condition of Postmodern Thought

1. Fredric Jameson, "Foreword" to *The Post-Modern Condition: A Report on Knowledge*, by Jean-Francois Lyotard, trans. G. Bennington and B. Massumi (Minneapolis: University of Minnesota Press, 1984), xii.

2. Lyotard, *The Post-Modern Condition*, 19.

3. Ibid.

4. Ibid. Lyotard cites C. Lévi-Strauss, *La pensée sauvage* (Paris: PLON, 1962); The English translation of this work is *The Savage Mind* (Chicago: University of Chicago Press, 1966).

5. Lyotard, *The Postmodern Condition*, 39. On Nietzsche's understanding of nihilism and the postmodern, see Mark Marren, *Nietzsche and Political Thought* (Cambridge: MIT Press, 1988).

6. See Arthur Kroker and David Cook, *The Postmodern Scene: Excremental Culture and Hyper-Aesthetics* (New York: St. Martin's Press; 1986).

7. Ihab Hassan, "POSTmodernISM," *New Literary History* 3:1 (1971), 5-30. But Nietzsche is mentioned obliquely in his *The Right Promethean Fire* (Urbana: University of Illinois Press, 1980).

8. Andreas Huyssen, *After the Great Divide: Modernism, Mass-Culture, Postmodernism* (Bloomington: Indiana University Press; 1986), 48ff.

9. William V. Spanos, *Repetitions: The Post-Modern Occasion in Literature and Culture* (Baton Rouge: Louisiana State University Press; 1987).

10. Wolfgang Welsch, "'Postmoderne': Genealogie und Bedeutung eines umstrittenen Begriffs," in *"Postmoderne" oder, Der Kampf um die Zukunft*, ed. Peter Kemper (Frankfurt am Main: Fischer, 1988), 9-36.

11. Friedrich Nietzsche, *Ecce Homo*, trans. W. Kaufmann (New York: Vintage Books, 1969), "Why I Write Such Good Books," sec. 1, p. 259.

12. Ibid., sec. 3, p. 264. Citation: *Thus Spake Zarathustra*, p. 3, "On the Vision and the Riddle," sec. 1.

13. Ibid, sec. 4, p. 265.

14. Ibid., sec. 7. p. 332.

15. Ibid., sec. 8. p. 333.

16. Ibid., sec. 9. p. 335.

17. Nietzsche's stylistics is a deconstructive strategy in advance of Derridean deconstruction. See Babich, "On Nietzsche's Concinnity: An Analysis of Style," *Nietzsche-Studien* 19 (1990), 59-80.

18. Linda Hutcheon, *A Poetics of Post-Modernism: History, Theory, Fiction* (New York: Routledge, 1988), and Charles Jencks, *What Is Post-Modernism?* 2d rev. ed. (London: Academy Editions/St. Martin's Press, 1987).

19. Georges Bataille, "Labyrinth," in *Inner Experience*, trans. L. Boldt (New York: SUNY Press, 1988), 81.

20. Umberto Eco, *The Postscript to the Name of the Rose*, trans. W. Weaver (New York: Harcourt Brace Jovanovich, 1984), 67.

21. Such a reprise is suggested by the Mediterranean or classical revival characteristic of so many American public and private-public buildings built at the end of the nineteenth-century and early in the twentieth.

22. For one example, see Robert B. Pippin's nuanced but prepostmodern "Nietzsche and the Origin of the Idea of Modernity," *Inquiry* 26 (1988) 154-80.

23. As Nietzsche expresses it, modern culture is the rational spiritualization/extirpation of the instincts. But because we remain self-unknowing, unconsciously conscious animals, the modern is to be understood as a state of "physiological self-contradiction." (*Twilight of the Idols*, "What the Germans— read: Moderns—Lack," sec. 41.) In *Beyond Good and Evil*, he speaks of this as the "collective degeneration of man," sec. 203.

24. "Today, on the contrary, we find ourselves entangled in error, *necessitated* to error" (Nietzsche, *Twilight of the Idols*, trans. R. J. Hollingdale [Harmondsworth, Middlesex: Penguin, 1968], "Reason in Philosophy," 5, p. 37.)

25. As most recent reviews of postmodernism repeat the logophile's retrieve of *modo, modernus*, that is, the etymology of the term 'modern', I will not recover this ground.

26. Nietzsche, *The Birth of Tragedy*, trans. W. Kaufmann (New York: Vintage Books, 1967), sec. 15, p. 97.

27. Ibid.

28. The scientists D. Bohme, I. Prigogine, E. Chargaff, and E. Morin, the sociologists of science B. Latour and K. Knorr-Cetina, the philosophers of science P. Heelan, I. Hacking, M. Galison, S. Toulmin, and others would confirm Lyotard's claims, if it is true that the implications of the literature surrounding the topic of the postmodern would also inspire waffling reservations.

29. The Nietzschean projects of both reconstructive, psychological *genealogy* and deconstructive, physiological *eschatology* are critical descriptions which require reflective distance on the temporal object of study for their only application. Thus the (Nietzschean) *named* genealogy (but not the temporal genealogy as such) and the (non-Nietzschean) *named* (Weberian) eschatology are postmodern constructs.

30. The term postmodern has, of course, a technical aesthetic significance for architects, art historians, and art critics.

31. Jencks, *What Is Post-Modernism?* 9.

32. In lived terms, like Nietzsche's textual self-deconstructive style or concinnity, postmodern double coding in art and literature seeks to "choose" to live a particular historical sophistication and learned limitations within that particular situation like a (clever and even decadent) "child."

33. Eco, *The Postscript to the Name of the Rose.*

34. Gadamer, "The Philosophical Foundations of the Twentieth Century," in *Philosophical Hermeneutics*, trans. D. Linge (Berkeley: University of California Press, 1977), 117.

35. David Carroll, *Paraesthetics: Foucault, Lyotard, Derrida* (New York: Methuem, 1987), 3.

36. Hutcheon, *A Poetics of Postmodernism*, 43.

37. If we may yet find such a needed recollective appropriation forbidding, the reason is that reading Nietzsche remains the elusive art that Nietzsche's interpreters tirelessly detail.

38. Nietzsche, *Beyond Good and Evil*, trans. R. J. Hollingdale (London: Penguin, 1973), sec. 22, p. 34. (hereafter cited as *BGE*.)

39. For a more detailed consideration of this possibility, see my "Nietzsche's Self-Deconstruction: Philosophy as Style," *Soundings* (Winter 1990). For another discussion of this same analgon between Nietzsche's style and Derridean deconstruction, see Rudolph Kuenzli, "The Signifying Process in Nietzsche's *The Gay Science*," in *Nietzsche: Literature and Values*, ed. V. Dürr, R. Grimm, and K. Harms (Madison: Monatsheft, University of Wisconsin 1988), and "Neitzsche's Zerography: *Thus Spoke Zarathustra*," *Boundary 2: Why Nietzsche Now? 9/10. (1981), 99-117.*

40. *BGE*, preface, 13.

41. *BGE*, sec. 233, p. 145.

42. *BGE*, sec. 206, p. 113.

43. *BGE*, sec. 245, p. 201.

44. *BGE*, Sec. 17, p. 24.

45. Heidegger, *Poetry, Language, Thought*, trans. A. Hofstadter (New York: Harper and Row, 1971), "Language," 191. See also n. 53 below.

46. Jacques Lacan, *Ecrits*, trans. A. Sheridan (New York: Norton, 1977), "Function and Field of Speech and Language," 71.

47. Sigmund Freud, *Jokes and Their Relation to the Unconscious*, trans. J. Strachey (New York: Norton, 1960), 115.

48. Lacan, *Ecrits*, "Agency of the Letter in the Unconscious," 172.

49. Frued, 115.

50. Ibid.

51. *BGE*, sec. 34, p. 47.

52. *NGE*, sec. 34, pp. 46-47.

53. In an inverse anticipation, Heidegger muses, "We cannot say 'Language speaks.' For this would be to say: 'It is language that first brings man about, brings him into existence.' Understood in this way, man would be bespoken by language" (*Poetry, Language, Thought*, "Language," 192).

54. Lacan, *Ecrits*, "The Function and Field of Speech and Language," 69.

55. Ibid., 40.

56. Cf. Lacan, *Ecrits*, 166.

Chapter 14: Nietzsche, Postmodernism, and Resentment

Parts of this essay were presented in a symposium of the North American Nietzsche Soceity held in December 1986.

1. David Hoy, "Foucault: Modern or Postmodern?" unpublished manuscript (University of California, Santa Cruz, 1968).

2. I will follow the practice of referring to those who exhibit postmodern tendencies as postmodern and to those who only talk about them as postmodernists. I do not pretend that this is a hard and fast distinction: many theorists are also practitioners and vice versa. But as so often in academic disputes, thought and action become confused. Nietzsche in particular seems to be more of a postmodernist than a postmodern, and his place in this discussion has much more to do with what he wrote and the way he wrote it than with the way he seems to have actually thought and lived, which were distinctively modern.

3. Alexander Nehamas, *Nietzsche: A Life in Literature* (Cambridge, Mass.: Harvard University Press, 1985).

4. "Truth and Lie in the Extra-Moral Sense" was never published by Nietzsche, although it was apparently written in the very early 1870s. See D. Breazeale, trans. and ed., *Philosophy and Truth: Selections from Nietzsche's Notebooks of the Early 1870's* (Atlantic Highlands, N.J.: Humanities Press, 1979).

5. Walter Kaufmann, *Nietzsche: Philosopher, Psychologist, Antichrist*, 4th ed. (Princeton: Princeton University Press, 1968). This classification is dramatically at odds with some more recent interpretations, for example, Alan Megill, *Prophets of Extremity: Nietzsche, Heidegger, Foucault, and Derrida* (Berkeley: University of California Press, 1985), who divides Nietzsche into an early modern phase and a later postmodernist phase. (I am arguing just the opposite, that the earlier Nietzsche struck postmodernist

themes and the later Nietzsche did not.) I should also mention a new (still unpublished) manuscript by Robert Ackerman (University of Massachusetts, Amherst, 1987), according to whom "only a nitwit" would argue that Nietzsche changed his mind so radically ("Nietzsche: A Frenzied Look").

6. Kathleen Higgins, *Nietzsche's Zarathustra* (Philadelphia: Temple University Press, 1987).

7. Ackerman, "Nietzsche: A Frenzied Look."

8. Robert Gooding-Williams, "Nietzsche's Pursuit of Modernism," *New German Critique* 20 (1987), 105.

9. Higgins, *Nietzsche's Zarathustra*, chap 7.

10. Bernd Magnus, "The End of the 'End of Philosophy'." See also his "Nietzsche and the Project of Bringing Philosophy to an End," *Journal of the British Society for Phenomenology* 14:3 (1983), 304ff.

11. David Hoy ("Foucault: Modern or Postmodern?") cuts the pie in quite a different way with particular reference to Foucault, but his argument is equally applicable to Nietzsche. According to Hoy, (1) postmoderns (unlike moderns) are willing to accept their inability to think "the great unthought" (Foucault's obscure term for self-validating, complete knowledge); (2) there is no single way of thinking, no singe Kantian categorical framework, in other words; (3) there is no privileged way of thinking; and (4) "nostalgia" (and the rhetoric of nostalgia), that is, "taking oneself too seriously," is rejected.

12. I have argued this thesis at length in my *History and Human Nature* (New York: Harcourt Brace Jovanovich, 1979).

13. "Philosophy as a Rigorous Science," in Husserl, *Phenomenology and the Crisis of Philosophy*, trans. Q. Lauer (Harper and Row, 1965), 1226.

14. Robert Gooding-Williams, "Nietzsche's Pursuit of Modernism," 95-96. These two "hands" seem perfectly compatible, if not ultimately identical. But one cannot help noting that if Willard van Ormand Quine, with his one-dimensional worship of science and utter contempt for any philosophy outside the narrow circle of postlogical positivism, represents postmodern philosophy, then the term truly is meaningless.

15. This topic has been elaborately discussed by Nehamas (*Nietzsche: A Life in Literature*) and by Magnus "The End of the 'End of Philosophy'," who argues that perspectivism should be taken as rhetorical rather than as a claim (which might then be taken to refer to itself). Maudemarie Clark has written a lively rejoinder to these arguments, as yet unpublished.

16. A good recent discussion is "On the Question of Nietzsche's 'Scientism'" by Beverly Gallo, who is at the University of California, The article is forthcoming in *International Studies in Philosophy* (1990).

17. See, for example, Walter Kaufmann's classic discussion of Nietzsche's revolutionary ethics (*Nietzsche: Philosopher, Psychologist, Antichrist*), but see also the discussion by Richard Wolin, "Modernism versus Postmodernism," *Telos* 62 (Winter 1984-85), and Magill, *Prophets of Extremity*.

18. Nietzsche, *The Antichrist*, trans. R. J. Hollingdale (Penguin, 1968) 156.

19. Max Scheler, *Resentment* (New York: Free Press, 1961).

20. Jürgen Habermas, "The Entry into Post-Modernity: Nietzsche as a Turning Point," trans. Lawrence (cited in Gooding-Williams).

21. Nietzsche, "On the Tarantulas," in *Thus Spoke Zarathustra*, II.7, trans. W. Kaufmann, *The Portable Nietzsche* (Viking, 1954).

22. Todd Gitlin, "Hip-Deep in Postmodernism," *New York Times*, November 6, 1988.

23. A particularly outrageous example of this self-conscious contradiction is Rosalind Krauss, "The Originality of the Avant-Garde: A Postmodernist Repetition," in *Art after Modernism*, ed. Wallis (New York: New Museum of Contemporary Art, 1984).

24. *Nation*, April 4, 1987.

25. Robert Ackerman, *Religion as Critique* (Amherst: University of Massachusetts Press, 1986).

26. Nietzsche, *Will to Power*, 461, trans. W. Kaufmann (Random House, 1967), 253-4.

27. Gitlin, "Hip-Deep in Postmodernism."

28. Ackerman, "Nietzsche: A Frenzied Look."

29. Ibid.

30. This apolitical irresponsibility has been broached with uncharacteristic tolerance by my colleague Douglas Kellner, who rightly contrasts the political programs of neo-Frankfurt School critical theory with the indulgences of postmodernism, aiming at what I find an implausible reconciliation between the two. See, for example, his "Postmodernism as Social Theory: Some Challenges and Problems," in *Theory, Culture, and Society*, vol. 5 (London: Sage, 1988).

31. Paul de Man, "Nietzsche's Theory of Rhetoric," *Symposium* (Spring 1974).

Notes on Contributors

BABETTE E. BABICH is Assistant Professor of Philosophy at Fordham University, The College at Lincoln Center. Her publications focus on Nietzsche and Heideger, with occasional readings of Derrida, Lacan, and Baudrillard, on the hermeneutic questions of art, author-deconstructive style, and posthumanist ethics. She is currently finishing a book on Nietzsche's perspectivalism and the philosophy of the natural sciences.

DEBRA B. BERGOFFEN, Professor of Philosophy at George Mason University, Fairfax, Virginia, has recently published "On the Advantage and Disadvantage of Nietzsche for Women" in *The Question of the Other*, "Seducing Historicism" in *International Studies in Philosophy*, and "Sophocles' *Antigone* and Freud's *Civilization and Its Discontents* in *American Imago*. She is currently exploring the question of the subject in the works of Freud and Lacan and examining the productive uses of reading the sayings of *Thus Spoke Zarathustra* as riddles.

MAUDEMARIE CLARK has taught at Columbia University and Colgate University, where she is Associate Professor of Philosophy. Her essays on Nietzsche have appeared in *Nietzsche-Studien* and *International Studies in Philosophy*. She has recently completed a book, *Nietzsche on Truth and Philosophy*.

REBECCA COMAY is Assistant Professor of Philosophy and Literary Studies at the University of Toronto. Her recently completed book on Heidegger and Hegel, *Underlining the Difference*, will be published by SUNY Press. She is currently working on a book concerning questions of art and politics in Heidegger and the Frankfurt School.

DANIEL W. CONWAY has taught at Stanford and Harvard Universities. He is currently Assistant Professor of Philosophy at the

341

Pennsylvania State University. His articles on Nietzsche have appeared in *Nietzsche-Studien, Political Theory, International Studies in Philosophy*, and *The Journal of the British Society for Phenomenology.* He is completing a book on the affirmative dimension of Nietzsche's thought.

CLAUDIA CRAWFORD teaches Humanities and Comparative Literature at the University of Minnesota. In addition to her recent book, *The Beginnings of Nietzsche's Theory of Language*, she has published articles on Nietzsche and literary theory in *Nietzsche-Studien, Substance, Enclitic*, and *American Imago.* She is currently working on a book-length study of Nietzsche and music.

ROBERT GOODING-WILLIAMS, Associate Professor of Black Studies and Philosophy at Amherst College, has published numerous articles and reviews and is presently at work on two books, *Nietzsche's Pursuit of Modernism* and *Dubois' Philosophy of Self-Consciousness.* He edited the 1987 *Praxis International* symposium on black neoconservatism and has been an editorial consultant for the *Journal of the History of Philosophy.*

KATHLEEN HIGGINS is Associate Professor of Philosophy at the Univeristy of Texas at Austin. She is author of *Nietzsche's 'Zarathustra'* and editor (with Robert C. Solomon) of *Reading Nietzsche.* Primarily interested in the relationshiop of aesthetic and ethical values, she has just completed a book on the ethical dimensions of musical experience and is co-editing books on ethics and on romantic love.

CLAYTON KOELB is Professor of German and Comparative Literature at the University of Chicago. He has written many essays on topics in literary criticism and theory and is author or editor of half a dozen books, including *The Incredulous Reader: Literature and the Function of Disbelief, Inventions of Reading: Rhetoric and the Literary Imagination* and *Kafka's Rhetoric: The Passion of Reading.* His work on Nietzsche has appeared in these books and in journals such as *boundary 2.*

GRAHAM PARKES is a member of the Philosophy Department at the University of Hawaii at Manoa, where he teaches courses in comparative philosophy, depth psychology, philosophy of literature and the visual arts, and modern German philosophy. He is the editor of two anthologies, *Heidegger and Asian Thought* and *Nietzsche and Asian Thought*, and is co-translator of a book by the Japanese philosopher Keiji Nishitani, *The Self-Overcoming of Nihilism*. He is currently working on a manuscript on Nietzsche's psychology and co-writing a screenplay for a four-part mini-series for public television entitled *Nietzsche: A Dangerous Life*.

CHARLES E. SCOTT is Professor of Philosophy and Director of the Humanities Center at Vanderbilt University. In addition to his books *The Language of Difference* and *The Question of Ethics*, he has published essays on Nietzsche in such journals as *The Review of Metaphysics* and *Research in Phenomenology*.

GARY SHAPIRO is Professor of Philosophy at the University of Kansas. He is the author of many articles on Nietzsche and of *Nietzschean Narratives*, co-editor of *Hermeneutics: Questions and Prospects*, and editor of *After the Future: Postmodern Times and Places*. He is currently completing a book tentatively titled *Alcyone: Nietzsche on Gifts, Noise and Women*.

ROBERT C. SOLOMON, who describes himself as "an unreconstructed crypto-modernist," is Quincy Lee Centennial Professor at the University of Texas at Austin. He is the author of *The Passions, In the Spirit of Hegel*, and *From Hegel to Existentialism*; editor of *Nietzsche*; and co-editor (with Kathleen Higgins) of *Reading Nietzsche*.

RICHARD H. WEISBERG, a frequent writer on Nietzschean ressentiment, holds doctoral degrees in both law and comparative literature. He has taught at the University of Chicago, practiced law in Paris and New York, and is now Professor of Law at the Benjamin N. Cardozo School of Law, Yeshiva University. He has written many articles treating the interrelations of legal and literary texts and is the author of *The Failure of the Word: The Protagonist as Lawyer in Modern Fiction* and *When Lawyers Write*.

Index